THE GUINNESS
BOOK OF
AIRCRAFT

THE GUINNESS
BOOK OF
AIRCRAFT

Records Facts and Feats

DAVID MONDEY
MICHAEL J.H. TAYLOR

Editor: Honor Head
Design and Layout: Eric Drewery
Picture Editor: Alex Goldberg

Published in Great Britain by Guinness Publishing Ltd,
33 London Road, Enfield, Middlesex

Typeset in 10/11 Goudy Old Style
by Ace Filmsetting Ltd, Frome, Somerset
Printed and bound in Great Britain by
Adlard & Son Ltd, Letchworth, Herts.

British Library Cataloguing in Publication Data
Taylor, Michael
    The Guinness book of aircraft.—5th ed.
    1. Aircraft. Flights, to 1987
    I. Title   II. Mondey, David
    629.13'09
    ISBN 0-85112-355-4

Contents

Introduction   7

Balloons and Airships   9

Rotorcraft   40

Parachutes, Kites and Gliders   63

Civil Aviation and Route Proving   73

Air Warfare and Military Aviation   132

Research and Experimentation   208

Valour and Achievement   222

Index   243

The Boeing B-47 Statojet gave the US Air Force its first mass produced jet bomber, with production ending in 1957. (The Boeing Company)

Introduction

In this, the fifth edition, great emphasis has been placed on introducing a layout much closer to that found in the parent *Guinness Book of Records*, for this is the aviation equivalent to that world-famous publication. It is now far easier for the reader to find facts on the 'first', 'largest', 'fastest', 'highest', 'longest', 'greatest' and 'most' within the text, which has a time-scale to encompass an Egyptian gliding bird thought to be around 2300 years old and the *Da Vinci 2* record-breaking human-powered helicopter of 1988.

As we approach the 21st century it is all too easy to take the attitude that everything exciting has been done before, that no challenge commensurate with those performed between the wars by Alcock and Brown, Lindbergh, Amy Johnson and so on remains for the taking. How wrong this attitude is. During nine cramped and hazardous days and nights in December 1986, Americans Dick Rutan and Jeana Yeager crewed their outrageously peculiar but outstandingly successful *Voyager* trimaran aeroplane on the first-ever non-stop and unrefuelled flight around the world. In true movie fashion, right at the start of the 26 986 mile (40 212 km) journey a problem occurred, when the lower wingtip surfaces were rubbed away as they made contact with the runway during the 14 200 ft (4328 m) take-off run from Edwards Air Force Base. However, the strength of the Magnamite graphite and Hexcel paper honeycomb wings proved incredible and the flight continued after the damaged and hanging winglets were deliberately shaken off. When *Voyager* landed again, only 106.14 lb (48.14 kg) of fuel remained, the two tiny 110–130 hp Teledyne Continental piston engines and a fuel-cap leak having consumed 1171.78 US gallons (975.7 Imperial gallons, 4435.66 litres) of fuel from 17 integral tanks. *Voyager* will never fly again and the project is said to have cost more than $2 million, but the fact that this huge sum was raised from the public and from commercial sponsorship shows that even today a pioneering spirit prevails.

Another epic flight occurred during 2–3 July 1987, when Britain's business superstar, Richard Branson, and Per Lindstrand crewed the world's largest ever hot-air balloon, *Virgin Atlantic Flyer*, on the first Atlantic crossing by this form of craft. Leaving Sugar Loaf, Maine, USA, in the early hours of 2 July, the balloon slowly reached a cruising altitude of 27 000 ft (8230 m). After 10 h 3 min flying, Branson and Lindstrand had bettered the previous distance record for hot-air balloons. However, proving once more that pioneering has its dangers, the balloon descended over Northern Ireland, scraped along the ground and ascended once more after fuel cells had been jettisoned to lighten the craft. Finally, the balloon came down in the sea. Both men had to leave the safety of the capsule when they found they could not release the envelope. Happily, they were rescued.

The above mentioned journeys are only two among many exciting and record-breaking flights that have occurred since the previous edition of this book went to press, with microlights (among others) adding a new dimension to long-distance challenges. Of course, record breaking is not the sole domain of private pilots, and commercial and military interests have established their own right to be in the book. In mid-1987 Boeing beat its pre-vious record for the world's best-selling commercial airliner, the Model 737 then ousting the Model 727 by a single aircraft. The same company was the first to fly a propfan engine (on a Model 727-100 in August 1986) and still offers the largest airliner in the Model 747 (the Soviet An-124, though in Aeroflot service, is a freighter). However, one of the attractions of aviation is that current records are sometimes held by the most unexpected aircraft, and the Short *Mercury* seaplane still holds a distance record it set in 1938, while no piston-engined aeroplane has ever flown higher than the Italian Caproni Ca 161 *bis* managed in the same year. Furthermore, the records established by the Soviet Kamov Vintokryl in 1961 and British-designed Fairey Rotodyne convertiplane two years earlier are unchallengeable, at least in the near future.

Although not achieving operational status, the Martin P6M-1 SeaMaster is remembered as the first large turbojet-powered flying boat. The first prototype flew on 14 July, 1955.

Balloons and Airships

The cumulative achievement in heavier-than-air flying by the 18th century can best be summed up as 'theoretical' rather than 'demonstrable'. Tiny ornithopters, helicopters and other models had attained little significant success but at least showed an awareness among the more enlightened scientific fraternity of the inadequacy of human muscles in relation to powered flight and the importance of methodical experimentation.

While such experiments continued, some thinking had earlier turned to the only other possible method of sustaining flight, that of lighter-than-air. The principle involved was not new, the fundamental understanding of why a body can float in liquid or gas going back more than 2000 years to the work of the Greek mathematician Archimedes of Syracuse. However, how to put the principle into practice had still to be worked out.

The invention of the air-pump by Otto von Guericke in the middle of the 17th century led indirectly to the first recorded design for a lighter-than-air craft. Francesco de Lana-Terzi envisaged a four-sphere airship, the idea being that the thin copper foil spheres (with air extracted to create vacuums) would weigh less than the volume of displaced air, thereby making them float if not tethered to the ground. Great interest was expressed in de Lana's concept, but many of the contemporary 'doubters', including some involved in rival heavier-than-air experimentation, proved more able to demonstrate the impossibility of de Lana's craft than to propose practical alternatives.

The first successful demonstration of a model hot-air balloon was made by another Jesuit priest, Bartolomeu Lourenço de Gusmão, who was born some fifteen years after de Lana's design was published. However, de Gusmão was not above making his own errors of judgement, and in 1709 had also shown drawings (and may have even constructed a model) of an intended full-size aircraft that coupled an ornithopter with a balloon sail or parachute, known as the *Passarola*.

More significant than even de Gusmão's model hot-air balloon to the future of lighter-than-air flying was the isolation of 'inflammable air' by English scientist Henry Cavendish in 1766. The gas, later named hydrogen by Lavoisier, offered the key to manned flight and could be manufactured in quantity by an expensive process of chemical reaction; ironically the inventors of a practical gas-holding craft (the balloon), Frenchman Étienne and Joseph Montgolfier, chose heated air as the lifting agent produced by the combustion of solid waste, though the first hydrogen balloon took to the air very soon after.

Due largely to the Montgolfier brothers' experiments in Paris, 1783 is viewed by historians as the foundation year of manned flight proper. Remarkably, the inherent dangers of carrying a 'bonfire' suspended below the balloon's envelope did not dampen the determination of the aeronauts that actually flew the man-carrying Montgolfier balloons. It is interesting to note that while the name Montgolfier is well remembered, the names of the men who piloted the balloons and thereby were exposed to the greatest dangers during these early flights are not generally known.

The possible perils of hot air as the lifting agent divided opinion between this and the use of hydrogen gas, of which the latter had the added benefit of offering the possibility of longer duration flights. History records that hydrogen won the day, though the safety of modern fuel cylinders, burners and flame-resistant fabrics such as Nomex have once again made hot-air ballooning an important aspect of the aviation scene.

A surprisingly short time elapsed before tentative ascents gave way to daring feats. This is particularly surprising when it is considered that the aeronauts were launching themselves into the unknown, at a time when fear of the sky still persisted. But complacency led to tragedy and two such daring flights ended in the first deaths of men and women aeronauts. The first men to lose their lives did so while attempting to cross the English Channel in a combination hot-air/hydrogen balloon, less than two years after the first manned ascent. The first woman aeronaut to die in a ballooning accident had been viewing her own firework party from the vantage point of a hydrogen balloon. In both cases the hydrogen gas ignited.

Few appreciate the scale of ballooning in the 19th century, for pleasure, sport, serious experimentation and observation. From the 1860s balloons filtered into military service, aided in the case of America by the Civil War. This war heralded three innovations that greatly enhanced the usefulness of balloons in military service. On 18 June 1861 the first telegraph message was transmitted from a tethered balloon to the ground, so opening the way for proper air-to-ground communications. The second innovation was the invention of the field-mobile hydrogen gas generating plant, using a process of dilute sulphuric acid reacting with iron and the gas purified by lime. The third was the adoption of a coal barge to transport and tow balloons, so introducing the aircraft carrier. However, the first major balloon operation took place between 1870 and 1871, when the defenders of Paris eluded the surrounding Prussian army by using hastily fabricated balloons to carry from the besieged city despatches, letters, persons and carrier pigeons. This operation led to the deployment (by the Prussians) of the first purpose-designed wagon-mounted anti-aircraft guns.

When it is appreciated that the period between 1895 and 1914 is termed 'the Golden Age' of ballooning, it becomes clear that this form of flying machine can claim a far longer period of continuous prominence than is the case for heavier-than-air machines. Moreover, the great interest in hot-air ballooning of recent years has brought ballooning close to the forefront of sport flying for a second time.

Modern balloons are still subject to the whim of the wind. It was this helplessness that first prompted early pioneers to use propellers and rudders to achieve propulsion and directional control. Attempts to navigate basically spherical balloons by such means lasted far longer than is often supposed, and it is well documented that the Swedish scientist and engineer, Salomon August Andrée, fitted 845 ft² (78.5 m²) of sail to a mast, foresail and jibs attached to his balloon *Ornen* prior to his ill-fated 1897 North Pole flight. Successful directional control was gained with the invention of the airship (correctly dirigible), which moved away from a spherical envelope but was far larger and much more expensive to construct. Despite greater control, early airships appeared to suffer many accidents which, with cost and size, partly explains why the balloon remained popular. Nevertheless, prior to 1915, with development and a great increase in size, the airship was regarded as the most comfortable and safe form of air travel, one suited to commercial operation, and the most destructive vehicle of war devised by man.

The last decade has seen some of the greatest exploits by balloons in the history of aviation. During 12–17 August 1978 the US balloon *Double Eagle II* established an absolute world duration record in Class A of 137 h 5 min 50 s, while *Double Eagle V* set an absolute distance record of 5208.67 miles (8382.54 km) on 9–12

November 1981, flying between Japan and California. More recently, in July 1987 the *Virgin Atlantic Flyer* became the first hot-air balloon to cross the Atlantic, also establishing a world distance record for this type of craft of 3075 miles (4948 km). In the field of dirigibles, on 5 June 1987 the US/UK Westinghouse/Airship Industries Sentinel 5000 was selected by US Naval Air Systems Command for development as an operational prototype airborne surveillance and targeting, early warning and communications airship, expected to be first flown in 1990. Only time will tell if the dirigible is due for the same kind of comeback as enjoyed by the balloon.

BALLOONS

Firsts:

The first recorded design for a lighter-than-air craft was attributed to the Jesuit priest Francesco de Lana-Terzi. Dated 1670, this comprised a wooden boat hull for three to four people, lifted into the air by four rope-tethered copper foil spheres from which the air had been extracted to create vacuums. A central mast with square sail was to provide propulsion and a hand-carried oar was to give directional control.

The first successful demonstration of a model hot-air balloon took place on 8 August 1709 in the Ambassadors' drawing-room at the Casa da India, Lisbon, in the presence of King John V of Portugal, Queen Maria Ann, the Papal Nuncio, Cardinal Conti (later Pope Innocent III), princes of the Court, members of the Diplomatic Corps, noblemen and courtiers. The balloon, made and demonstrated by Father Bartolomeu de Gusmão, consisted of a small envelope of thick paper, inflated with hot air produced by 'fire material contained in an earthenware bowl encrusted in a waxed-wood tray' which was suspended underneath. The balloon is said to have risen quickly to a height of 12 ft (3.5 m) before being destroyed by two valets who feared it might set the curtains alight. Suggestions that Gusmão became airborne later in a full-scale version of the balloon, although documented, cannot be substantiated. Interestingly, Gusmão later constructed a model glider.

Hydrogen was first isolated in 1766 by the English scientist Henry Cavendish, who referred to it

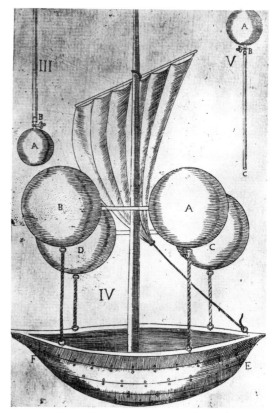

Drawing of de Lana's lighter-than-air craft, with four rope-tethered copper foil spheres intended to provide lift.

as 'inflammable air' or Phlogiston. The Royal Society was told of the gas, which is much lighter than atmospheric air.

The first person to demonstrate successfully the lifting properties of hydrogen gas was Italian Tiberius Cavallo (1749–1809), when in 1781 he filled soap bubbles with hydrogen gas and released them. Further attempts to 'fly' bladders filled with hydrogen gas were unsuccessful.

The first model hot-air balloon demonstrated by Joseph Montgolfier was a silk bag, which rose to the ceiling of a lodging house at Avignon, France, in November 1782.

The first balloon to ascend, capable of sustaining a weight equivalent to that of a man was a hot-air balloon made by the brothers Joseph and Étienne Montgolfier (1740–1810 and 1745–99 respectively). This balloon, calculated as being able to lift 450 lb (205 kg), was released on 25 April 1783, probably at Annonay, France, rose to about 1000 ft (305 m) and landed about 3000 ft (915 m) from the point of lift-off. The balloon had a diameter of about 39 ft (12 m) and achieved its lift using hot air provided by combustion of solid waste (probably paper, straw and wood) below the neck of the envelope.

The first public demonstration by the Montgolfier brothers was given in the market place at Annonay on 4 June 1783, when a small balloon of about 36 ft (11 m) diameter, constructed from linen and paper, rose to a height of 6000 ft (1830 m). This balloon travelled more than 1 mile (1.6 km) before landing.

The first free ascent by a hydrogen-filled balloon (unmanned) was made on 27 August 1783 from the Champ-de-Mars, Paris, when Jacques Alexandre César Charles (1746–1823) launched a 12 ft (3.5 m) balloon. It was filled with hydrogen that Charles had manufactured and was capable of lifting 20 lb (9 kg).

The balloon drifted for 45 min and came to earth at Gonesse, 15 miles (25 km) from Paris, where it was promptly attacked by a frenzied mob of panic-stricken peasants, who destroyed the 22 000 ft³ (620 m³) rubber-coated silk envelope.

The first living creatures to become airborne under a balloon were a sheep, a duck and a cock which were lifted by a 41 ft (13 m) diameter hot-air Montgolfier balloon at the Court of Versailles on 19 September 1783 before King Louis XVI, Marie-Antoinette and their Court. The balloon achieved an altitude of 1700 ft (520 m) before descending in the Forest of Vaucresson 8 min later, having travelled about 2 miles (3 km). The occupants were scarcely affected by their flight nor by their landing.

The first known award for an aviation feat was the Order of St Michel presented to the Montgolfier brothers by King Louis XVI after the balloon demonstration of 19 September 1783.

The first man carried aloft in a balloon, and therefore **the world's first aeronaut**, was François Pilâtre de Rozier. On 15 October 1783 he ascended in a tethered 49 ft (15 m) diameter Montgolfier hot-air balloon to 84 ft (26 m), the limit of the restraining rope. The hot air was provided by a straw-fed fire below the fabric envelope and the balloon stayed up for nearly 4½ min. Interestingly, the honour of being the first aeronaut had nearly gone to two criminals who, as proposed by King Louis XVI, might have gained their freedom by volunteering for the flight. After protests by de Rozier, he was given the opportunity to become airborne instead.

The first men carried in free flight by a balloon, the first pilot and passenger, and the first men to make an aerial journey were de Rozier and the Marquis d'Arlandes, who rose in the 49 ft (15 m) diameter Montgolfier balloon at 13.54 h on 21 November 1783 from the gardens of the Château La Muette in the Bois de Boulogne. These early aeronauts were airborne for 25 min and landed on the Butte-aux-Cailles, about 5½ miles (8.5 km) from their point of departure, having drifted to and fro across Paris. Their maximum altitude is unlikely to have been above 1500 ft (450 m).

The first public demonstration of a balloon in England was made by Italian Count Francesco Zambeccari on 25 November 1783, when an unmanned hydrogen balloon of some 10 ft (3.05 m) diameter was released in the Honourable Artillery Company's training ground in London. The balloon finally alighted at Petworth, Sussex.

The first men to be carried in free flight by a hydrogen balloon were Jacques Charles and one of the Robert brothers. The Robert brothers had been responsible for producing rubber-coated silk material, ideal for retaining the gas, and indeed had helped construct the balloon for the attempt. They ascended from the gardens of Les Tuileries, Paris, at 13.45 h on 1 December 1783, in a balloon 28 ft 2 in (8.6 m) in diameter before a crowd estimated at 400 000. The craft landed 27 miles (43 km) distant, near the town of Nesles. This flight can be said to have heralded the beginning of the end for the early hot-air balloon, having achieved a greater distance than was possible with the Montgolfier type.

The first reference to using a movable horizontal winged surface as a method of controlling balloons is attributed to David Bourgeois, in 1784.

The first unmanned hot-air balloon experiments in Germany were conducted by a monk, Ulrich Schiegg (1752–1810), at Ottobeuren in January 1784. Earlier still, at the end of the previous year, balloon experiments had begun in the Netherlands, though by whom is not clear.

The first unmanned hot-air balloon to be released in the United Kingdom was that constructed by Irishman Riddick. It was flown on 4 February 1784 from the Rotunda Gardens in Dublin.

The first manned balloon ascent in Italy was made on 25 February 1784, when Chevalier Paolo Andreani and brothers Augustin and Charles Gerli ascended in a Montgolfier balloon from Moncuco, near Milan.

Left   *Living creatures first take to the air in a balloon on 19 September 1783. Less than a month later man first flew.*

Right   *Francois Pilâtre de Rozier and the Marquis d'Arlandes undertook the first aerial journey on 21 November 1783, in a Montgolfier hot-air balloon. Note in this illustration that the ropes attached to the poles for captive flights hang loose. (Science Museum, London)*

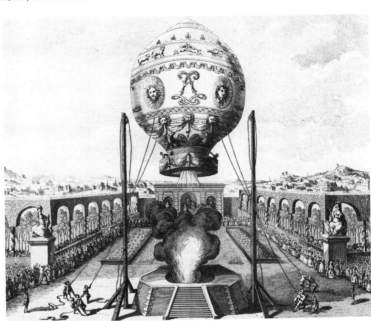

The first manned balloon flight in the United Kingdom was made on 15 April 1784, when Mr Rosseau and a ten-year-old drummer boy took off at 14.00 h from Dublin, Ireland, for a 2 h flight. They eventually landed at Ratoath. This marked also **the first occasion music was played from an aircraft**, as the boy beat a tune on a drum for at least an hour of the flight to indicate their position to the crowd below.

The first women to ascend in a balloon (tethered) were the Marchioness de Montalembert, the Countess de Montalembert, the Countess de Podenas and Mademoiselle de Lagarde, who were lifted into the air by a Montgolfier hot-air balloon on 20 May 1784 from the Faubourg-Saint-Antoine, Paris.

The first woman to be carried in free flight in a balloon was Madame Thible, who ascended in a Montgolfier with Monsieur Fleurant on 4 June 1784 from Lyon, France. The balloon, named *Le Gustav*, reached an altitude of 8500 ft (2600 m) in the presence of the King of Sweden.

The first manned balloon ascent in Austria was made on 7 July 1784, when Austrian J. Stuwer ascended from Vienna.

The first Scottish aeronaut was James Tytler, who made a balloon ascent from the Comely Gardens, Edinburgh, on 7 August 1784. However, he is better remembered for making an ascent in a home-made Montgolfier-type balloon on 25 August, this time from the city's Heriot's Garden. He is believed to have attained an altitude no greater than 500 ft (150 m).

The first aerial voyage by a hydrogen balloon over Great Britain was made by Vincenzo Lunardi of Lucca, an employee of the Italian Embassy in London. On 15 September 1784 he ascended in a 'charlière' (hydrogen balloon) from the Honourable Artillery's training ground at Moorfields, London, and flew northwards to the Parish of North Mimms (today the site of the village of Welhamgreen), Hertfordshire, where he landed his cat and jettisoned ballast. This caused him to ascend again and he finally landed at Standon Green End near Ware, Hertfordshire. On the spot where he landed stands a rough stone monument on which a tablet proclaims:

> Let Posterity know
> And knowing be astonished!
> That
> On the 15th day of September, 1784
> Vincent Lunardi
> of
> Lucca in Tuscany
> The first Aerial Traveller in Britain
> Mounting from the Artillery Ground
> in London
> And traversing the Regions of the Air
> For two Hours and fifteen Minutes
> in this Spot
> Revisited the Earth.
> On this rude Monument
> For ages be recorded
> That wonderous enterprize, successfully
> achieved
> By the powers of Chymistry
> And the fortitude of man
> The improvement in Science
> Which
> The Great Author of all Knowledge
> Patronising by his Providence
> The inventions of Mankind
> Hath generously permitted
> To their benefit
> And
> His own Eternal Glory

The first English aeronaut was James Sadler who, on 4 October 1784, flew in a home-made Montgolfier-type hot-air balloon of 170 ft (52 m) circumference at Oxford.

The first application of a propeller to a full-size man-carrying aircraft was recorded on 16 October 1784, when Jean-Pierre Blanchard added a small hand-operated six-blade propeller to the passenger basket of his balloon. As a means of propulsion it was, of course, completely ineffectual.

The first English aeronaut of a hydrogen balloon was also James Sadler, who ascended in such a craft from Oxford on 12 November 1784.

The first aerial crossing of the English Channel was achieved by the Frenchman Jean-Pierre Blanchard, accompanied by the American Dr John Jeffries. On 7 January 1785 they rose from Dover at 13.00 h and landed in the Forêt de Felmores, France, at approximately 15.30 h, having discarded almost all their clothes to lighten the craft *en route*. Their balloon was hydrogen-filled.

The first attempt to cross the Irish Sea by balloon was made by Richard Crosbie on 19 January 1785. Before a crowd of tens of thousands of onlookers, he set off in his hydrogen balloon from Ranelagh Gardens, Ireland. After a good start to the journey, Crosbie decided to postpone the actual sea crossing as darkness was setting in. He eventually landed safely at Clontarf. On 12 May the same year Crosbie made a second attempt at the crossing, but on this occasion the hydrogen balloon only just managed to lift off from the Dublin Barracks and was soon at rest again. Having yet again charged money for the opportunity of seeing him fly, probably making Crosbie **the first aviation entrepreneur**, he asked the crowd for a volunteer of smaller proportions than himself to attempt the crossing. Richard McGwire stepped forward and indeed took off. Fortunately, he was followed out to sea by a number of boats, which eventually plucked him from the water some miles out. On 19 July Crosbie made his last attempt to cross the Irish Sea by balloon. This might have succeeded but for a storm, and eventually Crosbie was rescued by a barge.

The first aeronaut to receive a knighthood for attempting an aerial journey was twenty-one-year-old Richard McGwire (see above).

The first woman to ascend in a balloon in England was Frenchwoman Mlle Simonet, who flew with Jean-Pierre Blanchard from the Barbican on 3 May 1785.

The first aeronauts to be killed while ballooning were François Pilâtre de Rozier and Jules Romain, who were killed while attempting to fly the English Channel from Boulogne on 15 June 1785 in a composite hot-air/hydrogen balloon. It is believed that, when hydrogen was vented from the envelope, the escaping gas was ignited, and the balloon fell at Huitmile Warren, near Boulogne.

The first British woman to travel by balloon in Britain was Mrs Letitia Anne Sage, who ascended in Lunardi's hydrogen balloon from St George's Fields, London, on 29 June 1785. Lunardi, who had proclaimed that he would be accompanied by three passengers (Mrs Sage, a Col Hastings and George Biggin), discovered that his balloon's

Richard Crosbie's final bid to cross the Irish Sea, 19 July 1785, ascending from Leinster Lawn. (National Library of Ireland)

lifting power was not equal to the task. Rather than draw attention to the lady's weight (by her own admission, she weighed more than 200 lb [90 kg]), he stepped down from the basket with Col Hastings. The balloon eventually came to earth near Harrow, Middlesex, where the two occupants were rescued from an irate farmer by the boys of that famous school.

The first manned balloon ascent in the Netherlands was made on 12 July 1785, when Frenchman Jean-Pierre Blanchard ascended from The Hague.

The first manned balloon ascent in Germany was made on 3 October 1785, when Frenchman Jean-Pierre Blanchard ascended from Frankfurt-on-Main. Other European nations in which he made the first balloon ascent include Switzerland.

The first manned balloon ascent in Belgium was made on 20 November 1785, when Frenchman Jean-Pierre Blanchard ascended at Ghent.

The first use of the word 'hydrogen' for the 'inflammable air' used in balloons was made by the French chemist Lavoisier in 1790.

The first free flight by a balloon in the United States of America was made on 9 January 1793 by the Frenchman Jean-Pierre Blanchard, who ascended in a hydrogen balloon from the yard of the old Walnut Street Prison, Philadelphia, and landed in Gloucester County, New Jersey, after a flight of 46 min. Among the vast crowd who turned out to witness this event were the President, George Washington, and four future presidents of the United States: John Adams, Thomas Jefferson, James Madison and James Monroe.

The first use of a man-carrying balloon in war (tethered) was in June 1794, deployed by the French Republican Army at Maubeuge, Belgium. On 26 June, during the battle of Fleurus, Capt Coutelle ascended in the balloon *Entreprenant* to make an aerial reconnaissance of the enemy, Coutelle had been sent to Maubeuge by the Committee of Public Safety but, on arrival, had nearly been executed as a spy by an officer of the French Army whose job it was to ensure that soldiers did not desert the fighting ranks. Both balloon companies attached to the Army were disbanded five years later.

In tethered flight above the battling armies, Capt. Coutelle of the French Republican Army makes the first ever aerial reconnaissance during the Battle of Fleurus, 1794. (Royal Aeronautical Society)

The first balloon ascent on a horse is generally believed to have been made by Frenchman Pierre Testu-Brissy, ascending from Meudon on 16 October 1798.

The first man to survive the destruction of his hot-air balloon while in flight was R. Jordarki Kuparanto who, on 24 July 1808, baled out of a Montgolfier balloon that had caught fire. Luckily Kuparanto had taken the precaution of ascending with a parachute as part of his equipment.

The first aerial crossing of the Irish Sea was accomplished on 22 July 1817 by Windham Sadler, son of James Sadler, the first English aeronaut. His journey took him between the Portobello Barracks and Holyhead, Wales.

The first woman aeronaut to be killed in a flying disaster was Madame Blanchard, widow of the pioneer French aeronaut Jean-Pierre Blanchard (who had died after a heart attack, suffered while ballooning, on 7 March 1809). Madame Blanchard was killed when her hydrogen balloon was ignited during a firework display at the Tivoli Gardens, Paris, on 7 July 1819.

James Sadler, the first English aeronaut, as engraved for the Dublin Magazine. (National Library of Ireland)

The first aeronaut to record 100 flights was undoubtedly the Englishman Charles Green (1785–1870) who, on 14 May 1832, ascended in a balloon for the 100th time, on this occasion from the Mermaid Tavern, Hackney, London. Green was the pilot of the *Great Nassau Balloon* during Robert Cocking's parachute descent of 24 July 1837.

The first long-distance voyage by air from England was made during 7–8 November 1836 by a hydrogen balloon named *The Royal Vauxhall Balloon*, crewed by Charles Green, Robert Holland MP and Monck Mason. They ascended from Vauxhall Gardens, London, and travelled 480 miles (772 km) to land near Weilberg in the Duchy of Nassau. The balloon was subsequently renamed the *Great Nassau Balloon*.

The first joint-stock company associated with ballooning was the Aeronautic Association, for which 4000 £2 shares were offered to the public in 1837. Expected to realize a profit of up to 200 per cent, the Association intended to construct the largest balloon to date, for 'promoting geographical surveys of some of the remaining undiscovered tracts of the globe, the first attempt to be directed to the unexplored regions of Africa'. The venture was unsuccessful.

The first recognized design for a kite-balloon, intended to be tethered to the ground and shaped to derive stability in high wind conditions, is generally attributed to the Frenchman Louis Godard, though another Frenchman, Abel Transon, expounded similar ideas much earlier, in 1844.

The first British aeronautical magazine was *The Balloon or Aerostatic Magazine*, published for the proprietors by B. Steill and edited by Henry Wells (pseudonym for Henry Tracey Coxwell). Priced 6d, the first edition of this monthly magazine appeared on 1 August 1845 and lasted just four issues.

The first balloon bombing raid was carried out on 22 August 1849, when Austrian unmanned hot-air balloons were launched against Venice. These caused little damage, despite each carrying a 30 lb (14 kg) bomb and time fuse.

The first balloon flight over the Alps was made between Marseilles and Turin on 7 October 1849 by M. F. Farban.

The first hydrogen balloon ascent in Australia was achieved on 29 March 1858 from the Cremorne Gardens, Melbourne, in a balloon named *Australasian*. This was flown by two men named Dean and Brown.

The first photographs taken from a tethered balloon were the work of Frenchman Félix Tournachon (1820–1910), better known as Nadar, in 1858.

The first long-distance balloon flight in America was made on 2 July 1859 by John C. Wise, John La Mountain and O. A. Gager, who covered 1120 miles (1800 km) from St Louis to Henderson, New York.

The first telegraph message transmitted from the air (and then relayed to the President of the United States) was keyed out by an official telegraph operator who accompanied the flamboyant showman Thaddeus Sobieski Constantine Lowe, during a tethered demonstration flight in the balloon *Enterprise* on 18 June 1861.

The first American Army Balloon Corps was formed on 1 October 1861 with a complement of 50 men under the command of Thaddeus S. C. Lowe who, following his demonstration flight, had been made Chief Aeronaut of the Army of the Potomac. The Corps had originally five balloons, the *Constitution, Intrepid, Union, United States* and *Washington*. Two more, the *Excelsior* and *Eagle*, entered service early in 1862. They were used for reconnaissance and artillery direction. The Corps was disbanded in mid-1863, almost two years before the end of the American Civil War.

The world's first aircraft carrier (defined as a waterborne craft used to tether, transport or launch an aircraft) was the *George Washington Parke Custis*, a coal-barge converted during the American Civil War in 1861 under the direction of Thaddeus S. C. Lowe for the transport and towing of observation balloons. The *G W Parke Custis* entered service with General McClellan's Army of the Potomac in November 1861, towing balloons on the Potomac River for the observation of the opposing Confederate forces.

Intrepid, one of the five original hydrogen balloons of the American Army Balloon Corps, was deployed for observation during the Battle of Fair Oaks in the Civil War on 31 May and 1 June 1862.

USS George Washington Parke Custis *on the Potomac River near Budd's Ferry, below Mount Vernon, in November 1861, deploying the balloon* Washington *to make a reconnaissance of the blockade. (US Navy)*

Inflation of the Civil War balloon Intrepid. *(US Air Force)*

On 11 December one of the balloons was used by the Corps to assist in the crossing of the river Rappahannock, probably the first time a balloon had been used in connection with crossing difficult terrain.

The first military use of balloons in an international war outside Europe was by the Brazilian Marquis de Caxias during the Paraguayan War of 1864–70. This atrocious conflict, which committed the combined forces of Brazil, Argentina and Uruguay against landlocked Paraguay, brought total disaster to the latter nation whose dictator, Francisco Solano López, ordered mass killings among his own people in a savage attempt to compel them towards victory. In the event Brazil occupied Paraguay until 1876; of about 250 000 Paraguayan male nationals before the war, only 28 000 survived in 1871.

The Prussian Army formed two lighter-than-air detachments in 1870, with the assistance of Englishman Henry Coxwell. These were deployed during the Franco-Prussian war (see below).

The first major balloon operation was carried out during the Franco-Prussian War of 1870–1. The Prussian Army had surrounded Paris and had cut off the city from the rest of France. Inside the city were a few skilled balloonists and material for balloon-making. In an attempt to get despatches out of Paris, Jules Duroug ascended in a balloon on 23 September 1870. He flew over the Prussian camp and landed at Evreux three hours later. He was followed by Gaston Tissandier, Eugène Godard and Mangin, who were all fired on. Meanwhile, inside Paris other balloons were being made from available material and sailors from the French Navy were being trained as pilots. Balloon ascents carried on until 28 January 1871, by which time 66 flights had been made, carrying about 110 passengers in addition to the pilots, 2½–3 million letters, and carrier pigeons to fly back to Paris with despatches. In mid-October 1870 a chemist, M. Barreswil, suggested the use of microphotography to allow each pigeon to carry a large number of messages. On 18 November **the first official pigeon post** was introduced between Tours and Paris. This microphotography system was reintroduced during the Second World War as the Airgraph service, coping with large volumes of forces and civilian airmail.

The first crossing of the North Sea was made from Paris, France, on 1 November 1870 in the hydrogen balloon *Ville d'Orléans*. The 774 mile (1246 km) journey ended at Blefjell in Norway.

The first attempt to fly across the Atlantic in a hydrogen balloon was made by John Wise in 1873. Sponsored by the *New York Daily Graphic*, the attempt had to be abandoned after only 41 miles (66 km) following an accident.

The first practical development of balloons in the British Army dates from 1878 when the **first 'air estimates'** by the War Office allocated the sum of £150 for the construction of a balloon. Capt J. L. B. Templer of the Middlesex Militia (later KRRC(M)) and Capt H. P. Lee, RE, were appointed to carry out the necessary development work. Although Capt Templer was thus the **first British Air Commander** and an aeronaut in his own right (and the owner of the balloon *Crusader*, which became the **first balloon used by the British Army** in 1879), the **first two aeronauts in the British Army** were Lt (later Capt) G. E.

British Army balloon at Frensham in 1890. (RAF Museum)

Grover, RE, and Capt F. Beaumont, RE, who had been attached as aeronauts to the Federal Army during the American Civil War from 1862. The **first British Army balloon**, a coal-gas balloon named *Pioneer*, was made during 1879, costing £71 from the £150 appropriation, and had a capacity of 10 000 ft³ (283.2 m³).

The first balloon ascent in Canada was made at Montreal on 31 July 1879 by a hydrogen balloon manned by Richard Cowan, Charles Grimley and Charles Page.

The first military use of a man-carrying balloon in Britain was that by a balloon detachment during military manoeuvres at Aldershot, Hampshire, on 24 June 1880. A balloon detachment accompanied the British military expedition to Bechuanaland, leaving on 26 November 1884 and arriving at Cape Town on 19 December. Another accompanied the expeditionary force to the Sudan, departing from Britain on 15 February 1885.

The first kite-balloon used in army manoeuvres was designed by August von Parseval, a German officer, and Bartsch von Sigsfeld, and used by the German Army in 1897.

The first attempt to carry out an exploration of the Arctic by free balloon was made on 11 July 1897, when Salomon August Andrée and two companions took off from Danes Island, Spitzbergen. Their 160 000 ft³ (4531 m³) capacity balloon had a sail attached to a complicated arrangement of drag ropes, with which it was hoped to steer the craft. Nothing was known of the explorers' fate until their bodies were discovered on White Island, Franz Josef Land, on 6 August 1930.

The first American pilot to be shot down in war was Sgt Ivy Baldwin, Army Signal Corps. In 1898 America and Spain went to war and Baldwin successfully persuaded the Army to deploy a balloon for observation. During the Battle of Santiago, Cuba, Baldwin ascended and gave important information on Spanish troop movements. Seeing the tethered balloon, and in the knowledge of the soldiers below, Spanish troops opened fire on the envelope and it dropped into water, causing only slight injuries to Baldwin. He eventually died in 1955.

The first ratified altitude record for balloons was that achieved on 30 June 1901 by Professors Berson and Suring of the Berliner Verein für Luftschiffahrt who attained a height of 35 435 ft (10 800 m). At the time of this record's ratification there was much controversy with those who still firmly believed that James Glaisher had achieved a height of 37 000 ft (11 275 m) on 5 September 1862; as instrumentation to confirm this altitude with any chance of accuracy did not exist at the time, ratification of the Berson and Suring record was upheld; this record remained unbroken for 30 years (although exceeded on a number of occasions by aeroplanes). Berson and Suring's record was beaten in 1931 when the Swiss physicist Prof Auguste Piccard, carried in a sealed capsule suspended beneath a balloon, made **the first balloon flight into the stratosphere** with an altitude of 50 135 ft (15 281 m). In the following year he increased this to 53 153 ft (16 201 m). On 11 November 1935 Capt Orvil Anderson and Capt Albert Stevens of the USA attained an altitude of 72 395 ft (22 066 m) in a balloon in which they ascended from a point 11 miles (17 km) south-west of Rapid City, South Dakota, and landed 12 miles (19 km) south of White Lake, South Dakota.

The first official balloon race in Great Britain, organized by the Aero Club, took place on 7 July 1906. Seven balloons competed, taking off from the grounds of the Ranelagh Club at Barn Elms, London. Winner of the event was Frank Hedges Butler, accompanied by Col J. C. and Mrs Capper.

The first international balloon race, and also **the first of the balloon races for the Gordon Bennett Trophy**, attracted an entry of 16 balloons. Flown from the gardens of the Tuileries, Paris, on 30 September 1906, it was won by Lt Frank P. Lahm of the US Army who covered a distance of 402 miles (647 km) before landing at Fylingdales Moor, near Whitby, Yorkshire.

Without doubt, the Gordon Bennett contest for a trophy and an annual prize of 12 500 francs, presented by the expatriate American James Gordon Bennett, became the most famous international balloon event.

On 15 June 1924 Lt Ernest Demuyter of Belgium, flying the balloon *Belgica*, won the trophy outright, having won also the two previous contests. His winning distance was 466 miles (750 km), reaching St Abbs Head, Berwick, Scot-

Right *33 lb bomb from a Japanese intercontinental balloon. (US Army)*

Below *Japanese rubberised silk balloon floating across the Pacific Ocean in late 1944, carrying a 33 lb anti-personnel bomb and incendiary weapons. (US Army)*

land. This distance, however, was one of the shortest in the first series of contests. Sportingly, the trophy was represented for competition, leading to the second series, won by Capt W. E. Kepner, US Army, on 30 June 1928; a third series, won in 1930 by W. T. van Orman of the USA; and a fourth series, with the 1938 and last contest being won by Janusz of Poland, with a flight of 1013 miles (1630 km).

The first international balloon race in Great Britain, on 30 May 1908, began at the grounds of the Hurlingham Club, Fulham, London. Thirty balloons competed, representing five European nations.

The first National Balloon Race held in America was won by John Berry and Paul McCullough on 5 June 1909. Their distance covered was about 378 miles (608 km).

The first operational use of intercontinental bomb-carrying balloons was made on 3 November 1944, when the Japanese initiated an assault on the United States. An ingenious constant-altitude device was intended to ensure that the balloon remained aloft in the prevailing jet stream which carried the balloons 6200 miles (9978 km) across the Pacific Ocean. Each carried a payload of one 33 lb (15 kg) anti-personnel bomb and two

incendiary weapons. More than 9000 of these balloons were launched, and it is estimated that approximately 1000 completed the crossing. Because of a self-destruct device, there were only 285 recorded incidents as a result of their use, and only six persons are known to have been killed by them.

The first ratified altitude record for a manned balloon of over 100 000 ft (30 480 m) was achieved by Maj David G. Simons, a medical

Major David G. Simons sitting inside the compact gondola before take off. (US Navy)

officer of the US Air Force, who reached an altitude of 101 516 ft (30 942 m) on 19–20 August 1957 in the 3 000 000 ft³ (84 950 m³) balloon *AF-WRI-1*. He took off from Crosby, Minnesota, on 19 August to gather scientific data in the stratosphere and landed at Frederick, South Dakota, the following day.

The first hot-air balloon record to be ratified by the FAI, a height of 9770 ft (2978 m), was achieved by B. Bogan in the USA on 13 September 1965.

The first crossing of the Swiss Alps by hot-air balloon was achieved on 21 August 1972 by Cameron A-140, crewed by Don Cameron and Mark Yarry. The flight was from Zermatt, Switzerland, to Biella, Italy.

The first transatlantic crossing by a gas balloon was achieved by *Double Eagle II*, crewed by Ben L. Abruzzo, Maxie L. Anderson and Larry M. Newman. This achievement, made between 12 and 17 August 1978, established new absolute world distance and duration records for gas balloons of 3107.62 miles (5001.22 km) and 137 h 5 min

50 s respectively, of which the duration record remains unbeaten.

The first non-stop balloon flight across the American continent was achieved by Fred Gorrell and John Shoecroft in the helium-filled balloon *Superchicken III*. Launched from Costa Mesa, Los Angeles, California, on 9 October 1981, a landing was made on Blackbeard's Island, Georgia, 55 h 25 min later. the distance covered was 2515 miles (4048 km).

The first transpacific crossing by gas balloon was achieved by *Double Eagle V*, between Nagashima, Japan, and Covello, California, USA, during 9–12 November 1981. (See also Longest.)

The first transatlantic crossing by hot-air balloon was achieved by *Virgin Atlantic Flyer*, crewed by Richard Branson and Per Lindstrand. The flight began at 0410 hours (local time) on 2 July 1987 from Sugar Loaf, Maine, USA, and the balloon first alighted near Limavady, Northern Ireland, on 3 July, regaining altitude after being dragged some 150 ft (46 m) but finally alighting in the sea approximately 1650 ft (500 m) off the coast.

Left   Historic photograph of the first transatlantic crossing by hot-air balloon, achieved by Virgin Atlantic Flyer during 2–3 July 1987. This is also the largest ever hot-air balloon.

Right   Commander Malcolm D. Ross established the current world altitude record for manned free balloons in May 1961. Prior to this, on 8 November 1956, he manned the US Navy's Stratolab Project balloon that was the first balloon to fly above 75,000 ft, actually reaching 76,000 ft (23,165 m). Shown is the aluminium gondola, completed by Winzen Research and General Mills Inc. (US Navy)

Largest:

The largest hot-air balloon constructed by the Montgolfier brothers, and the second-largest hot-air balloon ever was the *Flesselles*, which reputedly had a capacity of some 812 980 ft³ (23 000 m³). Flown on 19 January 1784, it carried seven passengers, including Joseph Montgolfier and Pilâtre de Rozier.

The largest balloon ever built was constructed by Winzen Research Inc, Minnesota, USA, with an inflatable volume of 70 000 000 ft³ (2 000 000 m³).

The largest non-rigid kite-balloon ever constructed was built by the French Aerazur company in the 1960s, with a volume of 529 720 ft³ (15 000 m³). This and others were employed for tests in the atmosphere of nuclear weapons.

The largest hot-air balloon ever flown was the *Virgin Atlantic Flyer*, with an envelope volume of 2 130 000 ft³ (60 314.8 m³), diameter of 166 ft (50.6 m) and height of 180 ft 5 in (55 m). (See also Firsts.)

Fastest:

The fastest manned hot-air balloon ever flown was the *Virgin Atlantic Flyer*, which achieved a computed speed of 153 mph (246 km/h) during its Atlantic crossing on 2–3 July 1987, having entered a jetstream at its cruising height of 27 000 ft (8230 m). (See also Firsts.)

Highest:

The current world altitude record for manned free balloons is held by Commander Malcolm D. Ross and Lt Commander V. A. Prather of the United States Navy Reserve, who, on 4 May 1961, ascended over the Gulf of Mexico to an altitude of 113 739.9 ft (34 668 m) in the Lee Lewis Memorial Winzen Research balloon.

The greatest altitude flown in a gas balloon by a woman is 20 262 ft (6176 m), achieved by Ms R. Peter of the Federal Republic of Germany on 30 July 1975.

The current women's world altitude record for hot-air balloons is 31 300 ft (9540.24 m),

achieved by Ms Carol Davis of the USA on 8 December 1979.

The current absolute world altitude record for manned hot-air balloons is 55 135 ft (16 805 m), achieved by Briton Julian Nott on 31 October 1980, flying a Cameron A-375 from Longmont, Colorado, USA.

The current world altitude record for manned pressurized balloons is 17 767 ft (5415.4 m), achieved by Briton Julian Nott in ULD 1 during 20–22 November 1984.

The current world altitude record for mixed gas/hot-air balloons is 14 573 ft (4442 m), achieved by Henk Brink of the Netherlands on 26 August 1985.

Longest:

The longest duration flight in a gas balloon by a woman is 40 h 13 min, achieved by Ms C. Wolf of the USA, from 20 November 1961.

The current women's world distance record for hot-air balloons is 228.03 miles (366.99 km), achieved by Ms Denise Wiederkehr of the USA in a Raven S-50 A on 23 March 1974.

The current women's world duration record for hot-air balloons is 11 h 10 min, achieved by Ms Denise Wiederkehr of the USA in a Raven S-50 A on 23 March 1974.

The current world duration record for manned, mixed gas/hot-air balloons is 96 h 24 min, achieved by Britons Donald Cameron and C. Davey between 26 and 30 July 1978.

The current world distance record for a manned balloon was established during 9–12 November 1981 by the helium-filled Raven balloon *Double Eagle V*. Crewed by Ben L. Abruzzo, Rocky Aoki, Ron Clark and Larry M. Newman, it travelled 5208.68 miles (8382.54 km) between Nagashima, Japan, and Covello, California, USA.

The longest distance flown in a gas balloon by a woman is 843.59 miles (1357.63 km), achieved by Ms Caplan of the USA from 8 October 1982.

The current world duration record for manned pressurized balloons is 33 h 8 min 42 s, achieved by Briton Julian Nott in the ULD-1 during 20–22 November 1984.

The current world distance record for manned pressurized balloons is 1485.98 miles (2391.46 km), achieved by Briton Julian Nott in the ULD-1 during 20–22 November 1984.

The current world distance record for manned mixed gas/hot-air balloons is 2521.36 miles (4057.732 km), achieved by H. Brink, E. Brink and W. Hageman of the Netherlands from 2 September 1986.

The longest endurance and greatest distance achieved by a manned hot-air balloon were 31 h 41 min and 3075 miles (4948 km) respectively, set by the *Virgin Atlantic Flyer* during its Atlantic crossing on 2–3 July 1987. (See also Firsts.)

The longest planned balloon flight is a round-the-world attempt, expected to last between 12 and 20 days. The pilot will be Briton Julian Nott, who holds the current world altitude record for hot-air balloons. The balloon, named *Endeavour*, is expected to journey continuously in a jetstream at an altitude of about 40 000 ft (12 190 m) and will have a pressurized cabin for the pilot (which was under construction in 1987). The date for the attempt, which will begin in Australia, had not been reported at the time of writing. A one-third scale balloon of *Endeavour*, known as the ULD-1, holds 24 international and world ballooning records and flew across Australia in a little over 33 h in November 1984. (See also Highest and Longest.)

Greatest:

The second but most famous air crossing of the North Sea was made during 12–13 October 1907 by the hydrogen balloon *Mammoth*, manned by Frenchman Monsieur A. F. Gaudron and two others. They ascended from Crystal Palace, London, and landed at Brackan on the shore of Lake Vänern in Sweden. The straight-line distance flown was about 720 miles (1160 km).

The greatest 'balloon buster' fighter pilot of the First World War and presumably any war was 2nd Lt Frank Luke of the 27th Aero (Pursuit) Squadron, American Expeditionary Force. His first victory over a balloon was on 12 September 1918, and in total he destroyed 15 balloons and 6 aircraft. He was killed in action on 28 September while on an unauthorized balloon-destroying mission, later receiving a posthumous Congressional Medal of Honor.

AIRSHIPS

Having become airborne in hot-air and hydrogen balloons, it was not long before the more inventive aeronauts attempted to overcome the unpredictable nature of ballooning by seeking ways and means of steering and propulsion. With these, the aeronaut would be able to travel in a direction other than that dictated by the wind. The result of propulsion was the airship, the accepted term for a powered lighter-than-air aircraft. An airship capable also of being steered and guided is correctly known as a dirigible, though 'airship' is the more commonly used name for all powered and steerable craft and both conventions are used below.

Firsts:

The first published design for a dirigible was that conceived by French Lt Jean-Baptiste Marie Meusnier, Corps of Engineers, in 1784. This was submitted to the Académie des Sciences but was never constructed. The design called for inner and outer envelopes, the latter to maintain the craft's steerable cigar shape when gas was released, and three large two-blade propellers were to provide propulsion, turned by 80 crew members prior to development of a suitable engine.

The first dirigible fitted with a ballonet, a small inner gastight compartment within the envelope which could be inflated with air to the desired volume or deflated to regulate altitude (ballonets were subsequently employed successfully for maintaining the envelope shape during variations in lifting gas volume and to adjust trim), was constructed by the Robert brothers. Based on the Meusnier concept, the craft flew for the first time on 15 July 1784 but was not particularly successful, this first flight ending with the crew piercing the envelope to relieve the dangerously high gas pressure. The dirigible is also remembered as **the first cylindrical lighter-than-air craft** and had a volume of 28 252 ft³ (800 m³).

The world's first powered, manned dirigible made its first flight on 24 September 1852, when the Frenchman Henry Giffard rose in a steam-powered balloon from the Paris Hippodrome and travelled approximately 17 miles (27 km) to Trappes. His average speed for the journey was 5 mph (8 km/h). The envelope was 144 ft (43.89 m) in length and had a capacity of 88 000 ft³ (2492 m³); the steam engine developed about 3 hp and drove an 11 ft (3.35 m) diameter three-blade propeller.

The world's first aircraft to be powered by an internal combustion engine was that built and

The world's first powered, manned dirigible was designed by Frenchman Henry Giffard and first flown on 24 September 1852. (Science Museum, London)

flown by Austrian Paul Hänlein in 1872. Approximately 164 ft (50 m) in length and 29 ft 6 in (9 m) maximum diameter, the 85 000 ft³ (2407 m³) dirigible was powered by a 5 hp Lenoir-type four-cylinder gas engine which consumed gas from the envelope. This turned a 15 ft (4.57 m) diameter propeller at about 40 rpm, using 250 ft³ (7.08 m³) of gas per hour. Only tethered flights were made and lack of capital prevented further development.

The first great German dirigible pioneer was Dr Karl Wölfert who, in 1880, ascended in a dirigible fitted with a small engine. His flying companion was Herr Baumgarten. Load distribution problems caused the dirigible to crash, prompting Baumgarten to abandon the project. However, Wölfert was not so discouraged and on 5 March 1882 he ascended in a dirigible at Charlottenburg, when he attempted unsuccessfully to propel it using a hand-turned propeller.

The first dirigible fitted with an electric motor was that flown on 8 October 1883 by Frenchman Gaston Tissandier. The motor was produced by Siemens and was powered by 24 bichromate of potash batteries.

The world's first fully controllable powered dirigible was *La France*, an electric-powered craft which, flown by Capt Charles Renard and Lt Arthur Krebs of the French Corps of Engineers, took off on 9 August 1884 from Chalais-Meudon, France, flew a circular course of about 5 miles (8 km), returned to its point of departure and landed safely. The 9 hp Gramme electric motor drove a 23 ft (7.01 m) four-blade wooden tractor propeller. A maximum speed of 14½ mph (23.5 km/h) was achieved during the 23 min flight.

The first successful use of a petrol engine in a dirigible was by Dr Karl Wölfert, who designed and built a small balloon to which he fitted a 2 hp single-cylinder Daimler engine in 1888. Its first flight was carried out at Seelberg in Germany on Sunday, 12 August that year, probably flown by a young mechanic named Michaël.

The first people to be killed in a dirigible accident were Dr Karl Wölfert and mechanic Herr Knabe, when *Deutschland*'s engine vaporizer set fire to the envelope, resulting in a gas explosion, on 14 June 1897.

The first all-metal dirigible, the German Schwartz *Metallballon*, made its only ascent on 3 November 1897.

The first floating dirigible hangar was that constructed in 1899 to house Zeppelin LZ 1, which floated on Lake Constance.

The first flight of a Zeppelin dirigible was made by Count Ferdinand von Zeppelin's LZ 1 on 2 July 1900. This flight, carrying five persons and lasting about 20 min, was from the floating hangar on Lake Constance and showed that the airship lacked control. LZ 1 was 420 ft (128 m) long, had a diameter of 38 ft 6 in (11.73 m) and a volume of 400 000 ft³ (11 327 m³). Power was provided by two Daimler engines, each rated at 16 hp.

An early demonstration of controlled flying in a dirigible was made on 19 October 1901, when Brazilian-born Alberto Santos-Dumont flew his airship No. 6 round the Eiffel Tower in Paris, France, winning a 100 000 franc prize. With an overall length of 108 ft (33 m), maximum diameter of 19 ft 6 in (6 m) and capacity of

22 200 ft³ (630 m³), it was powered by a 20 hp Buchet/Santos-Dumont water-cooled petrol engine, driving a two-blade propeller.

The first dirigible to be constructed and flown by an Englishman was the work of Stanley Spencer, whose non-rigid Spencer-Moering airship *Mellin* was launched in 1902. Envelope capacity was 30 000 ft³ (849.5 m³), length 93 ft (28.35 m) and power was provided by a 3½ hp Simms engine.

The first practical dirigible was designed by the Lebaudy brothers and first flew on 12 November 1903. The flight of 37 miles (60 km) was from Moisson to the Champ-de-Mars, Paris. This was the **first fully controlled air journey in history**.

The first dirigible bought by a government and suited for military service was the French Lebaudy brothers' number II enlarged. First flown in 1904, it was a semi-rigid with a capacity of 93 940 ft³ (2660 m³) and was powered by a single 40 hp Daimler engine. The Lebaudy II made a total of 12 flights.

The first of many Zeppelin dirigibles to be destroyed in bad weather was LZ 2, which had made its first and only ascent on 17 January 1906 and was lost in a gale while moored at Kisslegg the following day. (LZ 1 had been broken up after three flights, in 1901.)

Zeppelin LZ 3 was first flown on 9 October 1906. This became **the first military Zeppelin** on 20 June 1909, when it was handed over to the German Army as Z1.

The first airship used in parasite aeroplane experiments was the non-rigid Santos-Dumont 15, which had an envelope capacity of just 6568 ft³ (186 m³) and was unpowered.

The first British Army airship, Dirigible No. 1 (popularly known as *Nulli Secundus*), was first flown on 10 September 1907 with three occupants: Col John Capper, RE, pilot; Capt W. A. C. King, Adj of the British Army Balloon School; Mr Samuel Cody, 'in charge of the engine'. The engine was a 50 hp Antoinette. The airship was 122 ft (37 m) long, 26 ft (8 m) in diameter and

Left *Zeppelin LZ 1 in flight over Lake Constance on 2 July 1900. (Deutsches Museum)*

Right *Lebaudy airship at Versailles, having first flown in 1904. (Mme Moreau)*

Below *British Army airship* Nulli Secundus, *with Col Capper and Capt King already aboard. (Science Museum, London)*

had a capacity of 55 000 ft³ (1555 m³). The second and third Army airships were *Beta* (35 hp Green engine) and *Gamma* (80 hp Green engine) respectively.

The République was the first dirigible to be used by the French Army on manoeuvres, in 1908.

The first Italian Army dirigible was the semi-rigid SCA *Ibis*, launched in 1908. Envelope capacity was 97 115 ft³ (2750 m³), length 206 ft 8¼ in (63 m) and a speed of 31 mph (50 km/h) could be attained on the power of a single 100 hp engine.

The first Russian Army dirigible was named *Ljebedy*, a semi-rigid purchased from France. Launched in 1908, it had a capacity of 128 015 ft³ (3625 m³), was 203 ft 5 in (62 m) in length, and was powered by a single 70 hp Panhard engine.

The first dirigible used by the Austrian Army was the M1, an 81 224 ft³ (2300 m³) non-rigid airship built in Austria by Motor-Luftfahrzeug to the German Parseval PL4 Type B design and first flown in 1909. 165 ft (50 m) in length and powered by a single 75 hp Austro-Daimler engine, it could attain a speed of 28 mph (45 km/h).

The first Spanish military dirigible was the *España*, a non-rigid airship built by Astra in France and launched in 1909. Capacity was 148 322 ft³ (4200 m³), length 213 ft 3 in (65 m), and a speed of 28 mph (45 km/h) could be attained from the power of a single 110 hp Panhard engine. *España's* most important passenger was the King of Spain.

The first dirigible to be used to bring attention to a political cause was one flown over the British House of Commons by a suffragette on 21 June 1908, from which leaflets were dropped.

The first dirigible to be used by a commercial airline was Zeppelin LZ 6, which was first flown on 26 May 1909. (Details of the airline, Delag, can be found below.) LZ 6 was 472 ft (144 m) long, had a maximum diameter of 42 ft 6 in (13 m) and a volume of 565 035 ft³ (16 000 m³). Power was provided by a 145 hp Maybach and two 115 hp Daimler engines, giving a maximum speed of 37 mph (60 km/h).

The first International Airship Exhibition (ILA) was staged at Frankfurt/Main between July and October 1909. Zeppelin LZ 5 was flown to the exhibition.

The first occasion on which four people lost their lives in an air accident was on 25 September 1909, when the French dirigible *République* lost a propeller which pierced the gasbag; the craft fell from 400 ft (122 m) at Avrilly, near Moulins, the crew of four being killed.

The world's first commercial airline was formed as Delag (Die Deutsche Luftschiffahrt Aktiengesellschaft) by Count Ferdinand von Zeppelin on 16 October 1909. Between 1910 and November 1913 the airline carried more than 34 000 passengers between major German cities without injury, although, of the six original airships employed on the services, three were lost.

The first dirigible to fly from Continental Europe to Great Britain was the non-rigid Clément-Bayard II, which first flew in 1910. It had an envelope capacity of 22 445 ft³ (635 m³) and was powered by two 125 hp engines.

The first non-rigid dirigible to be moored by mast was the British Army's *Beta 1*, which first flew on 3 June 1910. This was also **the first British dirigible to have wireless telegraphy installed.**

The first occasion on which five people lost their lives in an air accident was on 13 July 1910 when a German non-rigid dirigible, of the Erbslön type, suffered an explosion of the gasbag and fell from 920 ft (280 m) near Opladen, Germany. The crew of five, including Oscar Erbslön, was killed.

The first dirigible to make the journey from London to Paris, and indeed the first to fly from England to France, was the British Willows III *City of Cardiff* on 4 November 1910, a non-rigid airship constructed by E. T. Willows.

The first Japanese Army dirigible was the non-rigid No. 1, built by Yamada and Heraka and launched in 1911. Capacity was 103 475 ft³ (2930 m³) and power was provided by a single 60 hp Wolseley engine. This was operated successfully as a training airship.

The first rigid dirigible with a wooden structure was the German Schütte-Lanz SL1, launched on 17 October 1911 and featuring laminated plywood girders. Capacity was 688 636 ft³ (19 500 m³), length about 430 ft (131 m), and a speed of 42 mph (68 km/h) could be attained on

the power of two 240 hp Mercedes engines. SL1 was taken into German Army service. The more successful and larger wooden SL2, launched in February 1914, used four 180 hp Maybach engines and had such advanced features as cruciform tail surfaces with elevators and rudders, and an enclosed control car near the nose for the flight crew. The SL2 was, therefore, **the first of the modern style rigid dirigibles**.

The first British rigid dirigible was the Vickers R1 *Mayfly*. It was 512 ft (156 m) long and was destroyed in a handling accident at Barrow on 24 September 1911 before making a single flight.

The first German naval rigid dirigible was Zeppelin LZ 14, military designated L1. Ordered in April 1912, the L1 was first flown on 7 October that year and during 13–14 October undertook a 900 mile (1450 km) proving flight. It was the success of this airship that led to the Navy's programme of airship construction for long-range military operations. LZ 14 had a capacity of 793 700 ft³ (22 475 m³), was 518 ft 2 in (158 m) in length and could attain a speed of 50 mph (80 km/h) on the power of three 165 hp Maybach engines. LZ 14 was lost during manoeuvres over the North Sea on 9 September 1913, with heavy loss of life. **LZ 14/L1 was the German Navy's first rigid airship loss.**

Above   American journalist Walter Wellman began an attempt to cross the North Atlantic in his hydrogen dirigible America *on 15 September 1910. After two days and nights, and many problems, the crew of five (plus a dog) was rescued by the British ship* SS Trent. *(Science Museum, London)*

Below   Zeppelin LZ 14, as L1 becoming the German Navy's first military Zeppelin and its first rigid airship to be lost. (M. B. Passingham)

The first airmail carried in Germany was flown on an experimental service between Darmstadt and Frankfurt-on-Main by the dirigibles *Schwaben* and *Gelber Hund*. This service lasted from 10 to 22 June 1912.

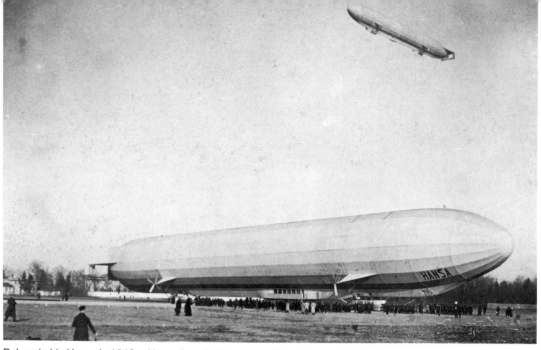

Delag airship Hansa *in 1912, with another airship approaching. (Deutsches Museum)*

The first international commercial airship service was begun by the Delag dirigible *Hansa* on 19 September 1912, flying between Hamburg, Copenhagen (Denmark) and Malmö (Sweden).

The first Zeppelin dirigible designed to be capable of reaching Britain in case of war (with a bomb load) and **the largest airship completed before the outbreak of the First World War** was LZ 18, designated L2 in German naval service. Launched on 9 September 1913, L2 was 518 ft 4 in (158 m) long and had a volume of 953 500 ft³ (27 000 m³). Power was provided by four 165 hp Maybach engines. Intended to be the first of 10 large dirigibles to equip two Navy units, it was lost, however, on 17 October 1913, when it caught fire while airborne. All 28 crew were killed.

The first successful mission by a German dirigible during the First World War was carried out on 12 August 1914, when L3 located the Dutch battleship *de Zeven Provincien* and destroyers close to the island of Terschelling, Waddeneilanden.

The first dirigible to be shot down by French infantry was *Dupuy-de-Lôme* on 24 August 1914, a French airship mistakenly identified as a Zeppelin.

The first Zeppelin dirigible with cruciform tail surfaces was LZ 27, designated L4 by the Navy,

first flown on 28 August 1914. After just under 50 flights it was destroyed during a forced landing in 1916.

The first airship raid on Great Britain was carried out on 19 January 1915 by three German Navy Zeppelins, L3, L4 and L6. They took off from Fuhlsbüttel and Nordholz. L6 was forced to return through engine trouble but L3 and L4 arrived over the Norfolk coast at about 20.00 h; nine bombs were dropped in the Great Yarmouth area at 20.25 h by L3, killing two persons and wounding three others. Meanwhile L4 had gone north-west towards Bacton and dropped incendiary bombs on Sheringham, Thornham and Brancaster as well as a high-explosive bomb on Hunstanton wireless station. Following that, it dropped bombs on Heacham, Snettisham and King's Lynn, where seven high-explosive bombs were dropped and an incendiary, killing two people and injuring 13. The two airships were both wrecked on the coast of Jutland on 17 February 1915, after running into a gale on their homeward journey from a mission to spot the British fleet.

The first dirigible with a volume of more than one million cubic feet was the German Navy's Schütte-Lanz SL3, which was completed in February 1915. Powered by four 210 hp Maybach engines, it was 502 ft 4 in (153 m) in length and had a volume of 1 144 200 ft³ (32 400 m³). This airship was lost in 1916.

Improved versions of the Royal Naval Air Service SS non-rigid airships came in the form of SS Zs from 1916. Sixty-six were delivered. Here an SS Z escorts a convoy over the North Sea. (Imperial War Museum)

The first British anti-submarine warfare dirigible was the non-rigid SS 1 (Sea Scout), built by Armstrong-Whitworth and launched in 1915. The first of 36 SS class airships used by the Royal Naval Air Service, it was 100 ft (30.48 m) in length and could attain a speed of 48 mph (77 km/h) on the power of a 70 hp engine in the nose of a car fabricated from the fuselage of a BE2c observation aeroplane. Sixty-six improved SS Zs followed from 1916.

The first partially successful attack on a submarine by an airship was performed in the early afternoon of 3 May 1915, when Zeppelin LZ 36 (L9) spotted four British submarines and managed to damage the conning tower of one, D4, by dropping five 50 kg bombs from an altitude of 3280 ft (1000 m).

The first air raid on London was by Zeppelin LZ 3 on 31 May 1915. The Kaiser had authorized bombing of London, east of the Tower, a few days before and on the night of the 31st 3000 lb (1360 kg) of bombs were dropped on north-east London, killing seven people and injuring 14 others.

The first French Navy dirigibles were the four Astra-Torres non-rigids designated AT 1 to AT 4, first flown in 1916. Each had a capacity of 229 545 ft³ (6500 m³), was powered by two 150 hp Renault engines and could attain a speed of 50 mph (80 km/h).

The first Zeppelin to be set on fire was LZ 47, during an attack on 21 February 1916.

The first airship to be brought down by air attack was Zeppelin LZ 37 on the night of 6–7 June 1915. In company with LZ 38 and LZ 39, the airship set out from Bruges to bomb London but adverse weather later forced them to alter course for their secondary targets—railways in the Calais area. LZ 37 was located and attacked by Flt Sub Lt R. A. J. Warneford of No. 1 Squadron, RNAS, flying a Morane-Saulnier Parasol from Dunkirk. Warneford's only means of attack were six 20 lb (9 kg) bombs; he followed the airship from Ostend to Ghent, being forced to keep his distance by fire from the airship's gunners. He made a single pass over the airship dropping all six bombs from about 150 ft (45 m) above it. The sixth exploded, and the airship fell in flames on a suburb of Ghent, killing two nuns. Only one member of Oberleutnant Otto van de Haegen's crew survived. Warneford returned safely to base after making a forced landing to repair a broken fuel line. He was informed the following evening that he had been awarded the Victoria Cross; he died 12 days later when the tail of a Henry Farman pusher biplane collapsed in mid-air.

The first Zeppelin to be shot down while over the British Isles was LZ 48 (German Navy designation L15). In the company of six other Zeppelins, it had taken off on 31 March 1916 to attack London and the south of England. Two Zeppelins soon turned back but the five remaining dirigibles continued. L15 had reached a point north of London by 10.30 p.m. when it was caught by searchlights near Dartford and hit by groundfire. The dirigible dropped bombs to gain height but was attacked by 2nd Lt A. Brandon, RFC, flying a BE2c biplane, who released explosive darts. L15 slipped away in the darkness but was in very bad shape. Attempting to limp home, it flew over Purfleet, where it was struck again by groundfire from an anti-aircraft gun. Unable to continue, L15 went down into the sea just off Kentish Knock Lightship, at Fundress. Taken in tow, it eventually sank off Westgate on the morning of 1 April. Two gold medals were made for Sir Charles Wakefield (then Lord Mayor of London) to commemorate the action, these being presented to Lance Corporal R. Rowe and a Purfleet officer, who were recognized as having shot down the L15.

The first German airship to be brought down on British soil was the Schütte-Lanz SL XI, which was attacked on the night of 2 September 1916 by Lt W. Leefe Robinson, RFC, using the newly-invented Pomeroy incendiary ammunition. It crashed in flames near Cuffley, Hertfordshire.

Robinson was awarded the VC. This action demoralized German airship crews, particularly because it had demonstrated the effectiveness of British defences, and is said to have prevented a large-scale airship attack on London. However, on the night of 23–24 September eleven Zeppelins raided England, three with London as their target. One airship, LZ 76 (L33), was hit by anti-aircraft fire and came down at Little Wigborough and another, LZ 74 (L32), was shot down by a British aircraft (flown by 2nd Lt Sowrey) over Great Burstead.

The first US Navy dirigible was the DN-1 (or A-1), constructed by the Connecticut Aircraft Company and flown for the first time (of only three flights) on 20 April 1917. Capacity was 150 000 ft³ (4247.5 m³), length 175 ft (53.34 m), and a speed of 35 mph (56 km/h) could be attained on the power of a single 140 hp Sturtevant engine; it had been built originally with two engines but was modified after it proved too heavy to leave the ground.

The US Navy's first dirigibles to be series produced were of the B series for anti-submarine warfare and training, each of the 17 airships (3 later enlarged) carrying the crew in converted aeroplane fuselages. Launched in 1917 and built by

Left *The wreck of German Navy Zeppelin L33 at Little Wigborough, attracting the attention of His Excellency the French Ambassador. (Imperial War Museum)*

Right *Shorts R-38 metal-framed airship under construction at Cardington in 1919. (Short Brothers)*

Goodyear, the Connecticut Aircraft Company and Goodrich, each B series craft (unmodified) had a capacity of 77 000 ft³ (2180 m³), was 160 ft (48.77 m) in length, and attained a speed of 45 mph (72 km/h) on the power of a single 100 hp Curtiss OXX-2 engine. **The first successful dirigible of the US Navy** was, therefore, the Goodyear B-1 acquired under the initial 14 March 1917 contract and first flown from Chicago, Illinois, to Wingfoot Lake, near Akron, Ohio, on 30 May 1917.

The worst losses suffered by the German Naval Airship Division on a single day of operational missions were five Zeppelins that failed to return to base on 20 October 1917. LZ 85 (L45) and LZ 96 (L49) force-landed in France, LZ 93 (L44) was shot down over France, LZ 89 (L50) was lost over the Mediterranean and LZ 101 (L55) force-landed in Germany. LZ 50 (L16) had also been wrecked the previous day. On 5 January 1918 five Navy dirigibles were destroyed in an explosion at the Ahlhorn sheds, raising the total number of airships lost to the German Navy in three months from October 1917 to twelve.

The last German airship attack on England which resulted in death or injury was made on 12 April 1918. Altogether, during the 51 Zeppelin airship raids on Great Britain during the war, 196 tons (199 tonnes) of bombs were dropped, killing 557 people and injuring many more.

The first airship crossing, and first two-way crossing of the Atlantic by any type of aircraft, were achieved by the British airship R-34 between 2 and 6 July (westward) and 9 and 13 July (eastward) 1919. Commanded by Sqn Ldr G. H. Scott, with a crew of 30, the R-34 set out from East Fortune, Scotland, and flew to New York, returning afterwards to Pulham, Norfolk, England. The total distance covered, 6330 miles (10 187 km) in 183 h 8 min, constituted a world record for airships.

Delag, the pre-war commercial airline flying dirigibles, reopened services on 24 August 1919 with the airship *Bodensee*, flying the route between Friedrichshafen and Berlin. However, this service was suspended on 1 December by order of the Allied Control Commission. Between these dates about 103 flights had been made, carrying 2400 passengers and 66 140 lb (30 000 kg) of cargo. Each flight carried 23 passengers.

The first dirigible with a volume of more than 2½ million cubic feet was the British Shorts R-38. Launched in 1921, it was **then the largest airship in the world**, with a length of 695 ft

(212 m), maximum diameter of 85 ft (26 m) and volume of 2 740 000 ft³ (77 600 m³). Power was provided by six Cossack engines with a total output of 2100 hp. It was destroyed when it broke up over Hull, England, on 24 August 1921. It was to have been sold to the United States and at the time of the disaster there were 16 Americans aboard in addition to the crew of 33. All the Americans and 28 of the British lost their lives.

The first airship to use helium gas instead of hydrogen was Goodyear C 7, one of 16 C series non-rigid airships ordered for the US Navy as coastal patrol and convoy craft. This made its first flight on 1 December 1921. The first C series airship, the C 1 launched in September 1918, was the first non-rigid dirigible to demonstrate the 'parasite' concept, when on 12 December 1918 it lifted a Curtiss Jenny biplane to an altitude of 2500 ft (760 m) and successfully released it. Previous experiments in Germany and Britain using the rigid airships L35 and R-23 had seen the air launch of an Albatros D.III and Sopwith Camel respectively. The Albatros had been released on 26 January 1918, making this **the first demonstration of the parasite fighter concept.** The first British parasite experiment was conducted on 6 November 1918.

The first Japanese naval dirigible was a non-rigid Vickers SS Twin type, launched in 1922. Of 100 000 ft³ (2832 m³) capacity, it was powered by two 100 hp Sunbeam engines and attained a speed of more than 60 mph (97 km/h). Unfortunately, No. 1 was destroyed by fire in its shed soon after, on 10 July 1922.

The US Navy's first rigid dirigible was the ZR-1 *Shenandoah* (see below).

The first helium-filled American rigid airship was the Zeppelin-type ZR-1 *Shenandoah*, which first flew on 4 September 1923 at Lakehurst, New Jersey, USA. On 3 September 1925 it was destroyed in a storm over Caldwell, Ohio, with heavy loss of life.

The first and only dirigible received by the US Navy from Germany as war reparations was the newly built LZ 126, known as ZR-3 *Los Angeles*. This was flown from Friedrichshafen to Lakehurst, USA, during 12–14 October 1924. A very successful airship that made well over 300 flights up to 1932, it was initially filled with hydrogen gas.

The first successful 'hook on' parasite experiment between a dirigible and an aeroplane was conducted between the US Army non-rigid and

ZR-1 Shenandoah, *the first helium-filled American rigid dirigible. (Smithsonian Institution)*

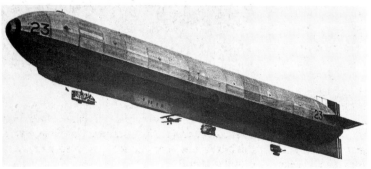

In 1918 both Germany and Britain carried out parasite fighter experiments using fighter biplanes released from airships. Britain began with a Sopwith Camel attached by hook to the R-23, the first airborne release taking place on 6 November. The fighter pilot on this occasion was Lieutenant R. .E Keys. (Imperial War Museum)

Above Norge, *the first airship to fly over the North Pole.*

Below *The ill-fated* Italia *ready for the North Pole flight in 1928. (Italian Ministry of Defence)*

helium-filled training dirigible TC-3 and a Sperry Messenger biplane on 15 December 1924. A previous attempt, by 1st Lt Clyde V. Finter on the 13th, failed when the aeroplane's propeller was damaged after striking the dirigible's 'hook on' trapeze structure.

The French rigid airship *Dixmude*, in fact Zeppelin LZ 114 (L72), received as war reparations, remained airborne for 118 hours and 41 minutes in September 1925, landing on the 25th. This was by far the greatest duration flight of the period.

The first airship flight over the North Pole was made by the Italian-built N-class semi-rigid airship N.1, subsequently named *Norge* by Roald Amundsen, who bought the airship for Arctic exploration. During the period from 11 to 14 May 1926, the *Norge* was flown from Spitzbergen to Teller, Alaska. Among the distinguished crew were Amundsen, Umberto Nobile and Lincoln Ellsworth, who dropped Norwegian, Italian and American flags at the Pole on 12 May. On 23 May

1928 Nobile set off in another attempt to fly over the North Pole, in the Italian dirigible *Italia*. This crashed on the return journey. Nobile survived this but Amundsen, who set out to rescue the crew of *Italia*, died.

The first airship flight round the world was accomplished by the German *Graf Zeppelin* between 8 and 29 August 1929. Captained by Dr Hugo Eckener, the craft set out from Lakehurst, New Jersey, and flew via Friedrichshafen, Germany, Tokyo, Japan, and Los Angeles, California, returning to Lakehurst in 21 days 5 h and 31 min. The total distance covered was more than 21 870 miles (35 200 km). Most successful of all the passenger-carrying airships, the *Graf* had flown well over a million miles and had carried a total of some 13 100 passengers before being scrapped at the beginning of the Second World War.

The last commercial airships to be developed by Great Britain were the R-100 and R-101. The latter crashed on 5 October 1930 at Beauvais, France, on a flight from Cardington, Bedfordshire, England, to Egypt and India. The accident, which destroyed the airship and killed 48 of the 54 occupants (including Lord Thomson, Secretary of State for Air, and Maj Gen Sir Sefton Brancker, Director of Civil Aviation), brought to an end the development of passenger-carrying airships in Great Britain. The R-101 was, however, the largest ever British airship, with a length of 777 ft (236.8 m) and volume of 5 508 800 ft³ (155 995 m³). The R-100 was designed by Barnes Neville Wallis (later Sir Barnes) for the Airship Guarantee Company. It was for this craft that he originated his unique geodetic form of basic airframe structure, used later in the construction of Vickers Wellesley and Wellington bomber aircraft. In a test on 16 January 1930 the R-100 achieved a speed of 81½ mph (131 km/h), making it **the fastest airship in the world**.

During July and August 1930 the R-100 made a double Atlantic crossing, flying between Cardington and Montreal, Canada. But, following the R-101 disaster, it was scrapped.

The first non-rigid dirigible to be fuelled with blaugas (German gas used for both fuel and envelope, comprising ethylene, methylene, propylene, butylene, hydrogen and ethane) was the US Navy airship K-1, built by Goodyear and launched in 1931. Capacity was 319 900 ft³ (9058.5 m³), length 218 ft (66.4 m), and a speed of 65 mph (105 km/h) could be attained from the power of two 330 hp Wright J-6-9 engines. The gas for fuel was contained in a ballonet.

The fastest airship in the world was the British R-100, which made a double Atlantic crossing in 1930.

The world's first fighter-carrying airship intended for operational service, USS *Akron*, was flown for the first time on 25 September 1931. This operated successfully with four Curtiss F9C-2 Sparrowhawk fighters until 4 April 1933 when it crashed into the sea off the New Jersey coast during a storm. (See below.) On 3 November 1931 *Akron* ascended with 207 persons on board, **the greatest number ever carried by an airship.**

The first and only American operational fighters to serve aboard airships were naval Curtiss F9C Sparrowhawk biplanes, which served on board the US airships *Akron* and *Macon* between 1932 and 1935. The prototype Sparrowhawk (*XF9C-1*) achieved the first 'hook-on' on the airship *Los Angeles* on 27 October 1931, and the first production aircraft hooked-on to *Akron* on 29 June 1932.

The final French Navy dirigible was the non-rigid Zodiac V12 of 1936 launch, which was designed to be towed while attached to its mooring mast to ease ground handling. Over 161 ft (49 m) in length, with an envelope capacity of 141 965 ft³ (4020 m³) and powered by two 270 hp Salmson engines, it could attain a speed of 64 mph (103 km/h).

Above USS Akron, *the first of two operational fighter-carrying airships.* Akron *was lost with 74 of its 78 crew on 4 April 1933 in a violent squall off Barnegat Light, NJ. (Goodyear Tire and Rubber Company)*

Below The prototype Sparrowhawk fighter, the *XF9C-1, being hoisted to the hangar inside the airship* USS Akron. *(US Navy)*

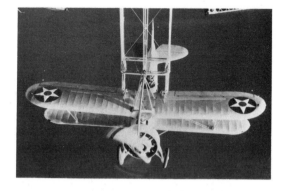

The last major airship disaster involved the destruction of the German *Hindenburg*, then the world's largest airship, on 6 May 1937. It was destroyed by fire when approaching its moorings at Lakehurst, New Jersey, USA, after a flight from Frankfurt, Germany. Thirty-five of the 97 occupants were killed in the fire which engulfed the

The final moments of Hindenburg, engulfed in flames at Lakehurst on 6 May 1937. (US National Archives)

nylon fabric envelope had a gross capacity of 96 000 ft³ (2718 m³) and was inflated by hot air generated by a propane gas burner carried in the lightweight tubular-metal gondola. More highly developed hot-air airships followed on from the Cameron.

The producer of the largest number of airships is the Goodyear Tire & Rubber Company, which has built well over 300; of these more than 250 were constructed for the US military services. The company also operates a fleet of airships, comprising three non-rigid craft for public relations and advertising.

Largest:

The heaviest bomb dropped by an aircraft by the end of 1914 weighed 661 lb (300 kg), released during experiments from the new German semi-rigid dirigible M IV, on 18 December 1914. This dirigible had been commissioned only days before.

The largest rigid dirigibles built in the United States of America were the Goodyear USS *Akron* and *Macon*. These identical craft had capacities of 6 500 000 ft³ (184 059 m³), were 785 ft (239.3 m) in length and were each powered by eight 560 hp German-built Maybach engines. (See also Firsts and Most.)

The largest rigid dirigible ever built was the German passenger craft LZ 130 *Graf Zeppelin II*. First flown on 14 September 1938, it had a capacity of 7 062 270 ft³ (199 981 m³), was 803 ft 10 in (245 m) in length, and was powered by four 1200 hp Mercedes Benz diesel engines. Officially, its last flight was made on 20 August 1939; in May and August 1939 it carried out radar spying missions against British interests. It was scrapped in April 1940.

The largest non-rigid airships ever built were four Goodyear ZPG 3-W early warning radar craft ordered for the US Navy. The first of these was launched on 21 July 1958 but crashed in 1960. All remaining craft were deleted in 1962. Each was 403 ft 4 in (122.9 m) long and had a volume of 1 516 300 ft³ (42 937 m³).

huge craft and which was attributed to the use of hydrogen—the only gas available to Germany owing to the United States' refusal to supply commercial quantities of helium. With its sister craft, the LZ 130 *Graf Zeppelin II*, it was the largest rigid airship ever built, with a length of 803 ft 10 in (245 m) and a volume of 7 062 100 ft³ (199 981 m³).

The first airship built in Britain following the R-101 disaster made its first flight at Cardington, Bedfordshire, on 19 July 1951. This was a small airship named *Bournemouth*, built by the Airship Club of Great Britain under the leadership of Lord Ventry.

The first German dirigible to use helium gas was the Ballonfabrik and Metallwerk *Trumpf III* non-rigid, launched in 1958. Of 158 916 ft³ (4500 m³) capacity and with a length of over 159 ft (48.5 m), it could attain a speed of 68 mph (110 km/h) on the power of two 180 hp Warner Scarab engines.

The world's first hot-air airship was first flown on 3 January 1973 at Newbury, England. Constructed by Cameron Balloons, D-96 (G-BAMK) was 100 ft (30.5 m) in length, with a maximum diameter of 45 ft (13.72 m). It was powered by a converted Volkswagen motorcar engine and had a speed of 17 mph (27.5 km/h). The lightweight

This photograph of Akron under construction gives a good idea of the huge size of the craft and its complex structure. (Goodyear Tire and Rubber Company)

ZPG-3-W early warning non-rigid airship (right) between the Goodyear Airdock's massive clamshell doors. (Goodyear Tire and Rubber Company)

Longest:

The FAI accredited world straight-line distance record for rigid dirigibles stands at 3967.137 miles (6384.5 km), established by the German airship LZ 127 *Graf Zeppelin* between 29 October and 1 November 1928. Captain was the legendary Dr Hugo Eckener.

The longest duration flight by a non-rigid dirigible without refuelling is 264 h 12 min, established between 4 and 15 March 1957 by a US Navy Goodyear ZPG 2 class craft. This flight, crewed by Cdr J. R. Hunt, Lt Cdr Robert S. Bowser and 12 others, began from South Weymouth NAS, Massachusetts, and ended at Key West, Florida. The distance flown was 9448 miles (15 205 km), a record for lighter-than-air craft.

The longest duration flight (without refuelling) by a fully equipped non-rigid dirigible on a mission is 95 h 30 min, achieved by the crew of a US Navy ZPG 2 airship between 25 and 29 March 1960. In command of the crew of 19 was Lt Lundi A. Moore.

Greatest:

The greatest name associated with dirigible design, and one that became synonymous with military airships, was that of Count Ferdinand von Zeppelin, who had his first design for a passenger-carrying airship rejected by the German gov-

ernment's technical commission in 1894. Not too discouraged, in the following year he was granted the first patent for his method of constructing rigid airships, and in 1896 he raised the princely sum of 800 000 Reichmarks to found the Joint Stock Company for Promotion of Airship Flight. Zeppelin died on 8 March 1917, having seen the heyday of the airship as a strategic bomber.

The greatest dirigible captain was undoubtedly Dr Hugo Eckener (born 1868), who joined Count Zeppelin prior to the first flight of LZ 3 in 1906 and subsequently headed the company after the Count's death. Among his many achievements was the development of *Graf Zeppelin* and *Hindenburg*. He died in 1954.

The greatest number of rigid airships operated by an armed service was the 69 Zeppelins and Schütte-Lanz craft flown by the German Naval Airship Division during the First World War. This service also suffered the greatest proportion of fatalities of any armed force, with approximately 40 per cent of its total personnel being killed.

The greatest number of persons carried by a dirigible stands at 207, achieved by US Navy rigid airship *Akron*, on 3 November 1931. (See also Firsts.)

The greatest number of persons carried across the Atlantic by dirigible stands at 117, performed in 1937 by Zeppelin LZ 129 *Hindenburg*.

Rotorcraft

In today's world, the helicopter fulfils a greater range of tasks than any other form of aircraft. Yet, in the first decade of the 20th century when powered aeroplanes were beginning to fly successfully, those that persisted with rotorcraft were believed misguided by some of the greatest aviation pioneers. However, the helicopter in toy and model forms appeared before the balloon, dirigible, glider proper and powered aeroplane, only being predated in the annals of aviation history by the rocket, kite and the inadequate wings of 'tower jumpers'.

Leaving aside the string-pull helicopter toys illustrated from the 14th century, the first documented reference to the possibility of propelling upwards a vehicle by means of rotating surfaces is attributed to Leonardo da Vinci (1452–1519), whose design sketches for such are believed to have originated in about the year 1500. Leonardo was otherwise devoted to the concept of flapping wings (i.e. the ornithopter) to achieve forward flight, and he was not aware of the lifting characteristics of aerofoils, nor was he acquainted with the properties of the propeller. As a result his design for a helicopter was based strictly on an 'air screw'—literally a rotating helical wing which would 'screw' its path upwards through the air.

Numerous attempts to evolve models of helicopters followed during the next four centuries, culminating in the unmanned models of W. H. Phillips who, in 1842, succeeded in launching a steam-driven craft whose rotating *blades* were propelled by tip jets.

It is perhaps useful here to interpose simple definitions of the helicopter and autogyro. Basically a helicopter achieves vertical flight by means of aerodynamic lift from rotor blades which are rotated under power; to eliminate torque (i.e. to prevent the fuselage of the aircraft from spinning uncontrollably on the axis of the rotor), either coaxial rotors, balanced sets of rotors or small tail-mounted rotors are geared to the power plant. Forward flight is achieved by tilting the rotor 'disc' so that its resulting thrust provides a degree of propulsion as well as lift.

An autogyro, on the other hand, is rather nearer to a conventional aeroplane in that forward motion is achieved by a conventional engine (either jet or piston engine-driven propeller); as forward motion is achieved the freely rotating rotor blades provide lift as aerofoils, enabling the autogyro to perform short, steep take-offs and landings.

Design and backward notes by Leonardo da Vinci for a corkscrew-rotor helicopter. (Science Museum, London)

Firsts:

The first helicopters to fly were small models powered by the string-pull method, the first of which appeared in the 14th century. One such toy was illustrated in a Flemish manuscript of 1325.

The first person to use the name 'helicopter' was Italian artist, philosopher and inventor, Leonardo da Vinci (1452–1519), whose knowledge of Greek translated spiral wing into *helix* and *pteron*. Among his aircraft designs was a helicopter intended to use a form of corkscrew rotor built from starched flaxen linen. One suggested form of power for the rotor was for the pilot to wind rope around the mast and then pull it to cause rotation in the established string-pull method already used for toys.

A clockwork-powered model helicopter, with two contra-rotating rotors, was constructed and flown in 1754 by the Russian Mikhail Vasilyevich Lomonosov. This was probably **the first self-propelled model helicopter.** (A similar type of model helicopter was constructed by Jacob Degen in 1816.)

The first recognized self-propelled model helicopter appears to have been that demonstrated on 28 April 1784, in France, by Launoy and Bienvenu. It consisted of a stick with a two-blade propeller at each end. The model was powered by a bowdrill arrangement; as the string of the bowdrill unwound the propellers counter-rotated. It was on this model that Sir George Cayley based his model helicopter in 1796, using a similar bowdrill arrangement but powering two four-blade rotors made from feathers.

The first model helicopter to use a pressure-jet system to drive the rotor was that flown by Englishman W. H. Phillips in 1842. Steam passed through the tips of the blades to turn the rotor.

The first attempt to produce a convertiplane (an aircraft that can achieve vertical flight supported by a rotor/rotors and horizontal translational flight using wings for lift) is generally attributed to Englishman Sir George Cayley. His Aerial Carriage, designed in 1843, had four circular wings (in pairs), mounted on outriggers from the boat-like wheeled fuselage. When the rotating wings were needed to provide lift, they were designed to open out into eight-bladed rotors. Forward propulsion was by two rear-mounted propellers.

Model of Sir George Cayley's Aerial Carriage of 1843. (Science Museum, London)

The first person to suggest the need for cyclic pitch control on helicopters was Italian G. A. Crocco, in 1906.

The first helicopter to lift a man from the ground was the French Breguet-Richet helicopter of 1907. Although the craft lifted off the ground at Douai, France, on 29 September that year, it did not constitute a free flight as four men on the ground steadied the machine with long poles which, while not contributing to the aircraft's lift, constituted a form of control restriction. Power was provided by a 50 hp Antoinette engine.

The first true free flight by a man-carrying helicopter was performed by Paul Cornu in his 24 hp Antoinette-powered twin-rotor (each 19 ft 8 in [6.0 m] diameter) aircraft near Lisieux,

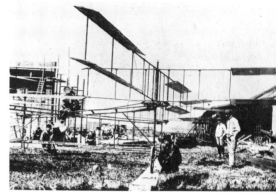

Top right   Breguet-Richet Gyroplane 1 *helicopter of 1907, showing the central 50 hp Antoinette engine and one of the multi-blade rotors.*

Right   Paul Cornu astride his 1907 twin-rotor helicopter. (Musée de l'Air)

Below   Dane Jacob Ellehammer stands by his cyclic control helicopter during its first flight in 1912, ready to switch off the ignition. This photograph was autographed two years later. (Royal Danish Ministry for Foreign Affairs)

France, on 13 November 1907. The flight, which lasted only 20 s, attained a height of 1 ft (0.3 m).

The first demonstration of a helicopter with basic cyclic control was the contra-rotating machine flown in 1912 by Dane Jacob C. H. Ellehammer. Power for the 24 ft 6 in (7.5 m) rotors was provided by a 36 hp radial engine.

Probably the first helicopter to be tested from water was the work of Frenchmen Papin and Rouilly. This had the unusual arrangement of the 80 hp Le Rhone engine powering a fan to produce air that was forced out of the single hollow rotor blade to cause rotation, while residual air was intended to provide directional control. Tested on Lake Cercey on 31 March 1915, the helicopter proved unstable and sank.

The first helicopter to be flown during the First World War intended for military use was the work of Oberstleutnant Stefan von Petroczy, Austrian Army Balloon Corps. His second full-size man-carrying helicopter was a large triple-outrigger machine with a cylindrical cockpit at its centre for an observer and gunner. One 120 hp Le Rhone engine was carried on each outrigger, all three powering a single pair of 19 ft 8 in (6 m) diameter contra-rotating rotors that turned beneath the cockpit. At all times the helicopter was intended to be tethered to the ground, being winched in and out as would an observation balloon. A parachute was carried which would be released mechanically should the rotor speed fall dangerously low. During tests, the helicopter remained in the air for approximately one hour and remained stable in 20 mph (33 km/h) winds.

The first helicopter to fly carrying three persons was built in Budapest by Dr Ing Theodor von Karman and Wilhelm Zurovec. The PKZ 1 was based upon the first full-size helicopter produced earlier by von Petroczy and thereby was powered by an electric motor, though the later machine featured four rotors. Completed in March 1918, it is thought that a total of four flights were made, on all but one with three persons on board.

The first full-size British helicopter to achieve partially successful free flights was produced by Louis Brennan and tested at Farnborough. The subject of great secrecy, the helicopter had a large two-blade rotor that was driven by tip-mounted four-blade propellers powered by a common

engine. The pilot was Robert Graham and approximately 70 free flights were made between 7 December 1921 and 2 October 1925, when the machine crashed due to control failure and the programme was abandoned. The maximum altitude achieved was about 10 ft (3 m). However, it is worth mentioning the little-known earlier British experiments conducted at the Leven Shipyard, Dumbarton, of William Denny Brothers. Here, work on developing a rotor suitable as the lifting surface of an aircraft began in 1905, culminating initially in the testing of a 25 ft (7.62 m) diameter silk and bamboo rotor in October 1906. Subsequent work encompassed also engines and gearbox, airframe, controls and much else, with a conventional elevator and rudder chosen to control the flight of the intended helicopter. Finally, the Denny helicopter weighed a massive 1577 lb (715 kg), due in part to the weight of the 40 hp V4 engine that powered six elm-framed rotors mounted in tandem pairs. Several tethered flights were achieved in 1912–13, up to a height of 10 ft (3 m). Unfortunately, the helicopter was destroyed in a gale before the First World War.

The first flight was recorded in France of the Oehmichen No. 2 multi-rotor helicopter on 11 November 1922. On 4 May 1924 Etienne

The secretly tested Brennan helicopter at Farnborough, with the designer standing and pilot Robert Graham in the cockpit.

Oehmichen established the **first helicopter 1 km distance record in a closed circuit**. However, compared to other helicopters then being tested elsewhere, the No. 2 was a huge and impractical design. Power was provided by a 180 hp Gnome engine, driving four primitive rotors carried on the cruciform structure and eight propellers intended to provide directional control.

The first successful gyroplane was the C.4 Autogiro, designed by Spaniard Juan de la Cierva and first flown on 9 January 1923. The secret of its success was in the adoption of flapping hinges joining the blades to the rotor head, and the C4 was therefore **the first practical rotorcraft of any type.**

The first demonstration of successful cyclic pitch control was by Argentinian Marquis de Pateras Pescara in his No. 3 helicopter that used a 180 hp Hispano-Suiza engine to power coaxial contra-rotating rotors. Each rotor had a four biplane blade arrangement (eight individual blades), the pitch of the blades being adjustable by warping. The pilot could thereby choose collective pitch and cyclic pitch control. On 18 April 1924 the Pescara No. 3 flew 2414 ft (736 m) at Issy-les-Moulineaux in France, setting a world record.

The RAF's first rotary-winged aircraft was an Avro-built Cierva C.6C, powered by a 130 hp Clerget engine. Completed in 1926, it did not join an active squadron but was used for trials.

The first two-seat autogyro, Juan de la Cierva's C.6D, made its first flight on 29 July 1927. On the following day, Spaniard de la Cierva became **the first passenger to be carried in an autogyro.**

The first rotating-wing aircraft to fly the English Channel was the Cierva C.8L Mark II (G-EBYY) Autogyro, flown by Juan de la Cierva with a passenger from Croydon to Le Bourget on 18 September 1928.

The first successful autogyro of American design was flown by Harold Pitcairn in Philadelphia on 19 December 1928.

The first Soviet autogyro to fly successfully (indeed the first Soviet rotary-winged aircraft of any type) was the KaSKr-1, which flew for the first time in September 1929. Designed by Nikolai Skrzhinskii and Nikolai Kamov, its fuselage was taken from a U-1 aeroplane.

The RAF's first operational rotary-winged aircraft were twelve Avro Rota Mk Is, licence-built Cierva C.30As, received during 1934 and 1935. Initially based at an Army co-operation training school, from 1940 they were operated by a Flight

The successful though impractical Oehmichen No 2 helicopter in flight. (Musee de l'Air)

Cierva C.8L Mark II Autogiro, the first rotorcraft to fly the English Channel.

from Duxford and then by No. 529 Squadron at Halton. No. 529 Squadron is remembered as **the RAF's only autogyro squadron**, surviving until October 1945. A civil British-registered C.30A was **the first autogyro with a pre-spin mechanism for the rotor**, allowing a 'jump' take-off.

The first US Army rotary-winged aircraft was the Kellett YG-1 autogyro, a military version of the civil KD-1 ordered in 1935 and powered by a 225 hp Jacobs R-755-1 engine. Other Kellett models followed, including the YG-1A and seven YG-1Bs.

The first-ever aircraft to make an intentional safe landing on the roof of a building was a Kellett KD-1B in May 1935 during an experimental airmail service, to commemorate the opening of the Philadelphia post office. (See 6 July 1939.)

The first helicopter to fly successfully was the French *Gyroplane Laboratoire*, designed by Louis Breguet and René Dorand. Fitted with a 350 hp Hispano-Suiza 9Q engine to drive two contra-rotating two-blade coaxial rotors, it demonstrated a speed of more than 60 mph (80 km/h) on 22 December 1935, climbed to an altitude of 519 ft (158 m) in 1936 and proved an endurance of more than an hour during a 27 mile (44 km) flight. It was destroyed in an air raid in 1943.

The first entirely successful helicopter in the world was the Focke-Wulf Fw 61 twin-rotor helicopter designed by Professor Heinrich Focke during 1933–34. The first prototype Fw 61 V1 (D-EBVU) made its first free flight on 26 June 1936 and was powered by a 160 hp Siemens-Halske Sh 14A engine. This aircraft, flown by

Gyroplane Laboratoire, *the first helicopter to fly successfully.*

Ewald Rohlfs in June 1937, established a world's closed-circuit distance record for helicopters of 76.025 miles (122.35 km) and a helicopter endurance record of 1 h 20 min 49 s. On other occasions it set an altitude record of 11 243 ft (3427 m) and a speed record of 76 mph (122 km/h). It gave a flying demonstration in the Berlin Deutschland-Halle during 1938 in the hands of the famous German woman test pilot Hanna Reitsch.

The first scheduled airmail service to be flown by a rotary-wing aircraft was recorded in the United States on 6 July 1939, by a Kellett KD-1B autogyro in service with Eastern Air Lines.

The first helicopter to go into limited production was the Focke-Achgelis Fa 223. The experimental Focke-Wulf Fw 61 (q.v.) was not exploited commercially, being too heavy structurally to carry a payload. Instead, a commercially developed derivative, the Fa 266 Hornisse, appeared in 1939 as a prototype six-seat civil transport helicopter. **This was the first real transport helicopter.** The Fa 266 made a free flight in August 1940 and was redesignated Fa 223 Drache, by which time it had changed into a military helicopter. By 1942 the Fa 223 was ready for operational trials although only two examples had flown because of Allied bombing. Because of the bombing, the factory had been moved from Bremen to Laupheim and eventually finished up in Berlin. By the end of the war only a small number of helicopters had flown, three of which were used for transport duties by Luft-Transportstaffel 40.

The first entirely successful helicopter was the German Focke-Wulf Fw 61.

Above   Kellet KD-1B, with 'First scheduled autogiro air mail route in the world' printed on its side.

Left   Third prototype Focke-Achgelis Fa 223 Drache. (Imperial War Museum)

Right   Focke-Achgelis Fa 330 Bachstelze, for towing behind submarines. This example ended up in America and was photographed in May 1946. (US Air Force)

The first successful and practical helicopters to be designed outside Germany were those of the Russian-born American Igor Sikorsky. His first successful helicopter was the Vought-Sikorsky VS-300, which featured full cyclic pitch control and was powered by a 75 hp engine. This made its first recognized free flight on 13 May 1940, although it had made a tethered flight on 14 September 1939. In May 1941 a 90 hp engine was installed and the VS-300 set up a new endurance record of 1 h 32 min 26 s. By 1942, after further improvement, the VS-300 became established as the first US successful and practical helicopter.

The first armed autogyro was the Soviet A-7Za, carrying three 7.62 mm PV-1 machine-guns. Production armed and unarmed A-7s were deployed operationally for reconnaissance and spotting and were used at the time of the German invasion, in 1941.

The first autogyros to be armed for ground and submarine attacks using bombs and depth charges, as well as for observation, were Japanese Kayaba Ka-1s, based on the Kellett KC-1A. First flown on 26 May 1941, examples of the Ka-1 joined the Army initially for observation but were later put on the deck of the *Akitsu Maru*, a converted cruiser, for coastal anti-submarine patrols. Power was provided by a 240 hp Argus As 10C engine and normal attack armament was two 60 kg bombs.

Undoubtedly the first helicopter to be tested from a ship's gun platform was one of 45 prototype and pre-production German Flettner Fl 282

Vought-Sikorsky VS-300, the first successful and practical helicopter designed outside Germany. (Sikorsky Aircraft)

Kolibris, which was experimentally flown from the cruiser *Köln* in 1942. The intended mass production of the Fl 282 was hindered by Allied bombing raids and only 24 were delivered, three being used by Luft-Transportstaffel 40.

The Focke-Achgelis Fa 330 Bachstelze was a single-seat gyro-kite designed in early 1942 and built by Weser-Flugzeugbau at Hoykenkamp near Bremen. Designed to be carried by Germany's ocean-going Type IX U-boats, it could be deployed when needed for observation duties, towed behind the surfaced submarine at a height of about 400 ft (122 m), to give its pilot a 25 mile (40 km) clear-weather field of view. It was, however, little used as U-boat crews believed it could pinpoint their position and also create crash-dive problems.

The first helicopter designed and built for military service was the Sikorsky XR-4, which first flew on 13 January 1942. Its delivery flight from Stratford, Connecticut, to Wright Field, Dayton, Ohio, a distance of 761 miles (1225 km), was the **first cross-country helicopter delivery flight**, accomplished between 13 and 18 May 1942. As a result of military trials at Wright Field, a small development batch of these helicopters was used for limited service and training during 1944–45 built on the first helicopter production line. R-4s were the first helicopters to fly in Alaska and Burma, first to be tried on board a US ship (1943), and the first to be flown by the British Fleet Air Arm.

The first jet-driven helicopters in the world were the Doblhoff/WNF 342 (V1–V4) helicopters, built in the suburbs of Vienna between 1942 and 1945 by the Wiener Neustadter Flugzeugwerke (WNF). The jet power was produced by mixing compressed air (provided from a compressor driven by a piston engine) with fuel, which was then channelled through the three hollow rotor blades and burnt in combustion chambers at the rotor tips. The V1 was flown first in the spring of 1943 but was damaged slightly by air raids during 1944. The V2 was derived from the rebuilt and modified V1, the V3 destroyed itself by vibration, but the V4 flew well before development was stopped in 1945.

Above   *World's first helicopter assembly line was set up by Sikorsky at Bridgeport to construct R-4Bs. (Sikorsky Aircraft)*

Left   *Sikorsky R-4B prepares to land on a ship's deck in the Pacific, 24 May 1945. (US Air Force)*

Arguably the first entirely successful coaxial rotor helicopter was the US Hiller XH-44, which was first demonstrated in public in August 1944.

The first helicopter with intermeshing rotors to be tested in the United States of America was the Kellett XH-8, first flown on 7 August 1944.

The first helicopters to be given USAAF 'R for Rotary-wing' military designations were the Platt-Le-Page XR-1 and XR-1A, ordered by the US government for evaluation and featuring twin rotors carried on wide outriggers.

The first successful tandem twin-rotor helicopter to be put into production was the Piasecki PV-3 (US Navy designation HRP-1) which first flew in March 1945. It was powered by a 600 hp Pratt & Whitney R-1340 Wasp engine and could fly at 120 mph (193 km/h). Designed to carry 10 persons, six stretchers or cargo, the first production HRP-1 'Flying Banana' was completed on 15 August 1947. Examples of this helicopter served initially with US Navy and Marine Corps experimental squadrons VX-3 and HMX-1.

The first helicopter to cross the English Channel was a Focke-Achgelis Fa 223 (No. 14) which

Right   Hiller XH-44 at San Francisco in August 1944. This was the first entirely successful coaxial rotor helicopter.

Below   Piasecki PV-3 as the prototype US Navy XHRP-1 'Flying Banana', first flown in March 1945.

arrived at Brockenhurst, Hampshire, in September 1945, piloted by a German crew of three. Fa 223 No. 14 had first flown in July 1943 and with No. 51 was confiscated by the Americans in May 1945. No. 14 was destroyed in October 1945 during evaluation trials.

The first-ever Type-Approval Certificate for a commercial helicopter was awarded for the Bell Model 47 on 8 March 1946; this aircraft made its first flight on 8 December 1945 and provided the design basis for a family of Bell helicopters that continued in production for close on 40 years.

The first US experimental delivery of airmail by helicopter began on 1 October 1946; the operations were carried out in the Chicago suburbs in a combined exercise by the US Post Office and the USAAF.

The first British-designed and -built production helicopter was the Bristol Sycamore, which first flew on 27 July 1947 and entered service with both the Army and Air Force. The Army versions were the HC10 ambulance and HC11 communications helicopters, the latter flying initially on 13 August 1950 and being delivered from 29 May 1951. The first RAF version, HR.12, was sent to St Mawgan for trials on 19 February 1952.

The world's first scheduled helicopter service was inaugurated on 1 October 1947 by Los Angeles Airways (LAA), using a Sikorsky S-51. The CAB had awarded LAA a temporary (three-year) certificate for mail carrying, on 22 May 1947.

The first helicopter built in Great Britain to enter service with the RAF was the Sikorsky-designed Westland/Sikorsky Dragonfly (the S-51 built under licence by Westland Aircraft Ltd at Yeovil, Somerset). The first Westland-built S-51 was for commercial use and flew in 1948. The RAF's first Dragonfly HC Mark 2 (WF 308) was powered by an Alvis Leonides engine and delivered in 1950; subsequent aircraft equipped No. 194 (Casualty Evacuation) Squadron, the RAF's first helicopter squadron, on 1 February 1953.

The first helicopter mail service in Great Britain was inaugurated on 1 June 1948 by British European Airways, with the Westland/Sikorsky S-51 (G-AKCU). Based at Peterborough, Northants, it served Norwich, Great Yarmouth and Kings Lynn.

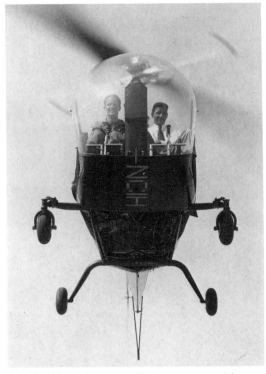

This Bell Model 47 was the first ever commercial helicopter to be awarded a Type-Approval Certificate. (Bell Helicopter Textron)

The first experimental night helicopter service was inaugurated on 14 February 1949 by British European Airways, flying the Westland/Sikorsky S-51 G-AKCU. The service, from Westwood, Peterborough, to Norwich, became regular from 17 October 1949 and continued until April 1950.

The first helicopter station in New York, which had been established at Pier 41 East River, became operational on 18 May 1949.

The United Kingdom's first night airmail services to be operated by helicopter began on 17 October 1949, the inaugural flight being made by BEA's Sikorsky S-51 G-AJOV, flown by Capt J. Cameron.

The first helicopter to have the engine mounted in the nose of the fuselage was the Sikorsky S-55, which first flew on 7 November 1949. This layout provided increased cabin area for the accommodation of passengers or cargo.

The first ramjet-powered helicopter to receive US certification was the Hiller HJ-1 Hornet of

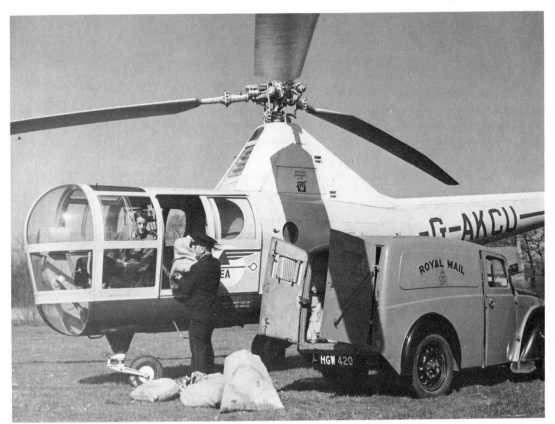

Above   *BEA Westland/Sikorsky S-51 G-AKCU which flew the first helicopter mail service in Great Britain.*

1950 appearance, a very small two-seat helicopter whose two-blade rotor was driven by tip-mounted 38 lb (17 kg) thrust Hiller 8RJ2B ramjet motors.

The Royal Navy's first all-helicopter squadron was No. 705, formed at Gosport, Hampshire, during 1950. Equipped with the Westland Dragonfly, this type of aircraft soon demonstrated its value for 'plane-guard' duties and ship-to-shore communications.

The first scheduled helicopter passenger services in the UK were those made between 9 and 19 May 1950 during the British Industries Fair. The services were flown between London and Birmingham by a Westland/Sikorsky S-51.

The first sustained and regular scheduled helicopter passenger services in the UK, between Liverpool and Cardiff, began on 1 June 1950. The service was operated by British European Airways with Westland/Sikorsky S-51s, but due to low demand was terminated on 31 March 1951 after carrying 819 passengers.

Below   *Hiller HJ-1 Hornet, the first ramjet-powered helicopter to receive US certification.*

The first tandem-rotor helicopter to gain CAA Type Approval was the McCulloch MC-4, which had first flown on 20 March 1951.

The US Navy's first ASW helicopter squadron, Squadron HS-1, was commissioned at Key West, Florida Keys, on 3 October 1951.

The first helicopter to use turboshaft engine power was a US Navy Kaman K-225 re-engined with a 175 shp Boeing YT50 and flown as such on 10 December 1951.

The first helicopter to use twin turboshaft engines was the re-engined Kaman HTK-1 128657, one of 29 piston-engined three-seat helicopters of this type received by the US Navy for training purposes from a September 1950 order.

The first twin-rotor twin-engined helicopter to be designed and flown in Britain, the Bristol Type 173 prototype (G-ALBN), was flown for the first time at Filton, Bristol, on 3 January 1952.

The first tandem-rotor helicopter received by the USAAF was the Piasecki H-21 Workhorse, first flown on 11 April 1952. Versions of the H-21 served in Arctic rescue, assault and cargo transport, and other roles from 1953. The main user of the H-21 was, however, the US Army, with whom it was better known as the Shawnee.

The first east–west crossing of the North Atlantic by helicopters was made in stages by two Sikorsky S-55s, between 13 and 31 July 1952.

The first French convertiplane was the Sud-Ouest SO 1310 Farfadet, which first flew as a helicopter on 8 May 1953. Seating was provided for a crew of two plus eight passengers. It combined the attributes of an aeroplane and helicopter by cruising on the power from a Turboméca Artouste II turboprop engine carried in the nose and with 'lift' provided by short wings and an autorotating rotor, while for transitional, vertical and hover modes the rotor was powered by a Turboméca Arius II turbo-compressor that supplied compressed air to the jet-driven rotor.

The Belgian airline Sabena operated the first international helicopter flight into central London on 7 July 1953. The flight was made by a Sikorsky S-55, between the Allee Verte Heliport in Brussels and London's South Bank Heliport near Waterloo.

The world's first international helicopter service was inaugurated on 1 September 1953 by the Belgian airline Sabena, flying Sikorsky S-55s. Services included flights from Brussels to Lille, Maastricht and Rotterdam.

Claimed to be the first rocket-powered rotary-wing aircraft to fly, on 13 May 1954, the American Kellett KH-15 research helicopter had a small liquid propellant rocket motor mounted at the tip of each of its main rotor blades.

The first tilt-rotor convertiplane to be flown was the Bell XV-3. Two examples were built, the first making its initial vertical flight on 23 August 1955. Powered by a single Pratt & Whitney R-985 engine of 450 hp, the XV-3 had a large fuselage that could accommodate four persons, and had

Above   *Sud-Ouest SO 1310 Farfadet, the first French convertiplane.*

Right   *Sabena Sikorsky S-55 taking on passengers at the Allee Verte Heliport in Brussels.*

Left   *The Korean War of the early 1950s established the helicopter as an indispensable workhorse. The little Bell Model 47 became known as the Korean Angel for its stretcher carrying of wounded from the front line to field hospitals. During three years of war some 23,000 United Nations wounded were carried by helicopter, about 18,000 by Model 47s alone.*

fixed wings of 31 ft 3½ in (9.54 m) span. The rotor/propellers were mounted at each wingtip and could be directed upward or forward by small electric motors for vertical or horizontal flight respectively. The first transition from vertical to horizontal flight was made on 18 December 1958; by 1966 more than 250 flights had been logged.

The US Navy's first helicopter assault carrier, the USS *Thetis Bay*, was commissioned on 20 January 1956.

The first rotating-wing aircraft to be literally a 'flying-boat' was the Bensen Model B-8B Gyro-Boat. Designed as a variant of the Gyro-Glider, this aircraft was basically a small dinghy that was fitted with a free-turning two-blade rotor and outer stabilizing floats (in later models). The Gyro-Boat would take off after being towed by a motorboat to a speed of 23 mph (37 km/h). The prototype first flew on 25 April 1956 and large numbers of these aircraft were built.

The first non-stop transcontinental flight across the USA by a rotary-winged aircraft was made during 23–24 August 1957. This was accomplished by a specially prepared Vertol H-21C 'Flying Banana' twin-rotor helicopter, flying from San Diego, California, to Washington, DC. During the flight, the H-21C was flight refuelled on four occasions by a U-1A Otter tanker aeroplane, using the looped hose method, and twice from the ground

while hovering. The overall flight took 31 h 40 min.

The first successful British convertiplane and first large VTOL transport was the Fairey Rotodyne, the prototype of which made its first flight on 6 November 1957. With accommodation for 40 passengers and a crew of two, the prototype Rotodyne Y was powered by two Napier Eland turboprop engines which were mounted below the fixed wings and drove tractor propellers. The large rotor mounted above the fuselage was driven by pressure-jets at the blade tips when required to be powered. In operation, the main rotor was usually powered for take-off and landing, but was allowed to autorotate in normal horizontal flight, the forward propulsion of the aircraft and much of the lift then coming from the turboprop engines and wings respectively. The first transition from vertical take-off to horizontal flight was made on 10 April 1958, and although potential operators were enthused with the Rotodyne, the project was cancelled under government economic cutbacks in 1962.

The first post-war German helicopter was the three-seat Borgward Kolibri I, designed by Heinrich Focke and flown for the first time on 8 July 1958 with Ewald Rohlfs at the controls. Power for this helicopter was provided by a 260 hp Lycoming VO-435-A1B piston engine.

The first specially designed anti-submarine

helicopter ordered for the Royal Navy was the Westland Wessex, developed from the Sikorsky S-58. Equipped with an automatic pilot, the Wessex could be operated by day or night in all weathers. Earliest first-line squadron to be equipped was No. 815, commissioned at Culdrose on 4 July 1961.

The first US helicopter unit to operate in Vietnam to assist South Vietnamese forces was the 57th Transportation Light Helicopter Company, which arrived in Tan Son Nhut in December 1961. Equipped with Piasecki H-21s, the Company was tasked with training South Vietnamese personnel to embark from helicopters.

The first support mission by US helicopters in Vietnam occurred on 23 December 1961, when H-21s of the US 57th Transportation Light Helicopter Company embarked 360 South Vietnamese troops on a search and destroy mission.

The first pilotless anti-submarine helicopter to enter service with the US Navy was the Gyrodyne QH-50A, in 1963; the Navy's drone helicopters each carried two homing torpedoes.

The first Fleet Air Arm helicopter used extensively from platforms on frigates, and smaller vessels, was the Westland Wasp. The first Small Ship Flight was formed on 11 November 1963. Though small, the Wasp could pack a hefty punch, carrying two homing torpedoes, or depth charges or air-to-surface missiles.

The first non-stop coast-to-coast helicopter flight across the North American continent was accomplished on 6 March 1965 by a Sikorsky SH-3A Sea King. The 2116 mile (3405 km) flight was made from the deck of the carrier USS *Hornet* at San Francisco, California, to the carrier USS *Franklin D. Roosevelt* at Jacksonville, Florida.

The first specially designed combat helicopter to go into large-scale service was the Bell Model 209 HueyCobra. First flown on 7 September 1965, six months after its development was started, the HueyCobra was designed as a two-seat armed combat helicopter for ground attack and escort duties, carrying guns, a grenade launcher, rockets and missiles. One of the main features of the HueyCobra is that its fuselage is only 3 ft 2 in (0.965 m) wide, making it a difficult target to hit by ground fire and easy to conceal beneath trees or with small camouflage nets. Production began with the AH-1G version for US Army service, delivered from June 1967. A total of 1078 AH-1Gs was built, beginning operations in August of that year. The current AH-1S version has a maximum speed of 141 mph (227 km/h) when carrying eight TOW anti-armour missiles.

The first non-stop transatlantic flights by helicopters were made during 31 May to 1 June 1967 by two Sikorsky HH-3Es *en route* to the Paris Air Show. Air-refuelled nine times during their 4270 mile (6872 km) flight from New York to Paris, the journey was accomplished in 30 h 46 min.

Left *The first successful British convertiplane and first large VTOL transport was the Fairey Rotodyne.*

Right *Bell AH-1G HueyCobra closing for a ground strike in Vietnam. (Bell Helicopter Textron)*

The US Navy's first helicopter mine counter-measures (MCM) squadron, HM-12, was established in late 1970. A special version of the Sikorsky S-65 twin-turbine helicopter was developed, with dual hydraulically powered winches to stream and retrieve the tow, and the first of these RH-53D helicopters was delivered to Squadron HM-12 during September 1973. The special equipment deployed by the tow was designed to destroy acoustic, magnetic or mechanical mines. More recently, in 1982 Sikorsky received a contract to develop a more advanced mine countermeasures helicopter based on the Super Stallion. The first of 32 MH-53E Sea Dragons was delivered to the US Navy on 26 June 1986 and operational deployment with HM-12 began on 1 April 1987.

The first non-stop transpacific flight by rotary-wing aircraft was that completed on 22 August 1970 by two Sikorsky HH-3C helicopters. These two aircraft covered a distance of 9000 miles (14 484 km), flight-refuelled *en route* by Lockheed Hercules tankers.

The first Soviet purpose-designed attack helicopter was the Mil Mi-24, known to NATO as *Hind*. Examples of the initial production version with a large enclosed flight deck for the crew of three, *Hind-A*, became operational in the early 1970s and two Soviet units were stationed in East Germany by early 1974. *Hind-D*, the first version to change to a crew of two in tandem individual cockpits, also features two later 2200 shp Isotov TV3-117 turboshaft engines, heavier armour protection, and improved armament that includes a 12.7 mm four-barrel Gatling machine-gun that can be used against ground and air targets. Pylons under the anhedral stub-wings allow the carriage of various weapon loads, typically four *Swatter* anti-armour missiles and four pods for up to 128 rockets in total. The main cabin of all Mi-24s can accommodate eight fully equipped assault troops. More than 2300 *Hinds* of all versions had been built for Soviet operation and export by 1988, and the helicopter was widely operated in Afghanistan.

The first occasion US Army HueyCobra attack helicopters fired TOW anti-armour missiles in action was during the spring of 1972. In April 1972 a number of the eight HueyCobras that had been modified to fire TOW missiles for trials under the Improved Cobra Armament Program (ICAP) were sent to Kontum in Vietnam to help meet an expected Viet-Cong offensive. By 27 June, they had flown 77 missions and had

Sikorsky MH-53E Sea Dragon towing a magnetic-influence hydrofoil vehicle. (Sikorsky Aircraft)

destroyed 39 armoured vehicles, trucks and guns without loss. Prior to this action each HueyCobra crew had launched only one TOW round in training.

The first round-the-world flight in a helicopter (in 29 stages) was achieved by Americans H. Ross Perot Jr and Jay W. Coburn flying Bell 206L LongRanger II *The Spirit of Texas*, between 1 and 30 September 1982. (See also Fastest.)

The first round-the-world solo flight in a helicopter (in stages) took place between 5 August 1982 and 22 July 1983. Australian pilot, Dick Smith, covered 35 258 miles (56 742 km) in his Bell JetRanger III *Australian Explorer.*

The first operational purpose-built armed attack helicopter of European design is the tandem two-seat Italian A 129 Mangusta, which first flew as a prototype on 15 September 1983 and

Left   *Mil Mi-24* Hind-A, identified by its cabin-style flight deck.

Below   *Ross Perot Jr and Jay W. Coburn with LongRanger II* The Spirit of Texas. *(Bell Helicopter Textron)*

joined Italian Army Aviation squadrons from 1988. Powered by two Rolls-Royce Gem 2 Mk 1004D turboshaft engines, it has a maximum dash speed of 196 mph (315 km/h), a normal maximum speed of 161 mph (259 km/h), and can carry eight TOW anti-armour missiles or other weapons.

The only modern purpose-designed attack helicopter featuring coaxial contra-rotating rotors is the new Soviet Kamov, known to NATO as *Hokum*. Little is yet known about this helicopter, which was at the development stage in 1987, though it is likely to be a tandem two-seater possessing a maximum speed in the 217 mph (350 km/h) range. US sources have stated their belief that *Hokum* could be intended mainly for all-weather air-to-air combat against other helicopters and some aeroplanes, using missiles and a fast-firing gun. If this proves to be correct, *Hokum* will become **the world's first purpose-designed air-to-air combat helicopter**.

The first Soviet attack helicopter designed from the start to have the tandem two-seat crew arrangement is the Mil Mi-28, known to NATO as *Havoc*. First becoming operational in 1987, the Mi-28 is believed to use similar engines to the Mi-24 (which see) and has a maximum

speed of around 186 mph (300 km/h). Armament includes a large gun under the nose and perhaps 16 anti-armour missiles or other weapons attached to stub wings.

The first composites-built human-powered helicopter designed and constructed to make an attempt to win the American Helicopter Society's $25 000 prize, is the *Da Vinci 2*, the work of students from the California Polytechnic University. To achieve this, the helicopter must hover for 60 s within a 10 m square and attain an altitude of 3 m. The *Da Vinci 2*, which will make the attempt in 1988, has **the largest rotor fitted to a helicopter**, with a diameter of 140 ft (42.67 m), made from foam, graphite and Tedlar. Tip-mounted two-blade propellers turn the rotor at just 6 rpm, undoubtedly making this the **slowest-turning rotor of any helicopter ever**.

Largest:

The largest rotor fitted to an engine-powered helicopter was 130 ft (37.62 m), used on the experimental American Hughes XH-17 flying-crane that first flew on 23 October 1952.

The largest helicopter flown anywhere in the world was the Soviet Union's Mil Mi-12, which

Agusta A 129 Mangusta, the first European purpose-built attack helicopter.

took to the air for the first time on 12 February 1969. A twin-rotor aircraft with an overall span over the rotor tips of 219 ft 10 in (67 m) and fuselage length of 121 ft 4½ in (37 m), it was powered by four 6500 shp Soloviev D-25VF turboshaft engines. First indication of the existence of this enormous helicopter to reach the West was in 1969, when the Soviet Union submitted to the FAI a number of payload-to-height records. Later, on 6 August 1969, the Mi-12 set a world record by lifting a payload of 88 636 lb (40 204.5 kg) to a height of 7398 ft (2255 m). No production followed.

The largest helicopter built outside of the USSR is the US Sikorsky CH-53E Super Stallion. This has a seven-blade main rotor of 79 ft (24.08 m) diameter that is powered by three 4380 shp General Electric T64-GE-416 turboshafts, a fuselage length of 73 ft 4 in (22.35 m) that can accommodate a crew of three and 55 troops or up to 30 000 lb (13 076 kg) of internal

Left *Hughes XH-17, which had a 130 ft rotor.*

Below *The largest helicopter ever flown was the Soviet Mil Mi-12. (Air Portraits)*

cargo, and weighs 73 500 lb (33 340 kg) when carrying an external payload. The prototype YCH-53E first flew on 1 March 1974.

Exceeding the record set previously by the Mil Mi-12, a Mil Mi-26 heavy-lift helicopter, crewed by G. G. Alfeurov and L. A. Indeev, lifted a total mass of 125 153.8 lb (56 768.8 kg) to a height of 2000 m on 3 February 1982 at Podmoscovnoe in the USSR. The Mi-26, of which development began in the early 1970s, is **the heaviest production helicopter flown anywhere in the world, and was the first to operate successfully with an eight-blade main rotor.** The prototype Mi-26 flew for the first time on 14 December 1977 and by autumn 1986 the Soviet forces had approximately 50 in service, with others delivered to India. Power is provided by two 11 240 shp Lotarev D-136 turboshaft engines, the main rotor diameter is 105 ft (32 m), and the fuselage length is about 110 ft 8 in (33.73 m). Accommodation is for a crew of five plus 85 troops or 44 090 lb (20 000 kg) of cargo. Gross weight is 123 458 lb (56 000 kg).

Fastest:

The current FAI world distance in a straight line record for autogyros is held by Briton Wg Cdr K. H. Wallis. Flying his WA-116/F from Lydd Airport, Kent, he flew 543.274 miles (874.315 km) to Wick, Scotland, on 28 September 1975.

The current FAI world speed record for convertiplanes: see Highest, 7 October 1961.

The current world speed record for helicopters over a 100 km closed circuit is held by a Soviet Mil Mi-6 piloted by Boris Galitsky. Set on 26 August 1964, the speed attained was 211.36 mph (340.15 km/h).

The current FAI world speed record in a 1000 km closed circuit is held by Soviet Galina Rastorgoueva in the Mil A-10 (Mi-24). Set on 13 August 1975, a speed of 206.7 mph (332.646 km/h) was attained.

The current FAI world speed record for helicopters in a 500 km closed circuit is held by American Thomas Doyle flying a Sikorsky S-76A. Set on 8 February 1982, a speed of 214.83 mph (345.74 km/h) was attained.

The current FAI world helicopter speed record for a round-the-world flight is held by Americans H. Ross Perot Jr and Jay W. Coburn at 35.4 mph (56.97 km/h). Flown from and back to Dallas, Texas, their Bell 206L LongRanger II *The Spirit of Texas* took between 1 and 30 September 1982 to establish the record.

The current FAI world speed record for autogyros is held by Briton Wg Cdr K. H. Wallis. Flying his WA-116/F/S on 14 October 1984, he achieved a speed of 117.80 mph (189.58 km/h).

Left *World speed record-holding Westland Lynx. (Westland Helicopters)*

Right *BERP III main rotor blades fitted to the 249 mph Lynx. (Westland Helicopters)*

The current FAI world speed record for helicopters is held by Briton Trevor Egginton in a Westland Lynx fitted with BERP III main rotor blades. Set on 11 August 1986, the Lynx attained 249.09 mph (400.87 km/h).

Highest:

The current FAI world records for altitude and speed in a straight line for convertiplanes are held by the Soviet Kamov Ka-22 Vintokryl. The former, established on 24 November 1961 at Bykovo, stands at 8491 ft (2588 m), while the speed record was set on 7 October 1961 at Joukovski-Petrovskoe over a 15/25 km course and stands at 221.4 mph (356.3 km/h). The pilot for the speed record was E. Efremov.

Above *The Soviet Kamov Ka-22 Vintokryl set the current FAI world altitude and speed in a straight line records for convertiplanes in 1961.*

Left *Wing Cdr Ken Wallis in his record-breaking WA-121/Mc at Boscombe Down on 20 July 1982, having bettered his previous altitude record.*

On 20 July 1982, Wg Cdr K. H. Wallis, flying from Boscombe Down, Wiltshire, attained an altitude of 18 516 ft (5643.7 m) in his Wallis WA-121/Mc which was powered by a Wallis-McCulloch engine of about 100 hp. This is the **current world altitude record for autogyros.**

The current world altitude record for helicopters of 40 820 ft (12 442 m) was established on 21 June 1972 by Jean Boulet of France, flying an Aérospatiale SA 315B Lama general-purpose helicopter. A Lama carrying out demonstration flights in the Himalayas during 1969 **also made the highest landings and take-offs that have been recorded,** at an altitude of 24 600 ft (7500 m).

The current FAI women's world altitude record for helicopters stands at 27 067 ft (8250 m), set by Soviet T. Zuyeva in a Kamov Ka-32 on 29 January 1985.

Longest:

The first helicopter to set an FAI accredited world record of over 1 km was an Italian machine designed by d'Ascanio (actually 0.67 mile; 1.078 km), in October 1930. The two two-blade contra-rotating rotors, plus the three variable-pitch propellers for longitudinal and lateral control, were driven by a 90 hp Fiat A-50 engine.

The current FAI world speed record for convertiplanes in a 100 km closed circuit is held by New Zealand, when on 5 January 1959 Sqn Ldr W. R. Gellatly and J. G. Morton flew at 190.9 mph (307.22 km/h) in the British-designed Fairey Rotodyne.

The current world distance in a closed circuit record for helicopters is held by American J. Schweibold in a Hughes OH-6A. Set on 27 March 1966, a distance of 1740 miles (2800.2 km) was flown.

The current FAI world distance in a straight line record for helicopters is held by American R. G. Ferry, who flew a Hughes OH-6A 2213 miles (3561.55 km) during 6–7 April 1966.

The current FAI women's world distance record for helicopters stands at 1387.03 miles (2232.218 km), set by Soviet I. Kopets in a Mil Mi-8 on 15 August 1969.

The current FAI world distance in a closed circuit record for autogyros is held by Briton Wg Cdr K. H. Wallis. Flying his WA-116/F on 13 July 1974, he flew 416.48 miles (670.26 km).

The current FAI women's world speed record for helicopters stands at 212.08 mph (341.32 km/h), set by Soviet Galina Rastorgoueva on 16 July 1975.

Worst:

The worst accident involving a helicopter took place on 10 May 1977 when 54 people were killed in an Israeli Sikorsky CH-53D Stallion at the West Bank.

Most:

The autogyro that has been produced in greater numbers than any other non-military rotorcraft is the Bensen B-8 Gyro-Copter, the prototype of which first flew on 6 December 1955. More than 5000 examples of the B-8M were built over the next three decades and the final version was usually powered by the 72 hp McCulloch Model 4318AX engine which gave it a maximum speed of 85 mph (137 km/h).

Following delivery of the company's 20 000th production helicopter, on 23 April 1974, Bell Helicopter's statistics showed that some 80 per cent of these had been delivered during the 10-year period from 1964. Sales of this proportion emphasize the enormous increase in the use of helicopters, particularly military use, that followed the post-war conflicts in Korea (the first war in which helicopters were widely used) and Vietnam.

The military force with the greatest number of helicopters on strength is the US Army, which has over 8500 helicopters of all kinds. The military transport section of the Soviet Air Force is thought to operate between 4100 and 4500 helicopters, including the largest helicopters in the world, of which a greater proportion can carry weapons.

Parachutes, Kites and Gliders

By comparison with the 'flash, bang, wallop' of modern military aircraft, or the exciting thunder of a Concorde supersonic transport overhead, the contents of this section of this book may appear comparatively uninteresting. However, deeper consideration will show this not to be the case, for parachutes, kites and gliders are the building blocks of aviation as we know it today and have their own, and most important, part in aviation history. Of even greater significance, they antedate what many enthusiasts may consider the more direct route to modern flight, via the balloon, airship and pioneering aircraft.

As the following pages record, the very earliest aviation artifact is the carved wooden model from Egypt which many believe could have been intended as a model glider, or the design for a larger version. Others have argued that it was more likely to be a crude, carved model of a bird, but as it almost certainly had cruciform tail surfaces (not a feature of any known ornithological species), the opinion is strengthened of those who believe it to be some form of, or design for, a flying machine. Gliders of one type or another, which attempted to adopt what appeared to be the most simple kind of flight used successfully by the birds, had a strong appeal to the early pioneers. Indeed, many of them slavishly copied the shape of a bird's wing, and the 'tower jumpers' were among the earliest to attempt gliding flight.

Clearly, the earliest parachutes were intended to permit some form of flight, for, in the absence of balloons or aeroplanes, there was nothing to escape from. Thus their first recorded use, during coronation celebrations of more than six hundred years ago, was to provide spectacle, a use that continued until the appearance of the early man-carrying balloons. Then, perhaps for the first time, the potential of a parachute for escape from damaged aircraft began to receive consideration, possibly dating from 22 October 1797 when the Frenchman Garnerin made a successful parachute descent from a balloon at a height of 2230 ft (680 m).

The practicality of the kite as a flying machine is first recorded by Marco Polo, who saw man-lifting kites being used in China during the 14th century. But even more important was the work of the Australian Lawrence Hargrave in the late 19th century, whose development of box kites and the design of strong and lightweight structures for them led directly to aircraft such as the pioneering

Engraving of Robert Cocking's parachute suspended below the Great Nassau Balloon. (The Science Museum, London)

designs of Alberto Santos-Dumont and the Voisin brothers in France. Before that, on 2 August 1899, Wilbur Wright had flown a kite of box form which could be controlled in flight by wing warping. This led to Orville and Wilbur Wright's gliders No. 1 and No. 2 of 1900 and 1901 respectively, both flown as a kite before being tested as a glider. But it was their highly successful No. 3 glider of 1902 that led directly to *The Flyer* which recorded the first man-carrying, powered and sustained flight on 17 December 1903.

Next time you see even the most unsophisticated home-made kite airborne on the wind, its restraining string in the hand of some bright-eyed boy or girl, remember that it represents a stepping stone to the whispering Airbus that is cruising overhead.

Firsts:

The first known model that could have represented a flying machine was a carved wooden bird, thought to be some 2300 years old. Originally discovered at Saqqara, Egypt, in 1898, and rediscovered in a storage box at the Cairo museum by Dr Khalil Messiha in 1972, it has a high-mounted wing with a finely carved aerofoil section, a body with the rear portion of narrow elliptical shape, and a deep vertical tail-fin with a groove for a horizontal surface.

Almost certainly the first recorded case of structural failure in flight, one that caused the death of Saracen of Constantinople, occurred in the 11th century. For his attempt at gliding flight he wore a cloak incorporating stiffening ribs, but unfortunately one of these ribs snapped and he plunged to the ground.

The first 'tower jumper' to achieve some measure of gliding flight was probably the English Benedictine monk Oliver of Malmesbury, in about AD 1020. Known as 'the Flying Monk', he jumped from Malmesbury Abbey with wings. A measure of gliding flight must have been achieved, as his only injuries were two broken legs. To Oliver can also be attributed **the first practical lesson in heavier-than-air gliding flight**, as his injuries convinced him of the necessity for tail surfaces attached to the feet.

The first recorded successful quasi-parachute jumps were made in China in 1306, as part of the celebrations during the coronation of Fo-Kin.

The first witnessed and properly recorded manned flights took place in Cathay (China) in the 14th century. These were recorded by the Venetian merchant traveller Marco Polo, while in Cathay with his father and an uncle. He witnessed man-carrying tethered kites and a translation of his report appears in *The Description of the World*, edited by A. C. Moule and P. Pelliot and published in London in 1938; it goes like this:

And so we will tell you how, when any ship must go on a voyage, they prove whether its business will go well or ill on that voyage. The men of the ship indeed will have a hurdle, that is a grating, of withies, and at each corner and side of the hurdle will be tied a cord, so that there will be eight cords, and they will all be tied at the other end with a long rope. Again they will find someone stupid or drunken and will bind him on the hurdle; for no wise man nor undepraved would expose himself to that danger. And this is done when a strong wind prevails. They indeed set up the hurdle opposite the wind, and the wind lifts the hurdle and carries it into the sky and the men hold on by the long rope. And if while it is in the air the hurdle leans towards the way of the wind, they pull the rope to them a little and then the hurdle is set upright, and they let out some rope and the hurdle rises. . . . The proof is made in this way, namely that if the hurdle going straight up makes for the sky, they say that the ship for which that proof has been made will make a quick and prosperous voyage, and all the merchants run together to her for the sake of sailing and going with her. And if the hurdle has not been able to go up, no merchant will be willing to enter the ship for which the proof was made, because they say that she could not finish her voyage and many ills would oppress her. And so that ship stays in port that year.

The first known design for a parachute proper was that by the Italian Leonardo da Vinci, dated about 1485. This square-section parachute was drawn to be hand held.

The first design for a parachute to appear in published form was to be found in *Machinae novae*, a Venetian work of 1595 by Fausto

Veranzio. This was a square cloth attached to a frame, the corners of which were roped to a body harness.

Perhaps the first sustained flight by a man-carrying glider was performed in the 17th century by Hezarfen Celebi of Turkey. Leaping from a tower at Galata, he is said to have covered some distance before meeting the ground.

The first documented parachute jump to be made successfully outside of China was that accomplished by an athlete in Siam during 1687. Detailed by M. de la Loubères, following a journey to Siam, the athlete is said to have jumped from height with two umbrellas, the handles of which were attached to his girdle.

The first demonstration in Europe of a quasi-parachute was given by the Frenchman Sebastien le Normand, who, in 1783, jumped from an observation tower at Montpellier (at a height equivalent to a first floor) under a braced conical canopy of 2 ft 6 in (0.76 m) diameter.

The first man in the world to identify and correctly record the parameters of heavier-than-air flight was the Englishman, Sir George Cayley, sixth Baronet (born 27 December 1773; died 15 December 1857). Sir George Cayley succeeded to the Baronetcy in a long and distinguished line of Cayleys whose origins are traceable back to Sir Hugo de Cayly, Knight, of Owby, who lived early in the 12th century. Sir William Cayley was created first Baronet by Charles II on 26 April 1661 for services in the Civil War. It was at Brompton Hall, near Scarborough, in the 1790s, that young George Cayley had carried out some of his early experiments with model aeroplanes. The following is a list of notable achievements by this remarkable scientist who was first to:

☐ set down the mathematical principles of heavier-than-air flight (i.e. lift, thrust and drag)
☐ make use of models for flying research, among them a simple glider—the first monoplane with fixed wing amidships, and fuselage terminating in vertical and horizontal tail surfaces; this was constructed in 1804
☐ draw attention to the importance of streamlining (in his definition of 'drag')
☐ suggest the benefits of biplanes and triplanes to provide increased lift with minimum weight

☐ construct and fly a man-carrying glider
☐ demonstrate the means by which a curved 'aerofoil' provided 'lift' by creating reduced pressure over the upper surface when moved through the air
☐ suggest the use of an internal-combustion engine for aeroplanes and constructed a model gunpowder engine in the absence of low-flashpoint fuel oil.

The first living creatures to descend by parachute from a balloon were animals released on 2 August 1791 over Vienna by the famous aeronaut Jean-Pierre Blanchard. (Following this and the release of a dog over Strasbourg, Blanchard made a parachute descent at Basle but broke a leg, in 1793.)

The first parachute descent ever performed successfully by man from a vehicle was accomplished by the Frenchman André Jacques Garnerin, who jumped from a balloon at 2230 ft (680 m), having ascended from the Parc Monçeau near Paris on 22 October 1797.

The first parachute descent in England was made by André Jacques Garnerin on 21 September 1802. However, he was injured in the descent, when one strap supporting the basket snapped.

The first man to bale out of a damaged aircraft with a parachute and survive was R. Jordarki Kuparanto who, on 24 July 1808, escaped from his Montgolfier hot-air balloon when it caught fire over Warsaw, Poland.

The first parachute descent from a balloon in America was that made by Charles Guille who, on 2 August 1819, jumped from a hydrogen balloon at a height of about 8000 ft (2440 m) and landed at New Bushwick, Long Island, New York.

The first public demonstration of a new form of parachute with an upside-down canopy to prevent oscillations, designed by Briton Robert Cocking and released from about 6600 ft (2000 m) on 24 July 1837, ended in tragedy. Lifted to height under the *Great Nassau Balloon*, the parachute, with Cocking underneath in a basket, descended well after release until the upper rim collapsed and he plunged to his death.

The first person to be carried aloft in a heavier-than-air craft in sustained (gliding) flight was a 10-year-old boy who became airborne in a glider constructed by Sir George Cayley at Brompton Hall, near Scarborough, Yorkshire, in 1849. The glider became airborne after being towed by manpower down a hill against a light breeze.

The first man to be carried aloft in a heavier-than-air craft, but not in control of its flight, was Sir George Cayley's coachman at Brompton Hall, reputedly in June 1853. A witness of the event stated that after he had landed, the coachman struggled clear and shouted, 'Please, Sir George, I wish to give notice. I was hired to drive, not to fly.' No record has ever been traced giving the name of either the 10-year-old or of the coachman. The decennial census of 1851, however, records the name of John Appleby as being the most probable member of Sir George's staff. With regard to the young boy, Sir George had no son or grandson of this age at the time of his experiments, so the first 'pilot' may have been a servant's son.

A first short free flight in a bird-form glider of his own design was made during 1857 by French sea-captain Jean Marie le Bris. This was made at Tréfeuntec, near Douarnenez, le Bris mounting his glider on a cart which was drawn along at speed to allow him to release the glider and make a short flight. His second attempt was less successful, the aircraft crashing and breaking his leg.

The first aircraft designed to save life was the man-carrying sea rescue kite developed by Irishman Cordner and first flown in 1859.

The first scientist correctly to deduce the main properties (i.e. lift distribution) of a cambered aerofoil was F. H. Wenham (1824–1908), who built various gliders during the mid-19th century to test his theories. In collaboration with John Browning, Wenham built **the world's first wind tunnel** in 1871 for the Aeronautical Society of Great Britain.

First exponent of the box-kite was Australian Lawrence Hargrave (1850–1915), who invented this mode of kite construction in 1893. This simple structure provided good lift and stability and formed the basis of early aeroplanes such as the French Voisin.

American-born Samuel Franklin Cody (1861–1913) made his first experiments relating to the construction and use of man-lifting kites at Farnborough (Hampshire) during 1899. This work led directly to development of the military

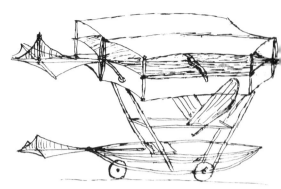

Sketch of the boy-carrying glider by Cayley himself. Note the triplane wings, combined elevator/rudder and the flapping power system. (The Science Museum, London)

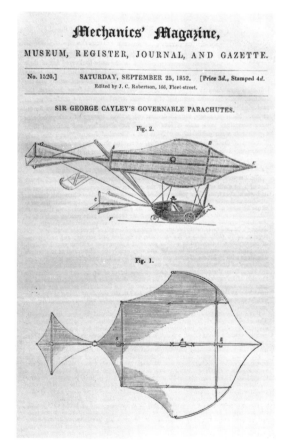

Cayley's 'governable parachute' man-carrying glider, published as a drawing in Mechanics Magazine in 1852. It was not built, but showed many design features of a workable aeroplane. (The Science Museum, London)

Samuel Cody on horseback, directing trials of one of his man-lifting kites.

observation kite, as used during the First World War.

The first test of their theories on the control of flight by wing warping was made by the Wright brothers (Wilbur and Orville) in August 1899, using a 5 ft (1.5 m) span biplane kite as the test vehicle.

The Wright brothers constructed and flew their first glider during 1900. This No. 1 glider, of biplane configuration, was flown also as a kite but had insufficient span. Using wing warping for lateral control, it was their first man-carrying aircraft and the first to be tested at the later famous Kill Devil Hills, North Carolina. Wing span was 17 ft (5.18 m). The Wrights' No. 2 glider was built in 1901. Of increased span, it was not as successful as hoped and resulted in the decision to undertake further research on aerofoils, using models. The No. 3 glider, built during August and September 1902, reflected this research and flew a great many times. This formed the basis of the powered *Flyer*.

The first glider flight from a balloon was performed by American Daniel Maloney on 29 April 1905. In a similar flight on 18 July Maloney lost his life.

The first parachute descent from an aeroplane in America was performed by Capt Albert Berry who, on 1 March 1912, jumped from a Benoist aircraft flown by Anthony Jannus at 1500 ft (460 m) over Jefferson Barracks, St Louis, Missouri.

The first parachute descent by a woman from an aeroplane was made by the 18-year-old American girl, Georgia ('Tiny') Broadwick who, using an 11 lb (5 kg) silk parachute, jumped from an aircraft flown by Glenn Martin at about 1000 ft (305 m) over Griffith Field, Los Angeles, California, on 21 June 1913.

The first parachute drop from an aeroplane over Great Britain was made by W. Newell at Hendon on 9 May 1914 from a Grahame-White Charabanc flown by R. H. Carr. Newell sat on a short rope attached to the port undercarriage, clutching his 40 lb (18 kg) parachute in his lap; when the aeroplane had climbed to 2000 ft (610 m) F. W. Gooden, seated on the lower wing, prised Newell off his perch with his foot! The parachute was 26 ft (7.9 m) in diameter and the drop occupied 2 min 22 s.

The first recorded free-fall jump from an aeroplane, before deployment of the parachute, was made by Leslie Leroy Irvin on 19 April 1919.

Above   Massive glider operations were conducted during the Second World War by both Allied and Axis powers as a method of transporting huge numbers of troops and their equipment by air. Among the biggest operations was the June 1944 D-Day Normandy landings, with hundreds of Allied gliders taking part. Here Halifax towing bombers prepare to haul some of the 250 or so Airspeed Horsa and 70 General Aircraft Hamilcar gliders used during the D-Day operations. (Imperial War Museum)

Left and below   The largest glider of the Second World War was the huge German Messerschmitt Me 321 Giant, with a wing span of 181 ft 3 in (55.24 m) and weighing 77,160 lb (35,000 kg) at take off (loaded). The immense towing power required to get it airborne eventually led to an armed six-engined version of the same aircraft, designated Me 323. Production totals for the Me 321 and 323 were 200 and 150 respectively. (MBB)

The first glider competition was held during 1920 at Rhon, Germany, organized by the Aero Technical Association of Dresden.

The first glider flight of more than one hour duration was made in Germany on 18 August 1922, by pilot Martens in a *Vampyr*.

The first American to escape from a disabled aeroplane by parachute was Lt Harold R. Harris, US Army, who on 20 October 1922 jumped from a Loening monoplane at 2000 ft (610 m) over North Dayton, Ohio.

Development of the first rotary-wing man-carrying glider intended as a pilot escape system was started by a team led by Raoul Hafner in the UK on 3 October 1940. Named the Rotachute, about 20 were built and tested but were not used.

The first glider to be towed across the North Atlantic was an RAF Hadrian (American Waco CG-4) transport glider piloted by Sqn Ldr Reginald G. Seys with a French-Canadian co-pilot, Sqn Ldr Fowler Gobeil. Its tug was an RAF Dakota, and during June 1943 it was flown in stages from Montreal to the UK in 28 h.

The first cross-Channel flight in a sailplane, between London and Brussels, was made by L. Welch on 12 April 1950.

The first UK National Hang-Gliding Championships were held on the South Downs at Steyning Hill (Sussex) on 13 July 1974. Highlighting the growth of hang-gliding as an aviation sport, more than 100 pilots attended this inaugural competition with some 80 gliders involved.

Largest:

The largest star formation of parachutists in free-fall to be approved under US Parachuting Association rules involved a team of 72 men. This was achieved at De Land (Florida) on 3 April 1983, the formation in free-fall being held for the required time of 3.4 s.

The largest all-woman free-fall formation of parachutists to be ratified by the FAI, one comprising 60 people, was made at De Land (Florida) on 24 March 1986.

The largest free-fall formation of parachutists to be ratified by the FAI, and one including both men and women, was that seen at Koksijde (Belgium) on 11 July 1987 in which a total of 126 people took part.

Highest, Longest and Greatest:

The longest recorded parachute descent was that by Lt Col William H. Rankin of the US Marine Corps who, on 26 July 1959, ejected from his LTV F8U Crusader naval jet fighter at 47 000 ft (14 326 m). Falling through a violent thunderstorm over North Carolina, his descent took 40 min instead of an expected time of 11 min, as he was repeatedly carried upwards by the storm's vertical air currents.

The longest recorded gap between two parachute jumps are probably those made by R. W. Mortimer of Folkestone (Kent). The first took place in Palestine during 1946, the next 28 years later on 9 September 1975 at Lympne (Kent) in

The first ejection-seat escape from a moving aeroplane while still on the ground was accomplished by Sqn Ldr J. S. Fifield on 3 September 1955, when he ejected from a modified Gloster Meteor 7 that was travelling at 120 mph (194 km/h). This shows Sqn Ldr Fifield moments before the Martin-Baker seat released a parachute.

preparation for a voluntary fund-raising project for a local charity.

The greatest altitude from which a successful emergency escape from an aeroplane has been reported is 56 000 ft (17 070 m). At this altitude, on 9 April 1958, an English Electric Canberra bomber exploded over Monyash, Derbyshire, and the crew, Flt Lt John de Salis and Flying Officer Patrick Lowe, fell free in a temperature of −70°F (−56.7°C) down to an altitude of 10 000 ft (3050 m), at which height their parachutes were deployed automatically by barometric control.

The greatest altitude from which a man has fallen and the longest delayed drop ever achieved by man was that of Capt Joseph W. Kittinger, USAF, over Tularosa, New Mexico, on 16 August 1960. He stepped out of a balloon gondola at 102 200 ft (31 150 m) for a free fall of 84 700 ft (25 816 m) lasting 4 min 38 s, during which he reached a speed of 614 mph* (988 km/h) despite a stabilizing drogue and experienced a minimum temperature of −94°F (−70°C). His 28 ft (8.5 m) parachute deployed at 17 500 ft (5334 m) and he landed after a total time of 13 min 45 s. The step by the gondola was inscribed 'This is the highest step in the world.'

The greatest free-fall parachute record by a man to be ratified by the FAI is that achieved by the Russian parachutist E. Andreev, near Volks, on 1 November 1962 with a free-fall distance of 80 380 ft (24 500 m).

The greatest height from which a group of British parachutists has made a delayed drop stands at 39 183 ft (11 942 m), achieved by five Royal Air Force parachute jumping instructors over Boscombe Down, Wiltshire, on 16 June 1967. They were Sqn Ldr J. Thirtle, Flt Sgt A. K. Kidd, and Sgts L. Hicks, P. P. Keane and K. J.

Teesdale. Their jumping altitude was 41 383 ft (12 613 m).

The greatest known landing altitude for a parachute jump was 23 045 ft (7134 m), the height of the summit of Lenina Peak on the border of Tadzhikistan and Kirgiziya in Kazakhstan, USSR. It was reported in May 1969 that 10 Russians had parachuted on to this mountain summit but that four had been killed.

The greatest straight-line distance in a single-seat glider to be ratified by the FAI was achieved on 25 April 1972. This was set by Hans Werner Grosse of West Germany, who piloted his Schleicher AS-W12 sailplane over a distance of 907 miles (1460 km). **The greatest distance for a two-seat glider** was achieved by S. H. Georgeson in New Zealand, on 31 October 1982, whose flight of 620.6 miles (998.76 km) was also FAI-ratified.

The greatest FAI-ratified glider heights attained by women in single- and two-seat sailplanes have now stood for a number of years. Both set in the USA, the oldest is the height of 35 463 ft (10 809 m) which Babs Nott and Hannah Duncan reached on 5 March 1975 in a Schweizer SGS 2-32 two-seater. Four years later Sabrina Jackintell's solo record was established in a Grob Astir CS, flown to a height of 41 460 ft (12 637 m) on 14 February 1979.

The greatest free-fall parachute record by a woman to be ratified by the FAI is that achieved by Russian parachutist E. Fomitcheva, near Odessa, on 26 October 1977 with a free-fall distance of 48 556 ft (14 800 m).

The greatest straight-line distance record set by a woman in a single-seat glider was achieved on 20 January 1980 by Britain's K. E. Karel, who piloted a standard 15 m Rolladen-Schneider LS3 sailplane over an FAI-ratified distance of 590 miles (949.7 km). **The women's two-seat glider record** is of much longer standing, having been set in the Soviet Union on 3 June 1967 by T. Pavlova and L. Filomechkina in a Blanik sailplane flown over a distance of 537.4 miles (864.86 km), also ratified by the FAI.

The greatest number of parachute jumps to be recorded within a period of 24 hours was a total of 250 made by US citizen David Huber at Issaquah, Washington, USA, 3–4 July 1985.

*The speed of 614 mph (988 km/h) reached by Kittinger during his fall represents a Mach No. of 0.93 in the Stratosphere and would have been reached at an altitude of about 60 000 ft (18 300 m); thereafter his fall would have been retarded fairly rapidly to less than 200 mph (322 km/h) as he passed through the Tropopause at about 36 000 ft (11 000 m). The speed of 614 mph (988 km/h) almost certainly represents the greatest speed ever survived by a human body not contained within a powered vehicle beneath the interface (i.e. within the earth's atmosphere).

The greatest FAI-ratified single-seat glider height record for men stands at 49 009 ft (14 938 m), which Robert R. Harris attained while flying a Grob G-102 in the USA on 17 February 1986. The two-seat record has remained unbroken since 1952 when on 19 March—and also in the USA—L. E. Edgar and H. E. Klieforth, in a Pratte-Read PR.GI sailplane, climbed to a height of 44 255 ft (13 489 m).

Most:

The most effective demonstration of the capability of his man-lifting kites was staged by English schoolteacher George Pocock. In 1827 he attached one of his kites to a road carriage and was pulled at speed between Bristol (Avon) and Marlborough (Wiltshire), a distance of some 31 miles (50 km).

The most northerly parachute jump was that made by American Dr Jack Wheeler on 15 April 1981, who landed on the polar ice cap at latitude 90° 00′ N.

The greatest FAI-ratified distance recorded for a hang-glider was that attained by Randy Haney of the USA who, flying an unpowered flexible-wing hang-glider on 2 June 1986, travelled 199.75 miles (321.47 km) from his take-off point.

One of the most amazing parachute rescues was that made by Gregory Robertson at Coolidge (Arizona) on 18 April 1987. In a multiple free-fall Debbie William collided with another parachutist at about 9000 ft (2745 m) and was knocked unconscious. Seeing the situation, Robertson manoeuvred alongside her and at a height of only 3500 ft (1065 m) managed to pull the ripcord of William's parachute, thus saving her life by a margin of about 10 s.

The three most outstanding pioneers of gliding flight, prior to successful powered flight, were the German Otto Lilienthal (1848–96), the Englishman Percy Sinclair Pilcher (1866–99) and the American Dr Octave Chanute (1832–1910). Their achievements may be summarized as follows:

Otto Lilienthal, German civil engineer, published a classic aeronautical textbook *Der Vogelflug als Grundlage der Fliegekunst* (The Flight of Birds as the Basis of Aviation) in 1899. Although he remained convinced that powered flight would ultimately be achieved by wing-flapping (i.e. in the ornithopter), Lilienthal constructed five fixed-wing monoplane gliders and two biplane gliders between 1891 and 1896. Tested near Berlin and at the Rhinower Hills near Stöllen, these gliders managed sustained gliding

At the height of his success, Otto Lilienthal pilots one of his gliders in 1894. (Deutsches Museum, Munchen)

Percy Pilcher flying his tailed Hawk glider. (The Science Museum)

A Chanute biplane glider in classic biplane configuration.

Octave Chanute. (Smithsonian institution)

flight; the pilot, usually Lilienthal himself, supported himself by his arms, holding the centre section of the glider. Thus, he could run forward and launch himself off the hills. During this period he achieved gliding distances ranging from 330 ft (100 m) to more than 820 ft (250 m). Although he had been experimenting with a small carbonic acid gas engine, he died on 10 August 1896 after one of his gliders crashed on the Rhinower Hills on 9 August before he could progress further with powered flight.

Percy S. Pilcher, British marine engineer, built his first glider, the *Bat*, in 1895 and flew that year on the banks of the River Clyde. Following advice by Lilienthal, as well as early practical experiments, Pilcher added a tailplane to the *Bat* and achieved numerous successful flights. This aircraft was followed by others (christened the *Beetle*, *Gull* and *Hawk*), the last of which was constructed in 1896 and included a fixed fin, a tailplane and a wheel undercarriage. It had a cambered wing with a span of 23 ft 4 in and an area of 180 ft² (7 m and 16.72 m² respectively). Pilcher had always set his sights upon powered flight and was engaged in developing a light 4 hp oil engine (probably for installation in his *Hawk*) when, having been towed off the ground by a team of horses, he crashed in the *Hawk* at Stanford Park, Market Harborough, on 30 September 1899, and died two days later.

Octave Chanute, American railroad engineer, was born in Paris, France, on 18 February 1832. His book *Progress in Flying Machines*, published in 1894, was the first comprehensive history of heavier-than-air flight and is still regarded as a classic of aviation literature. As well as providing a valuable information service for pioneers on both sides of the Atlantic, he began designing and building improved Lilienthal-type hang-gliders in 1896. After experimenting with multiplanes fitted with up to eight pairs of pivoting wings and a top fixed surface, he evolved the classic and successful biplane configuration. Flight-testing of his gliders was performed mainly by Augustus M. Herring (1867–1926), as Chanute was too old to fly himself. The Wright brothers gained early inspiration from *Progress in Flying Machines*, became close friends of Chanute, and learned from him the advantages offered by a Pratt-trussed biplane structure and, later, a catapult launching system for their wheel-less aircraft.

Civil Aviation and Route Proving

Civil aeroplanes formed the foundation upon which both commercial and military interests subsequently flourished. It is curious that, almost without exception, the earliest military sponsored projects failed (Ader's two-seat bomb carrier of 1897 and Langley's full-size *Aerodrome* of 1903, to name two of the better known), whereas others without military financial backing succeeded to varying degrees. There is no easy explanation for this and, indeed, civilians like the Wright brothers and Blériot subsequently exploited the military interest in their designs. But it did not end there. Aviation history has many later examples of civil innovation stealing the march on the military; the Bristol 142 six-passenger high-speed transport of 1935 led to the Blenheim bomber, while today's Concorde remains the world's only aeroplane to fly most of its life at supersonic speed.

Reaching back through centuries long past, accounts of intrepid tower jumpers who often as not leapt to their deaths clutching ill-conceived 'flying' apparatus, serve to show that man has always considered assisted flying possible. A glance skyward to see birds in flight was inspiration enough.

The first of the recorded tower jumpers was Bladud, the ninth king of Britain who, in about 843 BC, jumped to his death from the Temple of Apollo in Trinavantum (London) adorned with wings of feathers. Many centuries later, tower jumpers were still leaping off high places, with little chance of a second attempt at flight! Then, in the 11th century, two well-recorded leaps appeared to have shown some promise, although ending in one death and serious injury to the other would-be flier.

In the meantime, in China in the 4th century BC the kite had been invented for pleasure and war. In about 200 BC Chinese General Han Hsin used a kite to calculate the distance between his army and the enemy during a battle, and eight centuries later the Chinese are known to have used kites to pass military messages by semaphore. Amazingly, it was the kite that first gave man a taste of flying, as recorded in another section of this book.

Free flight was still the aim of most would-be fliers and an important step forward was made in AD 1250. In this year an English Franciscan monk named Roger Bacon completed a book entitled *Secrets of Art and Nature*, in which he mentioned 'Engines for flying, a man sitting in the midst thereof, by turning only about an Instrument, which moves artificiall Wings made to beat the Aire, much after the fashion of a Bird's flight'. At last the need for mechanical assistance had been appreciated, although Bacon's thoughts were directed to what we know today as the ornithopter with flapping wings. More than two centuries later the Italian Leonardo da Vinci also designed an ornithopter, giving further proof that it had been appreciated that man's muscle power without assistance was insufficient for flight. This was endorsed by the Italian Giovanni Borelli in 1680, in his book *De Motu Animalium*. Unfortunately, the ornithopter remained the number one concept for manned powered flight right up to the invention of man-carrying balloons, a dead-end concept that has still to be mastered in the late 20th century. Interestingly, whilst the ornithopter proved to be no way forward in itself, recent years have witnessed that engine power is not always necessary for powered and sustained flight. The development of pedal-power aircraft, albeit using modern technology in their configuration and construction, has shown that man's muscles can generate sufficient power for sustained flight if matched mechanically to a sufficiently lightweight and high-lift airframe.

It is generally accepted that Sir George Cayley (1773–1857) was the 'Father of Aerial Navigation'. Unlike the eminent persons mentioned previously, he believed that wings should be left to produce lift only and that another system of propulsion should be sought. This, instantly, rejected the ornithopter. He is credited with designing the first aircraft with a fixed and cambered wing, set at a modest angle of attack, a tail unit with horizontal and vertical surfaces, and a man-carrying body. Although a piloted aircraft of this general configuration and capable of powered flight was some decades away, the foundations for such a machine had been laid.

By accepting (as we do) that the Wright brothers' initial flight of 17 December 1903 was the first flight proper, injustices are heaped upon some other pioneers of the air that managed to achieve at least most of the proper criteria for flight and who are known, or are thought by some, to have flown over respectable distances prior to 17 December.

To understand why the Wrights are accepted as having been the founders of aeroplane flight proper, it is important to keep in mind a single word, *controllable*. Theirs was the first powered

aeroplane to succeed in making a sustained flight with the pilot having some real measure of control. Of course the term 'sustained' is relative to the period and indeed the first flight by the Wrights on 17 December was little more than a long leap into the air, lasting just 12 seconds from beginning to end.

But what of the other aviators? Among the pioneers who are credited with powered flight before the Wright brothers was the German civil servant from Hanover, Karl Jatho. His aircraft is normally referred to as a semi-biplane, having an unusually shaped bottom wing and a similarly configured but much smaller upper wing. No tailplane was fitted but between the wings were substantial rudder surfaces and elevators were carried. The small 9 hp petrol engine drove a paddle-like pusher propeller. On 18 August 1903 Jatho 'hopped' the aeroplane over a distance of 59 ft (18 m), which can barely be considered 'sustained'. However, in November he covered 195 ft (60 m). This, in fact, represents a flight more than 50 per cent longer in distance than the first made by Orville Wright on the 17th of the following month. However, this 'flight' on the Vahrenwalder Heide lacked that essential control, and was not the victim of discrimination on the basis that the Wright *Flyer* looked a real plane and the Jatho aerodyne appeared from its design capable of little more than marginal flight, though in truth it did lack the development potential of the *Flyer*. Also to be remembered is that on 17 December the *Flyer* was flown four times, the longest flight lasting nearly a minute.

If Jatho can be considered to have been a 'possible', then there were also 'probables' about whom far too little is known and therefore acknowledged. One such aviator was the American Lyman Gilmore who, in 1896, is said to have flown a steam-powered aeroplane on about a dozen occasions, the longest of these covering a distance of approximately 4 miles (6.4 km) after launch from a track. Certainly, Gilmore produced aeroplanes during this period that might have been capable of sustained flight. One, photographed when nearing completion, was a 60 ft (18.3 m) span airliner with heavily strut-braced bird-like wings, featuring a round-section fuselage (with windows) that offered interior seating for 10 passengers. Unfortunately, this giant was destroyed by fire while in its hangar. If the claim for Gilmore's 1896 steam-powered aeroplane could

Karl Jatho's semi-biplane, which flew 195 ft (60 m) just prior to the Wright brothers' first flights. (Historishchen Museums am Hohen Ufer)

be substantiated and officially recognized, aviation history would need to be rewritten. At the very least his steam plane must be a front-runner for the accolade 'the most successful early steam-powered aeroplane flown' (assuming it did!).

There is no doubt that the Wrights took a very professional attitude to flying, not only in the amount of original research carried out to achieve a satisfactory flying machine but also in terms of exploitation of their achievements. In March 1903 they patented an aeroplane design to protect their work, based on their No.3 glider, and between the close of 1903 and October 1905 they managed to perfect the *Flyer*. Then, extraordinarily, they stopped flying and began to capitalize on the *Flyer*. In January 1905, when the US government opened negotiations for the purchase of an aeroplane for military use, no other could come close to the *Flyer*, a position endorsed in mid-year with the appearance of the fully-controllable and refined *Flyer III*. Yet, by the time a Wright aeroplane was delivered to the US Army, the brothers were well on their way to losing their hitherto seemingly unassailable lead in design and performance. A further year and European aeroplanes were foremost.

Once powered heavier-than-air flying became a reality, and the first wars were fought using the aeroplane's unique skills, 1919 appeared to offer a bright new future; the peaceful exploitation of

flying could tentatively begin one of the greatest revolutions in popular mobility. Then came disillusionment. Somehow or other it had been overlooked that four terrible years of war would have to be paid for. The giant air fleets of the combatant nations and the enormous number of men, and indeed women, needed to support, maintain and fly them, were axed overnight. Major aircraft builders around the world found themselves without work, and many without hope of work just faded away. Those that believed there was a future for aviation fought for survival, revising their factories to manufacture urgently needed consumer goods until civil aviation could find its feet.

What had the First World War done for the emancipation of the aeroplane? Surprisingly little. By far the majority of all aircraft retained drag-inducing biplane structures, heavy fixed landing gear and open cockpits. The biggest change had come in the development of more reliable and more powerful engines, and the availability of such powerplant had, perhaps, made it easier for aircraft designers to build bigger and more effective aircraft without any significant improvement in design or technology. But the wide-scale use of military aircraft had made people more aware of aviation and its potential for civil use.

Jumping ahead, in 1945, for the second time in the brief historical period of less than three decades, the nations that had been involved in a major war began the process of facing up to a whole new range of problems. The return to peace was rather less of a shock than had been the case in 1919, with better plans for sailors, soldiers and airmen to be transformed back to civilians. But the six years of war had wrought tremendous changes in the field of aviation. Instead of the fairly parochial First World War, that which had just ended had been fought over a worldwide arena requiring the development of aircraft with far greater range capability. In the case of the United States, involved in European, Middle East and Far East theatres of action, it spurred the development of long-range transport aircraft, able to operate from, and to land-aerodromes.

Longer-range operations brought the evolution of better communications and navigation systems; the need to attack targets by day or night and in all weather conditions improved instrumentation and hastened the development of airborne radar for navigation. German and Allied research had shown that it would be possible to build new aeroplanes of increased speed and capability, and the development in Germany and Britain of gas turbine engines for aircraft propulsion meant that the powerplants needed by such advanced aircraft would soon be available.

All of this confirmed that the flying-boat was as dead as a dodo for future long-range world travel, and that a whole new generation of transport aircraft would need to be built to carry in peace the hundreds of thousands of ex-service men and women (and others) who had come to regard air travel as the norm.

Firsts:

The first powered model aeroplane to have flown is thought to have been that constructed in 1647 by the Italian Titus Livio Burattini, then residing at the court of King Wladyslaw IV of Poland. It is recorded to have had four sets of wings in tandem and a tail unit, the two centre pairs fixed and the forward and rear pairs for propulsion as an ornithopter. Drive was via springs. (Eight years later, Englishman Robert Hooke also flew a model ornithopter.)

The first man in the world to identify and correctly record the parameters of heavier-than-air flight was the Englishman, Sir George Cayley. (See also parachutes.)

The first modern aeroplane design, incorporating wire-braced constant chord wings (constructed using spars and cambered ribs, with double skinning), an enclosed fuselage for the crew and passengers and housing the power plant, propellers, a fixed tricycle landing gear, and a vertical tail and large-area tailplane, was the *Aerial Steam Carriage* (also known as the *Ariel*). Designed by Englishman William Samuel Henson (1812–88) from 1842, the design received a patent in 1843 and was expected to be built for service with the proposed Aerial Transit Company, **the first ever projected commercial airline**. The full-size *Aerial Steam Carriage* was to have had a span of 150 ft (45.72 m), a wing chord of 30 ft (9.14 m), and a length of about 84 ft 9 in (25.83 m), and the single 25–30 hp Henson steam engine was expected to drive two 10 ft (3.05 m) diameter six-blade pusher propellers. Although the subject of many engravings, it was never built. This is partly because of the failure of a scale model of the *Aerial Steam Carriage* to make a sustained flight. This model, with a span of 20 ft (6.10 m) and also steam powered, was tested between 1844 and 1847. Although launched using a ramp, it proved incapable of sustaining flight. Having seen the failure of his dreams, Henson emigrated to America in 1848. However, this model was **the first to be powered by a steam engine**.

The first powered model aeroplane to fly successfully is the subject of some controversy. The first claim is made for John Stringfellow, an associate of Henson who was to have been the co-founder of the Aerial Transit Company (had the founding of this public company for world-wide air travel been accepted more favourably). Continuing Henson's work, but using a 10 ft 6 in (3.20 m) span steam-driven model with curved wings, Stringfellow launched his model from a high cable at Chard, Somerset, England in 1848 but this is thought not to have sustained flight. However, Stringfellow is also remembered for a model triplane exhibited at the first aeronautical exhibition at Crystal Palace in 1868, which, although unsuccessful in flight, introduced the concept of superimposed straight wings on a model. (It should be remembered that the triplane concept in itself was not new, Cayley having produced a triplane glider with superimposed wings in 1849—see Gliders.)

The person credited with producing **the first powered model aeroplane to fly successfully** was Frenchman Félix du Temple de la Croix, who in 1857–8 flew a model powered successively by clockwork and steam.

The first design for a jet-propelled aeroplane in the modern sense (remembering the rocket-powered model bird designed by the Italian Joanes Fontana in about 1420, and before this the wooden model bird propelled by steam or compressed air jet demonstrated in about 400–350 BC by Greek-born Archytas of Tarentum, Italy) was produced by Frenchman Charles de Louvrie in 1865. Known as the *Aéronave*, it had a canopy-type wing supported on a strut above a wheeled cart which carried twin jetpipes through which vaporized oil or similar fuel was to have been burned and ejected. This was not constructed.

The Aeronautical Society of Great Britain was founded on 12 January 1866. In 1868 it staged the **first ever aeronautical exhibition**, held at Crystal Palace. The exhibits included model engines driven by steam, oil gas and guncotton.

The first design for a powered delta-winged aeroplane was that by Englishmen J. W. Butler and E. Edwards and patented in 1867. This was also the **first British design for a jet-propelled aeroplane**.

Undoubtedly the first ornithopter to fly successfully was completed in 1870 by Gustave Trouvé. This bird-like model was powered by revolver cartridges which, when fired, forced down the wings, which returned by springs. It was reported that flights of 195 ft (60 m) were possible.

The first powered man-carrying aeroplane to achieve a brief 'hop', after gaining speed down a ramp, was a monoplane with swept-forward wings built by Félix du Temple and piloted by an unidentified young sailor, at Brest in about 1874. The power plant was a hot-air or steam engine, driving a tractor propeller.

The first unmanned aeroplane to fly from level ground was the *Aerial Steamer*, designed and built by Englishman Thomas Moy. A tandem

Aeronautical Society's first exhibition at the Crystal Palace, 1868. Depicted among the exhibits is a Stringfellow triplane hanging from the roof. (The Science Museum, London)

wing craft with two six-blade pusher paddle-like propellers positioned between the wings and powered by a 3 hp steam engine, it lifted a few inches from the ground in 1875 in tethered flight from a circular track.

The four-stroke cycle gas engine was patented by Nikolaus Otto in Germany in 1876, and in 1877 he invented the four-stroke petrol internal combustion engine.

Among the first manned and powered aeroplanes to achieve a 'hop' flight after gaining speed down a slope was the huge monoplane built by Russian Alexander Fedorovich Mozhaiski and hopped in 1884. With a wing 74 ft 10 in (22.80 m) in span and 46 ft 7 in (14.20 m) in chord, and powered by a 20 hp steam engine driving a four-blade tractor propeller forward of the wings and a 10 hp steam engine driving two smaller pusher propellers inset in the wings, it was piloted by I. N. Golubev at Krasnoye Selo.

The first man-carrying aeroplane to achieve a powered 'hop' after rising from supposedly level ground was the bat-winged *Éole* monoplane built and flown by Clément Ader (1841–1925), at Armainvilliers, France, on 9 October 1890. Powered by an 18–20 hp steam engine, the *Éole* covered about 165 ft (50 m), but never achieved sustained or controlled flight. Ader's second aeroplane, the *Avion III*, was tested twice on 12–14 August 1897 but did not fly.

The first British powered aeroplane to fly tethered from a circular track, with a load equivalent to that of a pilot, was probably an early example of the *Multiplane*, a steam-powered multi-winged aeroplane designed by Horatio Phillips and flown at Harrow, England, with a 72 lb (33 kg) load in May 1893. This had 41 wings, each 19 ft (5.8 m) in span and with a chord of only 1½ in (3.8 cm). This type of wing set the pattern for his later successful aircraft.

The Aéro Club de France was founded in 1898.

The first man to achieve sustained powered flight with an unmanned heavier-than-air craft was the American Samuel Pierpont Langley (born 22 August 1834 at Roxbury, Massachusetts; died 27 February 1906, at Aiken, South Carolina). Mathematician and solar radiation physicist, Langley commenced building powered model aeroplanes during the 1890s, launching them from the top of a houseboat on the Potomac River near Quantico. His 14 ft (4.25 m) span models achieved sustained flights of up to 4200 ft (1280 m) from 6 May 1896 and incorporated a single steam engine mounted amidships, driving a pair of propellers. Langley's use of the name *Aerodrome* was derived incorrectly from the Greek

Left *Alexander Fedorovich Mozhaiski's twin-engined monoplane of 1884.*

Right *Model of Clément Ader's Éole.*

Far right *Langley full-size Aerodrome plunges towards the water. (Smithsonian Institution)*

αερο-δρομος (*aerodromos*) supposedly meaning 'air runner'; the word, however, is correctly defined as the location of a running event and cannot be held to mean the participant in a running event. Thus in the context of an *airfield* the word 'aerodrome', as originally applied to Hendon in Middlesex, England, is correct. In 1898 Langley was requested to continue his experiments with a $50 000 State subsidy and set about the design and construction of a full-scale version. As an intermediate step he built a quarter-scale model which, in June 1903, became **the world's first aeroplane powered by a petrol engine to achieve sustained flight**. His full-size *Aerodrome*, with a span of 48 ft (14.6 m) and powered by a 52 hp Manly-Balzer five-cylinder radial petrol engine, was completed in 1903, and attempts to fly this over the Potomac River with Charles M. Manly at the controls were made on 7 October and 8 December 1903. On both occasions the aeroplane fouled the launcher and dropped into the river. In view of the Wright brothers' success immediately thereafter, the American Government withdrew its support from Langley and his project was abandoned.

Perhaps now considered the most controversial aviation figure of 1901–2 was Bavarian born Gustav Whitehead, whose claimed aviation feats are not officially recognized and often divide opinion. On 14 August 1901 at Bridgeport, Connecticut (having emigrated to America), he is said to have piloted in sustained flight an aeroplane of his own design, covering a distance of about 880 ft (270 m) at an altitude of 50 ft (15 m). The single engine powered both the propellors and the landing gear wheels. On 17 January 1902 Whitehead is reported to have flown a controllable twin-engined flying-boat over a circular distance of about 7 miles (11 km), finally alighting on water. Other flights and achievements are said to have followed these. Photographs of Whitehead and his aircraft on the ground appeared in the press and he was the subject of many contemporary write-ups. Others stated thereafter that they saw him fly.

The first 'hop' from water by a seaplane was probably performed by Austrian Wilhelm Kress in a tandem-winged machine, powered by a 30 hp Daimler petrol engine, in October 1901. There is some doubt, as a few sources claim that he capsized the seaplane before leaving the water during the taxying phase. The trials were conducted on the Tullnerbach reservoir. This seaplane preceded Langley's full-size *Aerodrome* as **the first manned aeroplane fitted with a petrol engine**.

In Britain the Aero Club was founded on 29 October 1901, becoming the Royal Aero Club on 15 February 1910.

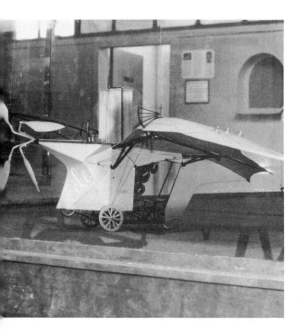

Wilbur Wright looks on as Orville guides the Flyer *on the first recognised powered, sustained and controlled flight by an aeroplane.*

The first aeroplane to achieve man-carrying powered, sustained flight in the world was the *Flyer*, designed and constructed by the brothers Wilbur and Orville Wright, which first achieved such flight at 10.35 h on Thursday, 17 December 1903, at Kill Devil Hills, Kitty Hawk, North Carolina, with an undulating flight of 120 ft (36.5 m) in about 12 s. Three further flights were made on the same day, the longest of which covered a ground distance of 852 ft (260 m) and lasted 59 s. It should be emphasized that these flights were the natural culmination of some four years' experimenting by the Wrights with a number of gliders, during 1899–1903. Details of the powered *Flyer* were as follows:

Wright Flyer No 1 (1903)
Wing span: 40 ft 4 in (12.3 m).
Overall length: 21 ft 1 in (6.43 m).
Wing chord: 6 ft 6 in (1.98 m).
Wing area: 510 ft² (47.38 m²).
Empty weight: 605 lb (274 kg).
Loaded weight: Approximately 750 lb (340 kg).
Wing loading: 1.47 ft/lb² (7.2 kg/m²).
Power plant: 12 bhp four-cylinder water-cooled engine lying on its side and driving two 8 ft 6 in (2.59 m) diameter propellers by chains, one of which was crossed to achieve counter-rotation. Engine weight with fuel (0.33 Imp gal), approximately 200 lb (90 kg).
Speed: 30 mph (approximately 48 km/h).
Launching: The *Flyer* took off under its own power from a dolly which ran on two bicycle hubs along a 60 ft (18 m) wooden rail.

The first full-size aeroplane to feature ailerons was a biplane flown by Frenchman Robert Esnault-Pelterie in October 1904.

The first aeroplane flight with a duration of more than five minutes was that by Wilbur Wright in the *Flyer II*, which covered 2¾ miles (4.4 km) on 9 November 1904.

The Aero Club of America was founded on 30 November 1905.

The world's first full-time air correspondent was Englishman Harry Harper, who began this position with the *Daily Mail* newspaper in 1906.

The first tethered sustained flight in Europe was made by the Danish engineer Jacob C. H. Ellehammer on 12 September 1906. Piloting a curious and primitive biplane fitted with a 20 hp radial engine, he covered about 140 ft (43 m) in circular flight, as the biplane was tethered to a post. For this the rudder had been fixed, making the flight uncontrollable by the pilot.

Santos-Dumont 14-bis tail first biplane, the first European aeroplane to make a sustained flight.

The first accredited sustained flight (i.e. other than a 'hop') achieved by a manned, powered aeroplane in Europe was made on 12 November 1906 by the Brazilian constructor-pilot Alberto Santos-Dumont (1873–1932), a resident of Paris, France, who flew his '14-bis' 722 ft (220 m) in 21.2 s. His aeroplane was in effect a tail-first box-kite powered by a 50 hp Antoinette engine, and this flight won for him the Aéro-Club de France's prize of 1500 francs for the first officially observed flight of more than 100 m. A previous flight, carried out on 23 October, covered 197 ft (60 m) and had won Santos-Dumont the Archdeacon Prize of 3000 francs for the first sustained flight of more than 25 m. Santos-Dumont's flight on 12 November was the first ever FAI recognized world record for distance flown. (See 26 October 1907.)

The first powered aeroplane flight in Great Britain, though not officially recognized, was almost certainly made by Horatio Phillips (1845–1924) in a 22 hp *Multiplane* in 1907. The aircraft had four of Phillips's unique narrow 'Venetian blind' wing-frames in tandem. It covered a distance of about 500 ft (152 m).

The first of many Daily Mail prizes offered for aeroplane achievements was one for a model aeroplane exhibition and competition held at the Agricultural Hall, London, on 6 April 1907. In a fly-off finish at Alexandra Palace, Alliott Verdon Roe was awarded £75 for the flight of his model biplane. With this prize, Roe went on to construct a full-size aeroplane.

The first aeroplane to be flown with cantilever wings was Louis Blériot's Type VI *Libellule*, which also featured wingtip ailerons. The Type VI made its first flight on 11 July 1907.

The second official distance record was set by Frenchman Henry Farman in the Voisin-Farman I at 2530 ft (771 m), on 26 October 1907. This aeroplane had first flown on 30 September. To be official as a world record, the achievement had to be recognized by the FAI, which had been established in France on 14 October 1905.

The first monoplane with tractor engine, enclosed fuselage, rear-mounted tail-unit and two-wheel main undercarriage with tailwheel was the Blériot VII powered by a 50 hp Antoinette engine. This was Louis Blériot's third full-size monoplane and was built during the autumn of 1907 and first flown by him at Issy-les-Moulineaux, France, on 10 November 1907. Before crashing this aeroplane on 18 December that year Blériot had achieved six flights, the longest of which was more than 1640 ft (500 m). This success confirmed to the designer that his basic configuration was sound—so much so that despite a 30-year deviation into biplane design, Blériot's basic configuration is still regarded as fundamentally conventional among propeller-driven aeroplanes of today.

The first US aeroplane company was formed on 30 November 1907 by Glenn Curtiss as the Curtiss Aeroplane Company.

The first circuit aeroplane flight made in Europe was undertaken by Henry Farman on 13 January 1908 in his modified Voisin biplane at Issy-les-Moulineaux when he took off, circumnavigated a pylon 1625 ft (500 m) away and returned to his point of departure. By so doing, Farman won the Grand Prix d'Aviation, a prize of 50 000 francs offered by Henry Deutsch de la Meurthe and Ernest Archdeacon to the first pilot to cover a kilometre. The flight took 1 min 28 s and, owing to the distance taken in turning, probably covered 4875 ft (1500 m).

The first aeroplane flight in Italy was made by the French sculptor-turned aviator Léon Delagrange in a Voisin in May 1908. At this time, aircraft built by the French brothers Gabriel and Charles Voisin were flown by two pilots, Henry Farman and Léon Delagrange. Henry Farman was born in England in 1874 and retained his English

citizenship until 1937 when he became a naturalized Frenchman. Having turned from painting to cycling before the turn of the century, he progressed to racing Panhard motor cars and at one time owned the largest garage in Paris. Gabriel Voisin later remarked that Farman possessed considerable mechanical and manipulative skill, whereas Delagrange 'was not the sporting type' and knew nothing about running an engine. Delagrange was killed flying a Blériot monoplane on 4 January 1910. Farman, having abandoned flying to pursue the business of aeroplane manufacture, died on 17 July 1958.

The first aeroplane flight in Belgium was made by Henry Farman, at Ghent, in May 1908.

The first passenger ever to fly in an aeroplane was Charles W. Furnas who was taken aloft by Wilbur Wright on 14 May 1908 for a flight covering 1968 ft (600 m) of 28.6 s duration. Later the same morning Orville Wright flew Furnas for a distance of about 2½ miles (4 km), which was covered in 3 min 40 s. Interestingly, it was only on 6 May that the Wrights had begun flying again after a three-year self-imposed absence.

The first passenger to be carried in an aeroplane in Europe was Ernest Archdeacon, the Frenchman whose substantial prizes contributed such stimulus to European aviation, who was flown by Henry Farman on 29 May 1908.

The first American to fly after the Wright brothers was Glenn H. Curtiss, who flew his *June Bug* for the first time on 20 June 1908. During this flight Curtiss covered a distance of 1266 ft (386 m) and exactly a fortnight later, on 4 July, he made a flight of 5090 ft (1550 m) in 102.2 s to win the *Scientific American* trophy for the first official public flight in the United States of more than 1 km.

The first aeroplane flight in Germany was made by the Dane J. C. H. Ellehammer, in his No IV machine at Kiel on 28 June 1908. However, this flight had a duration of only 11 s. A development of this aeroplane was flown by **the first German pilot**, Hans Grade, at Magdeburg in October 1908.

The world's first woman passenger to fly in an aeroplane was Madame Thérèse Peltier who, on 8 July 1908, accompanied Léon Delagrange at Turin, Italy, in his Voisin for a flight of 500 ft

Henry Farman pilots his Voisin-Farman I on a circular flight of over one kilometre, 13 January 1908. (Musée de l'Air)

Goupy I, the world's first full-size triplane to fly.

(150 m). She soon afterwards became the **first woman to fly solo**, but never was a qualified pilot.

The world's first full-size triplane to fly was the French Goupy I, which first took to the air on 5 September 1908. Built by Ambroise Goupy, it was powered by a 50 hp Renault engine. The later Goupy II, actually built by Blériot and first flown in March 1909, is recognized as the first of the classic tractor-engined biplanes.

The first flight in Europe of about 30 min duration was performed on 6 September 1908 by Léon Delagrange at Issy-les-Moulineaux, when he covered a distance of 15¼ miles (24.4 km) in 29 min 53 s.

The most important endurance flight to date was made by Wilbur Wright on 21 September 1908, when he covered 41⅓ miles (66.5 km) in France.

The first resident Englishmen to fly in an aeroplane (albeit as passengers) were Griffith Brewer (the first), the Hon C. S. Rolls, Frank Hedges Butler and Maj B. F. S. Baden-Powell, who were taken aloft in turn by Wilbur Wright in his biplane at Camp d'Auvours on 8 October 1908. Butler had founded the Aero Club of Great Britain, while Baden-Powell was Secretary of the Aeronautical Society. The 'resident' qualification is necessary here as of course the English-born, French-resident Henry Farman had been flying for more than a year by the time the four Englishmen were taken aloft by Wright.

The first European cross-country flight was made by Henry Farman on 30 October 1908, when he flew from Châlons to Reims, a distance of about 16 miles (26 km).

The first successful Russian aeroplane was the Gakkel-3 of 1909, designed by Yakov M. Gakkel.

The first German aviator to fly a German aeroplane was Hans Grade who, on 12 January 1909, flew a triplane of his own design at Magdeburg.

Probably the most successful monoplane designed and built before the First World War was the French Blériot XI, the work of Louis Blériot and first flown on 23 January 1909 while powered by a 30 hp REP engine.

The first aerodrome to be prepared as such in England was the flying-ground between Leysdown and Shellness, Isle of Sheppey (known as 'Shellbeach'), where limited established facilities were provided. It was opened in February 1909 by the joint effort of the Aero Club of Great Britain and Short Bros Ltd.

The first aeroplanes to be manufactured in series were six Wright biplanes produced by the British Short Brothers under an agreement concluded between Wilbur Wright and Eustace Short in February 1909. Therefore, Short Brothers was **the first aeroplane manufacturing company proper** in aviation history.

The first sustained, powered flight by an aeroplane in the British Empire was made on 23

Right *The Short Brothers' Leysdown factory, in which the first aeroplane production line was established in 1909 to build six Wright Model As. (Short Brothers)*

Below *The third Short-Wright Model A went to Frank McClean in October 1909. Having been returned to Shorts for modification, it reappeared in May 1910 with a new engine, wheels and a tailplane aft of the rudders. (Short Brothers)*

February 1909 by J. A. D. McCurdy, a Canadian, over Baddeck Bay, Nova Scotia, in the Aerial Experimental Association's biplane *Silver Dart*, which he had designed. He had made his own first flight at Hammondsport, New York, USA, the previous December.

The first aeroplane flight in Austria was made by the Frenchman G. Legagneux, at Vienna in April 1909 in his Voisin. **The first Austrian** to fly was Igo Etrich, in his *Taube* at Wiener-Neustadt in November of that year. This aircraft gave its name to the type in fairly widespread use by Germany at the beginning of the First World War.

The first cinematographer to be taken up in an aeroplane was at Centocelle, near Rome, on 24 April 1909, in a Wright biplane flown by Wilbur Wright.

The first resident Englishman to make an officially recognized aeroplane flight in England was J. T. C. Moore-Brabazon (later Lord Brabazon of Tara) who made three sustained flights of 450, 600 and 1500 ft (137, 180 and 450 m) between 30 April and 2 May 1909 at Leysdown, Isle of Sheppey, in his Voisin biplane. He had learned to fly in France during the previous year and on 30 October 1909 won the £1000 *Daily Mail* prize for the first Briton to cover a mile (closed circuit) in a British aeroplane—the Short No. 2 biplane. He was awarded the Royal Aero Club of Great Britain's Aviator Certificate No. 1 on 8 March 1910. Lord Brabazon died in 1969.

The first aeroplane flight in France of one hour endurance was performed by Frenchman Paul Tissandier in a Wright biplane on 20 May 1909. He also set the first official FAI world speed record for aeroplanes.

The first aeroplane to carry a pilot and two passengers was the Blériot XII, piloted on 12 June

1909 by Louis Blériot and with passengers Santos-Dumont and Fournier.

The first apprentice to an aeroplane manufacturing company was Howard (Dinger) Bell, who joined Short Brothers on 10 July 1909. His father, nicknamed 'Father Bell' by the employees, was the company's first foreman.

The first Briton to fly an all-British aeroplane was Alliott Verdon Roe (1877–1958), in his Roe 1 triplane on 13 July 1909 at Lea Marshes, Essex. Lack of funds to build the triplane had forced Roe to construct it from wood instead of light-gauge steel tubing, to cover the wings with paper and to use the same 9 hp JAP engine that had powered his unsuccessful biplane. The 100 ft (30 m) flight that was achieved on the 13th was much improved upon on the 23rd, when he flew 900 ft (274 m) at an average height of 10 ft (3 m).

Conquest of the English Channel. In response to an offer by the *Daily Mail* of a prize of £1000 for the first pilot (of any nationality) to fly an aeroplane across the Channel, **the first attempt** was made by an Englishman, Hubert Latham, flying an Antoinette IV. He took off from Sangatte, near Calais, at 06.42 h on Monday, 19 July 1909, but alighted in the sea after only 6–8 miles (10–13 km) following engine failure which could not be rectified in the air. He was picked up by the

French naval vessel *Harpon*. The occasion of this attempt was also the **first instance of wireless telegraphy being used to obtain weather reports**, the first report being transmitted from Sangatte, near Calais, to the Lord Warden Hotel, Dover, at 04.30 h on that morning.

Despite working furiously to get a replacement Antoinette, Latham was beaten by Louis Blériot. The Frenchman took off in his Blériot XI monoplane at 04.41 h, from Les Baraques, on Sunday, 25 July 1909, and landed at 05.17.5 h in the Northfall Meadow by Dover Castle to become **the**

Above   *Returning Hubert Latham's wrecked Antoinette to Calais after his unsuccessful attempt to be the first to fly the English Channel.*

Left   *Alliott Verdon Roe made history in his paper-covered triplane by becoming the first Briton to fly an all-British aeroplane.*

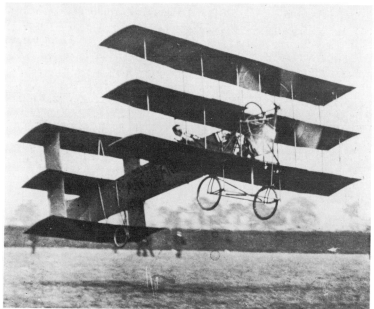

Louis Blériot's moment of triumph, having landed in Northfall Meadow after making the first aeroplane flight across the English Channel. (Air France)

first man to cross the English Channel in an aeroplane.

Latham made a second attempt to fly the Channel two days later (on 27 July), taking off at 05.50 h from Cap Blanc Nez. When only 1 mile (1.6 km) from the Dover cliffs, his engine failed and once again he had to alight in the sea.

The first woman passenger to fly in an aeroplane in England was Mrs Cody, wife of Samuel, who was taken up by her husband during the last week of July 1909 over Laffan's Plain, Hants, in the *British Army Aeroplane No 1.*

The first aeroplane flight in Sweden was made by the Frenchman Legagneux at Stockholm in his Voisin biplane on 29 July 1909.

The first passenger to be carried by an aeroplane in Canada was F. W. 'Casey' Baldwin who was taken aloft on 2 August 1909 at Petawawa, Ontario, in an aeroplane flown by J. A. D. McCurdy.

The first International Aviation Meeting in the world opened on 22 August 1909 at Reims, and lasted until 29 August 1909. Thirty-eight aeroplanes were entered to participate, although only 23 managed to leave the ground; the meeting also attracted aviators and aeroplane designers from all over Europe and did much to arouse widespread public interest in flying. The types of aeroplanes which flew were: Antoinette, Blériot

XI, Blériot XII, Blériot XIII, Breguet, Curtiss, Henry Farman, REP, Voisin and Wright.

The first aeroplane flight in Denmark was made by Léon Delagrange in September 1909.

The first pilot to be killed flying a powered aeroplane was Eugène Lefebvre, on 7 September 1909; he crashed while flying a new Wright Type A at Port Aviation Juvisy. Soon afterwards, on 22 September, Captain Ferber was killed when his Voisin hit a ditch while preparing for take-off.

The first Aviation Meeting held in Great Britain was that organized by the Doncaster Aviation Committee on the Doncaster Racecourse between 15 and 23 October 1909. This meeting was not governed by rules laid down by the FAI, nor was it officially recognized by the Aero Club of Great Britain. Twelve aeroplanes constituted the field, of which five managed to fly. **The first officially recognized meeting** was held at Squires Gate, Blackpool, between 18 and 23 October 1909, being organized by the Blackpool Corporation and the Lancashire Aero Club; seven of the dozen participants were coaxed into the air.

The first American woman passenger in an aeroplane was Mrs Ralph van Deman, who flew with Wilbur Wright on 27 October 1909.

The first major prize in Great Britain for all-British aviation activity was the £1000 offered by the *Daily Mail* to the first British pilot to complete a circular flight of 1 mile (1.6 km) in an all-British aeroplane. This prize was won by J. T. C. Moore-Brabazon on 30 October 1909 at Shellbeach when, flying the Short Biplane No 2, he achieved the one mile flight in a time of 2 min 36 s. Similar in configuration to the Short-built Wright biplanes, the Short No 2 differed considerably in detail and was powered by a 50–60 hp Green four-cylinder inline engine.

The first piglet to fly in a powered aeroplane in Britain took to the air as J. T. C. Moore-Brabazon's passenger on 4 November 1909. Intended to debunk the old adage that 'pigs can't fly', pig and pilot did admirably with a 3.5 mile (5.6 km) cross-country flight.

The first successful still photographs taken from an aeroplane were by M Meurisse, in December 1909, and showed the flying-fields at Mourmelon and Châlons. The aeroplane was an Antoinette piloted by Latham.

The first American monoplane to fly was the Walden III, designed by Dr Henry W. Walden and flown on 9 December 1909 at Mineola, Long Island, New York. It was powered by a 22 hp Anzani engine.

The first aeroplane flight in Australia was made by Colin Defries on 9 December 1909. Defries, a well-known racing driver, flew an imported Wright biplane over a distance of 1 mile (1.6 km) at a height of 35 ft (11 m) at Victoria Park Racecourse, Sydney, New South Wales.

The first passenger to be carried by aeroplane in Australia was Mr C. S. Magennis, who flew with Colin Defries on 10 December 1909.

The first aeroplane flight in Ireland was made by Harry G. Ferguson of Belfast on 31 December

The first Scottish aeroplane pilot was Mr. William H. Ewen, who gained pilot's certificate No. 63 in February 1911. His subsequent colourful flying career included making the first flight across the Firth of Forth in a Deperdussin monoplane on 30 August 1911, carrying airmail with Gustav Hamel, flying the English Channel in May 1912 and serving with the RFC/RAF. He died in 1947 at the age of 67.

J. T. C. Moore-Brabazon won a £1,000 Daily Mail prize for being the first Briton to make a circular one-mile flight in a British aeroplane, the Short No 2.

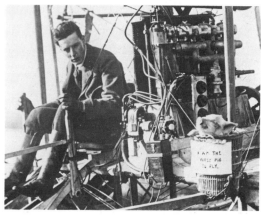

Winning a bet, Moore-Brabazon proveed that pigs can fly.

1909. The aeroplane was of his own design and manufacture; it resembled a Blériot, and was powered by an eight-cylinder 35 hp air-cooled JAP engine.

The first British woman to fly solo in an aeroplane was almost certainly Miss Edith Maud Cook, who performed various aerial acts under the name of Miss 'Spencer Kavanagh'. She achieved several solo flights on Blériot monoplanes with the Grahame-White Flying School at Pau in the Pyrenees in early 1910. She was also a professional parachute-jumper, known as 'Viola Spencer', and was killed after making a jump from a balloon near Coventry, England, in July 1910.

The first aeroplane meeting to be held in the USA was organized by the Aero Club of California at the Dominguez Field, Los Angeles on 10 January 1910.

The first Aviation Certificate awarded by the Royal Aero Club was received by Moore-Brabazon on 8 March 1910. The Aero Club had become the Royal Aero Club on 15 February 1910.

The first certificated woman pilot in the world was Mme la Baronne de Laroche, a French woman who received Pilot's Certificate No. 36 on 8 March 1910, having qualified on a Voisin biplane. She was killed in 1919 in an aeroplane accident.

The first night flights were made by Emil Aubrun, a Frenchman, on 10 March 1910 flying a Blériot monoplane. Each of the two flights began and ended at Villalugano, Buenos Aires, Argentina, and was about 12.4 miles (20 km) long.

The first aeroplane flight in Switzerland was made by Capt Engelhardt on 13 March 1910.

The first take-off from water by an aeroplane was made by Henri Fabre, a Frenchman, in his Gnome-powered seaplane *Hydravion* at La Mède harbour, Martigues, France, on 28 March 1910.

The first aeroplane flights in Spain were made by Gaudart, Poillot, Le Blond, Mamet and Olieslaegers between March and April 1910.

The first aeroplane to be 'forced down' by the action of another was the Henry Farman biplane of Mr A. Rawlinson during the Aviation Meeting at Nice, France, in mid-April 1910. Mr Rawlinson was flying his new Farman over the sea when the Russian Effimov passed so close above him (also in a Farman) that his downdraught forced the Englishman into the water. The Russian was fined 100 francs for dangerous flying.

The first recorded night flight in Great Britain was made by Claude Grahame-White from 27 to 28 April 1910, in an attempt to overhaul Louis Paulhan competing in the *Daily Mail* £10 000 London to Manchester race (which had to be started from a point within 5 miles of the newspaper's London offices and finish at a point within

5 miles of its Manchester offices). This was the first aeroplane event in Britain to offer a £10 000 prize. Paulhan, who eventually won despite Grahame-White's night flight, thus made the first London to Manchester aeroplane flight and the first straight line aeroplane flight in Britain of more than 100 km.

The first England to France and two-way crossing of the English Channel was accomplished by the Hon C. S. Rolls (the 'Rolls' of 'Rolls-Royce') flying a French-built Wright biplane on 2 June 1910. He took off from Broadlees, Dover, at 18.30.5 h, dropped a letter addressed to the Aéro Club de France near Sangatte at 19.15 h, then flew back to England and made a perfect landing near his starting-rail at 20.06 h. He was thus the **first man to fly from England to France in an aeroplane, the first man to make a non-stop two-way crossing, and the first cross-Channel pilot to land at a pre-arranged spot without damage to his aeroplane.**

The first Romanian aeroplane to fly was the *Vlaicu I* parasol-winged monoplane, designed by Aurel Vlaicu and flown on 17 June 1910. This date is marked as the National Aviation Day in that country.

The first British pilot to lose his life while flying an aeroplane was the Hon Charles Stewart Rolls (born in London, 27 August 1877, the third son of the first Baron Llangattock), who was killed at the Bournemouth Aviation Week on 12 July 1910 when his French-built Wright biplane suffered a structural failure in flight.

The first flight in Australia by an Australian in an indigenous aeroplane was made by John R. Duigan of Mia Mia, Victoria, on 16 July 1910 in an aeroplane constructed from photographs of the Wright *Flyer*. On that day Duigan flew only 28 ft (8.5 m), but on 7 October he covered 588 ft (179 m) at a height of about 12 ft (3.65 m).

The first mail carried unofficially in an aeroplane in Great Britain was flown by Claude Grahame-White on 10 August 1910 in a Blériot monoplane from Squires Gate, Blackpool; he did not reach his destination at Southport, having been forced to land by bad weather.

The first Channel crossing with a passenger was by Franco-American John B. Moisant and his mechanic in a Blériot two-seater aeroplane, from Calais to Dover, on 17 August 1910.

The first use of radio between an aeroplane and the ground was on 27 August 1910 when James McCurdy, flying a Curtiss, sent and received messages via an HM Horton wireless set at Sheepshead Bay, NY State.

The first American woman to fly solo in an aeroplane was Blanche Scott on 2 September 1910.

Left   Henri Fabre takes off from La Mède harbour in his Hydravion *seaplane, 28 March 1910. (Musée de l'Air)*

Right   M Christiaen in a Henry Farman biplane during the July 1910 Bournemouth Aviation Week. (The Science Museum, London)

The first air collision in the world occurred on 8 September 1910 between two aeroplanes piloted by brothers named Warchalovski at Wiener-Neustadt, Austria. One of the pilots suffered a broken leg. A passenger on one of the aircraft was the Archduke Léopold Salvator of Austria.

The first crossing of the Irish Sea was made by Robert Loraine who, flying a Farman biplane on 11 September 1910, set off from Holyhead, Anglesey. Although engine failure forced him down in the sea 180 ft (55 m) offshore from the Irish coast near Baily Lighthouse, Howth, he was generally considered to have been the first to accomplish the crossing.

The first flight over the Alps was made by the Peruvian Georges Chavez in a Blériot on 23 September 1910. His flight from Brig, Switzerland, to Domodossola, Italy, via the Simplon Pass, ended in disaster when he crashed on landing and was killed.

The first ever carriage of freight by air was undertaken on 7 November 1910. On this occasion it had been arranged between the Wright Company and the Morehouse-Martens Company of Columbus, Ohio, which operated an emporium named The Home Dry Goods Store, for two packages of silk to be transported by air between Dayton and Columbus to bring attention to a sale. A Wright Model B, at the last minute piloted by Philip O. Parmalee (see below), was used to carry nearly 542 yds of silk, at a cost to the company of $5000. Despite this carriage fee, the store made a profit of more than $1000, partly by cutting up some of the material and selling it in small pieces as souvenirs mounted on postcards.

The first British pilot to survive a spin (probably first in the world) was Fred Raynham who, flying an Avro biplane during 1911, stalled while climbing through fog. The stall occurred after he had stooped to adjust his compass as he thought that it was malfunctioning; the next he knew was that he was standing upright on the rudder pedals with his aeroplane whirling round. Quite how he recovered from the spin will never be known, for his recollection was that he *pulled the stick back*; notwithstanding this he caught sight of the ground and was able to perform a controlled landing.

The first flight in New Zealand by an aeroplane was made by a Howard Wright type biplane piloted by Vivian C. Walsh at Auckland on 5 February 1911. With his brother Leo, Vivian Walsh imported materials from England with which to build the aircraft and installed a 60 hp ENV engine. Vivian Walsh also made **the first seaplane flight in New Zealand** on 1 January 1914.

The first government (official) air-mail flight in the world was undertaken on 18 February

Left *Max Morehouse alongside the pilot for the first freight flight, Philip O. Parmalee (right).*

Right *Postmaster-General Hitchcock hands Earl L. Ovington the first official US air mail.*

1911 when the French pilot Henri Pequet flew a Humber biplane from Allahabad to Naini Junction, a distance of about 5 miles (8 km) across the Jumna River, with some 6500 letters. The regular service was established four days later as part of the Universal Postal Exhibition, Allahabad, India, the flights being shared by Capt W. G. Windham and Pequet. The envelopes of this first air-mail service were franked 'First Aerial Post, UP Exhibition, Allahabad, 1911' and are highly prized among collectors.

The first non-stop flight from London to Paris was made on 12 April 1911 by Pierre Prier in 3 h 56 min, flying a Blériot monoplane powered by a 50 hp Gnôme engine. Prier, who was Chief Flying Instructor at the Blériot Flying School, Hendon, took off from Hendon and landed at Issy-les-Moulineaux.

The first American woman pilot was Harriet Quimby who, on 2 August 1911, gained her licence. On 16 April 1912 she became **the first woman to fly an aeroplane across the English Channel**.

The first recorded carriage of freight by air in Britain was a box of Osram lamps carried on 4 July 1911 by a Valkyrie monoplane flown by Horatio Barber from Shoreham to Hove in Sussex, England, on behalf of the General Electric Company who paid £100 for the flight.

The first British woman pilot was Mrs Hilda B. Hewlett, who gained Pilot's Certificate No. 122 on 29 August 1911.

The first official mail to be carried by air in Great Britain was entrusted to the staff pilots of the Grahame-White and Blériot flying schools, who commenced carrying the mail between Hendon and Windsor on Saturday, 9 September 1911. The first flight was undertaken on that day by Gustav Hamel in a Blériot monoplane, covering the route in 10 min at a ground speed of over 105 mph (169 km/h) with a strong tailwind. The service lasted until 26 September, having been instituted to commemorate the coronation of HM King George V. The total weight of mail carried between the Hendon flying-field and Royal Farm, Windsor was 1015 lb (460.4 kg).

The first coast-to-coast flight across America was made by Calbraith P. Rodgers between 17 September and 5 November 1911. Rodgers, trying to win a $50 000 prize offered by William Randolph Hearst, flew from New York to Pasadena in a Burgess-Wright biplane. Making a series of short flights, he arrived at the destination 19 days outside the specified 30-day limit and so failed to qualify for the prize.

The first Italian air-mail service started on 19 September 1911 and covered Bologna, Venice and Rimini.

The first official carriage of mail by air in the USA was by Earl L. Ovington on 23 September 1911 in a Blériot-type monoplane known as the Queen monoplane. The journey of 6 miles (9.6 km) began from Nassau Boulevard, New York. Ovington became *Air Mail Pilot No 1*, a title given to him by Postmaster-General Hitchcock.

The first all-metal aeroplane to fly was the *Tubavion* monoplane built by the Frenchmen Ponche and Primard in 1912. A fatal accident brought its tests to a halt.

The first seaplane competition was held at Monaco in March 1912. Seven pilots attended (Fischer, Renaux, Paulhan, Robinson, Caudron, Benoit, Rugère), the winner being Fischer on a Henry Farman biplane.

The first of the great flying days at Hendon was held on 20 April 1912, when approximately 15 000 spectators paid to gain admission to the 6d, 1s and 2s 6d enclosures.

The first completed crossing from Great Britain to Ireland by aeroplane was achieved by Englishman Denys Corbett Wilson on 22 April 1912, flying across the St Georges Channel.

The first recognized flight in an aeroplane with a fully enclosed cabin for the pilot was made by A. V. Roe on 1 May 1912, in his Avro Type F.

The first American woman to be killed in an aeroplane accident was Julie Clark of Denver, Colorado, whose Curtiss biplane struck a tree on 17 June 1912 at Springfield, Illinois, and turned turtle. She had qualified for her Pilot's Certificate on 19 May 1912.

The first crossing of the English Channel by an aeroplane with a pilot and two passengers was made on 4 August 1912 by W. B. Rhodes Moorhouse (later, as a Lt in the Royal Flying Corps, the first British airman to be awarded the Victoria Cross, on 26 April 1915) who, accompanied by his wife and a friend, flew a Breguet tractor biplane from Douai, France, via Boulogne and Dungeness, to Bethersden, near Ashford, Kent, where they crashed in bad weather. Nobody was hurt.

The first man to fly underneath all the Thames bridges in London between Tower Bridge and Westminster was F. K. McClean who, flying the Short S.33 pusher biplane from Harty Ferry, Isle of Sheppey, on 10 August 1912, passed between the upper and lower spans of Tower Bridge, and then underflew all the remaining bridges to Westminster where he landed on the river. No regulations forbade this escapade, but the police instructed McClean to taxi all the way back to Shadwell Basin before mooring! On the return trip the aeroplane side-slipped soon after take-off and damaged one of the floats after hitting a barge. The machine was then towed into Shadwell Dock and dismantled for the return by road to Eastchurch.

The number of Pilots' Certificates which had been awarded in the world by the end of 1912 was 2490, though the number of actual pilots was slightly smaller as some had been awarded certificates in more than one country. One or two others had received certificates in countries which were not members of the Fédération Aéronautique Internationale. The massive superiority of France at this time is evident:

1	France	966	6 Russia	162
2	Great Britain	382	7 Austria	84
3	Germany	345	8 Belgium	58
4	United States of America	193	9 Switzerland	27
5	Italy	186	10 Holland	26

Left Frank McClean passes between the spans of Tower Bridge.

Right Le Grand, the first four-engined aeroplane to fly. (Sikorsky Aircraft)

11 Argentine		15 Hungary	7
Republic	15	16 Norway	5
12 Spain	15	17 Egypt	1
13 Sweden	10		
14 Denmark	8	Total	2490

The first Schneider Trophy Contest (more correctly titled 'La Coupe d'Aviation Maritime Jacques Schneider'), was included as one item of the second international Hydro-aeroplane Meeting held at Monaco during the two weeks beginning 3 April 1913. It created initially little interest, with only seven entries for the first contest, reduced to four starters after the eliminating trials. The course consisted of twenty-eight 10 km laps and this 1913 contest, flown on 16 April, was won by Maurice Prévost flying a 160 hp Gnome-powered Deperdussin. This pilot was under the impression that he should alight and taxi across the finishing line, but in fact this was invalid and it was required that he should fly the aircraft across the line. He was accordingly set off again to complete a further lap which, including a period spent ashore, deciding whether to continue or not, added about an hour to his time, so that his average speed is recorded in the official results as being 45.75 mph (73.63 km/h). Second was late-starter Roland Garros, flying a Morane-Saulnier monoplane powered by an 80 hp Gnome engine.

The first non-stop aeroplane flight between England and Germany was made by Gustav Hamel on 17 April 1913, flying a military-type Blériot XI monoplane between Dover and Cologne in a time of 4 h 18 min.

The first four-engined aeroplane to fly was the *Le Grand* ('The Great One', known also as *Russky Vityaz* or Russian Knight) biplane designed, and first flown on 13 May 1913 at St Petersburg, by Igor Sikorsky, then Head of the Aeronautical Department of the Russian Baltic Railway Car Factory at Petrograd. It had a wing span of over 92 ft (28 m) and was powered by four 100 hp Argus engines, originally mounted in tandem pairs but later in all-tractor configuration (from June). The first flight lasted under ten minutes. From *Le Grand* was evolved the Ilya Mourometz, which became the **first four-engined bomber to see active service**.

The first major British competition for seaplanes was the *Daily Mail* Hydro-Aeroplane Trial, started on 16 August 1913. The regulations stated a specified course round Britain, involving a distance to be flown of 1540 miles (2478 km) by an all-British aircraft before 30 August. Four aircraft were entered, but Samuel Cody was killed in a crash at Laffan's Plain on 7 August. F. K. McClean withdrew his Short S.68 due to engine trouble,

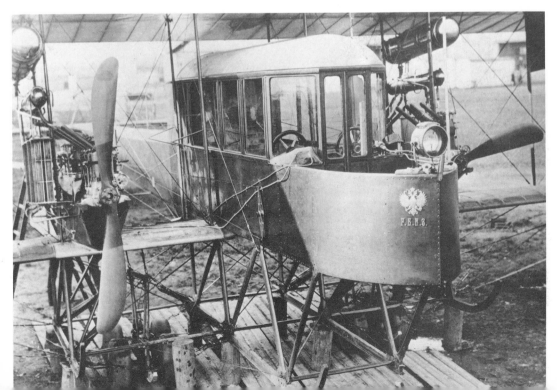

and the Radley-England Waterplane was scratched for the same reason. This left Harry Hawker, accompanied by his mechanic, H. A. Kauper, as the only contender. He left the water at Southampton at 11.47 h, in a Sopwith three-seater tractor biplane which was powered by a 100 hp Green six-cylinder inline engine. The route was from Southampton via Ramsgate, Yarmouth, Scarborough, Aberdeen, Cromarty, Oban, Dublin, Falmouth and back to Southampton. After an abortive attempt, which ended at Yarmouth owing to a cracked engine cylinder, Hawker took off again from Southampton on 25 August. He managed to fly round the course as far as Dublin when, just before alighting on the water, his foot slipped off the rudder-bar and the aircraft struck the water and broke up. The *Daily Mail* prize of £5000 was not awarded, but Hawker received £1000 as consolation.

The first pilot in the world to perform a loop was Lt Nesterov of the Imperial Russian Army who, flying a Nieuport Type IV monoplane, performed the manoeuvre at Kiev on 27 August 1913.

The first pilot to fly inverted in sustained flight (as distinct from becoming inverted during the course of the looping manoeuvre) was Adolphe Pégoud who, on 21 September 1913, flew a Blériot monoplane inverted at Buc, France. Notwithstanding the above definition, Pégoud's manoeuvre involved two 'halves' of a loop, in that he assumed the inverted position by means of a half-loop, and after sustained inverted flight recovered by means of a 'pull-through'. He thus did not resort to a roll or half-roll, which manoeuvre had not apparently been achieved at this time. As a means of acclimatizing himself for the ordeal of inverted flight, Pégoud had had his Blériot mounted inverted upon trestles and had remained strapped in the cockpit for periods of up to 20 min at a time!

The first air crossing of the Mediterranean was achieved on 23 September 1913 by a Morane-Saulnier monoplane piloted by Roland Garros, who flew 453 miles (730 km) from Saint-Raphaël, France, to Bizerte, Tunisia, in 7 h 53 min.

The first British aeroplane to beat all comers in a major international competitive event was the Sopwith Tabloid. Designed as a small, fast biplane scout aircraft, it first flew in the autumn of 1913. Official tests at Farnborough on 29 November 1913 showed it had exceptional performance, with a maximum rate of climb of 1200 ft (366 m)/min and a maximum speed of 92 mph (148 km/h). Its outstanding competitive success was its victory in the second contest for the Schneider Trophy held at Monaco on 20 April 1914 when, equipped as a floatplane, the aircraft was flown by Howard Pixton over the 280 km course at an average speed of 86.78 mph (139.66 km/h). After completing the race, Pixton continued for two extra laps to establish a new world speed record for seaplanes at 86.6 mph (139.37 km/h) over a measured 300 km course.

The first flight from France to Egypt was accomplished by Jules Védrines in a Blériot powered by an 80 hp Gnôme engine, between 29 November and 29 December 1913. Setting out from Nancy, France, his route was via Würzburg, Prague, Vienna, Belgrade, Sofia, Constantinople, Tripoli (Syria), Jaffa and Cairo.

The first scheduled airline using aeroplanes was the St Petersburg–Tampa Airboat Line, which

Left *Sopwith Tabloid, with Howard Pixton sitting on the lower wing.*

Right *First US experimental airmail service, begun on 15 May 1918 by the US Army Signal Corps. (US National Archives)*

started its operations on 1 January 1914, flying between St Petersburg and Tampa, Florida. The aircraft was a Benoist flying-boat piloted by Anthony Jannus. The operation lasted four months.

The first flight across the North Sea by an aeroplane was achieved by the Norwegian pilot Tryggve Gran flying a Blériot monoplane on 30 July 1914.

The last aviation sporting events to be held in Britain before the outbreak of the First World War took place at Hendon on 3 August 1914. They consisted of a cross-country and a speed handicap race, the former being won by R. J. Lillywhite, the latter by the American W. L. Brock.

NACA, the National Advisory Committee for Aeronautics, was founded in America on 3 March 1915.

The first American forest fire to be observed by aeroplane is thought to have been one blazing in Wisconsin, on 22 June 1915.

The first British airline company to be registered was Aircraft Transport and Travel Ltd, in London on 5 October 1916 by George Holt Thomas.

Official carriage of mail by aeroplane in Italy began on 22 May 1917, when military flights started between the cities of Turin and Rome.

The first French mail to be carried by aeroplane was flown between Paris, Le Mans and St Nazaire on 17 August 1917. A regular service was established thereafter.

The first variable-incidence variable-geometry

aeroplane in the world was the Swedish Pålson Type 1 single-seat sporting aircraft of 1918–19. It is said that the aircraft featured a system of cranks to alter the position of the biplane's top wing as well as its angle of incidence as a means of achieving optimum lift/drag in cruising flight. It is not known what success attended flight trials (if any).

The first scheduled regular international airmail service in the world was inaugurated between Vienna and Kiev, via Kraków, Lvóv and Proskurov on 11 March 1918. The service was principally for military mail and was operated with Hansa-Brandenburg CI biplanes, continuing until November 1918.

The first air crossing of the Andes was achieved by the Argentine army pilot Teniente Luis C. Candelaria, flying a Morane-Saulnier parasol monoplane on 13 April 1918 from Zapala, Argentina, to Cunço, Chile, a distance of approximately 124 miles (200 km). The maximum altitude was about 13 000 ft (4000 m). Candelaria had attended the fifth military flying course at El Palomar which commenced in September 1916.

The first experimental airmail service in the USA was flown by US Army Signal Corps Curtiss JN-4 and Standard J aircraft on 15 May 1918, between Washington, DC, and New York City. Lt Torrey H. Webb was the first pilot.

The first official airmail flight in Canada was flown on 24 June 1918 in a Curtiss JN-4 from Montreal to Toronto by Capt Brian A. Peck, RAF, accompanied by Corp Mathers.

The first flight from England to Egypt was accomplished by Maj A. S. MacLaren and Brig Gen A. E. Borton, flying a Handley Page O/400 bomber, between 28 July and 8 August 1918.

The first flight from Egypt to India was accomplished by Capt Ross M. Smith, Brig Gen A. E. Borton, Maj Gen W. Salmond and crew of a Handley Page O/400, between 29 November and 12 December 1918. Their journey took them from Heliopolis to Karachi.

The first US Army coast-to-coast flight across the USA was made by four Curtiss JN-4 Jennies between 4 and 22 December 1918. The points spanned were San Diego and Jacksonville.

The first passenger and mail services between London and Paris were initiated on 10 January

1919 by No. 2 (Communications) Squadron, RAF. Aircraft used were Airco (de Havilland) DH4As, which were DH4s modified to provide enclosed accommodation for two passengers. This service, intended for communications to and from the Peace Conference at Versailles, was terminated in September 1919.

The first sustained commercial daily passenger service was by Deutsche Luft-Reederei, which operated between Berlin and Weimar, Germany, from 5 February 1919. Aircraft used on the service were five-seat AEG biplanes and two-seat DFWs. The 120 mile (193 km) flight took 2 h 18 min.

The first airline passenger flight between Paris and London was made on 8 February 1919 by a Farman F60 Goliath, owned by the Farman brothers and piloted by Lucien Bossoutrot. As civil flying was not then permitted in the UK, the token payload consisted of military passengers, who flew from Toussus le Noble to Kenley. The flight is not recognized as a genuine scheduled operation.

The first purely commercial aircraft to be built for passenger carrying in Britain after the First World War, one of the first new civil types in the world, was the de Havilland DH16, the prototype of which flew for the first time in March 1919. The type entered service with Aircraft Transport and Travel Ltd in May. Altogether, nine DH16s were built by June 1920; the first six were powered by

the 320 hp Rolls-Royce Eagle VIII engine; the others had a 450 hp Napier Lion engine. Accommodation was for four passengers. The last DH16 was withdrawn from use in August 1923.

The first American international airmail was inaugurated between Seattle, Washington, and Victoria, British Columbia, Canada, by the Hubbard Air Service on 3 March 1919, using a Boeing Model CL-4S aircraft. The service was regularized by contract on 14 October 1920.

The first sustained regular (not daily) international service for commercial passengers

Above *Farman F60 Goliath on the historic first Paris–London airline passenger flight. (Air France)*

Below *Deutsche Luft-Reederei five-seat AEG JII biplane airliner. (Lufthansa Archiv)*

Father Bartolomeu de Gusmão demonstrates a tiny hot-air balloon to King John V of Portugal and other dignitaries, 1709.

Above   *The Ariel in full flight, as imagined by designer William Samuel Henson, 1843. (Robert Harding Picture Library)*

Left   *Wing Commander Wallis flies his record-breaking WA-116/F/S autogyro over a replica of the Wallbro monoplane of 1910.*

Opposite top   *Boeing Model 247, the first all-metal monoplane airliner with cantilever low-mounted wings, twin engines fitted with controllable-pitch propellers, and a retractable undercarriage. (The Boeing Company)*

Opposite bottom   *Restored Lockheed Vega* Winnie Mae *round-the-world record-breaker of the early 1930s. (Lockheed)*

Opposite top *Replica of Lindbergh's* Spirit of St Louis *solo transatlantic aircraft of 1927. (Paul Jackson)*

Opposite bottom *Luftwaffe Messerschmitt Bf 109 E-4/trop of I/JG 27, photographed in Africa in 1941. (MBB)*

Above *The prototype Fairchild Republic A-10A Thunderbolt II began a new trend for very heavily-armed, close-support aircraft. It is now a major USAF service type.*

Right *Group Captain James Edgar 'Johnnie' Johnson, Britain's top-ranking 'ace' fighter pilot of the Second World War. (Imperial War Museum)*

Above   *Chuck Yeager in the small cockpit of the Bell X-1 rocketplane.*

Left   *Convair XFY-1, an experimental turboprop-powered tail-sitting fighter of 1954. (General Dynamics)*

Opposite top   *The latest Swedish multi-role combat aircraft for service in the 1990s is the SAAB JAS 39 Gripen, which incorporates advanced design features and materials.*

Opposite bottom   *US Army Bell AH-1G HueyCobra attack helicopters between protective sandbags in Vietnam, September 1967. HueyCobras were the first ever purpose-designed attack helicopters. (US Army)*

USS Carl Vinson *with Tomcat fighters and other types on board, including two examples of the Douglas Skywarrior (front left, rear right), the heaviest aeroplane ever to serve as standard equipment on aircraft carriers. (US Navy)*

Left *Aircraft Transport and Travel Ltd de Havilland DH16 airliner.*

Below *Navy-Curtiss NC-4 flying-boat, the first aircraft to make a transatlantic crossing. (US Navy)*

was opened between Paris and Brussels by the Farman brothers on 22 March 1919. The fare for the 2 h 50 min flight was 365 francs. The pilot was again Lucien Bossoutrot. **The first Customs examination of passengers** took place at Brussels after the third of the weekly flights, on 6 April.

Civil flying in Britain restarted, after the First World War, on 1 May 1919, following publication of the Air Navigation Regulations.

The first British aeroplane to carry civil markings (K-100) was a de Havilland DH6 in 1919. It was sold to the Marconi Wireless Telegraph Co. Ltd, and used for radio trials; it became the second aircraft entered on the British Civil Register (as G-EAAB; see below).

The first British civil aeroplane (i.e. the first on the British Civil Register proper) was a de Havilland DH9 (G-EAAA, previously C6054), operated as a mailplane by Aircraft Transport and Travel Ltd in mid-1919, between London and Paris.

The first occasion on which newspapers were distributed by an aircraft on a daily basis was in May 1919. A Fairey IIIC seaplane was used on a week-long experimental freighting service to distribute the *Evening News* from the Thames, near Westminster Bridge, to coastal towns in Kent. This service saved about two hours' distribution time.

The first British Certificate of Airworthiness was issued on 1 May 1919 to the Handley Page O/400 (F5414) which thereafter became registered as G-EAAF, owned by Handley Page Air Transport Ltd.

The first transatlantic crossing by air was

achieved by the American Navy/Curtiss NC-4 flying-boat commanded by Lt Cdr A. C. Read between 8 May and 31 May 1919. Three flying-boats, the NC-1, NC-3 and NC-4, under the command of Cdr John H. Towers, had set out from Rockaway, New York, on 8 May. Only NC-4 completed the crossing, arriving at Plymouth, England, on 31 May, having landed en route at Chatham, Massachusetts; Halifax, Nova Scotia; Trespassey Bay, Newfoundland; Horta, Azores; Ponta Delgarda, Azores; Lisbon, Portugal; and Ferrol del Caudillo, Spain. The total distance flown was 3925 miles (6315 km) in 57 h 16 min flying time, at a speed of 68 mph (110 km/h). Both NC-1 and NC-3 were forced down on the sea short of the Azores, and NC-1 sank, its crew being rescued. NC-3, with Cdr Towers aboard, taxied the remaining 200 miles (320 km) to the Azores.

The first practical light aeroplane to be produced in Britain after the First World War was the Avro 534 Baby. The prototype crashed after its first take-off on 10 May 1919, but its 35 hp Green water-cooled engine was salvaged and installed in the second aircraft, which won the handicap section of the Aerial Derby on 21 June 1919.

The first regular civil air service in England was started by A. V. Roe and Co. on 10 May 1919 and discontinued on 30 September 1919. Using three-seat Avro aircraft, services were flown from Alexander Park, Manchester, to Southport, and also to Blackpool. One hundred and ninety-four scheduled flights were made during this period; the cost of a one-way flight was four guineas.

The first stage of a planned US transcontinental airmail service was inaugurated on 15 May 1919, between Chicago and Cleveland. Realizing that only a really long air route would show any advantage over surface transportation in terms of journey time, the US Post Office had purchased more than 125 ex-military aircraft, mostly de Havilland DH4Ms, with which it hoped to carry airmail between New York and San Francisco at the standard first class surface rate of 2 cents per ounce. The final link from Omaha to Sacramento, over the Rockies, was proved practicable on 8 September 1920. After months of careful planning, **the first coast-to-coast airmail service in the USA** left San Francisco at 04.30 h on 22 February 1921 and arrived at Mineola, Long Island, New York, at 16.50 h the following day. It was carried from San Francisco to North Platte, Nebraska, by a succession of pilots. At North Platte it was taken over by a pilot named Jack Knight, flying one of the open-cockpit DH4Ms. When he reached Omaha, weather conditions along the route were so bad that the pilot scheduled to fly the next stage to Chicago had not put in an appearance. So Knight carried on through the darkness to Chicago, over unfamiliar country,

becoming a national hero for 'saving the mail service'. A system of lighting for safer flying by night was installed along part of the route in 1923. Regular transcontinental night mail flights were inaugurated on 1 July 1924.

The first post-war aviation event to be held in Britain took place at Hendon on 7 June 1919, when Lt G. R. Hicks won a cross-country handicap race flying an Avro 504K.

The first non-stop air crossing of the Atlantic was accomplished on 14–15 June 1919 by Capt John Alcock and Lt Arthur Whitten Brown who flew in a Vickers Vimy bomber from St John's, Newfoundland, to Clifden, County Galway, Ireland. Powered by two Rolls-Royce engines, the Vimy was equipped with long-range fuel tanks and achieved a coast-to-coast time of 15 h 57 min. Total flying time was 16 h 27 min. Both Alcock

Above   Capt John Alcock and Lt Arthur Whitten Brown. (Aer Lingus)

Below   Alcock and Brown's Vimy leaves Newfoundland on the historic first ever non-stop air crossing of the Atlantic. (Aer Lingus)

and Brown were knighted in recognition of this achievement; Sir John Alcock, as Chief Test Pilot of Vickers, was killed on 18 December 1919 in a flying accident caused by bad weather near Rouen, France.

The world's first purpose-built all-metal commercial transport aircraft was flown in Germany. This was the F13 designed by Hugo Junkers, the prototype of which took to the air on 25 June 1919. Eventually, 322 were built up to 1932. Among the first to order the aircraft were SCADTA of Colombia and the US Post Office. Wing span was 58 ft 2¾ in (17.75 m), length with a 185 hp BMW engine 31 ft 6 in (9.60 m), and cruising speed was 87 mph (140 km/h).

The first London airport at which customs clearance could be obtained for outward bound flights was at Hounslow, Middlesex, in operation from July 1919.

The first non-stop flight between Rome and Paris was made on 14 July 1919 by an Italian Fiat BR light bomber.

The first flight across the Canadian Rocky Mountains, and also **the first airmail flight across the Rockies**, was made on 7 August 1919 in a Curtiss Jenny flown by Capt Ernest C. Hoy. He flew from Vancouver to Calgary via Lethbridge in 16 h 42 min.

The first two women passengers to fly on an airline service between England and France, on 26 August 1919, were carried in an aircraft of Handley Page Transport.

The first scheduled daily international commercial airline flight anywhere in the world was from London to Paris on 25 August 1919. It was made in a de Havilland DH16 flown by Cyril Patteson of Aircraft Transport and Travel Ltd, which took off from Hounslow with four passengers and landed at Le Bourget, Paris, 2 h 30 min later. The fare was £21 for the one-way crossing.

The first Schneider Trophy Contest to take place off the British coast was that flown at Bournemouth, Hampshire, on 10 September 1919. Fog turned the event into chaos and it was eventually abandoned. Guido Janello of Italy completed 11 laps, but as there was doubt concerning one of his turning points it was not allowed to count as a victory. As a gesture, Italy was asked to organize the next event. The 1919 contest at Bournemouth was the first in which an

Above   Pilot Henri Biard aboard the Supermarine Sea Lion, the Schneider Trophy seaplane prepared by R. J. Mitchell for the 1919 contest off Bournemouth.

Below   Junkers F13, the first purpose-built all-metal airliner. (Lufthansa Archiv)

aircraft was involved that had been especially prepared by R. J. Mitchell, a 24-year-old recruit of the Supermarine Company.

The first Dutch national airline, KLM (Royal Dutch Airlines), was founded on 7 October 1919. It is the oldest airline in the world still operating under its original name.

The first airline to provide food on its services was Handley Page Transport, on 11 October 1919, when it introduced lunch baskets at a cost of 3 shillings each.

The first American international scheduled passenger air service was inaugurated on 1 November 1919 by Aeromarine West Indies Airways between Key West, Florida, and Havana, Cuba. On 1 November 1920 the airline was awarded the first US foreign airmail contract.

The first flight from Britain to Australia was completed between 12 November and 10 December 1919 by two Australian brothers, Capt Ross Smith and Lt Keith Smith, with two other crew members. They set out from Hounslow, Middlesex, in a Vickers Vimy bomber powered by two Rolls-Royce Eagle engines, and flew to Darwin, a distance of 11 294 miles (18 175 km) in under 28 days with a Hounslow-Darwin flying time of 135 h 55 min. Their feat earned them the Australian government's prize of £10 000 ($40 000) and knighthoods. Sir Ross Smith was killed in a flying accident near Brooklands Aerodrome, England,

on 13 April 1922. By tragic coincidence, both Sir Ross and Sir John Alcock (famous for his Atlantic crossing, see above) were killed in Vickers Viking amphibians.

The first men to fly across Australia were Capt H. N. Wrigley and Lt A. W. Murphy, from Melbourne to Darwin in a BE2e between 16 November and 12 December 1919 in 46 h flying time.

The first Boeing commercial aircraft, the B-1 flying-boat of its own design, made its maiden flight on 27 December 1919.

The first aircraft with a practical form of retractable landing gear was the Dayton-Wright RB Racer, designed and built to compete in the 1920 Gordon Bennett Aviation Cup Race.

The first automatic pilot to be installed in a British commercial aircraft, the Aveline Stabilizer, was fitted in a Handley Page O/10 during 1920.

The Soviet Union's first internal airline service, between Sarapul and Yekaterinburg, was flown during January 1920 by demilitarized *Ilya Mourometz* bombers.

The first flight from Britain to South Africa was made between 4 February and 20 March 1920 by Lt Col Pierre van Ryneveld and Sqn Ldr Christopher Quintin Brand. They set out from Brooklands in a Vickers Vimy bomber but crashed at Wadi Halfa, Sudan, while attempting an

The four-man crew of the US Army Air Service Martin MB-1 bomber that circumnavigated the United States of America, November 1919. This is remembered as the 'Round the Rim' flight. (US Air Force)

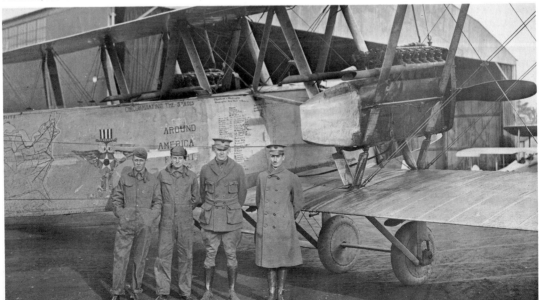

emergency landing. The South African government provided the pilots with another Vimy aircraft and after 11 days they set off again, only to crash at Bulawayo, Southern Rhodesia, on 6 March. Once again the government provided an aircraft, a war-surplus DH9, and on 17 March they set off again. Finally, on 20 March, they reached Wynberg Aerodrome, Cape Town. They received subsequently £5000 prize-money and were knighted by HM King George V.

The first regular use of Croydon as London's air terminal began on 29 March 1920. On that date the main airport facilities were transferred from Hounslow, Middlesex, to Croydon—or Waddon, as the airport was known originally. It was opened officially on 31 March 1921.

The first Australian commercial airline, QANTAS (Queensland and Northern Territory Aerial Service) was registered on 16 November 1920 for air taxi and regular air services in Australia. The company's first chairman was Sir Fergus McMaster (1879–1950), and its first scheduled services began on 2 November 1922 with flights between Charlesville and Cloncurry, Queensland.

The first Pulitzer Trophy Race was flown on 25 November 1920 from Mitchell Field, Long Island, New York. It was won by Capt Corliss C. Moseley flying a Verville-Packard 600.

The first fatal accident on a scheduled British commercial flight occurred on 14 December 1920 when a Handley Page O/400 crashed soon after take-off in fog at Cricklewood, London. Pilot R. Bager, his engineer and two passengers were killed, but four other passengers escaped.

The first solo coast-to-coast flight across the United States was recorded between 21 and 24 February 1921 by Lt William D. Coney of the US Army Air Service. His route, from Rockwell Field, San Diego, to Jacksonville, Florida, was completed in a flying time of 22 h 27 min.

The first and only Oxford versus Cambridge University Air Race ever staged was flown on 16 July 1921 and resulted in a flyaway victory for Cambridge. Each team flew three SE5as and the 129 mile (208 km) course of three laps lay along the route from Hendon via Epping and Hertford, returning to Hendon. Cambridge gained maximum points by achieving the first three places, the fastest lap being flown at an average speed of 118.55 mph (190.79 km/h). One of the Oxford aircraft failed to complete the course.

The first Air League Challenge Cup Race was flown at Croydon on 17 September 1921. Because there were then so few civil aircraft available for competitive events, it was decided to award the cup initially to RAF teams. The first winners were a team from No. 24 Squadron, then based at RAF Kenley, Surrey.

The first regular scheduled air services in Australia were inaugurated by West Australian Airways on 5 December 1921.

The first aircraft designed by the Soviet Union's Andrei N. Tupolev, the ANT-1 light sporting monoplane, was flown for the first time during 1922.

A South Atlantic flight attempt was started on 13 March 1922 by Portuguese pilots Capt Gago Coutinho and Capt Sacadura Cabral. Taking off from Lisbon in a Fairey IIIC, they arrived in Brazil on 16 June in the Fairey IIID *Santa Cruz*, the original aircraft having been wrecked *en route*.

The first air collision between airliners on scheduled flights occurred on 7 April 1922, between a Daimler Airways de Havilland DH18 (G-EAWO) flown by Robin Duke from Croydon, and a Farman Goliath of Grands Express Aériens flown by M. Mier from Le Bourget. The two aircraft, which were following a road on a reciprocal course, collided over Thieuloy-Saint-Antoine 18 miles (29 km) north of Beauvais. All seven occupants were killed.

The first coast-to-coast crossing of the United States in a single day was made by Lt James H. Doolittle who flew a modified DH4B from Pablo Beach, Florida, to Rockwell Field, San Diego, California, on 4 September 1922. Actual flying time to cover the 2163 miles (3480 km) was 21 h 19 min; elapsed time with a refuelling stop at Kelly Field, Texas, was 22 h 35 min.

The first King's Cup Air Race, over a course from Croydon, England, to Glasgow, Scotland, and return, was won during 8–9 September 1922 by Capt F. F. Barnard piloting a de Havilland DH4A.

The first German aeroplane to land in the UK post-war was a Dornier Komet four-passenger airliner (D-223) of Deutsche Luft-Reederei, which landed at Lympne Aerodrome, Kent, on 31 December 1922.

The first variable-pitch aeroplane propeller, designed by Turnbull in America, was demonstrated during 1923.

The Soviet Union's first state airline, Dobrolet, was established during March 1923, its initial operations carried out with assistance from the Air Force.

The first Czechoslovakian national airline, Ceskoslovenske Statni Aerolinie (CSA), began its first operations on 1 March 1923.

The first scheduled air service between London and Berlin was inaugurated by Daimler Airways on 10 April 1923, with intermediate landings at Bremen and Hamburg.

The first non-stop air crossing of the United States by an aeroplane was achieved on 2–3 May 1923 by Lts O. G. Kelly and J. A. Macready, USAAS, in a Fokker T-2 aircraft. Taking off from Roosevelt Field, Long Island, at 12.36 h (Eastern Time) on 2 May, they arrived at Rockwell Field, San Diego, California, at 12.26 h (Pacific Time) on 3 May. They overflew Dayton, Ohio; Indianapolis, Indiana; St Louis, Missouri; Kansas City, Missouri; Tucumcari, New Mexico; and Wickenburg, Arizona. The distance flown, 2516 miles (4050 km), was covered in 26 h 50 min. Kelly and Macready had also established a new world endurance record for aeroplanes, on 16–17 April 1923, flying the Fokker T-2 a distance of 2518 miles (4052 km) over a measured course in 36 h 5 min.

The first Grosvenor Challenge Cup contest, for British aircraft with engines of under 150 hp, was won on 23 June 1923 by Flt Lt W. H. Longton, RAF, flying a Sopwith Gnu.

The first use of electric beacons mounted on the ground, to provide flight directions for night flying operations, were introduced in the USA on 21 August 1923.

The first light-plane competition held in Great Britain was at Lympne, Kent, in October 1923, organized by the Royal Aero Club. The competition was for single-seat aircraft, and the prizes included £1000 offered by the *Daily Mail* and £500 by the Duke of Sutherland for the longest flight on one Imperial gallon of petrol made by an aircraft with an engine not exceeding 750 cc capacity. The prize money for the one-gallon flight was shared between Flt Lt Walter Longton, who flew an English Electric Wren, and Jimmy H. James in an ANEC monoplane, both flying 87.5 miles (140.8 km). Another prize of £500, offered by the Abdulla Company for the highest speed over two laps, was won in a Parnall Pixie by Capt Norman Macmillan, who attained an average speed of 76.1 mph (122.5 km/h).

The world's first aerial crop-dusting company, Huff Daland Dusters, was formed at Macon, Georgia, in 1924. It became named Delta Air Service, subsequently Delta Air Lines, when passenger services were initiated during 1929.

The first British national airline, Imperial Airways, was formed on 1 April 1924. This was the manifestation of the British government's determination to develop air transport, and the

company was to receive preferential air subsidies, having acquired the businesses of British Marine Air Navigation Co., Daimler Airways, Handley Page Transport and Instone Air Lines. Its fleet consisted of seven DH34s, two Sea Eagles, three Handley Page W8bs and one Vickers Vimy.

The first successful round-the-world flight was accomplished by two Douglas DWCs (Douglas World Cruisers) between 6 April and 28 September 1924. Four DWCs set out from Seattle, Washington, and two of them circumnavigated the world. The flagplane (named *Seattle* and piloted by the commander of the flight, Maj F. Martin) only reached Alaska, where it crashed on a mountain on 30 April; the crew returned to the USA. Another (the *Boston*) was forced to alight in the ocean near the Faeroes, and eventually sank after being cut loose from the crew's rescue ship, the USS *Richmond*. The crews of the two successful aircraft were as follows:

CHICAGO (Aircraft No. 2): Lt Lowell H. Smith, deputy flight commander and pilot; Lt Leslie P. Arnold, mechanic and second pilot.

NEW ORLEANS (Aircraft No. 4): Lt Erik Nelson, pilot and engineer officer; Lt John Harding Jr, mechanic and maintenance officer.

The total mileage by each of the two aircraft which completed the historic flight was 27 553 miles (44 340 km) and the elapsed time 175 days. The flying time was given as 371 h 11 min. It should be noted that this flight included the first staged crossing of the Pacific Ocean as well as the first staged east–west crossing of the North Atlantic. (Two of these aircraft are preserved to this day, one at the Smithsonian Institution in Washington,

the other in the Air Force Museum at Wright–Patterson Air Force Base.)

The first all-metal aircraft to be built in the Soviet Union, the ANT-2, made its maiden flight on 26 May 1924. Designed by Andrei N. Tupolev, its method of construction was based on that of the German Junkers types.

The first Light Aeroplane Competition for two-seat aircraft, organized by the Royal Aero Club, was held at Lympne, Kent, between 27 September and 4 October 1924. Lightest aircraft in the competition was the Hawker Cygnet, which had an empty weight of 373 lb (169 kg). Two examples were built, G-EBMB and G-EBJH, the former powered originally by a 34 hp British Anzani two-cylinder engine, the latter with a 34 hp ABC Scorpion, also of two cylinder configuration. The Cygnet was also Sydney Camm's first design for the H. G. Hawker Engineering Company. Winner of the competition, and the Air Ministry's £3000 prize, was Mr Piercy with the Beardmore Wee Bee monoplane, powered by a 32 hp Bristol Cherub engine.

The prototype of the de Havilland DH60 Moth, a small **two-seat biplane that revolutionized private flying** and was the true starting point of the flying club movement, was flown for the first time on 22 February 1925.

Henry Ford initiated **the first regular US air freight service**, linking Detroit, Michigan and Chicago, on 13 April 1925.

The first three-engined all-metal monoplane transport in the world to enter commercial

Left *A winner at the Lympne 'Motor Glider' competition of 1923 was the English Electric Wren. Many of the aircraft, though remarkable and economical, were nevertheless impractical.*

Right *Douglas DWC Chicago, one of two Air Service aircraft to complete the 1924 round-the-world flight.*

Left   *Sir Alan Cobham's de Havilland DH50, returning for a triumphant welcome.*

Right   *Fokker F.VIIA-3m Josephine Ford on exhibition.*

airline service was the Junkers G 23, four of which served with Swedish Air Lines (AB Aerotransport) on the Malmo–Hamburg–Amsterdam route from 15 May 1925. This aircraft, built in Germany and Sweden, provided the basis for the later and famous Junkers Ju 52/3m, and set the pattern for low-wing multi-engined monoplanes thereafter.

A contemporary of the above, and **another of the world's famous commercial airliners**, the Fokker F.VIIa-3m three-engined monoplane, flew for the first time in prototype form on 4 September 1925.

The first aeroplane flight between London and Cape Town was made by Alan Cobham, with his mechanic A. B. Elliott and cine photographer B. W. G. Emmott, in the second de Havilland DH50 that was built (G-EBFO). They left Croydon on 16 November 1925 and reached Cape Town on 17 February 1926. Cobham landed back at Croydon after the 16,000 mile (25 750 km) round trip on 13 March 1926. Three months later, on 30 June, Cobham and Elliott took off from the River Medway in the same aircraft, converted into a seaplane for the largely overwater flight to Australia and back. G-EBFO returned to a triumphant welcome on the Thames, at Westminster, on 1 October. The success was marred by the death of Elliott, who had been killed by a stray bullet fired by a bedouin while flying over the desert between Baghdad and Bazra on the outward leg. Cobham was knighted

for these flights, which pioneered future Empire air routes.

Flying a Dornier Wal flying-boat, Commandante Franco achieved **the first staged east–west air crossing of the South Atlantic** between 22 January and 10 February 1926.

The first commercial airmail flights in the USA were started on 6 April 1926 by Varney Speed Lines. These were flown between Pasco and Elko using Swallow biplanes.

The first aeroplane flight over the North Pole was accomplished by Lt Cdr Richard E. Byrd (USN) and Floyd Bennett, in the Fokker F.VIIA-3m *Josephine Ford* on 9 May 1926. The total distance flown was 1600 miles (2575 km).

The first successful passenger aircraft built in America was the Ford 4-AT Trimotor, which first flew on 11 June 1926. Powered by three 220 hp engines, it could accommodate 10 passengers and had a cruising speed of 105 mph (169 km/h). From 1926 to 1933, Ford built around 200 Trimotors, designated from 3-AT to 7-AT, and this aircraft was operated by many airlines.

The first known use of aircraft for violence in civil crime occurred on 12 November 1926, when three small bombs (which failed to explode) were dropped from an aeroplane on to a farmhouse in Williamson County, Illinois. The raid was carried out by a member of the Shelton gang, against members of the rival Birger gang, in a

Prohibition feud involving illicit supplies of beer and rum.

The first light aeroplane flight from London to Karachi, India, was flown by T. Neville Stack in the de Havilland DH60 Moth G-EBMO (Cirrus II engine), accompanied by B. S. Leete in a similar aircraft, G-EBKU, between 15 November 1926 and 8 January 1927.

The first non-stop solo air crossing of the North Atlantic was made by Capt Charles Lindbergh during 20–21 May 1927 in the Ryan NYP high-wing monoplane *Spirit of St Louis*. Taking off from Long Island, New York, on 20 May 1927, his epic flight to Paris of 3610 miles (5810 km) was accomplished in 33 h 39 min at an average speed of 107.5 mph (173 km/h).

Above   *Charles Lindbergh.*
Below   Spirit of St Louis.

The world's first charter flight, flown in both directions between Amsterdam and Jakarta, was completed between 15 June and 23 July 1927. The Fokker F.VIIa (H-NADP) was chartered by an American, W. van Lear Black, and flown a total out and return distance of 18 710 miles (30 111 km) under the command of Capt G. J. Geysendorffer.

The first non-stop flight between the United States and Hawaii was achieved by Lts Albert F. Hegenberger and Lester J. Maitland during 28–29 June 1927. Flying the US Army Fokker C-2 monoplane *Bird of Paradise*, they covered the 2407 miles (3874 km) from Oakland, California, to Honolulu, Hawaii, in 25 h 30 min.

The first flight by a light aircraft from London to Cape Town, South Africa, was accomplished by Lt R. R. Bentley, SAAF, flying the de Havilland DH60X Moth *Dorys*. Taking off on 1 September 1927, the flight was completed on the 28th of the month.

The first non-stop air crossing of the South Atlantic by an aeroplane was made on 14–15 October 1927. Capt Dieudonne Costes and Lt Cdr Le Brix flew the Breguet XIX *Nungesser-Coli* from Saint-Louis, Senegal, to Port Natal, Brazil, a distance of 2125 miles (3420 km) in 19 h 50 min.

The first air service by Pan American Airways was inaugurated on 19 October 1927 on the 90 mile (145 km) route between Key West, Florida, and Havana, Cuba.

The first solo flight from England to Australia was made by Sqn Ldr H. J. L. ('Bert') Hinkler in the Avro 581 Avian light aircraft prototype G-EBOV. Flying from Croydon to Darwin, between 7 and 22 February 1928, his 11 005 mile (17 711 km) route was via Rome, Malta, Tobruk, Ramleh, Basra, Jask, Karachi, Cawnpore, Calcutta, Rangoon, Victoria Point, Singapore, Bandoeng and Bima. His aircraft was placed on permanent exhibition in the Brisbane Museum.

The first flight by a woman from South Africa to England was achieved by Lady Heath in an Avro Avian III, flying from Cape Town to Croydon between 12 February and 17 May 1928. This was also **the first solo flight from South Africa to Britain** and, en route, **the first solo flight from the Cape to Cairo**.

The first solo return flight by a woman between London and South Africa was achieved by Lady Bailey who, in a de Havilland Moth (G-EBSF), left London on 9 March 1928. This aircraft was damaged beyond repair at Tabora a month later, but the pilot completed her flight to the Cape in a replacement Moth, G-EBTG. She subsequently toured round Africa before returning to London on 16 January 1929.

The first east–west air crossing of the North Atlantic, between Baldonnel, Ireland, and Greenly Island, Labrador, was recorded during 12–13 April 1928. This was achieved by Hermann Köhl, the Irish Capt J. Fitzmaurice and Baron von Hunefeld, flying the Junkers W33 *Bremen*.

The first west–east crossing of the Arctic was achieved by Capt G. H. Wilkins and Lt Carl B. Eielson flying a Lockheed Vega monoplane. Taking off from Point Barrow, Alaska, on 15 April 1928, they were within half an hour's flying time of their destination when they were forced by poor weather to land on Dead Man's Island. There they sheltered in the cabin of their aircraft for five days before taking off and landing at Spitzbergen on 21 April.

The Australian Flying Doctor Service was inaugurated on 15 May 1928, using the joint services of the Australian Inland Mission and QANTAS at Cloncurry. The first aircraft was the de Havilland DH50 *Victory*, modified to accommodate two stretchers; its first pilot was Dr K. H. Vincent Welsh. The founder of the service was the Rev. J. Flynn, OBE.

The first true trans-Pacific flight, discounting that of the Douglas World Cruisers, was that accomplished by the Fokker F.VIIB-3m *Southern Cross*, flown by Capt Charles Kingsford Smith and C. T. P. Ulm (pilots), accompanied by Harry Lyon (navigator) and James Warner (radio operator). Taking off from Oakland Field, California, on 31 May 1928, their route was via Honolulu, Hawaii, and Suva, Fiji, landing at Eagle Farm, Brisbane, on 9 June 1928. The flight covered 7389 miles (11 890 km), with a flying time of 83 h 38 min. The *Southern Cross* has been preserved and is displayed at Eagle Farm Airport. It was **the first aircraft ever to land in Fiji**.

The first air crossing of the Tasman Sea was made by the *Southern Cross* during 10–11 Septem-

Above *Fokker F.VIIB-3m* Southern Cross, *which made the first true trans-Pacific flight in 1928.*

Left *Charles Kingsford Smith.*

ber 1928. Again piloted by Charles Kingsford Smith and C. T. P. Ulm, the aircraft flew from Richmond Aerodrome, Sydney, to Wigram, Christchurch, New Zealand.

The first commercial air route between London and India was inaugurated by Imperial Airways on 30 March 1929. The route was from London to Basle, Switzerland, by air (Armstrong Whitworth Argosy aircraft); Basle to Genoa, Italy,

by train; Genoa to Alexandria, Egypt, by air (Short Calcutta flying-boats); and Alexandria to Karachi, India, by air (de Havilland DH66 Hercules aircraft). The total journey from Croydon to Karachi occupied seven days, for which the single fare was £130. The stage travelled by train was necessary as Italy forbade the air entry of British aircraft, an embargo which lasted several years and substantially frustrated Imperial Airways' efforts to develop the Far East route.

The first non-stop flight from Great Britain to India was accomplished by Sqn Ldr A. G. Jones Williams and Flt Lt N. H. Jenkins (pilot and navigator respectively) between 24 and 26 April 1929. Flying from Cranwell, Lincolnshire, to Karachi, India, in the Fairey Long Range Monoplane J9479, they covered the 4130 miles (6647 km) in 50 h 37 min. It had been intended to fly to Bangalore to establish a world distance record but the attempt was abandoned owing to headwinds. Another Fairey Long Range Monoplane, K1991, crewed by Sqn Ldr O. R. Gayford and Flt Lt G. E. Nicholetts, made **the first non-stop flight from England to South Africa**, between 6 and 8 February 1933. The total distance covered from Cranwell to Walvis Bay, South-West Africa, was 5309 miles (8544 km), which was completed in 57 h 25 min and set a new world distance record.

The first flight over the South Pole was made during 28–29 November 1929 by the Ford

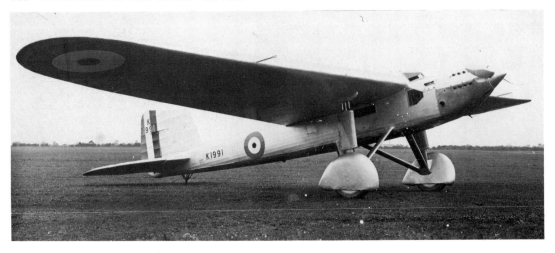

4-AT Trimotor *Floyd Bennett*. Its crew was Cdr R. E. Byrd, US Navy, with Bernt Balchen (pilot), Harold June (radio operator) and Ashley McKinley (survey).

The first solo flight by a woman from Great Britain to Australia was achieved by Amy Johnson, between 5 and 24 May 1930, flying the de Havilland DH60G Gipsy Moth *Jason* (G-AAAH) from Croydon to Darwin. This record remained unbeaten until 1934 when New Zealand airwoman Jean Batten, flying a de Havilland DH60M Moth (G-AARB) during the period 8–23 May 1934, took 14 d 22 h 30 min for the flight from Lympne, Kent, to Darwin, Australia, thus beating Amy Johnson's England–Australia record by more than four days.

The Boeing Company's first commercial monoplane, the Model 200 *Monomail*, made its first flight on 6 May 1930. This significant aeroplane, used as a mail/cargo carrier, introduced a cantilever low-set monoplane wing, retractable landing gear and other advanced features.

The first airline stewardess was Ellen Church, a nurse who, with Boeing Air Transport (later absorbed into United Air Lines), made her first flight, between San Francisco, California, and Cheyenne, Wyoming, on 15 May 1930.

The first east–west staged crossing of the North Atlantic in a flying-boat was achieved by a Dornier Wal piloted by Capt Wolfgang von Gronau. Taking off from the island of Sylt, on 18 August 1930, with co-pilot Edward Zimmer, Fritz

Albrecht (radio) and Franz Hack (mechanic), a landing in New York harbour was made on 26 August.

The first coast-to-coast all-air passenger service in the United States was inaugurated by Transcontinental and Western Air, between New York and Los Angeles, California, on 25 October 1930.

Imperial Airways' first monoplane airliner was the Armstrong Whitworth AW15 Atalanta, eight of which were built for the airline in 1931 and 1932. Accommodation was for nine passengers plus cargo or mail, and the aircraft were used on the Nairobi–Cape Town and Karachi–Singapore routes.

The first commercial air route between London and Central Africa was inaugurated on 28 February 1931 by Imperial Airways. The route lay from Croydon to Alexandria (using Argosy aircraft from Croydon to Athens, and Calcutta flying-boats from Athens to Alexandria via Crete), and from Cairo to Mwanza, on Lake Victoria (using Argosy aircraft). Passengers were taken only as far as Khartoum, mail being carried over the remainder of the route.

The first woman to fly solo from Brisbane, Australia, to London, England, was Australian Lores Bonney, flying a de Havilland DH60 Moth between 12 April and 21 June 1931.

A record round-the-world flight of 8 d 15 h 51 min was recorded between 23 June and 1 July 1931 by the Lockheed Vega *Winnie Mae*. Piloted

Left *Fairey Long-Range Monoplane* K1991, *which made the first non-stop flight between England and South Africa in 1933.*

Right *Boeing Model 200 Monomail. (The Boeing Company)*

Below *The first air stewardesses, with Ellen Church third from left.*

by Wiley Post, with Harold Gatty as navigator, the flight from and to New York covered a distance of nearly 15 500 miles (24 945 km) in about 106 flying hours, following a route via Chester (UK), Berlin, Irkutsk (Soviet Union) and Alaska.

Flying her Puss Moth G-AAZV *Jason II*, Amy Johnson achieved a **flight from England to Japan in less than nine days**. Taking off from Lympne, Kent, on 28 July 1931, she arrived at Tokyo on 6 August in a total flying time of 79 h.

The first non-stop flight from Japan to the United States was achieved by Hugh Herndon Jr and Clyde E. Pangborn flying a Bellanca mono-

plane. Taking off from Samushiro Beach, some 300 miles (483 km) north of Tokyo, on 4 October 1931, they landed at Wenatchee, Washington, on 5 October after 41 h 13 min.

Landing at Stag Lane aerodrome on 16 January 1932 in the DH80A Puss Moth G-ABJO, Wg Cdr R. H. McIntosh and the Hon Mrs R. Westenra completed a journey to Africa, around the continent and back to London. During the course of this trip they recorded **the first British flight across the Sahara, and the first by a lightplane.**

The first solo crossing of the North Atlantic by a woman was achieved by the American pilot Miss Amelia Earhart (Mrs Putnam). Taking off from Harbor Grace, Newfoundland, in a Lockheed Vega monoplane on 20 May 1932, she landed at Londonderry, Northern Ireland, on the following day.

The first east–west solo flight across the North Atlantic, from Portmanock Strand north of Dublin to Pennfield Ridge, New Brunswick, was achieved by J. A. Mollison. Flying the DH80A Puss Moth *The Hearts Content* (G-ABXY), he took off on 18 August 1932, recording a flight time of 31 h 20 min.

The first non-stop transcontinental flight by a woman across the United States, from Los Angeles, California, to Newark, New Jersey, was achieved by Amelia Earhart in a Lockheed Vega on 25 August 1932.

Above *Amelia Earhart with Mr McCallion, the first person to greet her after her solo Atlantic crossing. (Aer Lingus)*

Left *Amelia Earhart's Lockheed Vega where it stopped after her transatlantic crossing, just feet from a hedge in Springfield, Londonderry. (Aer Lingus)*

Below *Mollison leaves Dublin on his solo east–west crossing of the North Atlantic in* The Hearts Content *(Syndication International)*

Boeing Model 247, the first modern airliner.

Below The Marquess of Clydesdale's Westland PV-3 approaches Everest.

A Travel Air biplane with a steam engine power plant was flown successfully in the United States during 1933. Its Besler two-cylinder double-acting vee engine developed 150 hp at a boiler pressure of 1200 lb/in² (84.37 kg/cm²).

The true ancestor of modern airliners, with all-metal structure, cantilever low wings and retractable landing gear, was the Boeing Model 247, the prototype of which was flown on 8 February 1933. A total of 75 was built. The major production version was the Model 247D, powered by two 550 hp Pratt & Whitney Wasp engines driving controllable-pitch propellers. Cruising speed with ten passengers and 400 lb (181 kg) of mail was 180 mph (304 km/h).

Landing at Port Natal, Brazil, on 9 February 1933, after a flight from Lympne, Kent, in the Puss Moth *The Hearts Content*, J. A. Mollison had attained a remarkable series of achievements. He was **the first pilot to make a solo flight between England and South America, the first to fly the South Atlantic solo from east to west, and the first to have made solo flights across both the North and South Atlantic.**

The first flights over Mount Everest were made on 3 April 1933 by the Marquess of Clydesdale in a Westland PV-3, and by Flt Lt D. F. McIntyre piloting a Westland Wallace, each with one passenger.

The Douglas DC-1 first flew on 1 July 1933 at Clover Field, Santa Monica, California. Only one was built, flying mainly in TWA insignia. After service during the Spanish Civil War, it was written-off following a take-off accident near Malaga, Spain, in December 1940. From it were developed the famous DC-2 and DC-3, which established the reputation of Douglas as an airliner manufacturer.

The first solo flight around the world was achieved by Wiley Post between 15 and 22 July 1933, when he flew his Lockheed Vega monoplane, *Winnie Mae*, from Floyd Bennett Field, New York, for a distance of 15 596 miles

(25 099 km) in 7 d 18 h 49 min. His route was via Berlin, Moscow, Irkutsk and Alaska, back to New York. Post later pioneered the development of an early pressure suit during high altitude flights in *Winnie Mae*. He was killed in a crash in 1935, together with the famous comedian/philosopher Will Rogers.

Indian National Airways began **the first daily air service in India** on 1 December 1933, with inauguration of a passenger, freight and mail service between Calcutta and Dacca.

Above   *Wiley Post with his Vega Winnie Mae.*

Left   *In an attempt to fly non-stop from England to India, Sir Alan Cobham's Airspeed Courier used experimental in-flight refuelling techniques from a modified Handley Page W.10 tanker. Having taken off from Portsmouth on 24 September 1934, mechanical problems with the aircraft meant that the flight had to be abandoned at Malta. (Flight Refuelling Ltd)*

Below   Grosvenor House, *the first aircraft to cross the finishing line in the MacRobertson trans-World air race.*

The first regular internal airmail service in Great Britain was started by Highland Airways on 29 May 1934. The de Havilland Dragon G-ACCE, flown by E. E. Fresson, carried 6000 letters on this first flight from Inverness to Kirkwall, and the service operated thereafter on every weekday.

The first non-stop flight from Canada to England was made during 8–9 August 1934 by L. G. Reid and J. R. Ayling, flying the de Havilland Dragon (G-ACJM) *Trail of the Caribou*. Their flight, from Wasaga Beach, Ontario, to Heston, Middlesex, took 30 h 50 min.

The first 'trans-World' air race was the Mac-Robertson Race from England to Australia which started on 20 October 1934. In March 1933 the Governing Director of MacRobertson Confectionery Manufacturers of Melbourne, Sir Mac-Pherson Robertson, offered £15 000 in prize money for an air race to commemorate the centenary of the foundation of the State of Victoria. The race was won by one of three specially built de Havilland DH88 Comets. A two-seat low-wing monoplane, it was powered by two 230 hp Gipsy Six R engines, each driving a variable-pitch propeller of unusual design. Set in fine-pitch for takeoff, they were moved to the coarse-pitch cruise setting by compressed air after the machine was airborne and at suitable height; they could not be recycled back to the fine-pitch setting. Charles W. A. Scott and Tom Campbell Black were first to cross the finishing line at Flemington Racecourse, Melbourne in the DH88 *Grosvenor House* (G-ACSS), having completed the 11 333 miles (18 239 km) from Mildenhall, Suffolk, in 70 h 54 min 18 s at an average speed of 158.9 mph (255.7 km/h). Second home in the Handicap Race was, surprisingly, the Douglas DC-2 *Uiver* (PH-AJU) passenger transport aircraft of the Dutch airline KLM, flown by K. D. Parmentier and J. J. Moll.

The first flight by an aeroplane from Australia to the United States was made in the Lockheed Altair *Lady Southern Cross* by Sir Charles Kingsford Smith accompanied by Capt P. G. Taylor. Taking off from Brisbane on 22 October 1934, their flight ended successfully at Oakland, California, on 4 November after staging via Fiji and Hawaii.

The first regular weekly airmail service between Britain and Australia, from London to Brisbane via Karachi and Singapore, began on 8 December 1934. The participating airlines were Imperial Airways, Indian Trans-Continental Airways and Qantas Empire Airways. Mail which left London on 8 December reached Brisbane on 21 December.

The first woman in the United States to pilot an airmail transport aircraft on regular scheduled operations was Helen Richey. Her first scheduled flight, in a Ford Trimotor from Washington, DC, to Detroit, Michigan, was flown on 31 December 1934.

The first solo flight by a woman from Honolulu, Hawaii, to the United States was made by Amelia Earhart during 11–12 January 1935. Flying a Lockheed Vega, she landed at Oakland, California, after a flight lasting 18 h 16 min.

A privately sponsored civil aircraft that led to one of Britain's main bomber types of the early war years was the Bristol 142. Ordered by Lord Rothermere of the *Daily Mail* as a six-passenger high-speed transport aircraft, at a cost of around £18 500, the 142 was first flown on 12 April 1935. Powered by two 650 hp Bristol Mercury engines, it proved to have a maximum speed of 307 mph (494 km/h). This was some 80 mph (128 km/h) faster than the RAF's latest fighter, the Gloster Gauntlet. On seeing that the Air Ministry was suitably impressed with his aircraft, Lord Rothermere gave the 142 to the nation and named it *Britain First*. A bomber derivative was soon on the production line as the Bristol Blenheim.

The first through passenger air service between London and Brisbane, Australia, was inaugurated on 13 April 1935 by Imperial Airways and Qantas Empire Airways. The single fare for the 12 754 mile (20 525 km) route was £195. However, owing to heavy stage bookings, no through passengers were carried on the inaugural flight. The journey took 12½ days.

The first airline flight from the American mainland to Hawaii was made by a *Clipper* flying-boat of Pan American Airways during 16–17 April 1935. Taking off from Alameda, California, this was the airline's proving flight over this route, **representing the first stage in a trans-Pacific route from the US to the Philippines.**

The first solo air crossing of the South Atlantic by a woman was accomplished by New Zealand's

Jean Batten, flying a Percival Gull from Lympne, Kent, to Natal, Brazil, via Thies, Senegal, during the period 11–13 November 1935.

On 22 November 1935 and 21 October 1936, Pan American Airways inaugurated its first trans-Pacific mail service and passenger service respectively. The route was between San Francisco and Manila in the Philippines, via Honolulu, Midway Island, Wake Island and Guam, and took about six days. The aircraft used was the Martin 130 *China Clipper*, which was a high-wing monoplane flying-boat, powered by four 830 hp Pratt & Whitney Twin Wasp engines. Maximum cruising speed was 163 mph (262 km/h); range was 3200 miles (5150 km), and accommodation was for up to 43 passengers by day or 18 in a night sleeper layout.

The first flight of the Douglas DC-3 prototype was made on 17 December 1935, by Carl A. Cover from Clover Field, Santa Monica. A development of the DC-1 (Douglas Commercial No. 1) and DC-2, the DC-3 first entered service with American Airlines. Its inaugural passenger-carrying service was from Chicago, Illinois, to Glendale, California, on 4 July 1936. Certainly the most famous airliner in aviation history, some remain in civil and military service in 1988, 53 years after the prototype's first flight.

The first case in Britain involving the prosecution and punishment of an airline passenger for smoking on board an aircraft in flight was heard at Croydon, Surrey, on 17 March 1936. The passenger, who had travelled on an Imperial Airways Paris–London flight aboard the HP45 *Heracles*, was fined the sum of £10.

The original British Airways airline began using Gatwick Airport, Surrey, as its operating base on 17 May 1936.

The first Short C-class Empire flying-boat *Canopus* (G-ADHL) made its first flight on 3 July 1936 with John Lankester Parker, Short's Chief Test Pilot, at the controls. Its first flight with Imperial Airways was made on 30 October 1936. The Empire 'boats represented the last word in luxury air travel before the Second World War and, as their name implied, were flown on the Empire routes to Africa and the Far East. When 28 of these aircraft were ordered by Imperial Airways before the first aircraft was built, it **then represented one of the biggest gambles in commercial aviation history**.

The first Imperial Airways all-air trans-Mediterranean service was flown on 12 January 1937 by the C-class flying-boat *Centaurus* as the final leg on an India–UK service.

The first woman to fly solo from Brisbane, Australia, to Cape Town was Australian Lores Bonney in April 1937, flying a de Havilland DH60 Moth.

Left *Pan American Martin 130 Clipper flying-boats were instrumental in inaugurating commercial services over the Pacific.*

Right *Short C-class Empire flying-boat Canopus. (Short Brothers)*

Below *Blohm und Voss Ha 139 seaplane being catapult-launched from a depot ship.*

The inaugural flight of Britain's Empire Air Mail Programme was made on 29 June 1937, when the Imperial Airways C-class flying-boat *Centurion* (G-ADVE) left Southampton with 3500 lb (1588 kg) of unsurcharged mail.

The first North Atlantic trials involving the use of depot ships were started by Deutsche Lufthansa on 15 August 1937. These vessels were equipped to retrieve, refuel and catapult-launch four-engined Blohm und Voss Ha 139 seaplanes which had been developed specially for this purpose.

The first fully automatic landing by an aeroplane was made on 23 August 1937 at Wright Field, Ohio. This was accomplished by on-board equipment, without assistance from the pilot, and without radio control from the ground.

The first airmail and freight service between the United States and New Zealand was inaugurated on 23 December 1937 by the Pan American flying-boat *Samoa Clipper.*

The first flight refuelling test with a C-class Empire flying-boat of Imperial Airways was carried out under the supervision of Sir Alan Cobham, the founder of Flight Refuelling Ltd. The tanker used in these tests, started on 20 January 1938, was the Armstrong Whitworth AW 23 bomber/transport prototype which had been loaned to Flight Refuelling by the Air Ministry.

The first commercial use of composite aeroplanes in the world occurred during 21–22 July 1938, when the Short S21 *Maia* flying-boat and the Short S20 *Mercury* seaplane took off from Foynes, Ireland. The S20 upper component then separated and flew the North Atlantic non-stop to Montreal, Canada, with a load of mail and newspapers. It covered 2930 miles (4715 km) in 20 h 20 min, at an average speed of 140 mph (225 km/h). Numerous composite flights and separations were carried out and the pair of aircraft continued to operate on the Southampton to Alexandria air route until the outbreak of the Second World War. When launched from its 'mother-plane' *Maia*, the seaplane *Mercury* carried sufficient fuel to fly 5995.5 miles (9652 km) from Dundee, Scotland, to the Orange River, South Africa. In doing so, on 6–8 October 1938, it established a record that has never been beaten.

The first flight of a Danish airliner to the United Kingdom was made on 28 July 1938, the inaugural service made by the Focke-Wulf Fw 200 Condor *Dania* (OY-DAM) flying between Copenhagen and Croydon.

The first airliner with a pressurized cabin to enter service was the Boeing Model 307 Stratoliner, the prototype of which was flown for the first time on 31 December 1938. Derived from the B-17 Flying Fortress bomber, it was advertised as the first airliner to fly above most bad weather conditions because of its pressurized cabin. The first version to enter service, with Trans-Continental and Western Air in April 1940, was the Model 307B, accommodating 33 passengers.

The first regular airmail service over the North Atlantic began on 20 May 1939 with the departure of the Pan American Airways' Boeing 314 *Yankee Clipper* (NC18603) from New York.

The first transatlantic flight by a British prime minister was made by the Rt Hon Winston Churchill on 16–17 January 1942. The flight, between Bermuda and Plymouth, was made in the Boeing 314 flying-boat *Berwick* operated by British Overseas Airways Corporation (BOAC).

The first flight of an aircraft powered completely by turboprop engines was made by the 18th production Gloster Meteor F.1. Re-engined by Rolls-Royce with two RB.50 Trent turboprops, driving 7 ft 11 in (2.41 m) diameter five-blade propellers, it was flown for the first time on 20 September 1945.

The first post-war British survey flight to South America was made on 9 October 1945,

Left   *The Short-Mayo Composite, a method of extending the seaplane's range patented by Major R. H. Mayo and used successfully by Short Brothers/Imperial Airways. (Short Brothers)*

Right   *Silver City Airways' remarkable Bristol Freighter car/passenger airliner.*

Boeing Model 307 Stratoliner, the first pressurized airliner to enter service. (The Boeing Company)

when Capt O. P. Jones took off from Hurn, Hampshire, in the Avro Lancastrian G-AGMG.

The first regular British air service to South America was inaugurated on 15 March 1946, the service flown initially by Lancastrians.

The first transatlantic arrivals at London's Heathrow Airport, opened officially on 31 May 1946, were Lockheed Constellations of Pan American Airways and American Overseas Airlines.

The first US airmail to be carried by turbojet-powered aircraft was that flown on 22 June 1946, by two USAAF Lockheed P-80 Shooting Star fighters, from Shenectady to Washington D.C. and Chicago, Illinois.

The first non-stop flight between Hawaii and Egypt, over the North Pole, was made in a USAAF Boeing B-29 Superfortress on 6 October 1946, covering a distance of 10 873 miles (17 498 km).

The first aircraft to land on and take off from Mount Washington, New Hampshire, on 12 March 1947, was a ski-equipped Piper Cub flown by Carmen Onofrio.

The first car ferry flight operated by Silver City Airways was made on 14 July 1948, the Bristol Freighter G-AGVC making the initial flight carrying two cars.

The world's first turboprop-powered civil transport (when it entered airline service) was the prototype Vickers Viscount (G-AHRF), first flown on 16 July 1948.

A Vickers Viking carrying urgent medical supplies, and prevented by thick fog from taking off from Blackbushe, Surrey, on 30 November 1948, **became the first commercial aircraft to make use of the British wartime FIDO fog dispersal system** to become airborne.

The de Havilland DH106 Comet I, which was to

become the **world's first turbojet-powered airliner** when it entered airline service in 1952, was first flown in prototype (G-ALVG) form on 27 July 1949.

The 'Derry Turn' was evolved by John Derry, a test pilot of the de Havilland company, during 1949–50. It was a positive-G turn initiated by rolling in the opposite direction through 270°. A fairly spectacular manoeuvre, it was made possible only by the availability of sufficient excess engine power, allied with rudder control, to keep the nose of the aircraft up at the necessary late stage in the rolling manoeuvre.

The first turbine-powered airliner in the world to receive an Airworthiness Certificate

was the Vickers V630 Viscount prototype (G-AHRF), with Rolls-Royce Dart turboprop engines, which was awarded Certificate No. A907 on 28 July 1950. The following day British European Airways operated this aircraft to record **the world's first scheduled passenger service to be flown by a gas-turbine powered airliner**. However, this service was not sustained for a long period. Piloted by Capt Richard Rymer, the Viscount took off from London (Northolt) and flew to Paris (Le Bourget), carrying 14 fare-paying passengers and 12 guests of the airline. Capt Rymer was also **the world's first holder of a pilot's licence for a turbine-powered civil transport aircraft**.

The first solo trans-Polar flight was made on 29

Left *First flight of the prototype de Havilland Comet turbojet-powered airliner. (British Aerospace)*

Below *Prototype Vickers Viscount in BEA livery, 1950.*

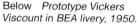

May 1951 in a North American P-51 Mustang by American C. Blair from Bardufoss, Norway, to Fairbanks, Alaska.

The first freight service operated by turbo-prop-powered aircraft, between Northolt and Hanover, was flown by Rolls-Royce Dart-engined Douglas DC-3s of BEA. The first flight was made on 15 August 1951 by G-ALXN *Sir Henry Royce*. This aircraft and a second DC-3, G-AMBD *Claude Johnson*, had been used for development flying of the Dart power plants introduced on the Vickers Viscount.

The world's first Certificate of Airworthiness for a turbojet-powered civil airliner was awarded to the de Havilland Comet I on 22 January 1952.

The world's first turbojet airliner to enter commercial service was the de Havilland DH106 Comet I, powered by four de Havilland Ghost 50 turbojet engines. **The world's first regular passenger service to be flown by turbojet aircraft** was inaugurated by British Overseas Airways Corporation on 2 May 1952, using the de Havilland Comet I G-ALYP between London and Johannesburg, South Africa. Its route was via Rome, Beirut, Khartoum, Entebbe and Livingstone, and the aircraft was captained in turn by Capts A. M. Majendie, J. T. A. Marsden and R. C. Alabaster. It carried 36 passengers and the total elapsed time for the 6724 miles (10 821 km) flight was 23 h 34 min. On 2 May 1953, a BOAC Comet I (G-ALYV) crashed near Calcutta after structural failure, with the loss of 43 lives. This was **the first fatal accident involving a turbojet airliner on scheduled service**. Subsequent accidents caused the grounding of Comets, on 8 April 1954. By the time of Comet 4 services, the aircraft's technology lead had been lost to the US Boeing 707.

The first commercial flights over the Polar regions between Europe and North America began on 19 November 1952. Flown by SAS (Scandinavian Airlines System) Douglas DC-6Bs, these first flights were unscheduled, but scheduled operations over this route were initiated during 1954.

The world's first fatal accident involving a turbojet airliner occurred on 3 March 1953 when *Empress of Hawaii*, the de Havilland Comet I CF-CUN of Canadian Pacific Airlines, crashed on take-off at Karachi, Pakistan. This occurred during the aircraft's delivery flight from London to Sydney, its intended operating base, and all eleven occupants were killed. It was stated that the accident was caused by the pilot lifting the aircraft's nose too high during take-off, thereby causing it to stall.

The first scheduled flight on BEA's London–Nicosia route, made by the Vickers Viscount V.701 *Sir Ernest Shackleton* (G-AMNY) on 18 April 1953, marked the beginning of **the world's first sustained passenger service to be operated by turboprop-powered airliners**.

The first woman in the world to fly faster than the speed of sound was Miss Jacqueline Cochran, pilot extraordinary and American cosmetics tycoon who, flying a Canadian-built version of the North American F-86 Sabre, exceeded the speed of sound on 18 May 1953, and on the same day established a world's speed record for women of 652 mph (1049 km/h).

The first US turbojet-powered transport aircraft, the Boeing Model 367-80 ('Dash-Eighty'), made its first flight as the prototype of a flight refuelling tanker/transport for the USAF on 15

Jacqueline Cochran, who became the first woman to fly faster than the speed of sound in 1953, went on to set many other aviation records. Here, she is greeted after establishing records in a Lockheed JetStar in 1962. In 1963 she flew a Starfighter to over 1,200 mph. (Lockheed)

Boeing Model 367-80, the first US jet transport. (The Boeing Company)

July 1954. Built extensively for the USAF in this form, it was to be developed simultaneously as the Boeing Model 707 civil transport, the founder member of a remarkable family of commercial transports now in worldwide use.

The first post-war landing in the UK by a German civil-registered aircraft was made on 15 April 1955. The aircraft was the Deutsche Lufthansa Convair CV-340 D-ACAD on a route proving flight. Lufthansa's first regular post-war air services to the UK began on 16 May 1955.

The first multi-engined airliner with its turbojet powerplant installed in pods, one on each side of the rear fuselage, was the French Sud-Est Aviation SE.210 Caravelle. The first of two prototypes made its maiden flight on 27 May 1955, powered by two 10 000 lb (4536 kg) thrust Rolls-Royce Avon RA.26 turbojets. This adoption of a rear-mounted engine installation was intended to ensure that the wing remained aerodynamically 'clean', free from the interference to airflow caused by wing-mounted engines and nacelles. The Caravelle was also **the first French turbojet-powered airliner.**

The first turbojet-powered airliner to enter service with Aeroflot was the Tupolev Tu-104, the prototype (SSSR-L5400) making its first flight on 15 June 1955. Its use on domestic routes was inaugurated by Aeroflot on 15 September 1956, thus the Soviet Union became the second nation in the world to introduce turbojet-powered civil transport aircraft. The use of the Tu-104 revolu-tionized Aeroflot's operations, these aircraft on long-range domestic routes providing a reduction of some 60 per cent in flight times by comparison with the piston-engined aircraft that they replaced.

The first non-stop flight by an airliner from London to Vancouver, on the Pacific Coast of Canada—a distance of 5100 miles (8208 km)— was completed by the turboprop-powered Bristol Britannia 310 G-AOVA on 29 June 1957.

The first transatlantic passenger service to be flown by turbine-powered airliners was inaugurated by BOAC on 19 December 1957, using Bristol Britannia 312 turboprop aircraft. The first flight from London to New York was by G-AOVC captained by Capt A. Meagher.

The first aircraft to be designed and built in the Chinese People's Republic, a twin-engined light transport designated Beijing (Peking) No. 1, made its first flight on 24 September 1958.

The termination of the Southampton–Madeira service of Aquila Airways, on 30 September 1958, represented **the end of UK commercial flying-boat operations.**

BOAC inaugurated the first transatlantic passenger services to be flown by a turbojet-powered airliner, the de Havilland Comet 4, on 4 October 1958. Simultaneous London–New York (Capt R. E. Millichap with G-APDC) and New York–London (Capt T. B. Stoney with G-APDB) services were flown.

Canadair CL-44D-4, with hinged tail swung open. (Canadair)

The first turbojet-powered airliner service linking South America and the UK was inaugurated by Aerolineas Argentinas on 19 May 1959, the service between Buenos Aires and London flown by a de Havilland Comet 4.

Australia's Qantas Empire Airways inaugurated its first trans-Pacific service with turbojet-powered airliners on 29 July 1959, when the Boeing 707-138 *City of Canberra* was flown from Sydney to San Francisco.

More than 30 years after being established as the hub of British civil aviation, London's Croydon Airport was finally closed down on 30 September 1959.

The first round-the-world passenger service by jet airliners was established by Pan American World Airways during October 1959. The inaugural service was flown by the Boeing 707-321 *Clipper Windward*.

The first nonstop flight between London and Bombay was recorded by a Boeing 707 during 20–21 February 1960, made during the course of the aircraft's delivery flight to Air India from the Boeing Company at Seattle, via London.

H ('Jerry') Shaw who had piloted KLM's first Amsterdam–London service on 17 May 1920, was carried as a passenger on KLM's 40th Anniversary flight on 17 May 1960.

The last scheduled service operated by a piston-engined aircraft from London Heathrow was that flown by a Douglas DC-3 on 31 October 1960. Operating on a flight from London to Birmingham, it was also the last scheduled service by a DC-3 to be flown by BEA.

The world's first aircraft to incorporate a hinged tail for rear loading, the Canadair CL-44D-4, was flown for the first time on 16 November 1960. Powered by four Rolls-Royce Tyne 515/10 two-shaft two-spool turboprops, each rated at 5730 ehp, it had a range of 5660 miles (9110 km) with a 37 300 lb (16 920 kg) payload. Its maximum payload was 66 048 lb (29 960 kg).

The first outsize transport conversion of a Boeing Stratocruiser, designed by Aero Spacelines and then designated B-377PG (later named Pregnant Guppy), made its first flight on 19 September 1962. Derived Super Guppies are used currently by Airbus Industrie to transport internationally built major assemblies of the Airbus to Toulouse for final assembly.

The first trans-Pacific solo flight by a woman was achieved between 30 April and 12 May 1963 by American Betty Miller. She flew from Oakland, California, to Brisbane, Australia, in four stages.

US airwoman Jerrie Mock became the first woman to complete a solo flight around the world when she landed at Columbus, Ohio, on 17 April 1964. This achievement had been completed in 29 days in her Cessna 180 lightplane, *Spirit of Columbus*.

Silver City Airways, which in mid-1948 had established the first UK cross-Channel car ferry, announced on 6 June 1964 that in its operations from that date a total of **one million cars had been carried between the UK and Europe.**

The McDonnell Douglas DC-9 twin-turbofan short/medium-range airliner, first flown on 25 February 1965, subsequently became **the second of the world's commercial turbine-powered airliners to exceed a sales total of 1000.**

The first British woman pilot to complete a solo round-the-world flight was Sheila Scott, who landed her Piper Comanche 260B *Myth Too* at London Heathrow on 20 June 1966. She also established a new round-the-world speed record in Class 3 and the longest solo round-the-world flight at that time of 33 d 3 min.

The delivery of a Model 707-120B to American Airlines on 5 June 1967 marked a significant milestone for The Boeing Company, this being **the 1000th jet airliner produced by the company.**

The first completely automatic approach and landing by a four-engined turbojet airliner with passengers on board was recorded by a Boeing Model 707-321B (N419PA) of Pan American Airways on 7 July 1967.

The first non-stop transatlantic flight by a turbine-powered executive jet was made on 5 May 1968. The flight from Teterboro, New Jersey, to London Gatwick, of 3500 miles (5633 km) was achieved by a Grumman Gulfstream II, powered by two Rolls-Royce Spey Mk 511-8 turbofan engines, each of 11 400 lb (5171 kg) thrust.

The world's first supersonic transport aircraft to fly was the Soviet Union's Tupolev Tu-144, the prototype of which (SSSR-68001) flew for the first time on 31 December 1968. On 26 May 1970 this prototype became the **world's first commercial transport to exceed a speed of Mach 2,** by flying at 1335 mph (2150 km/h) at a height of 53 475 ft (16 300 m). The maiden flight of the prototype was also **the first time that its Kuznetsov NK-144 turbofan engines had been tested in the air.** Then rated at 28 660 lb (13 000 kg) thrust without afterburning and 38 580 lb (17 500 kg) thrust with afterburning, the four turbofan engines of production aircraft were each rated at 44 090 lb (20 000 kg) thrust with afterburning. **Regular supersonic flights, the first in the world** by an aircraft of this category, were started by Aeroflot on 26 December

1975, but were confined to the carriage of freight and mail. The first scheduled passenger flights began on 1 November 1977 and a total of 102 flights had been made by 1 June 1978 when the service was terminated.

The world's first wide-body commercial transport aircraft was the Boeing Model 747 'jumbo-jet', the first of which flew on 9 February 1969 from Paine Field, near Seattle, Washington. The first commercial service with the 747 was inaugurated by Pan American Airways on its New York–London route on 22 January 1970. By mid-1987, a total of 677 of these aircraft had been delivered in a number of versions for the world's airlines and the USAF. In addition to standard passenger versions, combi or convertible variants are available for various and easily-changed permutations of cargo/passengers, as well as a purpose-designed freighter with a nose-loading door and a special cargo handling system. Other versions include the 747SP low-weight long-range passenger transport, and during 23–24 March 1976 one of these aircraft on delivery to South African Airways set a world record for non-stop distance flown by a commercial transport. Carrying 50 passengers, the aircraft was flown from Paine Field, Washington, to Cape Town, a distance of 10 290 miles (16 560 km). From 1 to 3 May 1976 a Pan American 747SP, commanded by Capt Walter H. Mullikin, completed a round-the-world flight in 1 d 22 h 0 min 50 s to set a round-the-world record speed of 502.84 mph (809.24 km/h). A 747SR short-range version was also made available.

The world's first supersonic commercial transport to operate regular scheduled passenger services is the British Aircraft Corporation/ Aérospatiale Concorde. The Aérospatiale 001 prototype made its first flight on 2 March 1969, and the BAC 002 flew for the first time on 9 April 1969. The Concorde test programme was the most comprehensive ever undertaken for a civil airliner, involving eight flight test aircraft plus two airframes for structural ground testing. Just prior to the type's entry into service, test aircraft had flown more than 5500 hours, of which more than 2000 hours were at supersonic speed. In route proving, test and demonstration flights, Concordes had then landed at 83 airports in 49 countries and had flown more than 5 million miles (8 million km). **The first passenger services were operated** on 21 January 1976, when simul-

Right   *The first Boeing Model 747, the world's first wide-body commercial airliner. (The Boeing Company)*

Below   *French prototype Concorde supersonic airliner. In 1988 Concorde remains the only aircraft (military or civil) to fly daily, and for most of its time while airborne, at supersonic speed.*

taneous take-offs were made by Air France's 205 from Paris to Rio de Janeiro, via Dakar, and British Airways' 206 from London to Bahrain. Prior to that, on 1 September 1975, the fourth production Concorde became **the first aircraft in the world to record two return transatlantic flights (London–Gander–London), or four transatlantic crossings in a single day**. Due to different forms of opposition, primarily from environmentalists, it was not until 22 November 1977 that Air France and British Airways were able to inaugurate services to New York.

The world's first scheduled jet service within the Arctic circle was inaugurated by Nordair on 19 March 1969, providing a weekly return service between Montreal, Canada, and Resolution Bay, Cornwallis Island.

The Daily Mail Transatlantic Air Race, held between 4 and 11 May 1969 to celebrate the 50th anniversary of the first non-stop crossing of the North Atlantic by Alcock and Brown, required the winner to record the shortest time to travel from the top of the Post Office Tower, London, to the top of the Empire State Building, New York. It was won by Lt Cdr Brian Davis, RN, flying in the reverse direction in a McDonnell Douglas Phantom II. His time of 4 h 46 min 57 s for the Atlantic crossing was then a record, and his point to point winning time was a remarkable 5 h 11 min.

The first airline in the world to introduce an inertial navigation system (INS) on scheduled passenger services was Finnair, on 20 October 1969, so dispensing with a navigator in the flight crew. In simple terms, an INS combines gyroscopes and accelerometers that provide data to a computer, and this in turn integrates the linear displacement from the start of the flight. Since the starting point is known, the INS can provide the exact position of the aircraft at all times, without any reference to an outside source.

An England–Australia Commemorative Air Race began on 18 December 1969, sponsored to mark the 50th anniversary of the first England–Australia flight by the brothers Ross and Keith Smith, as well as the bi-centenary of the discovery of Australia. It was won by Capts W. J. Bright and F. L. Buxton, flying the Britten-Norman BN-2A Islander G-AXUD.

The world's first all-paper man-carrying aircraft, assembled from paper, glue and masking tape as an aeronautical teaching aid at Ohio State University, flew on three occasions in August 1970. Towed into the air by a motor car, the all-paper glider had no wheels, but slid over the grass field on a fuselage undersurface of waxed corrugated paper. Maximum airspeed recorded was approximately 60 mph (96 km/h).

The first round-the-world cargo service was inaugurated by Trans-Mediterranean Airways on 14 April 1971.

In the course of its development programme, the French-built **Concorde 001 prototype made its first completely automatic approach and landing** at Toulouse on 13 May 1971.

During the period 11 June to 4 August 1971, the British airwoman Sheila Scott, flying a Piper Aztec D, achieved the **first flight to be made by a lightplane from Equator to Equator via the North Pole.**

In early May 1972, the Cessna Aircraft Company became **the first aircraft manufacturer in the world** to deliver its 100 000th production aircraft. Ten years later the figure had risen to the remarkable total of almost 172 000 aircraft, but this rate of acceleration has since fallen as a result of a recession in general avaiation activities and US liability laws. By the end of 1986 the total had risen to only 176,819 aircraft.

The Boeing Company announced on 22 September 1972 that with the receipt of its most recent order for the Model 727, placed by Delta Air Lines, this aircraft had become **the first jet-powered airliner in the world to reach a sales total of 1000.**

The first wide-body commercial transport aircraft produced by the aircraft industry of Europe was the Airbus Industrie A300 Airbus, the first example of which (F-WUAB) made its maiden flight on 28 October 1972. Bought initially by Air France, it entered service with this airline on its Paris–London route on 23 May 1974. A truly international project, the A300 is built primarily by Aérospatiale of France, Deutsche Airbus of Germany, Fokker in the Netherlands, CASA in Spain and British Aerospace in the United Kingdom; other European countries are also involved in some sub-contract work. A variant flown on 6 October 1981 was **the first wide-body transport aircraft in the world to be specially equipped for operation by a two-man flight crew**, and certification in this configuration was gained on 8 January 1982.

During its development programme, an Airbus Industrie A300B Airbus prototype recorded **the first fully automatic approach and landing to be made by the type**, on 8 May 1973.

The first no-booking guaranteed-seat air shuttle service in Europe was inaugurated on 12 January 1975 by British Airways. Operated by Hawker Siddeley Trident I airliners, it linked London Heathrow and Glasgow Airport, Scotland.

The first solo Australia–England flight in an aircraft of amateur construction was completed on 1 July 1976. This was achieved by Clive Canning, flying his home-built Thorp T-18 Tiger, a two-seat all-metal sporting aircraft for which more than 1300 sets of plans were sold. Just one month later, on 1 August 1976, Don Taylor set out to make a round-the-world flight in his Thorp T-18. This was completed successfully on 30 September 1976, the distance of 24 627 miles (39 633 km) completed in 171.5 flying hours, his T-18 becoming **the first home-built aircraft to circumnavigate the world.**

The prototype of the Il-86, **the Soviet Union's**

first wide-body jet transport aircraft, made its first flight from the old Moscow Central Airport of Khodinka on 22 December 1976. The Il-86, which has the NATO reporting-name *Camber*, is powered by four pylon-mounted Kuznetsov NK-86 turbofan engines, each of 28 660 lb (13 000 kg) thrust. With accommodation for up to 350 passengers, the aircraft is unusual in having three low-level airstair-type doors, through which passengers can enter at ground level to leave their coats and hand baggage on the lower deck, before climbing one of the three fixed staircases to the main cabin.

On 18 April 1978 the Vickers Viscount became **the first turbine-powered airliner to complete a quarter-century of regular commercial airline service**.

The first crossing of the English Channel by a powered hang-glider was recorded on 9 May 1978 by David Cook flying a Volmer VJ-23 Swingwing. Its McCulloch MC-101B piston engine had been installed by David Cook, enabling him to complete the crossing from Walmer Castle, Deal, to Blériot Plage, France, in a flying time of 1 hr 15 min.

The de Havilland Comet 4C G-BDIW made the **last revenue flight of the type** from London Gatwick Airport on 9 November 1980. Just over 31 years earlier, on 27 July 1949, the Comet I prototype had made its first flight. Early development flying and initial in-service use suggested that Britain had a world-beating aircraft that would be built in large numbers. Unfortunately for de Havilland this failed to materialize, and it was the Boeing Model 707 and its successors that captured the lion's share of the commercial market for jet airliners.

A woman's solo flight record between England and Australia was set by British pilot Judith Chisholm between 18 and 21 November 1980, flying a Cessna Turbo Centurion cabin monoplane. Although her 3 d 13 h record reflected the very considerable improvement in aircraft and facilities from the time that Jean Batten set the previous record, this in no way detracted from her achievement. She then set out from Australia to complete a solo round-the-world flight, landing back at London Heathrow on 3 December 1980. Judith Chisholm thus established a woman's solo round-the-world flight record of 15 d 22 min 30 s, halving the time set by Sheila Scott in 1966.

After operating the Boeing 707 for just over 22 years, Pan American Airways flew its last revenue service with this type of aircraft on 26 January 1981.

Offering large potential savings in fuel costs, an Avco Lycoming engine was modified to operate with liquefied petroleum gas (LPG). Installed in a SOCATA TB 10 Tobago lightplane, this engine became airborne for the first time on 15 May 1982.

The first flight across the Mediterranean by a microlight took place on 22 May 1983, by a French Aviasud Sirocco.

On 26 October 1958, Pan American inaugurated its first transatlantic services Boeing Model 707 jet airliner. Twenty-five years later, on 26 October 1983, this same route between New York and Le Bourget, France, was retraced by a 707 repainted in original colour scheme.

The first round-the-world flight by a microlight was completed in stages between September 1984 and March 1987 by Frenchman Patrice Franceschi in an Aviasud Sirocco. The 27 960 miles (45 000 km) took about 700 actual flying hours.

The first airliner to fly with a propfan engine was a Boeing Model 727-100 testbed aircraft, which carried a General Electric UDF (unducted fan) engine with two eight-blade fans of about 11 ft (3.35 m) diameter on its starboard side. This first flight took place on 20 August 1986.

The first aeroplane to fly around the world non-stop and unrefuelled was the Voyager Aircraft Inc *Voyager*, between 14 and 23 December 1986, a trimaran monoplane with high aspect ratio wings and constructed of composite materials that included Magnamite graphite and Hexcel honeycomb. Crewed on its 9 d 3 min 44 s westbound flight from and back to Edwards Air Force Base by Dick Rutan and Jeana Yeager, *Voyager* established world absolute distance in a straight line and closed circuit records by an aeroplane, of 24 986.664 miles (40 212.139 km).

Largest and Smallest:

The largest aeroplane to lift itself off the ground briefly in the 19th century was designed and built by Sir Hiram Maxim (1840–1916). Basically a biplane test rig with 4000 ft² (372 m²) of lifting area, it was powered by two 180 hp steam engines and ran along a railway track 1800 ft (550 m) long which was fitted with wooden restraining guard-rails to prevent the machine from rising too high.

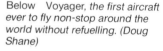

Left   *This Boeing Model 727-100 was the world's first airliner flown with a propfan engine.*

Below   *Voyager, the first aircraft ever to fly non-stop around the world without refuelling. (Doug Shane)*

On 31 July 1894, during a test run, the machine lifted about 2 ft (60 cm) before fouling the guardrails and coming to rest.

The largest flying-boat built between the wars was the Dornier Do X, the prototype of which made its maiden flight on 25 July 1929, at which time it was also **the largest aeroplane of any kind in the world**. Powered by 12 engines (initially 525 hp Siemens Jupiters, later 600 hp Curtiss Conquerors), mounted in tandem pairs on the 157 ft 5¾ in (48.00 m) monoplane wing, the Do X once carried (on 21 October 1929) a crew of ten and 159 passengers (nine of whom were stowaways). Altogether three Do Xs were built. The most famous flight was that made by the prototype from Germany to New York, which took from 2 November 1930 to 27 August 1931 because of damage to the wing and hull and lengthy stops at various places including Amsterdam, Calshot, Lisbon, the Canary Islands, Portuguese Guinea and Rio de Janeiro. In commercial terms the Do X was quite impracticable, and the two examples delivered to an Italian airline were never put into service. Although it had a respectable maximum speed of 134 mph (216 km/h), the Do X weighed 123 460 lb (56 000 kg) with full load and had a service ceiling of 1640 ft (500 m).

The world's largest aeroplane is the Soviet Antonov An-124 (NATO name *Condor*). The first prototype flew initially on 26 December 1982.

Production examples began operations with Aeroflot as long-range heavy-lift freighters in 1986 and military service is thought to have started in the following year. Powered by four 51 590 lb (23 400 kg) thrust Lotarev D-18T turbofans, it has a wing span of 240 ft 5¾ in (73.30 m), length of 226 ft 8½ in (69.10 m), a gross weight of 892 872 lb (405 000 kg), and can carry a 330 693 lb (150 000 kg) payload.

The world's smallest aeroplane is the *Baby Bird*, designed and built by Mr Don Stits. Flown in 1987 by retired US Navy pilot, Commander Harold Nemer, it is an unbraced high-wing monoplane

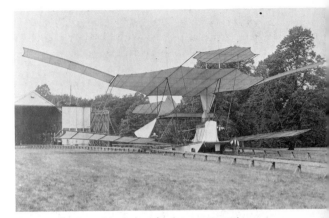

Above *Sir Hiram Maxim's epic steam-powered aeroplane of the 1890s, at Baldwyn's Park.*

Below *Dornier Do X at New York in 1931.*

Above *The largest aeroplane ever flown was the Hughes H4, which made a single flight of one mile duration (1.6 km), at an altitude of 70–80 ft (21–24 m), over Los Angeles Harbor on 2 November 1947. Funded and piloted by Howard Hughes, it reportedly cost him over $22 million to complete. Its wing span was 320 ft (97.54 m) and length 219 ft (66.75 m). Take off weight stood at 400,000 lb (181,436 kg).*

Left *Baby Bird, the world's smallest aeroplane to have flown. (Courtesy of Don Stits)*

with a wood and welded steel tube structure, fabric covered. Wing span is 6 ft 3 in (1.91 m), length 11 ft (3.35 m) and empty weight 252 lb (114 kg).

Fastest:

The world's first speed record over 100 km was established by the Englishman, Hubert Latham, during the Reims International Meeting between 22 and 29 August 1909. Flying an Antoinette (powered by a 50 hp eight-cylinder Antoinette engine) he covered the distance in 1 h 28 min 17 s, at an average speed of 42 mph (67 km/h). In so doing he won the second largest prize of the meeting amounting to 42 000 francs. Latham also won the altitude competition by reaching 508 ft (155 m). First prize went to Henry Farman who, flying a Gnôme-powered Farman, set up new world records for duration and distance in a closed circuit, covering 111.847 miles (180 km) in 3 h 4 min 56.4 s, winning 63 000 francs.

The first 'over 200 km/h' world speed record was set by Frenchman Maurice Prévost in the Deperdussin 'monocoque' of 1913 at Reims on 29 September 1913, at 126.666 mph (203.850 km/h). This was officially the fastest aircraft prior to the First World War, as no further records were set until 1920.

One of the most enduring speed records was that set on 23 October 1934 by Italian Francesco Agello flying a Macchi MC72 seaplane. Still unbeaten in 1988, this world speed record of 440.683 mph (709.209 km/h) in FAI sub-class C-2 was achieved in the Macchi seaplane which had been intended to compete in the Schneider Trophy Contest of 1931.

The current world speed in a closed circuit record for turboprop-powered aeroplanes is held by a Soviet Tupolev Tu-114, having attained 545.07 mph (877.212 km/h) on 9 April 1960. Piloted by Ivan Sukhomlin, the airliner was carrying a 25 000 kg payload.

Above *Probably the best remembered racing aeroplanes of all time were the two Gee Bee Super Sportsters of the 1930s, designed on the concept of the smallest airframe around the largest engine. On 3 September 1932, Major James H. Doolittle flew the Super Sportster R-1 to a record 294.418 mph (473.820 km/h) during the US National Air Races in Cleveland. Both the R-1 and R-2 (shown) eventually crashed, killing their pilots. Power was provided by a 730 hp Pratt & Whitney T3D1 radial piston engine.*

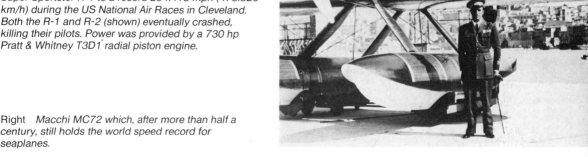

Right *Macchi MC72 which, after more than half a century, still holds the world speed record for seaplanes.*

The current world speed in a straight line record for piston-engined aeroplanes is held by American Frank Taylor in a modified Rolls-Royce/Packard Merlin V-1650-9 engined North American P-51D Mustang, at 517.06 mph (832.12 km/h). This was set on 30 July 1983.

The current world speed around the world record for jet-powered aeroplanes was established during 13–15 February 1984 by a Gulfstream III, piloted by American Brooke Knapp, at 512.83 mph (825.32 km/h).

The current world speed in a straight line record for microlights stands at 117.57 mph (189.21 km/h), set on 23 October 1935 by American David Green in a Monnett Moni.

The world's fastest flexwing aircraft is the British Pegasus Transport System Pegasus Flash microlight, which uses a 35 ft (10.67 m) flexwing and 39.4 hp Rotax 447 engine to achieve a cruising speed of 79 mph (127 km/h) and never-exceed speed of 88 mph (142 km/h).

Highest:

The first flight at an altitude of 1000 m (3280 ft) was achieved by Hubert Latham on 7 January 1910 at Châlons, France, flying an Antoinette VII monoplane.

The first pilot to fly at a height of over 1 mile was American Walter Brookins on 10 July 1910, when he piloted a Wright biplane at Indianapolis to about 6230 ft (1900 m).

The current world altitude record for piston-engined aeroplanes stands at 56 046 ft (17 083 m), established on 22 October 1938 by an Italian Caproni Ca 161*bis*.

The current world altitude record for microlights stands at 25 940 ft (7906.5 m), set by American Richard J. Rowley in a Mitchell U-2 Superwing.

Longest:

The longest flight by the end of 1908 was by

Wilbur Wright on 31 December 1908, at Camp d'Auvours, where he achieved a stupendous 77 miles (124 km) in 2 h 20 min. This won for him the Michelin prize of 20 000 francs—apart from breaking all his own records. Details of the longest flights made by Wilbur Wright in 1908 follow below, together with a list of the more significant flights made by other aviators that year.

The airline with the longest continuous record of scheduled services, Aerovias Nacionales de Colombia SA (Avianca), was founded on 5 December 1919.

The longest association of a navigator and pilot must be that recorded by William G. Crooks, who retired from regular communication flights for Hawker Siddeley Aviation on 30 June 1974. After service in the RAF from March 1942, he first crewed with pilot R. J. Chandler in April 1948. From then, until his retirement, William Crooks recorded 6554 h as navigator/radio operator on flights with R. J. Chandler.

The current world distance in a straight line record for seaplanes was established by Capt D. C. T. Bennett and 1st Officer I. Harvey in the Short-Mayo *Mercury* during 6–8 October 1938, at 5997.5 miles (9652 km). The flight, which began in Dundee, Scotland, ended at the Orange River, South Africa.

Farthest travelling amateur-constructed aircraft is almost certainly the original Volmer VJ-22 Sportsman two-seat amphibian designed by Volmer Jensen in the United States. First flown on 22 December 1958, it has since logged more than 1840 flying hours, covering a total distance equal to six times round the world.

The current world distance in a straight line record for microlights stands at 776.42 miles (1249.52 km), set by American Norman Howell in a Quickie on 9 April 1987.

The current world distance in a closed circuit record for jet-powered aeroplanes was set

---

Wilbur Wright

14 May 1908	Kill Devil Hills	5 miles	(8 km)	In 7 min 29 s.
8 August 1908	Hunaudières, France	—	—	Demonstration flight 1 min 45 s.
16 September 1908	Auvours, France	—	—	Flight taking 39 min 18 s.
21 September 1908	Auvours, France	41⅓ miles	(66.5 km)	First major endurance flight. Flew more than 100 times at this location.
3 October 1908	Auvours, France	34¾ miles	(56 km)	In 55 min 37 s.
10 October 1908	Auvours, France	46 miles	(74 km)	In 1 h 9 min 45 s, with M. Painleve as passenger.
18 December 1908	Auvours, France	62 miles	(99.8 km)	In 1 h 54 min 53 s. Climbed to 330 ft (100 m) to establish new altitude record.
31 December 1908	Auvours, France	77 miles	(124 km)	In 2 hr 20 min 23 s, to win Michelin prize and set up new world record.

Léon Delagrange

11 April 1908	Covered over 2½ miles (3.9 km) at Issy-les-Moulineaux.
23 June 1908	Covered 8¾ miles (14.08 km) in 18 min 30 s at Milan, Italy.
6 September 1908	Covered 15¼ miles (24.4 km) in 29 min 53 s at Issy-les-Moulineaux.
17 September 1908	Flight lasting 30 min 27 s at Issy-les-Moulineaux.

Henry Farman

13 January 1908	Covered a 1 km circuit in 1 min 28 s at Issy-les-Molineaux.
6 July 1908	Covered 12½ miles (20 km) in 20 min 20 s.
30 October 1908	Covered 17 miles (27.3 km) in 20 min on cross-country flight from Châlons to Reims.

Glenn H. Curtiss

4 July 1908	Covered 5090 ft (1550 m) in 1 min 42 s to win *Scientific American* trophy.

Volmer Jensen's VJ-22 Sportsman amphibian.

during 6–7 May 1987 by a Soviet Antonov An-124 piloted by Vladimir Terski, at 12 521.201 miles (20 150.921 km).

Greatest:

The world's greatest air tragedy occurred on 27 March 1977 when, in conditions of bad visibility, two Boeing 747s collided on the runway at Santa Cruz Tenerife, killing 583 people.

The commercial transport aircraft with the world's greatest sales total is the Boeing 737 twin-turbofan short-range airliner, which had received 1842 confirmed orders by 15 June 1987. This beat by one the previous record set by the Boeing Model 727 three-turbofan short/medium-range airliner.

The current world record for payload lifted to 2000 m stands at 377 473 lb (171 219 kg), set by a Soviet Antonov An-124 on 26 July 1985. The pilot was Vladimir Terski. (See also Largest.)

Most and Oldest:

Eleven passengers were first carried in an aeroplane on 23 March 1911 by Louis Breguet over a distance of 3.1 miles (5 km) at Douai, France, in a huge aircraft of his own design. **Twelve passengers were first carried in an aeroplane** on 24 March 1911 by Roger Sommer over a distance of 2625 ft (800 m) in a Sommer biplane powered by a 70 hp engine.

The oldest airline route still operated by the original airline company is the London–Amsterdam service which was first flown by KLM (Royal Dutch Airlines) on 17 May 1920. The aircraft used for the pioneer flight was an Eagle-engined DH16 (G-EALU) of Aircraft Transport and Travel, piloted by H. 'Jerry' Shaw. After that date, all early KLM services were operated by this British airline under charter.

The only mass hijacking of civil airliners involved a BOAC VC10, Swissair Douglas DC-8 and TWA Boeing Model 707. These were flown to a desert airstrip in Jordan known as Dawson's Field where, on 12 December 1970, they were destroyed by Palestinian guerillas.

The Boeing Company recorded a major production milestone on 3 August 1981, when the delivery of a Model 727-200 for service with Ansett Airlines of Australia represented the 4000th production jetliner to be delivered by the company.

The oldest airworthy airliner is a Fokker F.VIIA, on which the Aviadome Dutch national museum was to complete restoration in 1989.

Air Warfare and Military Aviation

Most aviation enthusiasts are all too easily 'hooked' by the excitement generated by military aviation, its subtle combination of speed, noise and spectacle too attractive to resist. It has always been so, the devotees gathering at air shows that began in the early days of flight and which, apart from the gap of a decade caused by two world wars, have continued unbroken to this day. Orville Wright is reported as saying in 1917: 'When my brother and I built and flew the first man-carrying flying machine, we thought that we were introducing into the world an invention which would make further wars practically impossible. What a dream it was; what a nightmare it has become.' In retrospect this seems somewhat naïve, for since time immemorial man has adapted for warlike purposes any invention which could speed his legs, extend the reach of his arms, or enhance his vision to ascertain the movements of his enemies. Following this line of thought, perhaps the earliest recorded adaptation of a flying machine for military use was some 200 years before the birth of Christ, when the Chinese General Han Hsin is reported to have used kites to measure the distance between his troops and an enemy position. There are many references to European use of kites during the 14th and 15th centuries to drop bombs on enemy strongholds, and only about a decade after the first manned flight (tethered) of a hot-air balloon this new aircraft had also been adopted for war use (observation, June 1794) and 55 years later bomb dropping (unmanned hot-air, 22 August 1849).

The wrecked Wright in which Lt Thomas Etholen Selfridge was killed, 17 September 1908.

Almost certainly the concentrated thought which the Wright brothers put into the realization of powered flight left little time for them to learn about the military use of balloons, and it is interesting to record the amazing speed of development of *The Flyer*. The real effort can be dated from 30 May 1899 when Wilbur wrote to the Smithsonian Institute asking for papers on aviation and details of books on the subject. 'I wish', he wrote, 'to avail myself of all that is already known and then if possible add my mite to help on the future worker who will attain final success.' Wilbur and Orville were to be the workers, flying an experimental wing-warping kite on 2 August 1899, their No. 1 glider in 1900, No. 2 in 1901, No. 3 in 1902 and *The Flyer* at the end of 1903.

This section details the major events of the brief 85 years that separate the Wright *Flyer* from the supersonic fighter of 1988. Highlights of the first half of this period must be the development of powerplants during the First World War, the Schneider Trophy Contests of 1913 to 1931 which inspired new structures and engines for high-speed flight, the introduction of gas turbines, radar and new weapon systems during the Second World War, climaxed by the awesome power of the nuclear weapons dropped over the Japanese cities of Hiroshima and Nagasaki on 6 and 9 August 1945 respectively. Tragically some 120 000 people were killed in these two attacks, a figure which must since have climbed higher as others died from the effects of exposure to radiation. If there is any justification for such a scale of human sacrifice, perhaps it can be found in recently declassified American planning documents for Operation 'Downfall', the invasion of Japan which had been scheduled to begin on 1 November 1945 (X-Day) with preliminary small-scale landings four days earlier. With Japan's home defence troops augmented by some 28 million members of the Japanese National Volunteer Combat Force, US planners anticipated the possible loss of 1 million of their troops, and with perhaps a minimum 2 million Japanese lives being lost before the nation would be forced to surrender.

Since 1946 the threat of all-out nuclear war has been sufficient to ensure an uneasy peace between East and West. But if recent efforts to reduce the number of nuclear missiles in the world's armouries eventually mature to eliminate all such weapons, it seems likely that military aviation will regain the importance that it held before the late 1950s, when missiles began to assume wide-scale use for combat, defence and strategic roles. If so, the aviation enthusiasts are likely to remain 'hooked' for many years to come . . . and enjoy every minute of it.

Firsts:

The first aerial bombers were bomb-carrying pennon kites, first illustrated in Europe in 1326.

The first contract for a military aeroplane was awarded to Clément Ader on 3 February 1892, to construct a two-seater capable of lifting a bomb-load of 165 lb (75 km). This contract was not fulfilled, as the aeroplane failed to fly at Satorg, France, on 14 October 1897.

The first specification for a military aeroplane ever issued for commercial tender was drawn up by Brig-Gen James Allen, Chief Signal Officer of the US Army, on 23 December 1907. The specification (main points) was as follows:

☐ Drawings to scale showing general dimensions, shape, designed speed, total surface area of supporting planes, weight, description of the engine and materials.

☐ The flying machine should be quick and easy to assemble and should be able to be taken apart and packed for transportation.

☐ Must be designed to carry two persons having a combined weight of about 350 lb and sufficient fuel for a flight of 125 miles.

☐ Should be designed to have a speed of at least 40 mph in still air.

☐ The speed accomplished during the trial flight will be determined by taking an average of the time over a measured course of more than 5 miles, against and with the wind.

☐ Before acceptance a trial endurance flight will be required of at least 1 h.

☐ Three trials will be allowed for speed. The place for delivery to the Government and trial flights will be Fort Myer, Virginia.

☐ It should be designed to ascend in any country which may be encountered in field service. The starting device must be simple and transportable. It should also land in a field without requiring a specially prepared spot, and without damaging its structure.

☐ It should be provided with some device to permit of a safe descent in case of an accident to the propelling machine.

☐ It should be sufficiently simple in its construction and operation to permit an intelligent man to become proficient in its use within a reasonable length of time.

The first tenders accepted by the US Army for military aeroplanes were received on 6 February 1908. These came from A. Herring, the Wright brothers and J. Scott. Contracts for these aircraft were signed four days later but only the Wright brothers eventually delivered an aeroplane for testing. Interestingly, on 15 February Captain Thomas Baldwin's tender for the US Army's first dirigible was delivered.

The first fatality to the occupant of a powered aeroplane occurred on 17 September 1908 at Fort Myer, Virginia, when a Wright biplane flown by Orville Wright crashed killing the passenger, Lt Thomas Etholen Selfridge, US Army Signal Corps. Wright was seriously injured. The accident happened during US Army acceptance trials of the Wright biplane and was caused by a failure in one of the propeller blades. This imbalanced the good blade, which tore loose one of the wires bracing the rudder-outriggers to the wings, and so sending the aircraft crashing to the ground from about 75 ft (925 m).

The first officially recognized aeroplane flight in Great Britain was made by the American (later naturalized British citizen) Samuel Franklin Cody in his *British Army Aeroplane No. 1*, powered by a 50 hp Antoinette engine. The flight of 1390 ft (424 m) was made at Farnborough, Hampshire, on 16 October 1908 and ended with a crash-landing, but without physical injury to Cody.

The first aeroplane flight of more than one mile in Britain was achieved on 14 May 1909 by Samuel Cody, who flew the *British Army Aeroplane No. 1* from Laffan's Plain to Danger Hill, Hampshire—a distance of just over 1 mile—and landed without incident. The Prince of Wales requested a repeat performance during the same afternoon, but Cody, turning to avoid some troops, crashed into an embankment and demolished the tail of his aeroplane.

Following the fatal accident of 17 September 1908, it was not until 27 July 1909 that Orville Wright (with Lieutenant Frank P. Lahm as passenger) was able to record at Fort Myer **the first official test of the US Army's first aeroplane**. During this flight a new two-man endurance record was established of 1 h 12 min 40 s. The second test was carried out on 30 July, the Army's Wright completing successfully the required 10 mile (16 km) cross-country flight.

The first aeroplane procured for service with the US Army was the Wright Model A biplane which, following satisfactory completion of the acceptance tests mentioned above, was accepted officially on 2 August 1909. Its basic price was $25 000, but as the cross-country flight had been completed at an average speed of 42.58 mph the Wright brothers were awarded a stipulated bonus of 10 per cent for each mile-per-hour in excess of 40, making the purchase price $30 000.

The first man to drop missiles from an aeroplane was Lt Paul Beck on 19 January 1910, when he released sandbags (representing bombs) over Los Angeles from an aeroplane piloted by Louis

Left *The British Army Aeroplane No 1 was methodically improved, leading to substantial increases in performance and flights of over 40 miles (64 km).*

Right *Ely leaves the deck of USS* Birmingham *on 14 November 1910 and the aircraft carrier for aeroplanes is born, but all hold their breath as he dives seaward while gaining flying speed. (US Navy)*

Far right *Ely completes the 'double' by making the first-ever landing on board a ship, this time the USS* Pennsylvania. *(US Navy)*

Paulhan. On 30 June, the same year, Glenn Hammond Curtiss dropped dummy bombs from a height of 50 ft (15 m) on the shape of a battleship marked by buoys on Lake Keuka.

The first military pilot to get the Brevet of the Aéro-Club de France was Lt Camerman on 7 March 1910, receiving Brevet No. 33.

The first French reconnaissance flight was undertaken by Lt Féquant in a Henry Farman biplane on 9 June 1910. The following day a Wright biplane was accepted into French Army service.

The first naval officer in the world to learn to fly was Lt G. C. Colmore, Royal Navy, who took flying lessons on the Short S.26 biplane at Eastchurch, England, at his own expense and was awarded British Pilot's Certificate No. 15 on 21 June 1910.

The first German active duty officer to receive a Pilot's Licence was Lt Richard von Tiedemann, a Hussar officer. He first flew solo on 23 July 1910.

The first patent for a device to allow a fixed machine-gun to be fired from an aeroplane was granted to German August Euler on 24 July 1910. Euler, who had also been **the first man in Germany to gain a pilot's licence**, later demonstrated his machine-gun mount on his biplane *Gelber Hund*.

The first military firearm to be fired from an aeroplane was a rifle used by Lt Jacob Earl Fickel, US Army, from a two-seater Curtiss biplane at a target at Sheepshead Bay, New York City, on 20 August 1910.

The first aeroplane to take off from a ship was a Curtiss biplane flown by Eugene B. Ely from an 83 ft (25 m) platform built over the bows of the American light cruiser USS *Birmingham*, 3750 tons (3810 tonnes), on 14 November 1910. It has often been averred that the vessel was anchored at the time of take-off; this is not correct as it had been proposed to take off as the ship steamed at 20 knots into the wind. In the event, the *Birmingham* had weighed anchor in Hampton Roads, Virginia, but, impatient to take off, Ely gave the signal to release his aircraft at 15.16 h before the ship was under way. With only 57 ft (17 m) of platform ahead of the Curtiss, the aircraft flew off but touched the water and damaged its propeller; the pilot managed to maintain control and landed at Willoughby Spit, 2½ miles (4 km) distant. As Ely became airborne from the cruiser, the *Birmingham* sent an historic radio message 'Ely's just gone.'

The first torpedo drop from an aeroplane was achieved in 1911 by the Italian Capitano Guidoni, flying a Farman biplane. The torpedo weighed 352 lb (160 kg).

The first explosive bombs deployed from the air by American pilots were those dropped by Lt Myron Sidney Crissy and Philip O. Parmalee, from a Wright biplane, during trials on 7 January 1911 at San Francisco, California.

The first aeroplane to land on a ship was also a Curtiss biplane flown by Ely, on 18 January 1911, when he landed on a 119 ft 4 in (36 m) long platform constructed over the stern of the American armoured cruiser, USS *Pennsylvania*, 13 680 tons (13 900 tonnes), anchored in San Francisco Bay.

It had been intended that the vessel would be under way during the landing, but the Captain considered that there was insufficient sea space to manoeuvre and the *Pennsylvania* remained at anchor. Despite landing downwind the Curtiss rolled to a stop at 11.01 h after a run of only 30 ft (9 m). Capt C. F. Pond is reputed to have remarked that 'this is the most important landing of a bird since the dove flew back to the Ark'. After lunch Ely successfully took off again from the *Pennsylvania* at 11.58 h and returned to his airfield near San Francisco.

The first aeroplane to perform a premeditated landing on water, taxi and then take off was a Curtiss 'hydroaeroplane' flown by Glenn Curtiss on 26 January 1911. He took off and then landed in San Diego Harbor, turned round and took off again, flying about 1 mile (1.6 km) before coming down near his starting point. A Curtiss A-1 'hydroaeroplane' was the US Navy's first aeroplane, first flown on 1 July 1911.

The first time an aeroplane was used in war was on 22 October 1911 when an Italian Blériot, piloted by Capitano Piazza, Italian Air Flotilla, made a reconnaissance flight from Tripoli to Azizia to view the Turkish positions.

The first bombs dropped from an aeroplane in war were small Cipelli grenades, hand-released from an Italian Air Flotilla aircraft (piloted by 2nd Lt Giulio Gavotti) over Turkish positions at Taguira Oasis and Ain Zara, on 1 November 1911.

The first single-seat scout aeroplane was the Farnborough BS1 of 1912, which was designed

mainly by Geoffrey de Havilland. Powered by a 100 hp Gnome rotary engine, this very advanced aeroplane demonstrated a speed of over 91 mph (147 km/h) over a mile course.

Another Farnborough aeroplane, the BE1, made **the first successful artillery-spotting flight** over Salisbury Plain in 1912.

The first officer of the Royal Navy to take off from a ship in an aeroplane was Lt Charles Rumney Samson who is said to have made a secret flight in a Short biplane from a platform on the bows of the British battleship, HMS *Africa*, 17 500 tons (17 780 tonnes), moored in Sheerness Harbour during December 1911. His first officially recorded take-off was from HMS *Africa* at 14.20 h on 10 January 1912, flying a Short S.38 biplane. Cdr Samson was appointed Officer Commanding the Naval Wing of the Royal Flying Corps in October 1912.

The first instance of a government ordering the grounding of a specific type of aircraft occurred in March 1912 when the French government ordered all Blériot monoplanes of the French Army to be prohibited from flying until they had been rebuilt so that their wings were braced to withstand a degree of negative-G. Five distinguished French pilots had been killed following the collapse of the Blériot's wings, but the ban was short-lived and the aircraft were flying again within a fortnight. The weakness was spotlighted by Louis Blériot himself who, despite the likely loss of prestige, published a short report explaining the weakness in his own aeroplanes. There is no doubt that his frankness increased—

Historic first, as Capitano Piazza stands in front of the Blériot that became the very first aeroplane used in war. (Italian Air Force)

rather than detracted from—his very high standing in aviation circles.

The first pilot in the world to take off in an aeroplane from a ship under way was Cdr Samson, who took off in a Short pusher biplane amphibian from the forecastle of the battleship HMS *Hibernia* while it steamed at 10.5 knots off Portland during the Naval Review on 9 May 1912. At the conclusion of the Review, Cdr Samson was one of the officers commanded to dine with HM King George V on board the *Victoria and Albert*.

The first American aeroplane armed with a machine-gun was a Wright Model B biplane flown by Lt Thomas de Witt Milling at College Park, Maryland, on 2 June 1912. The gunner, who was armed with a Lewis gun, was Capt Charles de Forest Chandler of the US Army Signal Corps.

The first military aeroplane trials to be held in Great Britain took place at Larkhill, Salisbury Plain, in August 1912. The most important section, the speed competition, was won by Samuel Franklin Cody flying his primitive *Cathedral* biplane. Of about 30 British and French aircraft that took part, the most advanced was the Farnborough BE2, a development of the BE1.

The first use of US Army Signals Corps aeroplanes during army manoeuvres was recorded on 10 August 1912.

The first pilot to perform, recover from and demonstrate recovery from a spin was Lt Wilfred Parke, Royal Navy, on 25 August 1912 while flying the Avro cabin tractor biplane during the Military Trials of that year. On this occasion Parke and his observer, Lt Le Breton, RFC, were flying at about 600 ft (183 m) and commenced a spiral glide prior to landing; finding that the glide was too steep, Park pulled the stick back, promptly stalled and entered a spin. With no established procedure in mind for recovery he attempted to extricate himself from danger by pulling the stick further back and applying rudder *into* the direction of spin, and found that the spin merely tightened. After carefully noting this phenomenon he decided, *when only 50 ft (15 m) from the ground*—and from disaster—to reverse the rudder, and the machine recovered instantly. Parke was able to give a carefully reasoned résumé of his corrective actions, thereby contributing immeasurably to the progress of aviation.

Above   *Cdr Charles Rumney Samson rises from HMS Hibernia to record the first ever aeroplane flight from a moving ship. (Short Brothers)*

Below   *Capt Charles de Forest Chandler holds the Lewis that put him in the record books for being the first person to fire a machine-gun from an aeroplane.*

The first officer of the Royal Flying Corps Reserves to be killed while engaged on military flying duties was 2nd Lt E. Hotchkiss (the Bristol Company's Chief Flying Instructor at Brooklands) who, with Lt C. A. Bettington, was killed on 10 September 1912 when their Bristol monoplane crashed on a flight from Salisbury Plain. The aircraft suffered a structural failure, after which the wing fabric started to tear away and the aircraft crashed near Oxford.

Germany formed its first Military Aviation Service on 1 October 1912. This lasted until just after the end of the First World War.

The first trials in America to determine the suitability of aeroplanes for anti-submarine warfare began on 26 October 1912, under the command of Lt John H. Towers.

The first British aeroplane designed and built as an armed fighting machine was the Vickers Destroyer EFB 1, ordered by the British Admiralty in November 1912 and displayed at the Olympia Aero Show in February 1913.

The first aeroplane to be successfully catapult-launched from a boat was a Curtiss A-1 Triad hydroaeroplane, piloted by Lt T. Ellyson, on 12 November 1912. The operation was performed from an anchored barge, at the Washington Navy Yard, using a compressed-air launcher invented by Capt W. I. Chambers.

The first Russian aeroplane with a machine-gun fitted was the Dux-1, a pusher-engined biplane intended for ground attack. This appeared in 1913.

The first aeroplane unit of the US Army, the 1st Aero Squadron, was formed on 5 March 1913.

The US Army's first aerial map (of the route from San Antonio to Texas City) was made by Lt T. C. Sherman who was riding as passenger in the aircraft flown by Lt T. D. Milling on 31 March 1913.

The first bombs to be dropped by aeroplane on an enemy warship were those released by Didier Masson, a supporter of General Alvarado Obregon, on Mexican gunships in the Guaymas Bay, on 10 May 1913.

The Sopwith Tabloid was **the world's first single-seat scout to enter production for military service.** Designed before the war and first flown during November 1913, a Tabloid won the 1914 Schneider Trophy contest and later became standard equipment of the early RNAS. Examples serving with the Eastchurch Squadron were armed with a wing-mounted machine-gun from February 1915.

The first ever aerial combat between aircraft took place in November 1913, when, over Mexico, an aeroplane piloted by Phillip Rader in support of general Huerta exchanged pistol shots with one flown by Dean Ivan Lamb operating with the forces of Venustiano Carranza.

The first French airmen to be killed on active service were Capt Hervé and his observer, named Roëland. During the colonial campaign in Morocco, early in 1914, they made a forced landing in the desert and were killed by local Arabs.

The first military operations involving the use of American aeroplanes were those during the Vera Cruz incident (Mexico) in April 1914, when five Curtiss AB flying-boats were carried to the port on board the battleship USS *Mississippi* and the cruiser USS *Birmingham*. The first such military flight was undertaken by Lt (Jg) P. N. L. Bellinger, who took off in the Curtiss AB-3 flying-boat on 25 April in order to search for mines in the harbour. The AB flying-boats flew on 43 consecutive days, and some damage was sustained from rifle fire. Bellinger's aircraft sustained the first damage by ground fire, on 6 May while on a reconnaissance flight, **the first US military aeroplane to be hit by enemy fire while on active service.**

The first air service of the US Army was established on 18 July 1914, when the Aviation Section was formed as part of the Signal Corps with a

Curtiss AB and Triad seaplanes at Pensacola Naval Aeronautic Station in March 1914, just prior to leaving for the Vera Cruz incident. (US Navy)

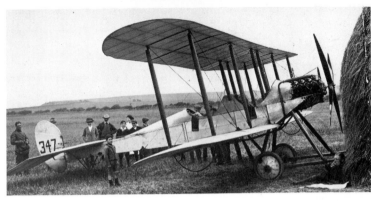

Above *Sikorsky* Ilya
Mourometz *heavy bomber.*
(Sikorsky Aircraft)

Right *BE2a No 347, the first
British aeroplane to land in
France at the beginning of the
First World War, with Lt Harvey-
Kelly having a quick smoke.*
(Imperial War Museum)

'paper' strength of 60 officers and 260 men, plus six aeroplanes. This superseded the Aeronautical Division of the Signal Corps.

The first standard naval torpedo dropped by a naval airman in a naval aircraft was a 14 in (35.6 cm) torpedo weighing 810 lb (367 kg), dropped by a Short seaplane flown by Sqn Cdr Arthur Longmore, RN (Royal Aero Club Pilot's Certificate No. 72), on 28 July 1914. This followed a similar demonstration by Short's test pilot, Gordon Bell, the previous day.

The first air operations undertaken by airmen of the Royal Navy during the First World War were reconnaissance flights by Eastchurch Squadron commanded by Wg Cdr Charles Samson in support of a Brigade of Royal Marines on the Belgian coast in August 1914.

The first British airmen killed on active service were 2nd Lt R. B. Skene and a mechanic R. K. Barlow, of No. 3 Squadron, RFC, on 12 August 1914. Flying from Netheravon to Dover to form

up for the Channel crossing, their aircraft, a Blériot two-seater of 'C' Flight, landed because of engine trouble. Shortly after taking off again, the aircraft crashed into trees and both occupants were killed.

The first German Air Service pilot to be killed on active service was Oberleutnant Reinhold Jahnow. He was fatally injured in a crash at Malmédy, Belgium, on 12 August 1914. He was holder of German Pilot's Licence No. 80, and a veteran of several reconnaissance flights for the Turks during the Balkan campaign of 1912.

The first British squadrons to fly over the English Channel to France after the outbreak of war were numbers 2, 3, 4 and 5, equipped with BE2s, Blériots and Farman biplanes; BE2s and Farmans; and Be8s and Avro 504s respectively, starting on 13 August 1914. The first of these aircraft to land was BE2a No. 347, flown by Lt H. D. Harvey-Kelly. Farmans of No. 4 Squadron were later **the first British armed aircraft to be flown in action**.

The first bombing attack of the First World War was made by an aeroplane flown by Lt Césari and Corp Prudhommeau, French Aviation Militaire, against the Zeppelin sheds at Metz-Frescaty, on 14 August 1914.

The first British reconnaissance flight over German territory was carried out by Lt G. Mappleback and Capt P. Joubert de la Ferté of No. 4 Squadron, RFC, flying a BE2a and a Blériot monoplane respectively. The flight took place on 19 August 1914.

The first RFC aeroplane to be brought down in action was an Avro 504 of No. 5 Squadron, piloted by Lt V. Waterfall, on 22 August 1914. The aircraft was shot down by rifle fire from troops in Belgium.

The first RFC 'air victory' was achieved on 25 August 1914, when Lt Harvey-Kelly flying an unarmed reconnaissance machine, in company with two other unarmed planes from No. 2 Squadron, forced a German two-seater to land.

The first aeroplane to be destroyed by ramming was an Austrian two-seater flown by Leutnant Baron von Rosenthal, rammed over the air base at Sholkiv on 26 August 1914 by Staff Capt Petr Nikolaevich Nesterov of the Imperial Russian XI Corps Air Squadron, who was flying an unarmed Morane Type M monoplane scout. Both pilots were killed. Nesterov (remembered also as the **first pilot to loop the loop**) was the Imperial Air Service's **first battle casualty**.

The first RNAS Squadron to fly to France after the start of the war was the Eastchurch Squadron, led by Wg Cdr C. R. Samson (the first British pilot to take off in an aeroplane from a ship). Arriving at Ostend on 27 August 1914, its equipment included two Sopwith Tabloids, three BEs, two Blériots, one Short seaplane, one Bristol biplane and one Farman biplane. The only armed aircraft attached to the Squadron was the Astra-Torres airship No. 3.

The first bombs to be dropped upon a capital city from an aircraft fell on Paris, on 30 August 1914. The pilot of the Taube monoplane is thought to have been Leutnant Ferdinand von Hiddessen, who dropped five bombs and a message on the Quai de Valmy, killing one woman and injuring two other people.

The first great land battle in which victory was generally attributed to aerial reconnaissance was the battle of Tannenberg, where 120 000 Russian soldiers and 500 guns were captured by German forces in late August 1914.

The first Japanese naval vessel converted to support seaplanes was the 7600-ton (7722 tonnes) *Wakamiya Maru*, converted in 1913. It began operations against German forces at Kiaochow Bay, China, on 1 September 1914, using Farman seaplanes. Dropping improvised bombs made from naval shells, the Farmans succeeded in sinking a German minelayer. The minelayer was **the first warship sunk from the air**.

The first British air raid on Germany was by four aircraft of the Eastchurch RNAS Squadron. On 22 September 1914 two aircraft took off from Antwerp to attack the airship sheds at Düsseldorf, two to attack the airship sheds at Cologne. Only the aircraft flown by Flt Lt Collet found the target—the sheds at Düsseldorf—and his three 20 lb (9 kg) Hales bombs, while probably on target, failed to explode. All aircraft returned safely.

The first French bomber Groupe was formed on 27 September 1914, equipped with Voisin pusher biplanes nicknamed 'Chicken Coops'.

The first aeroplane in the world to be shot down and destroyed by another was a German two-seater, possibly an Aviatik, shot down at Jonchery, near Reims on 5 October 1914 by Sergent Joseph Frantz and Caporal Quénault in a Voisin pusher of Escadrille VB24. The weapon used is believed to have been a Hotchkiss machine-gun.

The first successful British air raid on Germany took place on 8 October 1914. Sqn Cdr D. A. Spenser-Grey and Flt Lt R. L. G. Marix of the Eastchurch RNAS Squadron flew from Antwerp in Sopwith Tabloids (Nos. 167 and 168) to attack airship sheds at Düsseldorf and Cologne with 20 lb (9 kg) Hales bombs. Grey failed to find the target, bombed Cologne Railway Station and returned to Antwerp. Marix reached his target at Düsseldorf, bombed the shed from 600 ft (183 m) and destroyed it and Zeppelin LZ25/Z.IX inside. His aircraft was damaged by gunfire, and he eventually crash-landed 20 miles (30 km) from Antwerp, returning to the city on a bicycle borrowed from a peasant.

Voisin 'Chicken Coops' served throughout the First World War, despite its outdated design and poor performance. The Voisin X of 1918 used a 300 hp Renault engine to increase speed, carried a big 37 mm Hotchkiss cannon and up to 300 kg of bombs. Nine hundred were produced.

The first use of fléchettes as an aerial weapon occurred during autumn 1914 when deployed by aeroplanes of No. 3 Squadron RFC. Fléchettes were steel darts about 5 in (12.7 cm) in length and were dropped on enemy ground concentrations from containers each holding some 250. Casualties or damage were rare in such attacks.

The first British military aircraft insignia consisted of Union Jacks painted in rectangular and shield-shape forms on RFC aircraft. This was necessitated by the fact that RFC aircraft had been fired on by British and French groundtroops who (despite the adoption of Iron Cross insignia for German aircraft in September 1914) insisted they had mistaken them for German types. RNAS aircraft were instructed to bear the Union Jack on 26 October 1914. The roundel was adopted by the RFC from 11 December 1914, following the French example. On 11 December 1914 the RNAS adopted a roundel for the wings only – initially a red outer circle with a white centre.

The first ever strategic bombing raid by a formation of aircraft was launched on 21 November 1914 against the Zeppelin sheds at Friedrichshafen. Sqn Cdr E. F. Briggs, leading the attack, was accompanied by Flt Cdr J. T. Babington and Flt Lt S. V. Sippé, all on Avro 504s of the Royal Naval Air Service. The aircraft flew from Belfort in France, each carrying four 20 lb bombs, with which Zeppelin LZ32 (L7) was damaged in its shed and the gasworks destroyed. Briggs was wounded in the head by heavy defending machine-gun fire and taken prisoner.

The first operational seaplane unit of the Imperial German Navy was formed on 4 December 1914, moving to its base at Zeebrugge two days later.

The first operational four-engined bombers and reconnaissance aircraft were *Ilya Mouro-metz* biplanes, which equipped the Flotilla of Flying Ships (EVK), Russian Army, from 10 December 1914 (formation date of the EVK). This force eventually operated at a strength of between 40 and 50 of these giants. The total number of these bombers built was 73 and those not used for training made about 400 bombing raids, the first against a Polish target on 15 February 1915. Powered by 125–220 hp engines, the *Ilya Mourometz* could fly at 60–80 mph (97–129 km/h) and could carry up to 1500 lb (680 kg) of bombs. It carried up to 16 crew members and, as with the German R-Type bombers of 1918, routine servicing and minor repairs could be performed in flight.

The first aeroplane raid on Great Britain, by one aircraft, took place on 21 December 1914. Two bombs fell in the sea near Admiralty Pier at Dover.

The first bomb dropped by an enemy aircraft on British soil, and the second aeroplane raid on Great Britain, again by one aircraft, took place on 24 December 1914. One bomb exploded near Dover Castle.

The first Russian aircraft designed for air fighting was the two-seat Sikorsky S-16 biplane, which appeared in January 1915. Fitted with a type of synchronized machine-gun arrangement, S-16s were initially delivered in March to the EVK, as experimental escorts for the *Ilya Mourometz* bombers.

The first use of aeroplanes in military operations in South America was in February 1915, by the Brazilian Army in the State of Santa Catarina.

The first aeroplane to be designed and built for aerial fighting was the Vickers FB5 (Fighting Biplane No. 5) Gunbus. Armed with one forward-firing machine-gun, which was operated by a second crew member, the first examples of the FB5 were received by a unit in France on 5 February 1914, and the first FB5 fighter squadron (No. 11 Squadron RFC) joined the BEF on 25 July 1915.

The first naval vessel fully converted for aircraft duties, while still under construction, was HMS *Ark Royal*, and as such was the first ship in the world to be completed as an aircraft (seaplane) carrier. Launched in 1914, *Ark Royal* became the first aircraft carrier to operate aeroplanes against the enemy in Europe when, arriving at the entrance to the Dardanelles on 17 February 1915, one of her seaplanes was sent on reconnaissance against the Turks.

The first British bombing raid in direct tactical support of a ground operation occurred on 10 March 1915. It comprised attacks on railways bringing up German reinforcements in the Menin and Courtrai areas (Second Wing) and the railway stations at Lille, Douai and Don (bombed by the Third Wing), during the Neuve Chapelle offensive. The Divisional Headquarters at Fournes was also bombed by three aircraft of No. 3 Squadron piloted by Capt E. L. Conran, Lt W. C. Birch and Lt D. R. Hanlon.

The first single-seat fighter to destroy an enemy aircraft using a machine-gun that fired through the propeller disc was a French Morane-Saulnier, piloted by Roland Garros. Having first fitted deflector plates to the propeller to prevent the bullets from hitting the rotating blades, Garros claimed his first victory using this method on 1 April 1915. On 19 April Garros had to make an emergency landing behind German lines and his aircraft, along with its secret, was captured.

The first intentional air attack by an armed German aircraft on an armed enemy aircraft was made on 26 May 1915, when an armed Halberstadt C, crewed by Oberleutnant Kästner and Leutnant Langhoff, attacked and shot down a French Voisin biplane that was making a reconnaissance over the airfield at Douai.

The first single-seat fighter to enter service with the RFC was the Airco (de Havilland) DH2, the prototype of which made its first flight on 1 June 1915. Powered by a 100 hp Gnôme rotary engine, mounted in a 'pusher' configuration, the DH2 had a maximum speed of 93 mph (150 km/h) and was armed with one forward-firing Lewis machine-gun. It entered service with the RFC in early 1916, and was one of the fighters which ended the supremacy of the Fokker Eindecker. DH2s served until mid-1917, latterly in Palestine. About 400 were built.

The first fighter to be fitted with a successful synchronized machine-gun, firing forward between the propeller blades, was the German Fokker E series Eindecker. The first E.Is arrived at the Douai airfield on the Western Front for operational trials in July 1915. Eventually, about 425 'E' series monoplanes were built. None flew faster than 87 mph (140 km/h), but they caused such havoc in attacks on Allied aircraft that their activities for ten months in 1915–16 are remembered as the 'Fokker Scourge'. The inherently stable BE2cs of the RFC suffered particularly heavy casualties. First Eindecker victory was achieved on 1 August 1915 by Leutnant Max Immelmann, who had prepared for its use by flying a Fokker M8 on 30 July 1915. Previously, on 1 July, a Fokker M5K (considered the prototype to the E.I) had been flown by Leutnant Kurt Wintgens when he shot down a French Morane-Saulnier, probably **the first air victory using a synchronized machine-gun.** The 'scourge' ended only with the introduction into service of new Allied aircraft such as the RFC's DH2.

The first air attack using a torpedo dropped by an aeroplane was carried out by Flt Cdr C. H. Edmonds, flying a Short 184 seaplane from HMS *Ben-My-Chree* on 12 August 1915, against a 5000 ton (5080 tonne) Turkish supply ship in the Sea of Marmara. Although the enemy ship was hit and sunk, the captain of a British submarine claimed to have fired a torpedo simultaneously and sunk the ship. It was further stated that the British submarine *E14* had attacked and immobilized the

Right Morane-Saulnier Type N appeared in 1914. Fitted with a machine-gun and deflector plates on the propeller blades, it equipped French and British squadrons and allowed Roland Garros and Gilbert to become early 'aces'. (Imperial War Museum)

Below Fokker Eindecker, the first fighter with a synchronised machine-gun. This is an E.III. (Imperial War Museum)

ship four days earlier. However on 17 August 1915 another Turkish ship was sunk by a torpedo of whose origin there can be no doubt. On this occasion Flt Cdr C. H. Edmonds, flying a Short 184, torpedoed a Turkish steamer a few miles north of the Dardanelles. His formation colleague, Flt Lt G. B. Dacre, was forced to land on the water owing to engine trouble but, seeing an enemy tug close by, taxied up to it and released his torpedo. The tug blew up and sank. Thereafter Dacre was able to take off and return to the *Ben-My-Chree*.

The first sustained strategic bombing offensive was opened by Italy on 20 August 1915, following its declaration of war against Austria–Hungary on 24 May. Major aircraft type used in the early raids was the Caproni Ca 2 three-engined biplane (100 hp Fiat A10s), of which 31 were delivered in

1915 and 133 in 1916. The Ca 2 was used in the first Italian night bombing raids. It carried a crew of four.

The first launching of an aeroplane by catapult on board ship (excluding anchored barge), took place on 5 November 1915 when an AB-2 flying-boat was catapulted from the stern of the American battleship USS *North Carolina*, anchored in Pensacola Bay, Florida. On the following day AB-2, piloted by Lt Cdr Henry Mustin, was catapulted from USS *North Carolina* while the ship was moving.

The first product of the German Junkers company and **the world's first all-metal monoplane to fly** was the Junkers J1, which took to the air for the first time on 12 December 1915. Intended as a

reconnaissance and close-support aircraft, it had cantilever wings and the complete airframe was skinned in sheet iron. Power was provided by a 120 hp Mercedes DII engine. Only the single prototype was built.

The first major battle to see the use of large formations of fighter aircraft was Verdun, which began on 21 February 1916.

The first aeroplane involved in parasite fighter experiments (intended to be carried to within striking distance of a Zeppelin by a larger and longer-ranged aircraft) was the Bristol Scout, mounted on the upper wing of a Porte Baby flying-boat. On 17 May 1916 the Scout C (No. 3028) of this composite completed the first (and only) mid-air separation of this combination, climbing away from its carrier over Harwich and completing a successful flight and landing.

The first pilot of the Escadrille Américaine to gain an 'air victory' was Lt Kiffin Rockwell, while escorting bombers near Mulhouse on 18 May 1916; Rockwell himself was killed on 23 September. This famous French squadron manned by American pilots had formed only a month earlier, on 16 April; it was later to become known as the Lafayette Escadrille.

The first triplane fighter to enter service was the British Sopwith Triplane, a single-seater nick-named 'Tripehound'. The prototype flew for the first time on 28 May 1916. Later production aircraft were so successful that the Germans developed their own triplanes, leading to the introduction of the Fokker Dr I.

The first major fleet battle in which an aeroplane was used was the Battle of Jutland on 31 May 1916, when Flt Lt F. J. Rutland (accompanied by his observer, Assistant Paymaster G. S. Trewin) spotted and shadowed a force of German light cruisers and destroyers. Taking off from alongside HM seaplane carrier *Engadine* at about 15.10 h, Rutland sighted the enemy ships and continued to radio position reports to the *Engadine*.

The first American pilot to be killed in the First World War was Victor Emmanuel Chapman of the Lafayette Escadrille, who was shot down near Verdun on 23 June 1916.

The first German airship to be brought down on British soil was the Schutte-Lanz SL XI, which was attacked on the night of 2 September 1916 by a BE2c flown by Lt W. Leefe Robinson, RFC: see Lighter than air—dirigibles.

The first radio-guided flying-bomb was tested on 12 September 1916. It was called the 'Hewitt-Sperry biplane' and was built by Curtiss. Powered by a 40 hp engine, it was capable of covering 50 miles (80 km) carrying a 308 lb (140 kg) bomb-load.

The first submarine to be sunk by an aeroplane was the French submarine *Foucault*, on 15 September 1916, by an Austrian Löhner flying-boat.

The first Albatros D.I single-seat fighters were used operationally for the first time on 17 September 1916, under the command of Oswald Boelcke. This was the initial version of the famous Albatros D series fighters which, in early 1917, gave Germany its second period of air supremacy over the Western Front.

The first bombs to fall on London from an aeroplane were six small bombs dropped from a

Left   *AB-2 flying-boat in flight after the first catapult launch from USS* North Carolina *in Pensacola Bay. (US Navy)*

Right   *Curtiss-built Hewitt-Sperry radio-guided flying-bomb. (US National Archives)*

German LVG C11 on 28 November 1916, falling near Victoria Station. The pilot of the attacking aircraft was Deck Offizier P. Brandt.

The first flush-deck aircraft carrier in the world was HMS *Argus*, 15 775 tons (16 027 tonnes). Originally laid down in 1914 as the Italian liner *Conte Rosso*, she was purchased by Great Britain and launched in 1917, and completed in 1918. She featured an unrestricted flight deck of 565 ft (172 m) length and could accommodate 20 aircraft. She was ultimately scrapped in 1947. She was **the first carrier in the world to embark a full squadron of torpedo-carrying land-planes**, when in October 1918 a squadron of Sopwith Cuckoos was activated. They did not, however, see action.

The first intentional air victory achieved at night was gained on the night of 11 to 12 February 1917, by Leutnant Peter and Leutnant Frohwein flying a DFW CV. On this occasion they destroyed two bombers landing at Malzeville.

The first vessel in the world to be defined as an aircraft carrier (in the modern sense, i.e. equipped with a flying deck for operation of landplanes) was the light battle-cruiser HMS *Furious*. Construction of this ship began shortly after the outbreak of the First World War, it being intended to arm her with a pair of 18 in (457 mm) guns. In March 1917 authority to alter her design was issued, and at the expense of one of these huge guns she was completed with a hangar and flight deck on her forecastle. With a speed of 31.5 knots, she carried six Sopwith Pups in addition to four seaplanes. Her first Senior Flying Officer was Sqn Cdr E. H. Dunning. HMS *Furious* became the **longest-lived active carrier in the world.**

Sopwith Cuckoo torpedo seaplane.

Between 1921 and 1925 the midships superstructure was eliminated and she emerged as a flushdeck carrier displacing 22 450 tons (22 809 tonnes), with two aircraft lifts and an aircraft capacity of 33. Her overall length was 786 ft (239 m). After an extraordinarily active and exciting career in the Second World War (and a near head-on collision at night in the Atlantic with a troopship which passed so close as to carry away some of the carrier's radio masts), she was finally scrapped in 1949.

The first British unit to be established specifically for night bombing operations was No. 100 Squadron, RFC, which formed at Hingham (Norfolk) on 23 February 1917 and crossed to France on 21 March. It was based initially at St-André-aux-Bois where a week later the unit received its first aircraft, 12 FE2bs, and then moving to Le Hameau on 1 April 1917. Its first operations were two raids on the night of 5/6 April on Douai airfield, home base of the 'Richthofen Circus'. One FE2b failed to return, but four hangars were badly damaged by bombs.

The first German submarine to be sunk by an aeroplane was the U-36, attacked in the North Sea on 20 May 1917 by a Large America flyingboat piloted by Flt Sub-Lt C. R. Morrish.

The first mass bombing raid on England by Gotha heavy bombers was made on 25 May 1917, when 21 aircraft attacked several towns, including Folkestone and Shorncliffe. About 95 people were killed and 260 more were injured.

The first mass bombing raid on London was by German Gotha heavy bombers on 13 June 1917.

Fourteen bombers attacked an area around Liverpool Street Station, dropping 72 bombs and causing 162 deaths, with 432 people injured. **This was the worst bombing raid of the war** in terms of dead and injured. **The last major bombing raid on England in daylight** was on 12 August 1917.

The first German armoured aeroplane, designed for ground attack and low-level reconnaissance missions, was the Junkers J1 biplane, of which 227 were built. Fitted with 5 mm steel plating, the type entered service in the latter half of 1917 and was armed with three machine-guns.

The first landing in the world by an aeroplane upon a ship under-way was carried out by Sqn Cdr E. H. Dunning who flew a Sopwith Pup on to the deck of HMS *Furious* on 2 August 1917.

Above   *A German Gotha long-range heavy bomber being armed with 50 kg bombs. (US National Archives)*

Below   *Junkers JI armoured biplane. (Imperial War Museum)*

Left *Crew rush forward to grab Dunning's Pup fighter as it side-slips and lands onto HMS Furious.*

Below *Fokker Dr.I triplane fighters. (Imperial War Museum)*

Steaming at 26 knots into a wind of 21 knots, *Furious* thus provided a 47 knot headwind for Dunning who flew his Pup for'ard along the starboard side of the ship before side-slipping towards the deck located on the forecastle. Men then grabbed straps on the aircraft and brought it to a standstill. On 7 August Dunning attempted to repeat the operation in an even greater headwind but stalled as he attempted to overshoot and was killed when his aircraft was blown over the side of the ship.

The first enemy night bomber to be destroyed over Germany was shot down on the night of 8 to 9 August 1917 near Frankfurt-on-Main.

The first of Germany's new Fokker FI (Dr I) triplane fighters arrived at Courtrai on 21 August 1917. Lt Werner Voss was the first to fly one into action, destroying an RFC aircraft on 30 August.

The first mass bombing raid at night by Gotha aeroplanes on Britain was made on the night of 2 to 3 September 1917. The target was Dover.

The first raid on Britain by German 'R' type bombers was made on 17 September 1917. German Staaken R VI giant bombers were capable of dropping 1000 kg bombs, which were the largest bombs of the war.

The first RFC unit to be formed to carry out strategic bombing of targets inside Germany was the 41st Wing, which came into being on 11 October 1917.

The first Gotha bomber to be shot down at night during a bombing raid was destroyed in January 1918 by two Sopwith Camels of No. 44 Squadron, RFC, at Wickford, Essex. This proved that even at night the Gotha could be intercepted and stopped, and night raids on England ceased in May 1918.

The first US pilot to gain a victory while serving with an American squadron was Lt Stephen W. Thompson, in February 1918. His squadron, the 103rd Pursuit Squadron, had been formed from the Lafayette Escadrille on 18 February but was then still operating with French forces.

The first combat aeroplane to enter production in the United States was the British de Havilland DH4. The first machine was completed in February 1918.

The first US fighter squadron to arrive in France from America was the 95th Aero (Pursuit) Squadron, on 18 February 1918.

The first mission carried out by the newly-formed RAF (by combining the RFC and RNAS on 1 April 1918) was made on the same day by Bristol F2B Fighters of No. 22 Squadron.

The first American observation aircraft to fly over enemy lines were from I Corps Observation Squadron, on 11 April 1918.

The first American-trained pilots to shoot down enemy aircraft were 1st Lt Douglas Campbell and 2nd Lt Alan Winslow of the 94th Aero (Pursuit) Squadron, on 14 April 1918. Having taken off at 08.50 h, they intercepted an Albatros D V (flown by Corp Simon) and a Pfalz D IIIa (flown by Sgt Maj Wronieki) of Jagdstaffel 64 in the area of Toul, and shot both down. Both pilots survived. The first to fall was the Albatros, to the guns of Winslow. The American pilots flew Nieuport 28s. Campbell was the first US pilot serving under American colours to become an ace, gaining his fifth victory on 31 May 1918.

The first US bomber squadron of the AEF was formed in France on 18 May 1918, as the 96th Aero Squadron. The squadron's first raid was against the railway at Dommany-Baroncourt, on 12 June.

The first pilot to take off successfully from a towed barge in an aeroplane was the American-born Flt Sub-Lt Stuart Culley, RN, who on 1 August 1918 rose from a barge towed by HMS Redoubt at 35 knots. At 08.41 h on 11 August 1918 Culley took off from the barge while being towed off the Dutch coast and climbed to 18 000 ft (5500 m) to shoot down the German Zeppelin L53 using incendiary ammunition. He was thus the first (and probably the only) pilot to shoot down an enemy aircraft after taking off from a towed vessel. Landing in the sea along-side his towing destroyer, HMS Redoubt, he was rescued—and later awarded the DSO for his feat—and his Camel was salvaged by a derrick (invented by Col Samson). The only survivor of the Zeppelin baled out from 19 000 ft (5800 m)—almost certainly a record at that time.

The first US fighter patrol at night was undertaken by the 185th Aero (Pursuit) Squadron on 12 October 1918.

The First World War came to an end on the 11th hour of the 11th day of the 11th month, 1918.

The first US-designed fighter to enter large-scale production was the Thomas Morse MB-3, the prototype of which made its maiden flight on 21 February 1919.

The first military aircraft designed and built in Czechoslovakia, the Letov S1 reconnaissance and light bombing biplane, was introduced in 1919–20. Power was provided by a 260 hp Maybach Mb IVa engine and a total of 90 S1 and S2 versions was built. The SH-1 variant had a maximum speed of 120 mph (193 km/h).

The first American aircraft carrier to carry heavier-then-air craft was the USS Jupiter, an ex-collier of 11 050 tons (11 227 tonnes), which was converted during 1920 to provide a stem-to-stern flight deck. Later named USS Langley, it became the US Navy's first aircraft carrier when it was commissioned on 20 March 1922.

The first post-war world speed record was set in France on 7 February 1920 by Sadi Lecointe at a speed of 171.01 mph (275.22 km/h), flying a Nieuport-Delage 29.

The first Japanese fighter built for operation from an aircraft carrier was the Mitsubishi 1MF1, designed by the Englishman Herbert Smith. First flown in 1921, the 1MF1 proved very successful during flight trials.

Fll Sub-Lt Stuart Culley takes off from a barge towed behind HMS Redoubt. (Imperial War Museum)

Right *Vickers Vernon, the first aircraft designed as a troop transport.*

Below *USS* Langley *with its funnels lowered for aeroplane operations. (US Navy)*

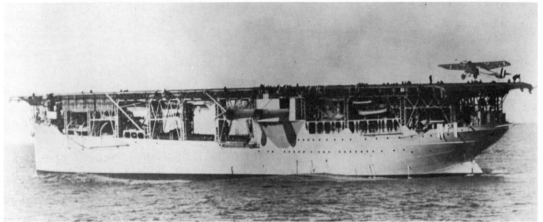

The US Army's first production armoured aeroplane, the Boeing GA-1, was flown for the first time during May 1921. In addition to very heavy protective armour plating, it carried eight 0.30 in machine-guns, a 37 mm Baldwin cannon, and ten 25 lb fragmentation bombs.

The first troop transport to be designed as such from the outset was the Vickers Vernon biplane. Production totalled 55, built in three versions with 360 hp Rolls-Royce Eagle VIII, 450 hp Napier Lion II and Lion III engines respectively, the first of them entering RAF service in August 1921.

The first purpose built aircraft carrier for the Imperial Japanese Navy was the *Hosho*, launched during November 1921 and commissioned on 27 December 1922. It survived the Second World War and was decommissioned after the Japanese surrender.

The first flight of the prototype Breguet 19
bomber/reconnaissance aircraft was made during May 1922. The Breguet 19 was one of the most extensively used military types of the 'between-wars' years.

The first over 200 mph world speed record was set by Sadi Lecointe on 20 September 1922, flying a Nieuport-Delage 29.

The first demonstration of radar signatures was made by technicians at Anacostia Naval Aircraft Radio Laboratory, USA, on 27 September 1922.

The first air control operation, in which an air force became entirely responsible for the internal security of a nation, began in October 1922. The RAF assumed responsibility for maintaining peace in Iraq, replacing the former large army garrison with two squadrons of Vernon transports, four of DH9As, one of Bristol Fighters and one of Snipe fighters.

The first take-off from an American aircraft carrier, the USS *Langley*, was made on 17 October 1922 by Lt V. C. Griffin flying a Vought VE-7SF fighter.

The first examples of the Czechoslovakian Aero A 11 were flown in 1923. This highly successful general purpose biplane, of which some 440 examples were built, established several duration records and, in 1926, one completed a 9320 mile (15 000 km) intercontinental flight.

The first take-off and landing on Japan's new aircraft carrier, the *Hosho*, were made in February 1923 by a Mitsubishi 1MF1 flown by a British pilot, Capt Jordan.

The first successful in-flight refuelling of an aeroplane was accomplished by Capt L. H. Smith and Lt J. P. Richter in a de Havilland DH4B on 27 June 1923 at San Diego, California. Smith and Richter established a new world endurance record by remaining airborne for 37 h 15 min 43.8 s from 27 to 28 August 1923, covering a distance of 3293.26 miles (5299.9 km) over a measured 50 km course at San Diego. Their DH4B was flight-refuelled 15 times.

The first six-engined American aircraft, the Barling XNBL-1 triplane bomber, was flown for the first time on 22 August 1923. Then the largest aeroplane in the world, it proved to be under-powered and no further examples were built.

The Soviet Union's first fighter aircraft to be built in series, the Polikarpov I-1 (Il-400) was flown for the first time in prototype form on 23 August 1923. A cantilever low-wing monoplane, it was then powered by an American Liberty engine.

The RAF's first new fighter after the end of the First World War, the Gloster Grebe biplane, entered service during October 1923.

First new Italian-designed fighter aircraft to be adopted by the Regia Aeronautica, the Fiat C.R.1 single-seat biplane fighter was demonstrated during this air force's annual review on 4 November 1924.

The first flight of the Gloster Gamecock prototype (J7497) was made during February 1925. In production form this aircraft was the **last biplane fighter of wooden basic structure to serve with the RAF**.

The first landing by night on an aircraft carrier was accomplished by Flt Lt Boyce, RAF, on 1 July 1926, piloting the Blackburn Dart N9804 to the deck of HMS *Furious*.

The first French aircraft carrier, named *Béarn*, was completed on 27 May 1927 after almost seven years of construction.

The first world speed record in excess of 500 km/h and 300 mph was established by Maj Mario di Bernardi of the Italian Air Force. Flying a Macchi M.52*bis* floatplane, he attained a ratified speed of 318.57 mph (512.69 km/h) on 30 March 1928.

Left Smith and Richter undertaking flight refuelling over Rockwell Field during their 37 hour endurance flight. (US Air Force)

Right The Handley Page Heyford was the RAF's last biplane bomber.

The world's first large-scale airlift evacuation of civilians was undertaken by transport aircraft of the Royal Air Force between 23 December 1928 and 25 February 1929. Five hundred and eighty-six people and 24 193 lb (10 975 kg) of luggage were airlifted from the town of Kabul, Afghanistan, during inter-tribal disturbances. They were carried over treacherous country using eight Vickers Victoria transports of No. 70 Squadron RAF, and a Handley Page Hinadai.

The first flight of the Gloster Gauntlet prototype was made during January 1929, and this interesting fighter proved to be the **last open cockpit biplane to serve with the RAF.** In November 1936 three Gauntlets of No. 32 Squadron were directed by experimental ground radar to intercept a civil airliner, this being **the world's first successful radar-controlled interception.**

The first electro-mechanical flight simulator was the Link Trainer which was patented on 14 April 1929. It comprised a replica of an aeroplane, with full controls and instruments, which did not leave the ground; instead it was 'attached' to a mechanical crab that traced a path over a large scale map in such a way as to represent heading, speed and time of the replica aircraft 'flown' by its occupant. Invented by Edward Albert Link, who sold his first model in 1919, it was adopted by the US Navy in 1931 and by the US Army in 1934. By 1939 there was scarcely an air force in the world that was not using Link Trainers. They can be regarded as the forerunners of today's complex flight simulators.

The first blind-flight take-off, level flight and landing was accomplished by Lt James H. Doolittle on 24 September 1929, at Mitchell Field, Long Island, New York.

The first flight of the Handley Page HP38 (J9130) prototype was made on 12 June 1930. Later named Heyford, it was **the last heavy bomber of biplane configuration to serve with the RAF.**

First flown in prototype form during October 1930, the Polish PZL P.7 fighter was to confer a unique reputation on the Polish Air Force when it equipped all of its fighter squadrons in 1933, thus making it **the first air force in the world to have only all-metal monoplane fighters in first-line service.**

Above   *PZL P.7a gull-wing fighters of Poland's 111 Squadron, 1st Air Regiment.*

The first monoplane heavy bomber to enter operational service with the RAF was the Fairey Hendon. First flown in prototype (K1695) form on 25 November 1930, it was not until 1936 that the first production examples were delivered to the RAF.

The first four-engined monoplane heavy bomber to enter service with the Soviet Air Force was the Tupolev TB-3 which, under the Tupolev bureau's designation ANT-6, had first flown as a prototype on 22 December 1930.

The first formation flight across the South Atlantic, from Portuguese Guinea to Natal, Brazil, was made on 6 January 1931 by ten Savoia-Marchetti S55 flying-boats, commanded by Italian Air Minister General Italo Balbo. In 1933, from 1 to 15 July, General Balbo led the first formation flight across the North Atlantic. Taking off from Orbetello, Italy, the 24 S55s flew to the Century of Progress Exposition in Chicago, their route being via Holland, Iceland, Labrador and New Brunswick, Canada.

The RAF's first fighter aircraft able to exceed 200 mph (322 km/h) in level flight, the Hawker Fury I biplane first entered service with No. 43 Squadron at Tangmere, Sussex, in May 1931. Powered by a 525 hp Rolls-Royce Kestrel IIS liquid-cooled engine and armed with two synchronized machine-guns, the Fury, designed by the late Sir Sydney Camm, had a top speed of 207 mph (333 km/h) at 14 000 ft (4270 m).

The first blind solo flight entirely on instruments (with no check pilot on board the aircraft) was accomplished by Capt A. F. Hegenberger when flying a Consolidated NY–2 trainer at Dayton (Ohio) on 9 May 1931.

The first over 400 mph speed record was set by Flt Lt G. H. Stainforth on 29 September 1931, his six runs over the set course averaging 407.5 mph (655.81 km/h). This was achieved in the Supermarine S.6B S1595 which, just over two weeks earlier on 13 September, had been flown by Flt Lt J. N. Boothman to win the Schneider Trophy Contest outright for Britain at an average speed of 340.08 mph (547.31 km/h).

The first twin-engined bomber to be designed for the clandestine German Luftwaffe was the

Above   Tupolev TB-3 heavy bomber used here for parachuting.

Below   The USAAC's first all-metal monoplane fighter was the Boeing P-26. Here the XP-936 first prototype (first flown on 20 March 1932) flies with the Boeing Y1B-9A, the USAAC's first all-metal monoplane bomber with a retractable undercarriage (prototype first flown 13 April 1931 but limited production only for trials).

Dornier Do 11. Designated originally Dornier Do F, the prototype first flew on 7 May 1932, disguised as the last of a batch of mail/cargo transport aircraft. Powered by two 650 hp Siemens-Jupiter engines, some 77 Do 11s were produced.

The first cantilever low-wing monoplane fighter to serve with the French Armée de l'Air was the Dewoitine D500. First flown in prototype form on 18 June 1932, the production aircraft did not begin to enter service until 1935 due to wing structural weakness. Variants included the D501 and D510 and many examples of the series were exported, China being the largest foreign operator with 34 D510s.

Designed and first flown as the Curtiss XF12C-1 parasol monoplane in 1933, this aircraft was almost immediately redesigned as a biplane and, as the SBC Helldiver, was **the last operational US biplane.** Remaining in production until 1941, at the time of the Japanese attack on Pearl Harbor in December 1941 the US Navy still had 186 Helldivers on strength.

Germany's first new post-war fighters, built to equip the secret Luftwaffe in the early 1930s, were the Heinkel He 51 and the Arado Ar 68. Many He 51s were built, in several versions, and 135 operated by the Spanish and German air forces during the Spanish Civil War. Their useful life in this role was curtailed when the Republican forces started flying the Russian Polikarpov I-15. The He 51B-1, powered by a 740 hp BMW VI engine, had a maximum speed of 205 mph (220 km/h). The first protoype Ar 68 flew initially in 1933; the major production version was the Ar 68E which

Prototype Dewoitine D500, first flown in mid-1932.

entered service from 1937, although small numbers of Ar 68Fs had entered service in 1935. Powered by a 690 hp Junkers Jumo 210D engine, the Ar 68E had a maximum speed of 208 mph (335 km/h).

The first aeroplane with retractable landing gear to be flown by the US Navy was the Grumman XFF-1 biplane fighter which, as the FF-1, began to enter service on 21 June 1933.

The first monoplane fighter with a fully enclosed cockpit and fully retractable landing gear to enter squadron service anywhere in the world was the Polikarpov I-16 Ishak ('Little Donkey'). The prototype was flown first on 31 December 1933, and deliveries of the Type I production fighter to Soviet squadrons began during the summer of 1934. The I-16 Type I was powered by a 450 hp M22 engine, and a top speed of 224 mph (360 km/h) at sea level, and was armed with two 7.62 mm ShKAS machine-guns.

Grumman FF-1 featuring a retractable undercarriage.

Polikarpov I-16s with M-25 engines. (Imperial War Museum)

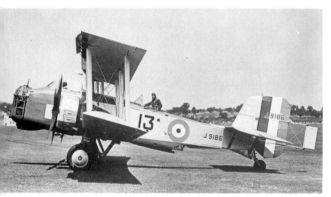

Boulton-Paul Overstrand bomber with power-operated turret. (Flight International)

Douglas TBD-1 Devastator carrier-based torpedo bomber.

The first RAF bomber incorporating a power-operated enclosed gun turret was the Boulton Paul Overstrand, 24 of which were built and entered service in 1934. Power was provided by two 580 hp Bristol Pegasus II M3 engines; a bomb load of 1600 lb (725 kg) could be carried.

The first German Army rocket, the A-1, was developed at Kummersdorf in 1933 but this never flew. Two A-2 rockets were fired from Borkum in December 1934 and achieved an altitude of about 8200 ft (2500 m). In April 1937 the Kummersdorf site was abandoned and von Braun took his team to Peenemünde on the Baltic coast. Here the A-3 and A-5 rockets were developed in preparation for the A-4. It was better known as the V-2, the initial V standing for *Vergeltungswaffe* ('reprisal weapon'). The first so-called 'reprisal weapon' was the V-1 flying bomb, better known to the British as the 'Doodlebug'.

The first American naval aircraft to feature hydraulically operated folding wings, and also the US Navy's first carrier-based monoplane torpedo-bomber to enter production, was the Douglas TBD Devastator. First flown in prototype form on 15 April 1935, the first production TBD-1s were delivered to US Navy Squadron VT-3 on 5 October 1937. Of 75 Devastators on strength with the US Navy on 3 June 1942, 37 were lost during the Battle of Midway (see below), Squadron VT-8 entirely destroyed and another squadron decimated in combat with Japanese Zero fighters. Following this action the type was withdrawn from operational use.

The first German monoplane fighter into squadron service with a fully enclosed cockpit and fully retractable landing gear was the Messerschmitt Bf 109B-1. The prototype Bf 109V-1 (D-IABI) was first flown on 28 May 1935, powered by a 695 hp British Rolls-Royce Kestrel V engine. The first production Bf 109B-1s were delivered to Jagdgeschwader 2 'Richthofen' in the spring of 1937, and this version was the first of the series to become operational in Spain with the Legion Condor during the Civil War. The B-1 model was powered by a 635 hp Junkers Jumo 210D engine, had a top speed of 292 mph (470 km/h) at 13 100 ft (4000 m), and was armed with three 7.92 mm MG 17 machine-guns.

The first American monoplane fighter into squadron service with a fully enclosed cockpit

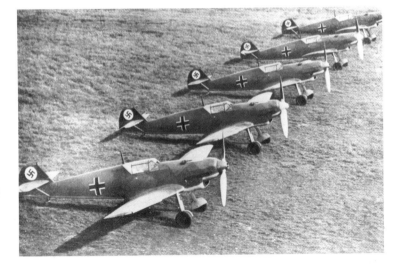

Right Luftwaffe Messerschmitt Bf 109B-1 fighters in 1936. (MBB)

Below Hawker Hurricane fighters of No 56 Squadron at the height of the Battle of Britain, July 1940. In this most famous air battle of all time, Hurricanes claimed more victories than any other British fighter. (Imperial War Museum)

and fully retractable landing gear (into fairings) was the Seversky P-35, the prototype of which was evaluated at Wright Field during August 1935. The production model, of which deliveries began in July 1937, was powered by a 950 hp Pratt & Whitney R-1830-9 engine. It had a top speed of 281 mph (452 km/h) at 10 000 ft (3050 m), and was armed with one 0.5 in and one 0.3 in machine-gun.

The first French monoplane fighter into squadron service with a fully enclosed cockpit and fully retractable landing gear was the Morane-Saulnier M-S 406. The M-S 405, from which the series was derived, first flew on 8 August 1935, and was the first French fighter aircraft able to exceed a speed of 250 mph (402 km/h)

in level flight. The first production M-S 406 (N2-66) flew for the first time on 29 January 1939, and by 1 April 1939 a total of 27 had been delivered to the French Air Force.

The first British monoplane fighter into squadron service with a fully enclosed cockpit and fully retractable landing gear was the Hawker Hurricane. It was also the RAF's first fighter able to exceed a speed of 300 mph (483 km/h), and the first of its eight-gun monoplane fighters. The prototype was flown for the first time on 6 November 1935, and initial deliveries of production aircraft were made to No. 111 Squadron at Northolt, Middlesex, during December 1937.

First moves to institute Shadow Factories in

Britain were made in April 1936, initially to establish aircraft engine production by motor car engine manufacturers. The scheme was later adopted for the production of aircraft.

The first indication of the beginning of the Spanish Civil War came on 18 July 1936 with simultaneous revolt of 12 military garrisons in Spain and of 5 in Spanish Morocco.

The first large-scale military airlift began on 21 July 1936, when Junkers Ju 52/3m bomber/transports were used over a period of about six weeks to ferry some 7350 Nationalist troops, with their artillery and other equipment, from Morocco to Spain at the beginning of the Spanish Civil War.

The first multi-engined bombers of the clandestine German Luftwaffe to be used in combat were specially converted Junkers Ju 52/3m transports, each of which could carry a maximum bombload of 3,307 lb (1500 kg). Operating with the Legion Cóndor pending the delivery of Dornier Do 17 and Heinkel He 111 bombers, **the first action by these aircraft occurred on 14 August 1936** when bombs were dropped on a Republican column advancing to the south of Madrid.

The first Japanese Army Air Force low-wing monoplane fighter, and first with an enclosed cockpit, was the Nakajima Ki-27. The first prototype made its initial flight on 15 October 1936, and production aircraft entered combat in Manchuria during 1938.

The first intensive air bombardment of a city during the Spanish Civil War occurred on 6 November 1936, when Nationalist attacks were made on Madrid in attempts to dislodge Republican troops.

First seeing combat in 1937 during the Sino-Japanese war while operating from the carrier *Hosho*, the Nakajima A4N1 fighter had entered service with the Imperial Japanese Navy during 1935. Considered obsolete by the outbreak of the Pacific War in late 1941, the A4N1 was the **Japanese Navy's last carrier-based biplane fighter**.

The first monoplane to enter service with the Fleet Air Arm was the Blackburn Skua dive-bomber, of which the prototype was first flown on 9 February 1937. Deliveries of production aircraft began in November 1938; a total of 165 was built, these remaining in service until 1941.

The first two-seater fighter with a power-operated four-gun turret to serve with the RAF, the Boulton Paul Defiant, was first flown in prototype form on 11 August 1937.

The first Italian monoplane fighter into service with a fully enclosed cockpit and fully retractable landing gear was the Macchi C200 Saetta ('Lightning'). First single-seat fighter designed by Dr Mario Castoldi, the prototype was flown first on 24 December 1937. Deliveries of production aircraft began in October 1939, and these were powered by the 870 hp Fiat A74RC38 radial engine, giving the C200 a maximum speed of 313 mph (505 km/h) at 15 750 ft (4800 m).

The first monoplane fighter to equip a US Navy squadron was the Brewster F2A Buffalo,

flown for the first time in XF2A-1 prototype form during December 1937.

The UK's first purchasing mission in the United States left Britain on 20 April 1938 and was under the leadership of Air Cdre A. H. Harris. Its task was to assess and procure (if suitable) any aircraft which could speed the re-equipment of the RAF.

First flown in prototype (K8854) form on 23 September 1938, the Supermarine Sea Otter was **the company's last production biplane flying-boat**. It remained in production until July 1946 and, built to a total of 292, **was the last biplane to serve with the Fleet Air Arm**, which retained it in use until the early 1950s.

Flown for the first time on 1 June 1939, entering service with the Luftwaffe in August 1941 **and first engaged in combat with RAF Spitfires on 27 September 1941**, the Focke-Wulf Fw 190 is regarded as one of the classic fighter aircraft of the Second World War. Their first major deployment was to provide an air umbrella for the German battleships *Gneisenau* and *Scharnhorst* and the cruiser *Prinz Eugen* during their 'Channel-dash' on 12–13 February 1942.

The first successful use of air-to-air rockets against aeroplanes is believed to have taken place on the afternoon of 20 August 1939 when five Polikarpov I-16 Type-10 fighters, each fitted with underwing rails for eight 82 mm RS 82 rockets, went into action against Japanese fighters over the Khalkin Gol area of Mongolia. The unit, commanded by Capt Zvonariev, claimed the destruction of two Mitsubishi A5M fighters on this occasion.

The first American-built aircraft to be used operationally by the RAF during the Second World War was the Lockheed Hudson, which entered service with No. 224 Squadron at Gosport in the Summer of 1939. A Hudson operated by this squadron scored the first British victory over a German aircraft in the Second World War, directed Naval forces to the prison ship *Altmark*, and took part in the hunting of the battleship *Bismarck*. On 27 August 1941 a Hudson of No. 269 Squadron caused submarine U-570 to surrender to it: the first U-boat captured in a solely RAF operation.

The first occasion that a British aircraft crossed the German frontier during the Second World War was on 3 September 1939 when Blenheim IV (N6215) of No. 139 Squadron, flown by Flying Officer A. McPherson, and carrying Cdr Thompson, RN, and Corp V. Arrowsmith, photographed German naval units leaving Wilhelmshaven.

The first leaflet raid over Germany in the Second World War was carried out by three Whitley IIIs of No. 51 Squadron and seven Whitley IIIs of No. 58 Squadron on the first night of the war, 3 to 4 September 1939. Approximately six million propaganda leaflets were dropped on targets in the Ruhr and over Bremen and Hamburg.

The first British aircraft to drop bombs on enemy targets during the Second World War was a Blenheim IV (N6204), flown by Flt Lt K. C.

Left *Junkers Ju 52/3mg3e bombers of 1/KG 152 'Hindenburg', in 1936.*

Right *Prototype Macchi C200 Saetta fighter.*

Doran, leading a formation of five aircraft from No. 110 (Hyderabad) Squadron in a raid on the German Fleet in the Schillig Roads, off Wilhelmshaven, on 4 September 1939. A formation of five Blenheims from No. 107 Squadron also took part in the attack.

The first British aircraft to attack a German U-boat during the Second World War was an Avro Anson I of the RAF's No. 500 (County of Kent) Squadron then based at Detling. On 5 September 1939, this aircraft made a bombing attack on the enemy submarine.

The first German aircraft to be shot down by British aircraft during the Second World War was a Messerschmitt Bf 109E, destroyed by Sgt F. Letchford, air gunner of a Fairey Battle (K9243) of No. 88 Squadron, Advanced Air Striking Force of the RAF, over France, on 20 September 1939. The first Fleet Air Arm victory followed when three Dornier Do 18s of *Küstenfliegergruppe* 506 were sighted by a patrol of Swordfish aircraft flying from HMS *Ark Royal* over the North Sea on 26 September 1939. Nine Skuas were launched immediately from the carrier and these succeeded in forcing one of the Dorniers (Werke Nr 731, of 2 *Staffel*, Kü F1 Gr 506) down on to the sea in German Grid Square 3440. The German four-man crew was later rescued and made prisoner on board a British destroyer.

The first British bombers to fly over Berlin in the Second World War were Armstrong Whitworth Whitleys of No. 10 Squadron, which dropped propaganda leaflets during the night of 1–2 October 1939.

The first German aircraft shot down by an RAF aircraft operating from the United Kingdom during the Second World War was a Dornier Do 18 flying-boat destroyed by a Lockheed Hudson of No. 224 Squadron. This occurred on 8 October 1939 during a patrol by the RAF aircraft over Jutland.

The first German aircraft shot down over British soil during the Second World War was a Junkers Ju 88A-1 of I/KG30, piloted by Hauptmann Pohl, and destroyed over the Firth of Forth by a Spitfire of No. 603 (City of Edinburgh) squadron on 16 October 1939.

The first enemy aircraft shot down by RAF fighters on the Western Front during the Second World War was a Dornier Do 17 destroyed over Toul on 30 October 1939. The victorious pilot was Pilot Officer P. W. Mould, flying a Hurricane of No. 1 Squadron.

The first long-range anti-shipping squadron of the German Luftwaffe was formed in November 1939. In the absence of a more suitable aircraft, the unit was equipped with the Focke-Wulf Fw 200 Condor long-range civil transport. One of these aircraft, *Immelmann III* (D-2600), was Adolf Hitler's personal transport. Though not ideal for military service, the Fw 2000 was responsible for the destruction of an immense number of Allied merchant ships. The Condor unit I/KG40, controlled by the German Navy, claimed more than 363 000 tons (368 800 tonnes) of shipping destroyed during one six-month period.

The first four-engined attack bomber to be designed for the Japanese Navy, and the first aircraft with retractable tricycle landing gear to be built in Japan, was the Nakajima G5N Shinzan which flew for the first time in December 1939. Designed and built after examination of the American Douglas DC-4E prototype, it was found to have indifferent performance and only six were completed.

The first loss suffered by the Finnish Air Force during the 'Winter War' with the Soviet Union in 1939–40 was Sergeant Kukkonen who, flying a Fokker D XXI of Fighter Squadron HLeLv24 near Viipuri, was shot down by his own anti-aircraft guns on 1 December 1939.

The first aerial victory claimed during the 'Winter War' between Finland and Russia was that of Lt Eino Luukkanen on 1 December 1939; flying a Fokker D XXI (*FR-104*) of Fighter Squadron HLeLv24, he destroyed a Russian SB-2 bomber.

The first British naval fighter to be armed with a power-driven gun turret was the Blackburn Roc. Aircraft of this type entered service with the Fleet Air Arm in February 1940, but did not serve on board aircraft carriers. Proving unsatisfactory, they were retired in 1943.

The first British air combat victory of the Second World War to be recorded by a gun-camera was that showing the attack on and destruction of a Heinkel He 111 on 22 February 1940. This was achieved by Sqn Ldr Douglas

Farquhar of No. 602 (City of Glasgow) Squadron flying a Spitfire over Coldingham, Berwickshire.

The first Royal Air Force aircraft to drop bombs deliberately on German soil during the Second World War is believed to have been an Armstrong Whitworth Whitley (N1380, DY-R) of No. 102 Squadron based at Driffield, Yorkshire. This squadron, in company with Whitleys of Nos 10, 51 and 77 Squadrons, and Handley Page Hampdens of No. 5 Group, attacked the German mine-laying seaplane base at Hornum on the night of 19–20 March 1940.

The first British bombs to fall on the German mainland in the Second World War were dropped by eight or nine Whitleys of Nos 77 and 102 Squadrons, which attacked enemy lines of communication leading to Southern Holland on the night of 10–11 May 1940.

The first eight-gun fighter to enter service with the Fleet Air Arm was the Fairey Fulmar, which began to equip No. 808 Squadron at Worthy Down in June 1940. Fulmars played a conspicuous part in the defence of convoys to Malta and Northern Russia.

First Allied aircraft to bomb Berlin during the Second World War was a Centre NC 223.4 civil transport (F-ARIN *Jules Verne*) which had been developed for transatlantic operations with Air France. Converted for operation as a bomber, on the night of 7–8 June 1940 this aircraft followed a circuitous route carrying a 4409 lb (2000 kg) bombload which it dropped on Berlin before returning over Germany and north-east France to land at Orly after a 13 h 30 min flight.

The first regular-serving American pilot to die in action during the Second World War was Pilot Officer William M. L. Fiske, RAF, who on 17 August 1940 died of wounds suffered in action the previous day at Tangmere, Sussex, during the Battle of Britain.

The first Japanese monoplane fighter with a fully enclosed cockpit and fully retractable landing gear to enter squadron service was the Mitsubishi A6M2, known popularly as the Zero-Sen. The A6M1 prototype was flown first on 1 April 1939, and the '12-Shi fighter project', as it had been known, was adopted officially by the Imperial Japanese Navy on 31 July 1940, under the designation A6M2 Type 0 Carrier Fighter Model

1.1. The Zero was first used operationally on 19 August 1940, when a formation of 12 aircraft, led by Lt Tamotsu Yokoyama, escorted a force of bombers attacking Chungking.

The first Second World War bombing attack on London was made by the Luftwaffe on the night of 24–25 August 1940.

First flown in NA-73 prototype form on 26 October 1940, the North American P-51 Mustang was to become one of the best known Allied fighter aircraft of the Second World War with more than 15 000 being built. Designed to meet a British requirement for use in Europe, in its most extensively produced versions (the P-51D/K) it became regarded as one of the classic fighter aircraft of the war.

The first air victory scored in the Greek–Italian campaign of 1940–41 was achieved by a Greek pilot of No. 21 Squadron of the Royal Hellenic Air Force. Flying a Polish PZL P24, he destroyed an Italian aircraft north of Yannina on 1 November 1940.

The first organized transatlantic ferry flights of aircraft built in the United States, for service with the Allied nations involved in the Second World War, began on 10 November 1940.

The first American-built fighter aircraft in British service to destroy a German aircraft in the Second World War were two Grumman Martlets of the Royal Navy. Patrolling over Scapa Flow on 25 December 1940, Martlets of No. 804 Squadron, flown by Lt L. V. Carver, RN, and Sub-Lt Parke, RNVR, intercepted and forced down a Junkers Ju 88. Known in US Navy service as the F4F Wildcat, this was Grumman's first monoplane fighter. Its first operational use in US Navy service was in the defence of Wake Island.

The first British single-seat monoplane fighter to serve on board aircraft carriers of the Royal Navy was the Hawker Sea Hurricane. The type equipped No. 880 Squadron in January 1941 and was embarked in HMS *Furious* in July of the same year. They were used also aboard merchant ships and a number of small naval catapult ships under the 'Catafighter' scheme. Their first success in this role came on 3 August 1941 when the Sea Hurricane of HMS *Maplin*, flown by Lt R. W. H. Everett, RNVR, shot down a German Fw 200 Condor.

The first airborne operation carried out by British paratroops in the Second World War had the codename 'Operation Colossus'. On 10 February 1941 the paratroops were dropped by Whitley Vs of Nos 51 and 78 Squadrons in an unsuccessful attack against the viaduct at Tragino, Campagna, Italy.

The first RAF squadron to fly four-engined bombers operationally during the Second World War was No. 7, which used three of its new Short Stirlings (led by Sqn Ldr Griffith-Jones) to bomb oil storage tanks at Rotterdam on the night of 10–11 February 1941.

The first 4000 lb 'block buster' bomb to be used operationally by the RAF was dropped by a Wellington of No. 149 Squadron, during an attack on Emden on 1 April 1941.

The first aircraft designed as a jet fighter, and also the first twin-engined jet aircraft, was the German Heinkel He 280. The first prototype, the 280V-1, was first flown on 2 April 1941 powered by two Heinkel HeS 8 turbojets, each developing approximately 1102 lb (500 kg) static thrust. Maximum level speed of the He 280V-5, with HeS 8A engines of 1650 lb (750 kg) static thrust, was demonstrated to be 510 mph (820 km/h) at

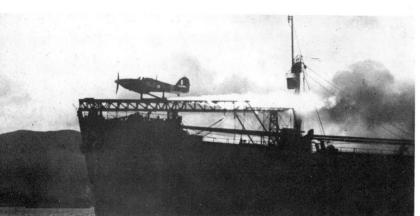

Left *Sea Hurricane Ia 'catafighter' of the Merchant Service Fighter Unit. (Imperial War Museum)*

Below *The RAF's first four-engined monoplane bomber was the Short Stirling. (Charles E. Brown)*

First flown in 1969 as the world's first wide-body airliner, the Boeing Model 747 has been so successful that twenty years on no replacement aircraft has been produced.

Left *Yuriy Gagarin, the world's first man in space.*

Opposite top *The fastest military aircraft in the world is the Lockheed SR-71A strategic reconnaissance aircraft, which can fly above Mach 3 for half its mission time. (Aviation Pictures)*

Opposite bottom *The largest aeroplane in the world is the Soviet Antonov An-124. (Aviation Pictures)*

Below *Shuttle spacecraft Colombia made its first 36-orbit test flight in April 1981. Between 28 November and 8 December 1983 it established the current duration record in Class P for aerospacecraft, of 10 days, 7 hours, 47 mins and 24 seconds, having previously set (in 1982) both the distance record and the greatest mass lifted to altitude record. (NASA)*

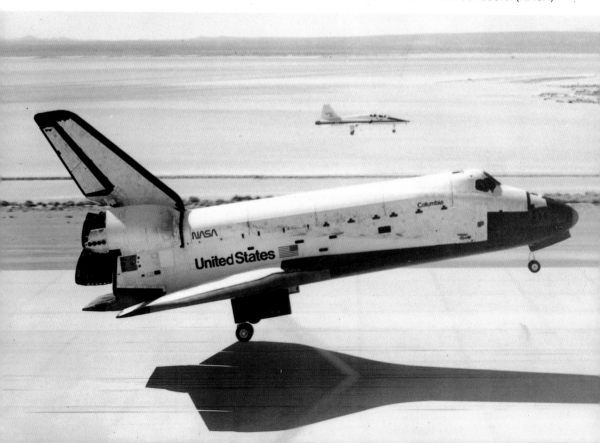

Above *The largest
helicopter in the world is the
Soviet Mil Mi-26. (Ken
Brookes)*

Left *The first European
wide-body airliner was the
Airbus Industrie Airbus A300.
The major current version is
the A300-600 (as illustrated).*

Right *The US Army's
newest and most powerful
attack helicopter is the
McDonnell Douglas (Hughes)
AH-64A Apache, seen here
carrying eight Hellfire anti-
armour missiles and rocket
launchers in addition to its
30mm cannon. (McDonnell
Douglas)*

Opposite top   The Bell XV-15 tilt-rotor research aircraft combines the best features of an aeroplane and a helicopter, with its engines and rotors able to turn upward for vertical flight and swing forward for high-speed horizontal flight. Maximum speed is 382 mph (615 km/h).

Opposite bottom   The most popular new western fighter is the General Dynamics F-16 Fighting Falcon. Already more than 2,000 have been built and current orders include many for foreign air forces. (General Dynamics)

Below   The RAF's latest fighter is the Panavia Tornado F.Mk 3. This example, belonging to No 229 OCU, is escorting a missile-armed BAe Hawk trainer. (British Aerospace)

Grumman X-29A FSW (forward swept wing) technology demonstrator first flown on 14 December 1984 is intended to research the benefits of this unusual configuration. (Grumman Aircraft)

19 680 ft (6000 m). It did not achieve production status, being abandoned in favour of the Messerschmitt Me 262.

The first combat mission flown by the Boeing B-17 Flying Fortress was a daylight raid at 30 000 ft (9150 m) against Wilhelmshaven by three aircraft of No. 90 (Bomber) Squadron, RAF, on 8 July 1941. Twenty B-17Cs had been supplied to the RAF, and were used by that service under the name Fortress I. From 1942 onwards about 200 B-17F and B-17G aircraft were delivered to the RAF, which designated the 'Fs' as Fortress II and IIA, the 'Gs' as Fortress III. All of the II and IIA aircraft served with Coastal Command's Very Long Range force for mid-Atlantic patrol.

The first single-engined American aircraft equipped with a power-operated gun turret, and also the first to carry a 22 in (55.9 cm) torpedo, was the Grumman TBF Avenger. First flight of an XTBF-1 prototype was made during August 1941. The first operational use of production aircraft was at the Battle of Midway, on 4 June 1942, when five out of six aircraft deployed were lost. Despite this inauspicious start, the Avenger became one of the most outstanding naval aircraft of the Second World War. Almost 10 000 were built, of which nearly 1000 served in 15 first-line squadrons of the British FAA.

The first RAF fighter capable of exceeding a speed of 400 mph (644 km/h) was the Hawker Typhoon, which entered squadron service with No. 56 at Duxford in September 1941. Armed with four 20 mm cannon, and able to carry two 1000 lb bombs or eight 60 lb rocket-projectiles beneath its wings, the Typhoon became famous for 'train-busting' activities and devastated German *Panzer* divisions at Caen and the Falaise gap after the Allied invasion of Europe.

The first RAF Coastal Command aircraft to be equipped with ASV Mk II long-range radar were the Whitleys of No. 502 Squadron. On 30 November 1941 one of the Squadron's aircraft, a Whitley VII (Z9190), made the Command's first ASV 'kill', sinking U-206 in the Bay of Biscay.

The first Japanese attack on the US Pacific Fleet and shore installations at Pearl Harbor, Hawaii, was made on 7 December 1941. The attack, made without any previous declaration of war, brought immediate reaction from the United

The full strike potential of carrier aircraft was demonstrated for the first time on 7 December 1941, when Aichi D3As of the Imperial Japanese Navy began the attack on the US Navy base at Pearl Harbor. (US National Archives)

States, which declared war on Japan on 8 December. This marked the beginning of the Pacific War and American participation in the Second World War.

The first British combined operation against Europe during the Second World War was mounted to gain knowledge of the capability of German radar installations. British air, land and sea forces were used on 27–28 February 1942 to take vital components from a radar station at Bruneval, northern France.

The first German U-boats to be destroyed by the United States Navy during the Second World War were sunk on 1 and 15 March 1942. These sinkings were achieved by Lockheed PBO-1 Hudson aircraft of the US Navy's VP-82 Squadron, based at Argentia, Newfoundland.

The first combat operation carried out by Avro Lancaster heavy bombers was a mine-laying sortie flown by No. 44 (Bomber) Squadron, based at Waddington, Lincolnshire, over the Heligoland Bight on 3 March 1942. Their first night bombing attack was recorded when two of No. 44 Squadron's aircraft took part in a raid on Essen on the night of 10–11 March 1942. The first of many famous raids involved 12 aircraft of Nos 44 and 97 Squadrons led by Sqn Ldr J. D. Nettleton, which made a low-level daylight attack on the MAN Diesel factory at Augsburg on 17 April 1942. Their first operation with the Pathfinder Force was made on the night of 18–19 August 1942.

The first RAF aircraft to have the British H2S

Left   With heavy seas and an overcast sky, Doolittle's small group of B-25 Mitchell bombers take off from USS Hornet on the final leg to Japan. (US Air Force)

Right   Yorktown burning after being bombed during the Battle of Midway. (US Navy)

blind bombing radar system installed (on 27 March 1942) was the Handley Page Halifax V9977. This radar, in conjunction with the metal foil strips known as Window which were dropped from the air to confuse enemy radar, was **first used with devastating success in an attack on Hamburg** on 24–25 July 1943.

The first United States air attack on the Japanese mainland was made on 18 April 1942. This occurred when 16 North American B-25 Mitchell bombers led by Lt Col James Doolittle were flown off the US Navy carrier USS *Hornet* to raid Tokyo and other targets. Unable to return to their carrier, most aircraft landed in China.

The first naval battle in which the issue was decided by aircraft alone was the Battle of the Coral Sea, fought on 7–9 May 1942, between US Navy Task Force 17 and Vice-Admiral Takeo Takagi's Carrier Striking Force (part of Vice-Admiral Shigeyoshi Inouye's Task Force MO). The battle was fought to prevent Japanese support of an invasion of Port Moresby and to disrupt plans to launch air strikes against the Australian mainland. In this respect the battle must be considered to have been an American victory, although the large American carrier USS *Lexington* was sunk—**the first American carrier to be lost in the Second World War**. The Japanese carrier *Shoho* was attacked and sunk by Dauntless and Devastator aircraft from the *Lexington* and *York-town*, becoming **the first Japanese aircraft carrier to be destroyed by American airmen**. A total of 69 American naval aircraft was lost during the battle, while the Japanese losses amounted to about 85 aircraft and some 400 naval airmen (many of whom went down with the *Shoho*). The

Japanese carrier *Shokaku* was also damaged severely, but was able to limp home for repairs. The loss of experienced airmen and the absence of the *Shokaku* critically weakened Japanese naval forces that were to be involved in the vital Battle of Midway, fought 4–7 June 1942.

The first 'thousand bomber' raid against a German target was mounted by RAF Bomber Command. In the attack against Cologne on the night of 30–31 May 1942, 1046 aircraft were involved, of which 599 were Vickers Wellingtons.

The first and only time a Japanese fixed-wing aircraft attacked the continental USA during the Second World War occurred during June 1942. The aircraft, a Yokosuka E14Y1 ('Glen') light submarine-based reconnaissance floatplane launched from the Japanese submarine I-25, dropped four incendiary bombs on the wooded Oregon coast.

First night attack on a German U-boat in which a Leigh light was used to illuminate the target was made on the night of 3–4 June 1942 by a Vickers Wellington of No. 172 Squadron, RAF.

The first major naval battle of the Pacific War to confirm the lethal capability of an aircraft carrier strike force was that known as the Battle of Midway, fought off Midway island during 3 and 4 June 1942. In a first shattering blow, dive-bomber squadrons from the USS *Enterprise* and *Yorktown*, attacking from opposite directions to confuse Japanese defences, scored lethal hits on the Japanese carriers *Akagi*, *Kaga* and *Soryu*; within minutes they were blazing and out of action. Only *Hiryu*, some miles distant, had escaped but within the next two hours was spotted

by scout planes from *Yorktown* and quickly put out of action by dive-bombers from the *Enterprise*. Before this happened, however, *Yorktown* had been damaged severely by aircraft from *Hiryu*, and was later sunk by the Japanese submarine I-168 while under tow for repair in Hawaii. From that moment the Japanese fleet no longer held the initiative; not only had Japan lost four of her six first-line aircraft carriers, but very large numbers of experienced naval airmen.

The first aerial victories claimed during the 'Continuation War' between Finland and the Soviet Union, which broke out in June 1941, were two Soviet DB-3 bombers shot down by six Fokker D XXIs over the Riihimaki railway junction in the first air battle, which probably took place on 25 June 1942.

The first German turbojet-powered aircraft to enter operational service was the Messerschmitt Me 262A. The first flight of the Me 262V-1 prototype, powered by a single 1200 hp Junkers Jumo piston-engine, was made on 18 April 1941. It was not until 18 July 1942 that the first flight with two turbojet engines was recorded, these being Junkers 109-004A-0 turbojets, each of 1848 lb (840 kg) static thrust. The first production aircraft had 109-004B-1 turbojets of 1980 lb (900 kg) thrust, which provided a maximum level speed of about 539 mph (868 km/h) at 23 000 ft (7000 m).

The Me 262A-2a Sturmvogel (Stormbird) fighter-bomber variant is believed to have entered service with Kommando Schenk in early July 1944, moving to Juvincourt in France on 10 July 1944 to begin operations with six aircraft. This suggests that the Me 262 was the first turbojet-powered combat aircraft to enter operational

Messerschmitt Me 262A-2a Sturmvogel jet fighter in 1944. (MBB)

service. The Me 262A-1a Schwalbe (Swallow) entered operational service on 3 October 1944; a test unit was expanded and renamed Kommando Nowotny under the command of the Austrian ace, Major Walter Nowotny, and became operational on that date. One of the two Staffeln of the unit was based at Achmer, the other at Hesepe.

The first exploratory use of the RAF's Pathfinder Force was made on the night of 16–17 August 1942 to mount an attack on Emden, Germany. The official formation of the Pathfinder Force, under the command of Air Cdre D. C. T. Bennett, had only been completed on the previous day, 15 August.

The first Boeing B-17E to arrive in Britain was allocated to the USAAF's 97th Bombardment Group. This unit made its first operational sortie in Europe on 17 August 1942, when 12 B-17Es attacked Rouen.

First aircraft in the world to be equipped with

crew ejection seats as standard, and also the Luftwaffe's first operational aircraft with retractable tricycle landing gear, was the Heinkel He 219, first flown in prototype form on 15 November 1942. A twin-engined night fighter, the He 219 became operational during June 1943.

The first operational use of rocket-powered and remotely controlled missiles took place on 17 August 1943, when the Luftwaffe carried out anti-shipping attacks on British vessels in the Bay of Biscay. The aircraft used for the raid were Dornier Do 217E-5s of II/KG 100, which launched Henschel Hs 293A-1 missiles. On 27 August 1943 an Hs 293 sank the Royal Navy corvette HMS Egret in the Bay of Biscay.

The first air raid on a rocket research establishment was carried out by RAF bombers on the night of 17–18 August 1943 against Peenemünde. This followed air reconnaissance that had confirmed in June the existence of large rockets at the establishment.

The first specially designed anti-submarine patrol aircraft for the Japanese Navy was the Kyushu Q1W Tokai, the prototype of which made its first flight in September 1943. Only a few Q1W1s entered service before the war's end, these being equipped with radar and magnetic anomaly detection (MAD) equipment.

The first major warship to be sunk by air-launched missile was the Italian battleship Roma, struck by two Ruhrstahl/Kramer Fritz X-1 radio-controlled missiles launched from Luftwaffe Do 217K-2 bombers of III/KG 100 on 9 September 1943. Roma was one of many ships on their way to be surrendered to the Allies, and another, the Italia, was damaged by a Fritz X-1. As a matter of record, III/KG 100 had flown its first operational mission with Fritz X-1s over the Mediterranean on 29 August 1943.

The first operational use was made by the RAF of a 12 000 lb bomb, dropped by a Lancaster bomber on the Dortmund–Ems Canal on the night of 15–16 September 1943.

The first operational carrier-based fighter in the world with tricycle landing gear was the Grumman F7F-1 Tigercat. The first of two XF7F-1 prototypes made its first flight in December 1943, but rapidly changing requirements and alterations to specification meant that production

aircraft entered squadrons too late to see operational service in the Second World War. A two-seat night-fighter variant (the F7F-2N) was also produced.

The first turbojet-powered fighter to enter operational service with the USAAF/USAF was the Lockheed P-80 (later F-80) Shooting Star. The first XP-80 prototype (44-83020) was flown for the first time on 8 January 1944, but although the Shooting Star was too late to see service in the Second World War, it was deployed operationally with considerable success during the Korean War.

The first night bombing attack to be made from a US aircraft carrier was recorded on the night of 17–18 February 1944, when 12 TBF-1C Avengers from the USS Enterprise attacked Truk Island in the Pacific Ocean.

Making its first major daylight attack on Berlin, the USAAF deployed some 660 heavy bombers and escorting aircraft in this mission flown on 6 March 1944.

The first British twin-engined aircraft to land on the deck of an aircraft carrier was the pre-production prototype of the de Havilland Sea Mosquito (LR359) which, flown by Lt Cdr E. M. Brown, RN, landed on board HMS Indefatigable on 25 March 1944. Production Sea Mosquito TR33s first entered service with No. 811 Squadron at Ford, Sussex, in August 1946.

The world's first operational rocket-powered fighter was the Messerschmitt Me 163 Komet, first flown as a prototype under full power by Heini Dittmar at Peenemünde, Germany, on 13 August 1941. On one early flight Dittmar far exceeded what was then the official world speed record, attaining a speed of 571 mph (919 km/h); on 2 October 1941, after having been towed to altitude, he started the rocket motor and 2 min later recorded a speed of 623.85 mph (1004 km/h) in level flight. It was the success of these early trials that led to the Me 163 being developed as an operational rocket-powered interceptor. The first (and only swept-wing) rocket-engined aeroplane to enter operational squadron service with any air force was the Messerschmitt Me 163B-1 Komet interceptor fighter. It was powered by a Walter 109-509A-2 rocket motor, using the liquid propellants known as T-Stoff (hydrogen peroxide and water) and C-Stoff (hydrazine hydrate, methyl alcohol and water) to give a maximum static thrust of 3300 lb (1500 kg). Maximum speed of the Komet in combat was about 600 mph (965 km/h). The swept-wing, tailless Me 163B-1a was armed with two 30 mm MK 108 cannon; some machines are known to have carried various experimental armament systems in addition. The Komet equipped only one combat unit, Jagdgeschwader 400, which comprised eventually three Staffels. The whole unit was concentrated on Brandis in July 1944, and the first operation was flown against a group of B-17s on 16 August 1944, without any of the US bombers being destroyed. Although approximately 300 of these rocket-powered interceptors were built, JG 400 claimed only nine Allied aircraft destroyed and two probables before the units were disbanded in early 1945.

The first operational use of composite combat aeroplanes was by the German Luftwaffe, during the Allied liberation of France in June–July 1944. Devised originally under a programme designated 'Beethoven-Gerät', it was known subsequently as the 'Mistel-Programm'. The biggest problem was to develop an effective system by which the pilot of the single-seat upper aircraft could control and effect separation of the two components. Initial operational Mistel Is comprised an upper piloted Bf 109F-4 and a lower Ju 88A-4 which carried a warhead containing 3800 lb (1725 kg) of high explosive. The weapon was first issued to 2 Staffel of Kampfgeschwader 101, commanded by Hauptmann Horst Rudat, which was formed in April 1944. The first operational use of the device, known unofficially as *Vater und Sohn* (Father and Son), was on the night of 24–25 June 1944, when five Mistels were deployed against Allied shipping in the Seine Bay. Later versions of the composite had Focke-Wulf Fw 190s as the upper component.

The first operational use of napalm incendiary material was made on 17 July 1944 by USAAF Lockheed P-38 Lightnings making an attack on a fuel depot at Coutances, France.

The first jet aircraft to enter operational service with the RAF was the Gloster Meteor Mk I, powered by two 1700 lb (771 kg) thrust Rolls-Royce W2B/23 Welland I turbojet engines. Twenty Meteor Is were built, one of which was exchanged for an American-built Bell Aira-

Messerschmitt Me 163B-1 Komet with rocket motor firing. (MBB)

comet—**the first US-designed and built jet fighter.** Three others were used for development purposes and the remainder (EE213–EE222, and EE224–EE229) were delivered to No. 616 Squadron. The first two aircraft were delivered on 12 July 1944 to the Squadron, based at Culmhead, Somerset, under the command of Wg Cdr A. McDowall. The first combat sortie was flown from Manston by the Squadron on 27 July 1944 against V1 flying bombs but was unsuccessful owing to gun-firing difficulties. **The first combat success** was scored on 4 August 1944 by Flying Officer Dean who, after his guns had jammed, flew alongside the enemy bomb and, by tipping it with his wing, forced the missile into the ground. The aircraft was EE216.

The world's first piston-engined aircraft to attain a speed of more than 500 mph was a specially prepared Republic XP-47J Thunderbolt (43-46952) powered by a 2100 hp Pratt & Whitney R-2800-57 engine. This occurred on 4 August 1944 when a speed of 504 mph (811 km/h) was recorded.

The first loss of a jet aircraft in aerial combat is thought to have taken place on 28 August 1944, when Maj Joseph Myers and Lt M. Croy of the 78th Fighter Group, US 8th Air Force, were credited with the destruction of an Me 262 operated by the Kommando Schenk.

The first country in the world to be subjected to an assault by ballistic rocket missiles was France. On the morning of 8 September 1944 the first V-2 rocket was fired against Paris. At about 18.40 h on the same day the **first V-2 to land in**

The world's first operational jet bomber was the German Arado Ar 234 Blitz, which became operational in the autumn of 1944.

Above   Bomb-laden Mitsubishi Zero prepares to take off from a Philippine airfield on a kamikaze mission in October/November 1944. (US Navy)

Right   USS Saratoga in flames, having been struck by a Japanese kamikaze aircraft on 21 February 1945. (US Navy)

Britain fell in Chiswick, London, killing two people and injuring ten. The last rocket to fall in Britain was at Orpington, Kent, at 16.54 h on 27 March 1945, killing one person and injuring twenty-three. Between the two dates 1115 rockets struck Britain (of which about 500 hit London), killing 2855 and seriously injuring 6268. **The worst incident** is believed to have occurred when a V-2 fell upon a Woolworth store at Deptford, killing 160 and injuring 135. **The worst-hit country** was, however, Belgium, more than 1500 rockets being launched against Antwerp alone.

The first aerial victory against another piloted aircraft to be gained by the pilot of a jet aircraft has never been identified positively, but was certainly achieved during the first week of October 1944 by a pilot of Kommando Nowotny, the target being a Boeing B-17 Flying Fortress of the US 8th Air Force.

The first aviation unit formed specifically for suicide operations was the *Shimpu* Special Attack Corps, a group of 24 volunteer pilots commanded by Lt Yukio Seki, formed within the 201st (Fighter) Air Group, Imperial Japanese Navy, during the third week of October 1944. The unit, equipped with Mitsubishi Zero-Sen single-seat fighters, was formed for the task of diving into the flight decks of American aircraft carriers in the Philippines area, with a 250 kg bomb beneath the fuselage of each fighter. (*Shimpu* is an alternative pronunciation of the Japanese ideographs which also represent *kamikaze*, 'Divine Wind', the name applied more generally to Japanese suicide

operations.) The first successful suicide attack was made on 25 October 1944 when five Zeros, flown by members of the Special Attack Corps, sank the US escort carrier *St Lo*, and damaged the carriers *Kalinin Bay*, *Kitkun Bay* and *White Plains*. According to Japanese accounts the last sortie by suicide aircraft was flown on 15 August 1945, by seven aircraft of the Oita Detachment, 701st Air Group and led by Adm Matome Ugaki, commander of the 5th Air Fleet. United States records fail to confirm a *kamikaze* operation on this date, but they do list a total of 34 American naval vessels sunk and 288 damaged from the beginning of the suicide aircraft operations as mentioned above; those sunk included 3 escort aircraft carriers, 13 destroyers and a destroyer escort. The total number of suicide aircraft expended to gain these results are believed to be as follows:

	Sorties	Aircraft returned	Expended
Philippines area	421	43	378
Formosa area	27	14	13
Okinawa area	1809	879	930
Totals	2257	936	1321

It has not proved possible to distinguish between actual suicide aircraft and escort fighters in the Okinawa operations and this must necessarily invalidate the total figures to some extent. A rough estimate would show that the usual ratio of escort fighters to suicide aircraft on most sorties was about three to two, although late in the campaign many sorties were flown entirely without escort. (See also 1 April 1945.)

The first trans-Pacific incendiary balloon attacks against the continental USA: see Balloons and Airships (3 November 1944).

The first jet fighter ace in the world has not been identified positively, but it is thought that he was one of the pilots of the Kommando Nowotny. The unit was withdrawn from operations following the death in action of Maj Walter Nowotny on 8 November 1944, and later provided the nucleus for the new fighter wing, Jagdgeschwader 7 'Notwotny'; III Gruppe JG 7 became operational during December 1944. Hauptmann Franz Schall is known to have scored three aerial victories on the day of Nowotny's death, and served subsequently with 10 Staffel, JG 7; it is therefore entirely possible that he was the first pilot in the world to have achieved five confirmed aerial victories while flying jet aircraft. Other known jet aces of the Second World War are listed below. The fragmentary records which survived the final immolation of the Luftwaffe in 1945 prevent the preparation of a complete list, and the following should be regarded only as a framework for further research:

Oberstleutnant Heinz Bar (JV 44)	16
Hauptmann Franz Schall (10/JG 7)	14
Major Erich Rudorffer (II/JG 7)	12
Oberfeldwebel Hermann Buchner (III/JG 7)	12
Hermann Buchner (III/JG 7)	—
Leutnant Karl Schnorrer (II/JG 7) not fewer than	8
Leutnant Rudolf Rademacher not fewer than (II/JG 7)	8
Major Theodor Weissenberger (Staff/JG 7)	8
Oberleutnant Walter Schuck (3/JG 7)	8
Oberst Johannes Steinhoff (Staff/JG 7, JV 44)	6
Major Wolfgang Spate (Staff/JG 7)	5
Leutnant Klaus Neumann (JV 44)	5

The first major air attack on Tokyo was that made on 24 November 1944. This was mounted by Boeing B-29 Superfortresses of the USAAF's 21st Bomber Command, a total of 88 B-29s being despatched on this operation from their base on the Mariana Islands.

The first widespread operational use of air-to-air rockets against aeroplanes was by the Luftwaffe, probably by III/JG7 either in late 1944 or early 1945. The R4M unguided rockets, of which 24 were carried on racks under the wings of Messerschmitt Me 262A-1b fighters, were 55 mm folding-fin missiles aimed through a standard Revi gunsight. Fired in salvoes their effect was devastating, especially against the American formations of B-17 Flying Fortress and B-24 Liberator bombers.

The first turboprop-powered aircraft to fly in the USA, albeit with a mixed powerplant, was the Consolidated XP-81 escort fighter prototype flown on 7 February 1945. This aircraft had a conventionally mounted turboprop engine driving a tractor propeller, plus a turbojet engine mounted in the rear fuselage.

The first interceptor designed to be piloted, rocket-powered and vertically launched was the German Bachem Ba 349 Natter, which was first launched as an unmanned prototype on 18 December 1944. The first piloted test flight took place on 28 February 1945, which was not successful and the pilot, Oberleutnant Lothar Siebert, was killed. Three launches in March were, however, successful and the Natter was thereafter approved for deployment against Allied aircraft flying over Germany. However, no Natter was used operationally. Designed to be semi-expendable, armament was 24 × 73 mm unguided rockets packed into the nose.

The first test-drop of the 22 000 lb 'Grand Slam' bomb was made from an Avro Lancaster on 13 March 1945. This first operational drop of this bomb was made by Sqn Ldr C. C. Calder of No. 617 (Bomber) Squadron, flying Lancaster BI (Special) PD112. The bomb was dropped on the Bielefeld Viaduct on 14 March 1945, smashing two of its spans.

The first single-seat carrier-based dive-bomber and torpedo-carrier in the US Navy, the Douglas AD-1 Skyraider was developed too late to see operational service in the Second World War. First flown on 18 March 1945, the Skyraider was to prove an important naval aircraft in the Korean and Vietnam conflicts. When supplied to the British Royal Navy under the MAP, it filled a unique position as an airborne early-warning aircraft. Designated AEW1 in British service, the Skyraiders were also the last piston-engined fixed-wing aircraft in first-line service with the FAA.

The first purpose-designed suicide aircraft and the only rocket-powered aircraft to be used operationally outside Germany was the Japanese Yokosuka MXY-7 Ohka. This single-seater was powered by three small solid fuel rocket motors, which were ignited after the aircraft had been air launched from a carrier bomber and had travelled some distance in gliding flight. The first operational sortie by Ohkas was carried out on 21 March 1945 but was not successful. The first successful Ohka missions were flown on 1 April 1945, when the American battleship USS *West Virginia*, the British aircraft carrier HMS *Indefatigable* and other ships were damaged. On 12 April an Ohka sank the American destroyer USS *Mannert L. Abele* off Okinawa.

The first twin-engined single-seat fighter to operate from carriers of the Royal Navy was the de Havilland Sea Hornet F20, the prototype Sea Hornet (PX212) making its first flight on 19 April 1945. Aircraft of this type equipped No. 801 Squadron, and were embarked in HMS *Implacable*

Above   *The Bat radar-guided air-to-surface missile. (Associated Press)*

Right   Enola Gay, *from which the first atomic bomb was dropped on Japan. (The Boeing Company)*

in 1949, remaining in service until the squadron was re-equipped with Sea Furies in 1951. Production aircraft were powered by two 2030 hp Rolls-Royce Merlin 133s or 134s, and had a maximum speed of 467 mph (752 km/h) at 22 000 ft (6700 m).

The first American air-to-surface radar-guided missile was the Bat, an unpowered glide-bomb developed by Hugh L. Dryden. Carrying a 1000 lb (454 kg) warload, the missile was about 12 ft (3.65 m) long and, on being launched from its carrier aircraft, used radar to home on its target. It possessed a range of about 20 miles (30 km), and in April 1945 one such missile succeeded in sinking a Japanese destroyer at this range.

The world's first operational atomic bomb was dropped on the Japanese city of Hiroshima on 6 August 1945, carried by the B-29 Superfortress *Enola Gay*, captained by Col Paul W. Tibbets Jr. A second operational atomic bomb was deployed three days later, carried by the B-29 Superfortress *Bock's Car* captained by Maj Charles W. Sweeney, and dropped on the city of Nagasaki. These two devastating air attacks quickly brought an end to Japanese resistance and the signature of the surrender documents aboard the battleship USS *Missouri* (anchored in Tokyo Bay) brought an official end to the Pacific War on 2 September 1945.

The first American aeroplane to land under jet power on a ship was a Ryan FR-1 Fireball compound fighter, fitted with a conventionally mounted Wright R-1820-72W radial piston-

engine as well as a General Electric I-16 turbojet installed in the rear fuselage. This combination had resulted from US Navy doubts of the suitability of jet-powered aircraft for carrier operations. Flown by Ensign Jake C. West on to the escort carrier USS *Wake Island* on 6 November 1945, it had been intended to fly on using the reciprocating engine, but this failed on the approach and West landed under jet-power. **The first US (all-) jet aircraft to land on an aircraft carrier**, on 21 July 1946, was the McDonnell FD-1 Phantom prototype, which landed on the USS *Franklin D Roosevelt*. Production aircraft were redesignated subsequently FH-1.

The first American surface-to-air anti-aircraft guided missile was the Western Electric SAM-A-7 Nike-Ajax, development of which was started by Bell Telephone Laboratories in 1945. Before the weapon entered service more than 1500 test rounds were fired, and by 1959 10 000 had been

delivered. Its place was taken in 1959–60 by the Nike-Hercules.

The first two post-war world absolute speed records were established by Gloster Meteor F4

Above *The FD-1 Phantom approaches USS* Franklin D. Roosevelt *on 21 July 1946, to record the first landing of a US pure jet aircraft on a carrier deck. (McDonnell Douglas)*

Left *Royal Australian Air Force Meteor F8 jet fighters of No 77 Squadron in Korea.*

Left   *One of the first two Soviet jet fighters to enter service was the Mikoyan-Gurevich MiG-9.*

Right   *Martin XB-48 six-jet bomber.*

fighters. On 7 November 1945 Gp Capt H. J. Wilson established a record speed of 606 mph (975 km/k) at Herne Bay, Kent, flying the Meteor EE454 *Britannia*. On 7 September 1946 Gp Capt E. M. Donaldson raised the record to 616 mph (991 km/h) near Tangmere, West Sussex, in Meteor EE549. The three Meteors allocated to the re-formed RAF High Speed Flight (EE548-550), which was to make the attempt to set a new speed record in 1946, had their wings clipped, reducing wing span from 43 ft 0 in (13.11 m) to 37 ft 2 in (11.33 m). Unfortunately, it was discovered that this reduced their maximum speed by almost 58 mph (93 km/h) and full-span wings were used for the record attempt. Because the clipped-wing modification improved structural integrity, as well as rate of roll, it subsequently became standard on all but the earliest F4s. In 1948 Meteor F4s superseded F3s in the RAF's first-line fighter squadrons until they, in turn, were supplanted by F8s. In May 1950, the F4s which equipped No. 222 Squadron at Leuchars became the first jet fighters to be based in Scotland. Meteor F8s first entered service with No. 245 Squadron at Horsham St Faith, Norfolk, on 29 June 1950. The Meteor F4 was powered by two 350 lb (1587 kg) thrust Rolls-Royce Derwent 5 engines, the F8 by 3600 lb (1633 kg) thrust Derwent 8s. Meteor F8s of the Royal Australian Air Force were the only British jet fighters to see action in the Korean War.

The world's first pure jet aircraft to operate from an aircraft carrier was a de Havilland Vampire I, the third prototype (LZ551) which had been modified for deck-landing trials. It was first landed on HMS *Ocean*, a light fleet carrier of the Colossus Class, by Lt Cdr E. M. Brown, RNVR, on 3 December 1945. The first deck landing was followed by trials in which 15 take-offs and landings were made in two days.

The Mikoyan MiG-9 and the Yakovlev Yak-15 were the first Soviet pure jet aircraft, both flown in prototype form on 24 April 1946. The Yak-15, designed by Alexander S. Yakovlev, was the first jet fighter to enter squadron service with the Soviet Air Forces when delivered to the IA-PVO in early 1947. Powered by a single RD-10 turbojet (a Russian adaptation of the German Jumo 004B engine) developing initially 1875 lb (850 kg) thrust, it was armed with two 23 mm Nudelman-Suranov NS-23 guns and had a top speed of 488 mph (786 km/h) at 16 400 ft (5000 m). Like the first Tupolev jet bombers, the Yak-15 was also the result of adapting a piston-engine airframe for jet propulsion. The prototype retained the wings, cockpit, tailplane and tailwheel landing gear of a Yakovlev Yak-3, the new engine being mounted in the forward fuselage. This meant that the jet efflux was below the pilot's cockpit, and production aircraft had the fuselage undersurface protected by heat-resistant stainless steel. It meant also that the first batch of production aircraft had an all-metal tail-wheel. This proved unsatisfactory, and the Yak-15 was retrofitted with tricycle landing gear. A member of the company test team in 1947 was Olga Yamschikova, **probably the first woman in history to fly a turbojet-powered fighter aircraft**.

The first high-speed twin-engined strike aircraft designed specifically to operate from aircraft carriers of the Royal Navy was the Short Sturgeon. Originating from a wartime requirement, to operate from *Ark Royal* and *Hermes* class carriers, the war's end resulted in the Sturgeon being completed to satisfy a gunnery training and

target-towing role. The first prototype made its maiden flight on 7 June 1946.

The first American pure jet aeroplane to operate from a carrier was the McDonnell FH-1 Phantom, first operating from the USS *Franklin D Roosevelt* on 21 July 1946. It was **also the first jet fighter to serve with first-line squadrons of the US Navy and the US Marine Corps.**

The first recorded use of an ejection seat, to enable a man to escape from an aircraft in flight, occurred on 24 July 1946. This was the date when the first experimental live ejection was made, using a Martin-Baker ejection seat installed in a Gloster Meteor. With the aircraft travelling at 320 mph (515 km/h), 'guinea pig' Bernard Lynch ejected at a height of 8000 ft (2440 m). In subsequent tests, Lynch made successful ejections at 420 mph (675 km/h) at heights up to 30 000 ft (9145 m). It should be noted that the wartime Heinkel He 219 Uhu (Owl) **was the first operational aircraft to be equipped with ejection seats**; while no dates have been recorded, it is known that some lives were saved by this equipment in the He 219.

The first manned test of an American ejection seat was made by Sgt L. Lambert, USAAF, who was ejected from a Northrop P-61 Black Widow on 17 August 1946. The two-seat aircraft was travelling at 300 mph (483 km/h) at 7800 ft (2375 m).

The first post-war long distance record for aeroplanes was set by a modified Lockheed P2V-1 Neptune maritime reconnaissance aircraft, the *Truculent Turtle*, which flew a distance of 11 236 miles (18 082 km) between 29 September and 1 October 1946. On 7 March 1949 a later-version P2V-2 took off from the carrier USS *Coral Sea* at the then record take-off weight from a ship of 74 000 lb (33 566 kg).

The first six-turbojet bomber to fly in America was the Martin XB-48. Only two prototypes were built, the first of them flown on 22 June 1947, and both were powered by six wing-mounted Allison J35 turbojet engines.

The Soviet Union's first jet-powered bomber to fly, on 24 July 1947, was the Ilyushin Il-22. However, early flight tests proved disappointing and its development was abandoned.

The first Soviet jet bomber to achieve very limited production status was the Tupolev Tu-12, little more than a Tu-2 piston-engined bomber re-engined with gas-turbines. The prototype probably flew for the first time on 27 July 1947, powered by two 3525 lb (1600 kg) thrust RD-10 engines, derived from the Junkers 004B. Power plant of the later aircraft consisted of RD-500 engines, the Russian equivalent of the Rolls-Royce Derwent 5, which developed 4410 lb (2000 kg) thrust.

Free from Army control for the first time since its foundation, the United States Army Air Force became an independent member of the new unified US armed services on 18 September 1947, receiving the title United States Air Force.

The North American F-86 Sabre, which was to become **the USAF's first sweptwing fighter, and its first fighter able to exceed a speed of Mach 1 in a shallow dive**, was flown for the first time in XP-86 prototype (NA-140) form on 1 October 1947.

The first launch of a ballistic missile in the USSR was made on 30 October 1947, when a reconstructed German V-2 was fired from Kazakhstan. (At the close of the Second World War, Soviet forces had captured Peenemünde, the secret German rocket research establishment, together with missiles and technical data.) The V-2 formed the basis of the first Soviet ballistic missile, deployed with an improved missile known as Pobeda which had a range of 559 miles (900 km). The Pobeda was designed under the direction of Sergey Korolev and the first test missile was launched in 1948. It was in mass production by 1950 and subsequently was allocated the code name *Shyster* by NATO. Pobeda missiles were also the first to be used in launching experiments with dogs, between 1949 and 1952. The first Soviet intercontinental ballistic missile was test launched successfully in August 1957.

The world's first aircraft to fly on the power of a single turboprop engine was the Boulton Paul P.108 Balliol, a three-seat advanced trainer for service with the RAF. It was first flown with its Armstrong Siddeley Mamba turboprop engine on 24 March 1948.

The world's first turbojet-powered aircraft to exceed a speed of Mach 1 was the YP-86A prototype of the North American F-86 Sabre which, on 25 April 1948, attained supersonic speed in a shallow dive.

The first wind tunnel with a test section having a continuous capability of 3000 mph (4828 km/h) was that activated by the USAF at Aberdeen, Maryland, announced as being operational on 23 May 1948.

The first deliveries of food and other supplies into West Berlin were made on 26 June 1948 by Douglas C-47s of the USAF based near Frankfurt. This marked the beginning of the Berlin Airlift (or Operation 'Vittles' as it was known to the USAF) and also of the **first major post-war 'Cold War' confrontation between East and West.**

The first east–west crossing of the North Atlantic by turbojet-powered aircraft was made by six RAF de Havilland Vampire F.Mk 3s on 14 July 1948, flying via Iceland and Greenland.

First transatlantic deployment of a USAF jet fighter unit (the 56th Fighter Group) **and the first west–east crossing of the North Atlantic by turbojet-powered aircraft** was achieved in 9 h 20 min on 20 July 1948. This involved 16

Lockheed F-80 (formerly P-80) Shooting Stars which were *en route* to Fürstenfeldbruck, Germany via the UK.

The USAF's first turbojet-powered all-weather interceptor was the prototype of the Northrop XF-89 Scorpion, which recorded its first flight at Edwards AFB, California, on 16 August 1948. The Scorpion entered USAF service in 1950.

The first European swept-wing jet fighter to enter operational service after the Second World War was the Swedish Saab J-29. It first flew on 1 September 1948 and joined the Day Fighter Wing F13 of the Flygvapnet near Norrkoping in May 1951. Nicknamed *Tunnan* (Barrel) and powered by a British de Havilland Ghost turbojet of 4410 lb (2000 kg) thrust, the J-29B possessed a top speed of 658 mph (1059 km/h) at 5000 ft (1525 m) or Mach 0.90 at the tropopause.

The first four-jet bomber to fly in the United States was the North American NA-130, as the XB-45 Tornado prototype, and first joining the 47th Bombardment Group at Barksdale AFB, Louisiana in November 1948 it was **also the first operational jet bomber to serve with the USAF.**

The prototype of **the first indigenous French jet fighter** recorded its first flight on 23 January 1949. This was the Dassault MD.450 Ouragan of which 350 were delivered to the Armée de l'Air in the 1950s.

The first non-stop round-the-world flight was accomplished between 26 February and 2 March

Left   *Soviet operated V-2 ballistic missile.*

Right   *The first European operational swept-wing jet fighter was the Swedish Saab J-29. (Saab-Scania)*

1949. This was made by the Boeing B-50 *Lucky Lady II* with a crew commanded by Capt James Gallagher, USAF, and covering a distance of 23 452 miles (37 742 km) in 94 h 1 min. Taking off from and landing back at Carswell AFB, Texas, the B-50 was flight-refuelled four times.

The first turbojet-powered all-weather interceptor to serve with the USAF's Air Defense Command was the Lockheed F-94 Starfire, first flown in YF-94 prototype (48-356) form on 1 July 1949.

The first use of an ejection seat by a US airman for an emergency escape from an aircraft was recorded on 9 August 1949. This occurred when Lt J. L. Fruin of the US Navy parted company with his McDonnell F2H-1 Banshee which was travelling at some 575 mph (925 km/h) over South Carolina.

The first aircraft in the world powered by a coupled twin-turbine engine driving contra-rotating co-axial four-blade propellers was the Fairey Gannet, first flown on 19 September 1949. The unusual power plant was an Armstrong Siddeley Double Mamba, each of its two sections driving one propeller. Half of the engine could be shut down and its propeller feathered to provide a more economical cruise power setting.

The first aircraft to carry more than 100 passengers in flight across the North Atlantic was a USAF C-74 Globemaster I of MATS. Landing at Marham, Norfolk, after a non-stop flight from the US on 18 November 1949, the Globemaster had carried a total of 103 passengers and the aircraft's crew.

First American-built aircraft to enter RAF service after the Second World War were ex-USAF B-29 and B-29A Superfortresses, given the RAF designation Washington B1. No. 149 Squadron at Marham was the first squadron to receive these aircraft, in March 1950, and a total of 88 entered RAF service.

Following the end of the Second World War the first major East–West military confrontation occurred when the Communist forces of North Korea crossed the 38th Parallel to invade South Korea on 25 June 1950, marking the start of the Korean War. The USAF's Japanese-based Far Eastern Air Forces were immediately directed to the area to evacuate US nationals and provide initial support to the South Koreans.

The first victory by an American pilot in the Korean War occurred on 27 June 1950, when Lt William Hudson with radar observer Lt Carl Frasee in the North American F-82G Twin Mustang 46-383 shot down a North Korean Yakovlev Yak-9 north-west of Seoul.

The first operation in the Korean War by Boeing B-29 Superfortresses was made on 27 June 1950 when aircraft of the USAF's 19th Bombardment Group attacked railway installations and the Han river bridges at Seoul.

The first US bomber strike into North Korea occurred on 28 June 1950, when Douglas B-26s of the 8th Bomber Squadron, 3rd Bomb Group, made an attack on railway installations at Munsan.

The first US Navy jet fighter to take part in air combat was the Grumman F9F-2 Panther, several

Left *Panther jet fighters on board USS* Valley Forge *line up for take off on a strike mission against targets in North Korea, July 1950. (US Navy)*

Right *The single B.Mk 2 model Valiant V-bomber.*

of which took off from the carrier USS *Valley Forge* off Korea on 3 July 1950 and went into action against North Korean forces. A US Navy pilot of a Grumman Panther shot down a MiG-15 on 9 November 1950, and thus became the first US Navy pilot to shoot down another jet aircraft. The Panther was the first jet fighter designed by the Grumman Corporation, and the first two XF9F-2 prototypes were powered by imported Rolls-Royce Nene turbojets of 5000 lb (2268 kg) thrust.

The first US Marine Corps air operation in support of the South Koreans was flown from the escort carrier USS *Sicily* on 3 August 1950. This occurred when Vought F4U-4 Corsairs of squadron VMF-214 made a rocket and bomb attack on Chinju.

The first non-stop crossing of the North Atlantic by a turbojet-powered fighter aircraft was recorded on 22 September 1950, when a Republic EF-84E Thunderjet with hose-and-drogue flight refuelling capability flown by Col David C. Schilling, USAF, flew from the UK to Limestone, Maine. The flight was achieved by making three in-flight refuellings *en route*.

The first aerial victory to be gained by the pilot of one jet aircraft over another was achieved on 8 November 1950, when Lt Russel J. Brown Jr of the 51st Interceptor Wing, USAF, flying a Lockheed F-80C, shot down a MiG-15 fighter of the Chinese People's Republic air force over Sinuiju on the Yalu River, the border between North Korea and China.

The first turbojet-powered night fighter to enter service with the RAF, serving with No. 29

Squadron at Tangmere, Sussex, in January 1951, was the Meteor NF11, developed by Armstrong Whitworth.

The first jet aircraft to fly the North Atlantic non-stop and unrefuelled was an English Electric Canberra B.Mk 2 on 21 February 1951, which was flown from Britain to Baltimore and was later purchased by the USAF to become the first Canberra to carry American markings. Canberras were the first jet bombers produced in Britain and the first to serve with the RAF. The type had the unique distinction of being the first aircraft of non-US design to enter operational service with the USAF after the end of the Second World War. USAF approval for licence-production of the Canberra by the Glenn L. Martin Company was given on 6 March 1951, leading to a pre-production batch of eight B-57As (the original USAF designation), the first of these making its first flight at Baltimore, Maryland, on 20 July 1953.

The first west European fighter to be dived supersonically, on 23 February 1951, was the French Dassault MD.452 Mystère prototype. When the type entered service with the Armée de l'Air in 1955, and by then powered with the SNECMA Atar turbojet, **it was the nation's first completely indigenous jet fighter.**

The first jet bomber to be produced in the UK, and the first to serve with the RAF when it became operational in May 1951, was the English Electric Canberra. The prototype Canberra, the A.1, was first flown in prototype form on 13 May 1949.

The first (and only) **use of air-dropped torpedoes during the Korean War** occurred on 1

May 1951. These were deployed by US Navy Douglas Skyraiders and Vought Corsairs flying off the USS *Princeton* to attack the flood gates of the Hwachon dam.

The first British V-bomber (so-called from the wing leading-edge plan-form) was the Vickers Valiant, of which the prototype (WB210) first flew on 18 May 1951. Two Mark 1 and one Mark 2 prototypes were built, and were followed by 104 production aircraft, the first of which (WP199) flew on 21 December 1953. They were powered by various versions of the Rolls-Royce Avon axial-flow turbojet, four such engines being located in the wing roots. The Valiant entered RAF service with No. 138 Squadron at Gaydon, Warwickshire, in early 1955 and afterwards equipped Nos 7, 49, 90, 148, 207, 214 and 543 Squadrons.

The first surface-to-surface weapon to enter service with the US Air Force was the Martin TM-61A Matador 'flying-bomb' which joined Tactical Missile Wings in the USA, Germany, Korea and Taiwan from 1951. By 1957 Martin's Baltimore factory had delivered 1000 Matadors.

The distinction of being **the world's first jet night fighter squadron** belongs to the RAF's No. 25 Squadron which, when based at West Malling (Kent) during July 1951, was equipped with de Havilland Vampire NF.Mk 10s.

The first single-seat sweptwing interceptor jet fighter to enter service with the RAF was the Supermarine Swift, the prototype (WJ960) of which was flown for the first time on 5 August 1951.

The first ballistic missile to enter service in the United States was the Firestone SSM-A-17

Corporal, a liquid-fuelled rocket-propelled (un-boosted) missile which entered service with the US Army during the early 1950s and subsequently with the British Army. It had a range of about 75–100 miles (120–160 km). Corporal had been designed in 1951 and was the first army missile with a warhead of a kiloton.

The first standardized jet fighter to serve in FAA first-line squadrons was the Supermarine Attacker, which was also the first aircraft powered by the Rolls-Royce Nene turbojet. The type entered service with No. 800 Squadron at Ford, Sussex, on 22 August 1951, and this was the FAA's first operational jet squadron. When withdrawn from first line service, the Attackers were transferred to RNVR air squadrons: when No. 1831 Squadron received these aircraft on 14 May 1955, it became the first jet fighter squadron of the RNVR.

The first British delta-wing interceptor fighter, and the first twin-jet delta fighter in the world, was the Gloster Javelin. First flight of the prototype (WD804) was made by Sqn Ldr W. A. Waterton on 26 November 1951. **The Javelin was also the RAF's first purpose-built all-weather interceptor fighter.** The use of the delta-wing posed many aerodynamic problems, early flights suffering from control surface vibration and buffeting. On the 99th flight, on 29 June 1952, both elevators were lost following violent flutter. By superb flying, Waterton managed to control the aircraft in pitch, by means of the variable incidence tailplane, and bring it in to a fast landing, which caused the landing gear to collapse. For his skill and courage in saving the aircraft and its flight recorder, Waterton was awarded the

George Medal. **The first production Javelin FAW1** (XA544), powered by two 8150 lb (3697 kg) thrust Armstrong Siddeley Sapphire AS Sa6 turbojet engines, made its first flight on 22 July 1954. First deliveries to No. 46 Squadron at Odiham, Hampshire, began in February 1956.

The first operational pilotless long-range ground-to-air interceptor was the Boeing IM-99 Bomarc. The first prototypes, designated XF-99s, were tested in 1952. Launched vertically, the Bomarc was powered by two Marquardt RJ43-MA ramjets and incorporated a Westinghouse guidance system. Its cruising speed was Mach 2.8 and maximum range varied from 200 miles (320 km) for the IM-99A to 400 miles (640 km) for the IM-99B.

IM-99B Bomarc pilotless long-range ground-to-air interceptor.

The first operational inflight refuelling of combat aircraft was recorded on 29 May 1952. This involved 12 Republic F-84E Thunderjets of the USAF's 159th Fighter-Bomber Squadron which had taken off from Itazuke (Japan) to attack a target at Sariwon; following the attack they made a rendezvous with KB-29 tankers over Taegu, taking on sufficient fuel for the return flight to their base.

The first turbojet-powered aircraft to complete a non-stop trans-Pacific flight was a North American RB-45 reconnaissance aircraft of the USAF which was flown from Elmendorf AFB (Alaska) to Yokota AB (Japan) on 29 July 1952.

The world's first large bomber to have a delta-wing plan-form was the Avro Vulcan B.1, the prototype of which (VX770) flew for the first time on 30 August 1952. Production aircraft entered service with RAF Bomber Command in May 1956, equipping No. 230 Operational Conversion Unit at Waddington, Lincolnshire, and the type was to record more than a quarter-century of operational use with the RAF. The Vulcan was the second aircraft in the RAF's V-bomber programme, the third and last being the Handley Page Victor which was flown in prototype (WB771) form for the first time on 24 December 1952.

The first North Korean jet aircraft to be shot down at night, a Yakovlev Yak-15 on the night of 3 November 1952, fell to the guns of a Douglas F3D-2 Skynight. This was a US Marine Corps aircraft crewed by Major William T. Strattio Jr with Master-Sergeant Han C. Hoglind as his radar operator.

The US Navy's first angled-deck aircraft carrier, the USS *Antietam*, began operational flight testing with Navy aircraft on 12 January 1953.

The world's first fighter aircraft capable of sustained supersonic speed in level flight, the North American F-100 Super Sabre, was flown for the first time in YF-100A prototype form on 25 May 1953.

The first transatlantic deployment of the USAF's Boeing B-47 Stratojet bomber by Strategic Air Command was accomplished during the period 3–5 June 1953. This involved aircraft of the 306th Bomb Wing which staged through Limestone AFB (Maine) *en route* to RAF Fairford (Gloucestershire).

The first British transport aircraft designed specifically to air-drop heavy loads, and also the RAF's largest aircraft at the time of its introduction, was the Blackburn Beverley. Powered by four 2850 hp Bristol Centaurus 173 engines, the prototype (WZ889) flew for the first time on 14 June 1953. Able to carry a payload of almost 22 tons (22.4 tonnes), Beverleys began to equip No. 47 Squadron Transport Command in March 1956.

The first air disaster involving the death of more than 100 people occurred on 18 June 1953, when a USAF C-124 Globemaster II transport crashed on take-off from Tachikawa AFB (Tokyo) killing a total of 129 crew and passengers.

The world's first 'over 700 mph' speed record was set at 715.60 mph (1151.64 km/h) on 16 July 1953. This was achieved by Lt Col W. F. Barnes, USAF, flying a North American F-86D Sabre.

Above *USS* Antietam, *the first aircraft carrier with an angled deck.*

Left *No 74 Squadron, RAF, Lightning fighters.*

The RAF's first indigenous swept-wing fighter, the **Supermarine Swift F.Mk 1**, entered service with No. 56 Squadron at RAF Waterbeach on 13 February 1954. The aircraft was found to have a number of shortcomings and was soon withdrawn from service in the interceptor role.

The first turbojet powered all-weather fighter to serve with the Royal Navy was the de Havilland Sea Venom, which first entered service with No. 890 Squadron, which re-formed at Yeovilton, Somerset, on 20 March 1954. At the end of 1958 three Sea Venoms of No. 893 Squadron carried out the first firings of Firestreak missiles by an operational fighter squadron of the Royal Navy.

The first supersonic operational carrier-borne naval interceptor in the world was the Grumman F11F-1 Tiger of the US Navy. Designated originally F9F-9, this was changed after the first three production aircraft had been delivered and, in 1962, was designated finally F-11. The prototype, powered by a Wright J65-W-6 turbojet rated at 7800 lb (3538 kg) thrust, flew for the first time on 30 July 1954. The F-11A was capable of a speed of 890 mph (1432 km/h) in level flight at 40 000 ft (12 200 m), and was armed with four 20 mm cannon. Two or four Sidewinder missiles could be carried on underwing pylons. F11F-1s entered service with the US Navy's VA-156 Squadron in March 1957. Two F11F-1s were powered by 15 000 lb (6805 kg) thrust General Electric J79-GE-3A engines, and demonstrated Mach 2 performance in level flight.

The first supersonic single-seat fighter to serve with the RAF, the English Electric (later BAC) Lightning, designed by W. E. W. Petter, flew for the first time on 4 August 1954, piloted by Wg Cdr R. P. Beamont. Entering operational service with No. 74 Squadron at Coltishall, Norfolk, in July 1960, it was the first RAF fighter capable of speeds in excess of Mach 2, and the RAF's first integrated weapons system. During the research which led to its construction, Britain's first transonic wind tunnel was built.

The first man to escape from an aeroplane flying at supersonic speed and live was George Franklin Smith, test pilot for North American Aviation Corporation, who ejected from an F-100 Super Sabre on 26 February 1955 off Laguna Beach, California. After failure of the controls in a dive, Smith fired his ejector seat at an indicated speed of Mach 1.05 or more than 700 mph (1125 km/h). After being unconscious for five days Smith made an almost complete recovery from his injuries and within nine months had been passed fit to resume flying.

The first jet fighter in the world with a variable-incidence wing was the Chance Vought (subsequently Ling-Temco-Vought, or LTV) F-8 Crusader supersonic air-superiority fighter of the US Navy. The operation of such a high-performance aircraft from the deck of an aircraft carrier meant that to achieve an acceptable landing speed an excessive nose-up attitude would result. The use of a variable-incidence wing provided the necessary compromise. The first of two XF8U-1 prototypes, powered by a Pratt & Whitney J57-P-11 turbojet engine, made its first flight on 25 March 1955. Deliveries of the production Crusader, under the designation F-8A, began to VF-32 (US Navy Fighter Squadron 32) on 25 March 1957, serving originally at sea aboard the USS *Saratoga*. This initial production version was powered by a J57-P-12 or -14 engine, providing a maximum level speed of 1100 mph (1770 km/h) at 40 000 ft (12 200 m). Armament comprised four 20 mm cannon and, on early models, a fuselage pack of 32 air-to-air rockets. Later F-8As carried two fuselage-mounted Sidewinder missiles.

First US Navy unit to receive the Douglas A3D Skywarrior carrier-based attack bomber was squadron VAH-1 based at NAS Jacksonville (Florida) on 31 March 1956. More than 30 years of operational use has given the Skywarrior an honoured place in Navy history as **its most versatile carrier-based aircraft**.

The first operational overflight by a Lockheed U-2 reconnaissance aircraft was made on 4 July 1956. Taking off from Wiesbaden (Germany) the U-2's route took it over Moscow, Leningrad and the Soviet Baltic Sea coast.

The first member of the RAF to survive a supersonic ejection (and the second man in the world) was Flying Officer Hedley Molland who escaped from a Hawker Hunter fighter on 3 August 1955. Flying at 40 000 ft (12 200 m), the aircraft went into an uncontrollable dive. All of Flying Officer Molland's efforts to regain control failed, and by the time he ejected his stricken machine was travelling at an estimated Mach 1.10, its height about 10 000 ft (3050 m). Descending in the sea he was picked up by a tug, and recovered in hospital from his injuries which included a broken arm (caused by flailing in the slipstream) and a fractured pelvis.

The world's first parachute escape from an aircraft travelling at speed on the ground was achieved by Sqn Ldr J. S. Fifield, on 3 September 1955, at Chalgrove airfield, Oxfordshire. This occurred when he was ejected from the rear cockpit of a modified Gloster Meteor 7, piloted by Capt J. E. D. Scott, Chief Test Pilot of Martin-Baker Ltd, manufacturers of the ejection seat. The speed of the aircraft at the moment of ejection was 120 mph (194 km/h) and the maximum height reached by the seat was 70 ft (21 m) above the runway.

The first supersonic tactical fighter-bomber to be designed as such, and in operational form one of the USAF's most important weapons in Vietnam, the YF-105A prototype of the Republic F-105 Thunderchief was flown for the first time on 22 October 1955. Exceeding Mach 1 during this flight, the definitive F-105D had a maximum speed in excess of Mach 2 and all-weather capability resulting from its fully integrated automatic flight and fire control systems.

The USAF's first operational delta-winged aircraft was the Convair F-102A Delta Dagger which entered service initially with the 327th Fighter Interceptor Squadron at George AFB (California) in April 1956; it had first flown in YF-102A prototype form on 24 October 1953.

The first air-to-air guided missile to be adopted by the US Air Force was the Hughes GAR-1 Falcon, six of which were carried in wing-tip pods on the Northrop F-89H Scorpion all-weather fighter. They entered operational service in 1956.

The world's first known air-transportable hydrogen bomb was dropped on 21 May 1956, from a Boeing B-52B flying at 50 000 ft (15 240 m) over Bikini Atoll in the Pacific.

Northrop F-89H Scorpion with Falcon missiles attached to the wingtip pods.

Convair B-58 Hustler, the USAF's first supersonic bomber.

The first turbojet aircraft in the world to be used in the military transport role was a modified version of the de Havilland Comet Series 2, the first of which was delivered to RAF Transport Command at Lyneham, Wiltshire, on 7 July 1956.

The first-ever firing of a nuclear-tipped air-to-air missile was carried out on 19 July 1956 when a Northrop F-89J Scorpion discharged a Douglas MB-1 Genie at 15 000 ft (4500 m) above Yucca Flat, Nevada, in the USA. This missile incorporated a warhead of about 1.5 kilotons yield and the fighter turned away sharply to avoid the missile's blast. The warhead was detonated after having travelled about 3 miles horizontally, but USAF observers standing directly below the explosion reported no immediate ill-effects from fall-out.

The first practical steps towards the creation of the post-war Luftwaffe came on 1 February 1956, when the West German Ministry of Defence initiated a pilot training scheme. The actual formation date of the Luftwaffe der Deutschen Bundesrepublik was on 24 September 1956.

The first British atomic bomb was dropped by a Vickers Valiant (WZ366) of No. 49 (Bomber) Squadron, RAF, captained by Sqn Ldr E. J. G. Flavell, over Maralinga, Southern Australia, on 11 October 1956.

First military aircraft to land on the ice at the South Pole was a US Navy Douglas R4D on 31 October 1956. Rear Admiral G. L. Dufek (in command) and his crew of seven were the first men to stand on that spot since January 1912.

Becoming the USAF's first supersonic bomber when it entered service in early 1960, the XB-58 prototype of the Convair B-58 Hustler, a four-turbojet delta-wing medium-bomber, was flown for the first time at Fort Worth, Texas, on 11 November 1956.

B-52B Stratofortress lands back at March AFB, having made the first non-stop round-the-world flight by a turbojet aircraft.

The first non-stop round-the-world flight by turbojet-powered aircraft, made by three USAF Boeing B-52B Stratofortresses, was completed on 18 January 1957 after a flight of 45 hr 19 min. Commanded by Maj Gen Archie J. Old, USAF, the 24 325 mile (39 147 km) flight was made at an average speed of 537 mph (864 km/h).

The first British hydrogen bomb was dropped by a Vickers Valiant of No. 49 (Bomber) Squadron, captained by Wg Cdr Hubbard, on 15 May 1957. The bomb was detonated at medium altitude over the Pacific in the Christmas Island area.

Initial examples of the Boeing KC-135A, **the USAF's first turbojet-powered aircraft designed as a tanker/transport aircraft**, were delivered to the 93rd Air Refuelling Squadron at Castle AFB (California) on 28 June 1957.

The world's first true stand-off bomb to achieve operational status was the Bell GAM-63 Rascal on which, under the original designation XB-63, work started in 1946. Powered by three liquid-fuel rockets, this bomb was first delivered to the US Strategic Air Command at Pinecastle Air Force Base, Florida, on 30 October 1957, and was carried operationally under Boeing DB-47E Stratojet bombers of SAC. Its warhead was either atomic or thermonuclear, as required, and its range was about 100 miles (160 km).

The first 'over 2000 km/h' world speed record, later ratified at a figure of 1403 mph (2259.18 km/h), was established over Southern California on 16 May 1958 by Capt W. W. Irvin, USAF, flying a Lockheed F-104A Starfighter.

The first swept-wing single-seat fighter to be built for the Royal Navy, and the first to be capable of low-level attack at supersonic speed, attained in a shallow dive, was the Supermarine Scimitar. The first operational squadron, No. 803, was formed at Lossiemouth, Scotland, in June 1958. The Scimitar was also the first British naval aircraft to have a power operated control system.

The first West European aircraft to demonstrate a speed of Mach 2 in level flight, on 24 October 1958, was the first pre-production example of the Dassault Mirage IIIA interceptor.

The first American missile with intercontinental range was the Northrop SM-62 Snark, an aeroplane-configured missile with a thermonuclear warhead and capable of a range of more than 6300 miles (10 140 km). Snark first became operational in 1959, with the 702nd Strategic Missile Wing, Presque Isle Air Force Base.

Achieving his first solo flight in a turbojet-powered trainer, on 13 March 1959, Aviation Cadet E. R. Cook became the US Navy's first student pilot to do so without previous experience in a propeller-driven aircraft.

The first non-stop flight between the UK and Cape Town (with two inflight refuelling contacts) was made by the Vickers Valiant B.Mk 1 XD861 of the RAF's No. 214 Squadron. Commanded by Wing Cdr M. J. Beetham, the 6060 mile (9753 km) flight was completed in 11 h 29 min on 9 July 1959.

The first aircraft to be brought down by a surface-to-air missile (SAM) while overflying the Soviet Union, on 1 May 1960, was a Lockheed U-2 reconnaissance aircraft piloted by Francis Gary Powers. The ability of the Soviets to intercept such a high-flying aircraft brought a major re-think in the mode of deployment of strategic aircraft.

The USAF's first supersonic bomber aircraft, the Convair B-58A Hustler which had a maximum speed of Mach 2, entered service on 1 August 1960 with the USAF's 43rd Bomb Wing at Carswell AFB, Texas. The Hustler had unusual self-contained emergency escape capsules that could be used at the aircraft's maximum speed and on 28 February 1962 the first manned test of one of these capsules was carried out, when Warrant Officer Edward J. Murray was ejected from a Hustler travelling at 595 mph (909 km/h) at 20 000 ft (6100 m). After a controlled time a parachute was deployed automatically to bring the capsule and its occupant safely to the ground. In a third test, on 8 June 1962, a capsule containing the chimpanzee Zena was ejected successfully at 1060 mph (1706 km/h), and this landed without causing any harm to its occupant.

The first sortie of the 'Looking Glass' programme was flown on 3 February 1961, a mission under which the USAF's Strategic Air Command has kept an ACP (airborne command post) aircraft continuously in the air since that date. Early operations were flown by Boeing KC-135As, but specialist variants of the EC-135 are now used in this role.

The first non-stop flight from Britain to Australia was made in a 20 h 30 min period during 21–22 June 1961. This was achieved by the Avro Vulcan B.Mk 1A XH481 of the RAF's No. 617 Squadron, under the control of Sqn Ldr M. G. Beavis and his crew, the 11 500 mile (18 507 km) route involving flight refuelling contacts over Cyprus, Pakistan and Singapore.

The world's first specially designed low-level strike aircraft was the Blackburn NA39, subsequently named Buccaneer. The S1, powered by de Havilland Gyron Junior turbojets, first entered operational service with the FAA's No. 801 Squadron at Lossiemouth in July 1962. The developed S2 version, with more powerful Rolls-Royce Spey turbojets, also entered service with No. 801 Squadron, on 14 October 1965. Prior to that, on 4 October 1965, the first production aircraft (XN974) became the first FAA aircraft to make a non-stop crossing of the North Atlantic without flight refuelling. The 1950 miles (3138 km) from Goose Bay, Labrador, to RNAS Lossiemouth were flown in 4 h 16 min.

The first confirmation that Soviet medium-range ballistic missile sites were being installed on Cuba came on 14 October 1962, after a reconnaissance flight made by Maj Steve Hayser, USAF, in a Lockheed U-2. It was not until 20 November 1962 that agreement for their removal was finalized by the USA and Soviet Union.

The first British aircraft designed from the outset as a military transport, and the world's first military transport with a fully automatic landing system, was flown in prototype (G-ASKE later XR362) form as the Short SC.5 on 5 January 1964. The type entered service as the Belfast C.Mk 1 on 20 January 1966 when the first aircraft was delivered to No. 53 Squadron at Brize Norton, Oxfordshire.

The first action to mark full US involvement in the Vietnam War was made on 5 August 1964 when aircraft of the US Navy's 7th Fleet carriers USS *Constellation* and *Ticonderoga* attacked torpedo boats and their bases along the North Vietnam coastline. This was in retaliation for attacks by North Vietnam torpedo boats against the destroyer USS *Maddox* on 2 August.

The first flight of the USAF's variable-geometry Mach 2+ tactical fighter-bomber, the General Dynamics F-111A, was made at Fort Worth, Texas, on 21 December 1964. This was accomplished with the wing locked at a sweepback of 26°, and the first flight with the wings actuated through the full sweep from 16° to 72.5° was accomplished on 6 January 1965. Although their initial operational use in Vietnam appeared to be a failure, the aircraft has since been developed as a valuable component of the US armed forces.

The first massive air strike against targets in North Vietnam was launched by the United States under Operation 'Rolling Thunder' on 2 March 1965; this first attack, on an ammunition base at Xom Ban, was carried out by 110 aircraft. The US Navy became involved in 'Rolling Thunder' operations for the first time on 26 March when aircraft from the USS *Coral Sea* and *Hancock* attacked radar stations near Vinh Son.

The first US combat victories in the Vietnam War (against Mikoyan MiG-17s) were gained on 17 June 1965 when Cdr L. C. Page and Lt J. E. D. Batson in McDonnell Phantom IIs of US Navy squadron VF-21, flying off USS *Midway*, destroyed two of a flight of four.

Three B-52 Stratofortress bombers fly towards their targets in Vietnam. (US Air Force)

The first Boeing B-52 Stratofortress mission of the Vietnam War was made on 18 June 1965 when 27 aircraft of the 7th and 320th Bomb Wings attacked Viet-Cong targets with conventional HE bombs.

The first US Air Force combat victories of the Vietnam War were gained on 10 July 1965 by two McDonnell F-4 Phantom IIs crewed by Captains K. E. Holcombe, T. C. Roberts, A. C. Clark and R. C. Anderson. Members of the USAF's 45th Tactical Fighter Squadron, they destroyed two MiG-17s over Vietnam.

The first Lockheed SR-71 reconnaissance aircraft was delivered to the USAF's Strategic Air Command at Beale AFB (California) on 7 January 1966. With the ability to fly at a speed of Mach 3 plus and at heights in excess of 85 000 ft (25 910 m), this aircraft has since become widely known for its 'spy-plane' capabilities.

The first US attack against Hanoi, on 29 June 1966, was by Republic F-105 Thunderchiefs of the USAF's 355th and 388th Tactical Fighter Wings, led respectively by Maj James Kasler and Lt-Col James R. Hopkins.

A first hovering flight by a Hawker Siddeley Harrier development aircraft was made at the company's Dunsfold (Surrey) airfield on 31 August 1966. The first production example of what had then become known as the Harrier GR.Mk 1 was flown initially on 28 December 1967, and the type was to become the world's **first jet-powered V/STOL combat aircraft to gain full operational status** when Harrier GR.Mk 1s

joined the RAF's No. 1 Squadron at RAF Wittering in July 1969.

The first (and only) US airborne combat assault of the Vietnam War took place as Operation 'Junction City' on 22 February 1967, in which 845 paratroopers of the 173rd Airborne Brigade were dropped by 14 Lockheed C-130 Hercules transports.

The first US aerial mining operation of the Vietnam War was carried out on 26 February 1967 by Grumman A-6A Intruders of US Navy squadron VA-35.

The first successful operational use of the Walleye guided bomb was made on 11 March 1967 when Cdr H. Smith flying a US Navy Douglas A-4 launched one against a military barracks at Sam Son.

The first supersonic (in level flight) carrier-based interceptor fighter to serve with the Royal Navy was the McDonnell Douglas F-4K Phantom II (RN designation Phantom FG.1), of which the first three were delivered to RNAS Yeovilton, Somerset, on 29 April 1968. The Phantom FG.1, which equipped No. 892 Squadron, was **also the FAA's last air superiority fighter**, a fact indicated by the Omega symbol on the tail fin (the last letter of the Greek alphabet). The Phantoms of No. 892 Squadron served aboard the carrier HMS *Ark Royal* until this vessel was withdrawn from service in 1978.

First European air force to introduce the Lockheed P-3B Orion ASW aircraft into operational service was the Royal Norwegian Air Force which, on 10 April 1969, received the first of an order for five.

The first transatlantic crossing by a Hawker Siddeley Harrier GR.Mk 1 was recorded on 28 April 1969, this RAF aircraft flown from Northolt (Middlesex) to Floyd Bennett Field, New York.

The first land-based pure-jet aircraft in the world to be built for anti-submarine duties and long-range maritime patrol, the Hawker Siddeley Nimrod, developed from the de Havilland Comet 4C, entered service with RAF Strike Command on 2 October 1969. Powered by four Rolls-Royce RB.168-20 Spey Mk 250 turbofan engines, each of 12 140 lb (5507 kg) thrust, it has a typical operational endurance of 12 h.

The first significant development of the gunship aircraft was seen when the initial example of the Lockheed AC-130A (or Gunship II) went into action over the Ho Chi Minh trail on 27 February 1968. Armed with four 0.3-in Miniguns and four 20-mm Vulcan cannon, these aircraft played a major role by taking a heavy toll of Communist supplies and personnel.

The first man in space, Soviet cosmonaut Col Yuri Gagarin, was killed in a flying accident on 28 March 1968 while piloting a Mikoyan MiG-15UTI near Kirzhatsk, to the north of Moscow.

The first of the new purpose-designed Transall C.160D medium-range military transports was delivered to the German Luftwaffe on 26 April 1968.

Hawker Siddeley flew for the first time on 28 June 1968 the initial production example (XV226) of the Nimrod maritime reconnaissance aircraft. As the Nimrod MR.Mk 1 the type entered service in November 1970, equipping first No. 206 Squadron at RAF Kinloss, Morayshire.

Lockheed flew the first example of the C-5A Galaxy heavy logistics transport aircraft on 30 June 1968. At that time the world's largest landplane to have flown, the first of them for service with the USAF was handed over officially on 17 December 1969.

Equipped with the first US aircraft designed specifically for counter-insurgency (COIN) operations, the North American OV-10A Bronco, US Marine Corps squadron VMO-2 arrived at Da Nang (South Vietnam) on 6 July 1968. The OV-10A proved invaluable in this theatre, used primarily for helicopter escort, forward air control and reconnaissance missions.

The first USAF mission in support of the Laotian government was flown by Boeing B-52s during 17–18 February 1970. This attack was mounted against North Vietnamese and Pathet Lao positions on the Plain of Jars.

Japan's first military jet transport of indigenous design and manufacture was flown for the first time on 12 November 1970. This was the first of two XC-1 prototypes which were designed and built by the Nihon Aeroplane Manufacturing Company; C-1 production aircraft for service with the JASDF were built by Kawasaki.

On 21 November 1970 USAF and USN aircraft made the first major air strike against North Vietnam since 1 November 1968 (when President Lyndon B. Johnson had declared an end to the bombing of targets in North Vietnam). Enemy installations at Mu Gia and Ban Kari were attacked by some 300 aircraft.

The first VTOL fixed-wing combat aircraft to enter service with any of the US armed forces, the first Hawker Siddeley AV-8A Harrier was handed over officially to the US Marine Corps on 6 January 1971.

Japan's first supersonic aircraft of indigenous design and manufacture is the Mitsubishi T-2 twin-turbofan advanced trainer, in service with the JASDF. Flown initially in XT-2 prototype form on 20 July 1971, it was first flown supersonically in level flight on 19 November 1971. A single-seat close support version designated F-1 has been developed from this aircraft and the first of two prototypes was flown initially on 3 June 1975.

The first jet aircraft to be built in Brazil was the EMBRAER EMB-326GB Xavante (Servant) trainer and ground attack aircraft. Assembled under licence from Aermacchi of Italy, the first Brazilian-built example was flown initially on 3 September 1971, and the type serves with the Brazilian Air Force as the AT-26 Xavante.

The first aircraft to be flown in the United States with a fly-by-wire control system, on 29 April 1972, was a specially-equipped McDonnell Douglas F-4 Phantom II. Such a system replaces the conventional mechanical linkage for the operation of flight control surfaces by wires carrying electrical signals. Fly-by-wire offers many advantages, being lighter in weight, providing greater redundancy because cable runs can be duplicated or triplicated, and is ideal for integration with computer-controlled automatic flight control systems.

The first Chinese National aircraft of indigenous design and construction, the AIDC (Aero Industry Development Centre) XH-C-1A turboprop-powered trainer prototype, was flown for the first time on 23 November 1973 in Taiwan.

The first General Dynamics YF-16 lightweight fighter prototype (72-01567), for competitive evaluation against the Northrop YF-17, made its official maiden flight on 2 February 1974; on 11 March 1974 this aircraft was **flown at a speed of Mach 2 for the first time.** Selection of this aircraft by the USAF for production as the F-16 (later named Fighting Falcon) has led to **the largest single-aircraft production programme in the world** involving more than 100 major contractors and about 4000 sub-contractors; these supply assemblies and components for the General Dynamics plant at Fort Worth (Texas) as well as the European production lines in Belgium and the Netherlands. The USAF, which currently plans to procure 3047 F-16s, saw the first example enter service with the 388th Tactical Fighter Wing at Hill AFB (Utah) on 6 January 1979, and initial operational capability was attained by this unit's 4th TFS in October 1980. The first European-built F-16s were delivered to the air forces of Belgium, the Netherlands, Norway and Denmark on 26 January 1979, 6 June 1979, 25 January 1980 and 26 January 1980 respectively.

The first prototype of the Panavia multi-role combat aircraft (MRCA) made its first flight at Manching, Germany, on 14 August 1974. Designed to meet the requirements of the air forces of the Federal Republic of Germany, Italy and United Kingdom, and of the German Navy, the MRCA, since named Tornado, is a twin-engined two-seat supersonic aircraft. Its variable-geometry wings and advanced avionics, giving all-weather terrain-following capability, provide the necessary flexibility to meet the requirements of the user nations.

The first operational deployment of the Grumman F-14A Tomcat carrier-based fighter occurred on 17 September 1974, when the USS *Enterprise* with US Navy F-14 squadrons VF-1 and VF-2 included in its complement sailed from San Francisco, California.

The first detailed technical knowledge gained by the West of the Mikoyan MiG-25 'Foxbat' Mach 3 interceptor occurred during September 1976 when a Soviet pilot defected to the West in one of these aircraft.

The first overseas deployment of US Marine Corps Hawker Siddeley AV-8A Harriers began on 6 October 1976 when USMC squadron VMA-231 aboard the carrier USS *Franklin D. Roosevelt* sailed to join the US 6th Fleet in the Mediterranean.

The first McDonnell Douglas F-15A Eagle fighters to be stationed in Europe were those of the USAF's 36th Tactical Fighter Wing which left Langley AFB (Virginia) on 27 April 1977 *en route* to Bitburg, West Germany.

The first example (XZ450) of the British Aerospace Sea Harrier, a navalized version of the RAF's Harrier, **was flown initially on 20 August 1978.** The first production aircraft for the Royal Navy was handed over officially on 18 June 1979.

The first Fairchild A-10A Thunderbolt II 'tank busters' for service with the USAF in Europe were received during January 1979 by the 81st Tactical Fighter Wing at RAF Bentwaters, Suffolk. They were used initially for combat training over Germany.

The first of the ski ramp-equipped 'Invincible' class, HMS *Invincible* began sea trials with the Royal Navy on 26 March 1979. Her intended complement of aircraft was five British Aerospace Sea Harriers and 10 Westland Sea King Helicopters.

The first British Aerospace Sea Harrier for service with the Royal Navy was handed over on 18 June 1979. The first ship trials were carried out aboard HMS *Hermes* during November of that year. **First used in combat** during the Falkland Islands campaign (2 April to 14 June 1982), 28 Sea Harriers operating from HMS *Hermes* and HMS *Invincible* made 2380 sorties and destroyed 27 enemy aircraft in air-to-air combat without loss resulting from air-to-air combat.

The first stage of Soviet involvement in Afghanistan began on 24 December 1979 with Mikoyan MiG-21 and MiG-23 fighters providing escort to the large numbers of transport aircraft which airlifted some 5000 troops of the 105th Airborne Guards Division into Kabul.

The first pre-emptive air strikes by the Iraqi air force against Iranian air bases, oil installations and the capital (Tehran) on 22 September 1980 marked the beginning of the 'Gulf War'.

The first USAF unit to become operational with the 'Pave Tack' weapon delivery system (on 15 September 1981) was the 494th Tactical Fighter Squadron based at RAF Lakenheath, Suffolk. A laser transmitter/receiver and a precision optical sight is incorporated in the 'Pave Tack' pod.

The first hardened aircraft shelters in the United Kingdom, built at Honington, Suffolk, and intended to protect the occupying aircraft from nuclear blast, were put into use for the first time on 9 November 1981.

The first fully automatic landing to be achieved by the McDonnell Douglas F/A-18 Hornet was made on 22 January 1982 at the Naval Air Test Center, Patuxent River, Maryland.

The first of 18 Boeing E-3A Sentry AWACS (airborne warning and control system) **aircraft for use by NATO** was delivered on 22 January 1982, the last of them on 25 April 1985.

The first phase of what was to become known as the Falklands war began on 2 April 1982 when the armed forces of Argentina began an invasion of the Falkland Islands. British reaction saw the main elements of a British Task Force (including the carriers HMS *Hermes* and *Invincible*) sail from Portsmouth (Hampshire) on 5 April.

RAF Harriers and Navy Sea Harriers and Sea King on board HMS Hermes, *flagship of the Falklands Task Force. (Ministry of Defence)*

A Royal Navy Sea Harrier recorded the type's first combat victory on 1 May 1982, when a Dassault-Breguet Mirage IIIEA of the Argentine air force was destroyed by a Sidewinder missile.

The first British air attack against Argentine positions on the Falkland Islands was made on 1 May 1982. This first of a series of 'Black Buck' operations saw the single Vulcan B.Mk 2 XM607 drop a stick of 21 1000 lb bombs diagonally across the runway of Port Stanley airfield. This attack, launched from Ascension Island and involving inflight refuelling for both the out and return flights, **takes its place in aviation history as the longest operational bombing mission**.

The first in-strength landing of UK forces on the Falkland Islands was made on 20 May 1982 with essential air cover provided by the Navy's Sea Harriers; little more than three weeks later, on 14 June, all Argentine forces on the islands surrendered.

The first combat unit to become operational with the McDonnell Douglas F/A-18 Hornet naval strike fighter, on 7 January 1983, was the US Marine Corps squadron VMFA-314 based at MCAS El Toro, California.

The first of the USAF's rewinged Lockheed C-5A Galaxy transport aircraft made its first flight at Marietta (Georgia) on 9 February 1983, being delivered back to the USAF on 28 February. The new wings, designed to overcome fatigue problems with those incorporated in the original structure, were installed subsequently on the remaining 76 in-service Galaxies.

First service introduction of the new McDonnell Douglas/British Aerospace AV-8B Harrier II V/STOL close-support aircraft for the US Marine Corps took place on 12 January 1984. This occurred when the first of 12 pre-production aircraft was handed over officially to the USMC at Cherry Point, North Carolina.

The RAF's first Vickers (British Aerospace) VC10 inflight refuelling tanker unit was established at RAF Brize Norton (Oxfordshire) on 1 May 1984. This saw No. 101 Squadron being reformed and equipped initially with VC10 K.Mk 2 tankers.

The first Dassault-Breguet Mirage 2000 air-superiority fighters were declared operational with the Armée de l'Air on 2 July 1984. This was at Dijon-Longvic where the first squadron to equip with the type, Escadron de Chasse 1/2 *Cigognes*, put on a 10-aircraft demonstration flight.

The first production example of an advanced version of the General Dynamics Fighting Falcon, the F-16C which incorporates many improvements, was handed over to the USAF at Fort Worth (Texas) on 19 July 1984.

The first operational test and evaluation of the USAF's new LANTIRN (Low-Altitude Navigation and Targeting Infra-Red system for Night) was made by three General Dynamics F-16 Fighting Falcons on 15 October 1984. In tests that were regarded as 'highly successful', it was found easily possible to make night sorties at treetop height while travelling at some 500 mph (805 km/h).

The first production example of the Rockwell B-1B long-range strategic bomber for service with the USAF made a successful first flight at Palmdale (California) on 18 October 1984.

For the first time a team from outside the United States won the prestigious Curtis E. LeMay and John C. Meyer trophies (awarded on 2 November 1984) for skill and accuracy in bombing operations. This was achieved by the RAF's No. 617 Squadron participating in the USAF's 'Giant Voice' competition.

The first Harrier II to be built in Britain was flown for the first time at the Dunsfold (Surrey) airfield of British Aerospace on 30 April 1985. Under the designation Harrier GR.Mk 5, this aircraft was one of the 62 then scheduled for service with the RAF (now 96 required).

The first airport on the Falkland Islands able to accept wide-body aircraft was opened officially by HRH Prince Andrew on 12 May 1985. Known as Mount Pleasant airport, **the first wide-body transport to land there (on 1 May) had been an RAF Lockheed TriStar** following a proving flight from the UK via Ascension Island.

The first Rockwell B-1B long-range strategic bomber entered operational service on 7 July 1985. Its service entry had been delayed by some serious shortcomings (some of them still unresolved) before delivery was made to the 96th Bomb Wing of the USAF's Strategic Air Command at Dyess AFB, Texas.

The first flight following conversion to K.Mk 1 tanker configuration was made on 9 July 1985 by the first (ZD950) of six Lockheed TriStar 500s purchased from British Airways for service with the RAF. The first example for RAF use was handed over officially in a ceremony at the Marshall of Cambridge (Engineering) facility on 24 March 1986.

The first (56-5601) of four flying prototypes of the Kawasaki XT-4 two-seat intermediate jet trainer/liaison aircraft recorded the type's maiden flight on 29 July 1985. The procurement of some 200 production T-4s is anticipated to replace the Lockheed T-33As and Fuji T-1A/Bs in Japan Air Self-Defence Force service.

The first Lockheed C-5B Galaxy heavy-lift transport made a successful first flight on 10 September 1985. While generally similar to the C-5A Galaxy, the new version has as standard all modifications and improvements incorporated in the C-5A during service with the USAF since 1970.

A first proof of growing US capability against enemy satellites in space was given on 13 September 1985 when a USAF McDonnell Douglas F-15 Eagle launched an anti-satellite missile (ASAT) which successfully destroyed an inert US satellite in Earth orbit.

A first major retaliation against alleged Libyan-inspired terrorist activities saw aircraft of the US Air Force (Europe) and the US Navy attack targets in Libya (at Benghazi, Benina, Sidi Bilal and Tripoli) on the night of 14/15 April 1986.

The first four-turbofan VIP transport to serve with The Queen's Flight of the RAF, the first of two British Aerospace 146 CC.Mk 2 aircraft was handed over officially to the Royal Air Force at Hatfield (Hertfordshire) on 23 April 1986.

For the first time a Boeing B-52H Stratofortress of the USAF carried its maximum load of 20 ALCMs (air-launched cruise missiles), a weapon load of some 64 000 lb (29 030 kg). This occurred during a flight from Carswell AFB (Texas) to Edwards AFB (California) on 10 May 1986.

The first occasion that the Mikoyan MiG-29 'Fulcrum' was seen on the ground outside of WarPac borders was on 1 July 1986, when six of these advanced Soviet aircraft paid a courtesy visit to Rissala AB, Finland.

The first passenger-carrying non-revenue service was flown from the new London City Airport to Paris (Charles de Gaulle) on 14 October 1987; this was made by a de Havilland Canada DHC-7 Dash 7 operated by Brymon Airways. **The first revenue services were flown on the official opening date, 26 October 1987**, with Brymon Airways and Eurocity Express (both using Dash 7s) providing links with Plymouth (UK), Brussels and Paris.

The first RAF unit to be declared operational with the Panavia Tornado F.Mk 3, an advanced air defence fighter, was No. 9 Squadron on 1 November 1987. It is planned that six more RAF squadrons will become equipped with this new combat aircraft.

Largest:

The largest bombers to serve with the Russian army during the First World War were the Sikorsky *Ilya Mourometz* series, the largest of them being the IM-Ye1 (six built) with a wing span of 102 ft 10.25 in (31.35 m) and a length of 59 ft 8.5 in (18.20 m). The first true military variant was the IM-B, which entered service in 1914, and was thus **the first four-engined heavy bomber to enter service with any of the world's air forces**.

The largest German aeroplane to be used operationally during the First World War was the Zeppelin-Staaken R VI, a four-engined giant bomber with a wing span of 138 ft 5.4 in (42.20 m) and a length of 73 ft 6 in (22.10 m), the first of 18 entering service in June 1917. Powered by four 245 hp Maybach Mb IV or 260 hp Mercedes D IVa engines, the R VI had a maximum speed of 84 mph (135 km/h).

The largest and first four-engined British bomber of the First World War was the Handley Page V/1500 biplane, first flown during May 1918, which had a wing span of 126 ft (38.40 m) and a length of 64 ft (19.50 m).

The largest aeroplane force assembled during the First World War for a single military operation was that used during the battle for the Saint-Mihiel salient between 11 and 15 September 1918. In command of 1483 fighter, observation and bombing aircraft was Gen William Mitchell of the US Army Air Service.

The largest Japanese military aircraft built between the wars was the Mitsubishi Ki-20, the basic design of which originated in Germany as the Junkers G 38. The first Ki-20 was completed in secrecy during 1931; by 1934 it had been joined by five others, the later examples built from Japanese components. The Japanese Army Air Force was not impressed by the aircraft, and the Ki-20s never saw action. Each had a wing span of 144 ft 4 in (44.00 m).

The largest French bomber to enter service between the wars was the Farman F221 which, with its derivatives, was the mainstay of the French bomber force for several years. Production began in 1934 with 12 F221s. Later versions included the F222, F222/2, F223 and F2233. The F221 had a wing span of 118 ft 1½ in (36 m) and was powered by four 800 hp Gnome-Rhône 14 Kbrs engines. Maximum speed was 185 mph (297 km/h).

The largest number of losses suffered by an air force in a single day's offensive operations, as a result of air combat and anti-aircraft gunfire, is believed to have been that of the Luftwaffe on 10 May 1940. On this day Germany invaded the Netherlands and Belgium and was opposed simultaneously by the air forces of Belgium, France, Great Britain and Holland. The Norwegian campaign, by then nearing its end, also claimed a small

Fokker D XXI 241 was one of 9 Dutch fighters that fought 9 Messerschmitt Bf 109s on 10 May 1940, with 4 or 5 of the German aircraft shot down for the loss of 241 itself.

number of German victims on that day. According to its own records the Luftwaffe lost on 10 May:

	Destroyed	Damaged
Dornier Do 17 bombers	26	7
Dornier Do 18 flying-boat	1	
Dornier Do 215 reconnaissance aircraft	2	
Fieseler Fi 156 artillery support aircraft	22	
Heinkel He 111 bombers	51	21
Henschel Hs 123 dive-bomber		1
Henschel Hs 126 reconnaissance aircraft	1	3
Junkers Ju 52 transports	157	
Junkers Ju 87 dive-bombers	9	
Junkers Ju 88 bombers	18	2
Messerschmitt Bf 109 fighters	6	11
Messerschmitt Bf 110 fighters	1	3
Other types	10	3
Totals	304	51

Aircrew casualties amounted to 267 killed, 133 wounded and 340 missing; other Luftwaffe personnel casualties (Flak, engineers, etc) amounted to 326 killed or missing.

Apart from the historical interest of these figures, they indicate conclusively that the operations undertaken by the Luftwaffe on this day represented the true beginning of the *Blitzkrieg* against substantial opposition. On 10 May Germany suffered losses in excess of all previous cumulative losses since 1 September 1939, including the Polish campaign. Losses suffered by the Luftwaffe during the invasion of Poland may be summarized as follows:

	Aircraft	Aircrew		
Period	destroyed	killed	wounded	missing
1–8 Sept	116	128	68	137
9–13 Sept	34	15	15	15
14–18 Sept	23	24	32	14
19–27 Sept	30	54	18	4

The largest flying-boat to attain operational status during the Second World War was the German Blohm und Voss Bv 222 Wiking. Designed as a transatlantic civil transport for Lufthansa, the prototype (D-ANTE) first flew on 7 September 1940, but was quickly impressed into war service as a cargo transport. The final Bv 222C

version had a wing span of 150 ft 11 in (46 m), gross weight of 108 000 lb (48 990 kg) and was powered by six Junkers Jumo 205C engines.

The largest airborne assault mounted by the Luftwaffe during the Second World War was operation 'Mercury', the landing of 22 750 men on the island of Crete beginning at 07.00 h on 20 May 1941. The Luftwaffe used 493 Junkers Ju 52/3m aircraft and about 80 DFS 230 gliders. The assault was made by 10 000 parachutists, 750 troops landed by glider, 5000 landed by Ju 52/3ms and 7000 by sea. The operation, although regarded as a brilliant success, cost Germany about 4500 men killed and some 150 transport aircraft destroyed or badly damaged, and effectively brought Luftwaffe paratroop operations to an end.

The largest military flying-boat built in Great Britain was the Short Shetland, of which only two prototypes were built. The first, designated Shetland I (DX166), flew for the first time on 14 December 1944, piloted by John Lankester Parker with Geoffrey Tyson as co-pilot. Designed for long-range maritime reconnaissance, both Shetland prototypes were powered by 2500 hp Bristol Centaurus engines, and their wing spans were 150 ft 4 in (45.82 m). The Shetland I had a maximum take-off weight of 125 000 lb (56 700 kg) and attained a maximum level speed of 263 mph (423 km/h). The first prototype was later destroyed by fire at its moorings. With the end of the war in sight it was decided to complete the second prototype as a civil transport, which was given the designation Shetland II. It was allocated the last constructor's number issued by Shorts at Rochester, S1313, and had the civil registration G-AGVD. It flew for the first time on 17 September 1947 and completed its preliminary trials, but lack of commercial interest in flying-boats after the end of the Second World War meant that it was scrapped in 1951 without ever having carried a fare-paying passenger.

The largest flying-boat to serve with the US Navy was the Martin JRM Mars. Twenty JRM-1 transports were ordered in January 1945 but only five were built, plus one heavier JRM-2. With a wing span of 200 ft (60.96 m) and gross weight of 165 000 lb (74 842 kg) in the JRM-2, the Mars flying-boat had a maximum speed of 225 mph (362 km/h). It was converted after the war for water-bombing of forest fires.

Prototype Martin Mars flying-boat, first flown on 3 July 1942.

The largest military flying-boat built in Germany during the Second World War was the Blohm und Voss Bv 238. The single prototype, powered by six Daimler-Benz DB 603 engines, was first flown in March 1945. Intended to fill a long-range reconnaissance or transport role, the Bv 238 had a wing span of 197 ft 4½ in (60.17 m) and a maximum loaded weight of 176 370 lb (80 000 kg).

The largest bomber aircraft to serve with the USAF, and the largest operational bomber aircraft in the world in terms of wing span (230 ft/70.10 m) was the Convair B-36, first flown in XB-36 prototype form (42-13570) on 8 August 1946. They took part in a number of interesting experiments before the type was retired from service by Strategic Air Command on 12 February 1959.

The largest US airborne operation before the United States became actively involved in the Vietnam conflict occurred on 27 April 1964. In this action Sikorsky UH-34 helicopters of the US Marine Corps (with escorting Bell UH-1B gunships of the US Army) airlifted 420 South Vietnam troops to attack Communist positions on the Laotian border.

In early November 1967 the RAF used some 50 transport aircraft to withdraw British troops from Aden, **becoming involved in its largest transport operation since the Berlin Airlift** of 1948–49. This occurred when Britain gave up its sponsorship of the South Arabian Federation of Arab Emirates which had been set up in 1959.

The largest US landplane ever flown, in terms of overall dimensions and bulk, the Lockheed C-5A Galaxy, made its maiden flight on 30 June 1968. On 17 December 1984 one of these aircraft set a US national record for the greatest take-off weight, a total of 920 836 lb (417 684 kg), this including a payload of 245 731 lb (111 462 kg) which it lifted to a height of 2000 m to set an international payload-to-height record that was ratified by the FAI.

Then the world's largest ship, the US Navy's new nuclear-powered aircraft carrier USS *Nimitz* completed a test cruise on 14 August 1975 prior to embarking on its first overseas deployment to European waters.

The largest value order for military aircraft from a British manufacturer since the end of the Second World War was that finalized between British Aerospace and Saudi Arabia's Ministry of Defence and Aviation on 26 September 1985. Valued at some £3 to 4 billion it covered the supply of 72 Panavia Tornado fighters, 30 British Aerospace Hawk and two Jetstream 31 aircraft for training, plus 30 Pilatus PC-9 trainers supplied via British Aerospace.

The largest military flying-boat in current service is the Japanese Shin Meiwa SS-2. Operated by the Japanese Maritime Self-Defence Force (JMSDF) under the designations PS-1 and US-1, signifying anti-submarine flying-boat and air–sea rescue amphibian respectively, the prototype of this four turboprop-powered aircraft made its first flight in the PS-1 configuration on 5 October 1967. With a wing span of 108 ft 8¾ in (33.14 m), the PS-1 has a maximum take-off weight of 94 800 lb (43 000 kg) and maximum ferry range of 2948 miles (4744 km). The first US-1 was delivered to the JMSDF on 5 March 1975.

The de Havilland DH4 was the first British aircraft produced for day bombing and proved the most successful light bomber of the First World War. First flown in August 1916, it joined operational squadrons the following year. Various engines were fitted, the largest being a 375 hp Rolls-Royce Eagle VIII which allowed a maximum speed of 143 mph (230 km/h), faster than German fighters.

Edward Rickenbacker of the 94th Aero Squadron, America's top-ranking 'ace' of the First World War, with his SPAD XIII. (US Air Force)

Fastest Italian aircraft of the First World War was the Ansaldo SVA 5 Primo.

Fastest:

The fastest British and French operational combat aircraft of the First World War appear to have been the British Airco DH4 day bomber (when Eagle VIII powered) and the French SPAD XIII fighter, with speeds of 143 mph (230 km/h) and 138 mph (222 km/h) respectively.

The fastest Italian operational aircraft of the First World War was probably the Ansaldo SVA 5 Primo reconnaissance and bombing biplane which was flown first during the summer of 1917. The maximum speed of this aircraft with the standard 220 hp SPA 6A engine was 143 mph (230 km/h), but variants tested with other powerplant installations achieved even higher speeds.

The fastest operational fighter in German service during the First World War was the Fokker D VIII parasol-wing monoplane, with a maximum speed at sea level of nearly 127 mph (204 km/h).

The fastest fighters developed by Germany during the First World War, but flown only in prototype form, were almost certainly the AEG D I biplane and Siemens-Schuckert D VI parasol-wing monoplane, both with a maximum speed of nearly 137 mph (220 km/h).

The fastest light bomber of the mid-1920s was the Fairey Fox. The prototype was first flown on 3 January 1925, powered by a 480 hp Curtiss D12 engine, and had a maximum speed of 156 mph (251 km/h). The first of 28 production Foxes were delivered in August 1926 to No. 12 Squadron RAF, which has since used a fox's head as a badge. Much faster than other bombers of their time, Foxes could outpace then-current fighters. No further production was undertaken for the RAF, but later versions were built in Belgium by Avions Fairey, and some of these were used in action against the invading German forces in 1940.

The fastest aircraft to fly before the Second World War was a special development of the German Messerschmitt Bf 109 single-seat fighter. Bf 109s in Luftwaffe service at the outbreak of war included B, C, D and E series aircraft, the last with a maximum speed of 354 mph (570 km/h). However, on 26 April 1939, a much-changed Me 209 (Bf 109R) flew at Augsburg, Germany, at an FAI

RAF Mosquito B IVs of No 105 Squadron at Marham in 1942.

accredited speed of 469.22 mph (755.138 km/h), setting a record that was not beaten by another piston-engined aeroplane until 30 years later.

The fastest aircraft in RAF Bomber Command for an entire decade, from November 1941 until introduction of the English Electric Canberra in 1951, was the de Havilland Mosquito. Entering squadron service with No. 105 at Swanton Morley, Mosquitos made their first operational sortie on 31 May 1942, four aircraft making a surprise attack on Cologne just a few hours after the first 1000-bomber raid. Too fast to be intercepted during much of its wartime service, the Mosquito had the lowest loss rate of any aircraft in Bomber Command. Fighter variants of the Mosquito were no less successful, the Mk VI being the most extensively built, entering service with Fighter Command as a day and night intruder. Mosquitos served also as night fighters, responsible for home defence, and on the night of 14–15 June 1944 **the first V1 flying bomb to be shot down** was destroyed over the English Channel by a Mosquito of No. 605 Squadron flown by Flt Lt J. G. Musgrave.

The fastest piston-engined fighter designed for the Luftwaffe, the Dornier Do 335, demonstrated a maximum speed of 474 mph (763 km/h) at 21 000 ft (6400 m). First flown in September 1943, the Do 335 Pfeil had a unique engine layout, one Daimler-Benz DB 603 being mounted conventionally in the nose, with a second DB 603 mounted in the rear fuselage and driving a pusher propeller through an extension shaft. It was developed too late to enter operational service.

The fastest twin piston-engined combat aircraft in the world to reach operational status was the de Havilland Hornet fighter which had a maximum speed of 485 mph (780 km/h) in 'clean' combat configuration. Powered by two 2070 hp Rolls-Royce Merlin 130 engines, the Hornet was armed with four 20 mm cannon, could carry up to 2000 lb (907 kg) of bombs or rockets on underwing pylons, and had a maximum range of over 2500 miles (4025 km). It was first flown by Geoffrey de Havilland Jr on 28 July 1944, but did not reach the first RAF squadron—No. 64 (Fighter) Squadron at Horsham St Faith, Norfolk—until May 1946, after the end of the Second World War. The Hornet was **the fastest piston-engined fighter to serve with the RAF** and also **the last piston-engined fighter to serve with RAF first-line squadrons**.

The fastest military aircraft in service is the Lockheed SR-71A two-seat strategic reconnaissance aircraft, first flown on 22 December 1964. Relying upon height and speed to provide invulnerability from interception, the SR-71A is capable of more than Mach 3 at optimum altitude. **SR-71As hold both of the world absolute speed records** (straight line and closed circuit), and one set a New York–London transatlantic record of 1 h 55 min 32 sec.

The fastest (and almost certainly the only) father and son to have individually flown an aircraft at a speed of more than Mach 3 in level flight are Lt Gen James M. Keck, USAF (Retd) and Maj Thomas J. Keck, USAF. Both flights were made in the Lockheed SR-71A strategic reconnaissance aircraft, father (James M.) flying first on 15 January 1975 and son (Thomas J.), assigned to Beale AFB (California) as an SR-71 pilot, making his first flight on 21 October 1977.

The fastest non-stop air-refuelled round-the-world flight was that made during the period 12–14 March 1980 by two Boeing B-52H Stratofortresses of the USAF's Strategic Air Command. This circumnavigation, completed in 42 h 30 min, was an operational deployment during which reconnaissance and surveillance tasks were carried out.

The fastest piston-engined aircraft is a modified North American P-51D Mustang, powered by a 3000 hp Rolls-Royce/Packard Merlin engine. This was flown by Frank Taylor on 30 July 1983 to set an FAI ratified record speed of 517.06 mph (832.12 km/h).

Highest:

The highest known interception by an unpressurized aircraft, its pilot G. W. H. Reynolds unaided by a pressure suit and breathing only a conventional oxygen supply, was that made at 49 500 ft (15 090 m) in a specially prepared Spitfire VC operating from No. 103 MU near Alexandria, in late August 1942. A Ju 86P-2 high-altitude pressurized aircraft was destroyed in this interception.

The highest altitude attained by an air-breathing aircraft, which is also the current world absolute altitude record ratified by the FAI, is 123 524 ft (37 650 m). This was set on 31 August 1977 by Alexander Fedotov in the Soviet Union, flying the specially prepared Mikoyan Ye-266M.

Longest:

One of the longest-serving aircraft designed during the First World War was the two-seat Bristol Fighter. The type first became operational on the Western Front in early April 1917 and wartime production amounted to no fewer than 3101 aircraft, with post-war production continuing until 1927. Many of these late-production aircraft were exported, and those acquired for the Royal New Zealand Air Force remained in service until 1936. The F2B Mk II version, powered by a 280 hp Rolls-Royce Falcon II engine, had a maximum speed of 125 mph (201 km/h).

The longest non-stop and unrefuelled distance flown by military aircraft prior to the

Sqn Ldr Kellett (with dog).

Second World War was a flight of 7158.5 miles (11 520 km) from Ismailia (Egypt) to Darwin (Australia), which also set a new world distance record. This was achieved during 5–7 November 1938 by two Vickers Wellesleys of the RAF's Long Range Flight, captained by Sqn Ldr R. G. Kellett and Flt Lt A. N. Combe.

The longest production run of any US fighter of the Second World War was that of the Vought F4U Corsair, first flown on 29 May 1940, at which time it was the most powerful naval fighter in the world. Initial deliveries to VF-12 (US Navy Fighter Squadron Twelve) began on 3 October 1942, the type remaining in production until December 1952. It was thus the last American piston-engined fighter to remain in production. Fastest of the series was the F4U-5N, powered by a 2300 hp Pratt & Whitney R-2800-32W radial engine with a two-stage supercharger, which gave a maximum level speed of 470 mph (756 km/h) at 26 800 ft (8168 m). In service with the British Fleet Air Arm on board HMS *Victorious*, Corsair Mk IIs took part in the attacks on the German battleship *Tirpitz* on 3 April 1944, this being the first operation flown with Corsairs from an aircraft carrier.

The longest non-stop but air-refuelled flight then made by an RAF aircraft, set by a Vickers Valiant B.Mk 1 of No. 214 Squadron, covered a distance of 8500 miles (13 679 km) in a circuit around the UK during 2 to 3 March 1960. It was in effect a rehearsal for a UK–Singapore non-stop flight, the distance of 8110 miles (13 052 km) accomplished in 15 h 35 min during 25–26 May 1960 in a Valiant captained by Sqn Ldr J. H. Garstin.

The longest non-stop and unrefuelled distance flown by a military aircraft was 11 337 miles (18 245.05 km) between Okinawa (Ryukyu Islands) to Madrid (Spain) during 10–11 January 1962. Setting a new world absolute distance record, this was accomplished by a Boeing B-52H Stratofortress of the USAF captained by Maj Clyde P. Evely.

The longest point-to-point operational sortie achieved by a bomber aircraft was that flown by an RAF Avro Vulcan B.Mk 2 on 30 April/1 May 1982. Captained by Flt Lt Martin Withers the aircraft took off from Wideawake airfield, Ascension Island to drop its load of 21 1000 lb bombs across the runway of Port Stanley airfield, Falkland Islands. Some operational sorties flown by USAF Boeing B-52s during the Vietnam War may have been very similar in length, approaching a total distance of 8000 miles (12 875 km), but were not point-to-point operations against a single target.

The longest non-stop air-refuelled sortie by a mixed flight of some 20 Harriers and Sea Harriers was that flown on 8 May 1982, from RNAS Yeovilton (Somerset) to Ascension Island, accomplished in a time of 9 hours.

Greatest:

The flying-boat produced in the greatest numbers was the Consolidated PBY Catalina. Excluding production in Russia, 1196 Catalina flying-boats and 944 amphibians were built, serving with the air forces and airlines of more than 25 nations. The prototype was first flown on 28 March 1935, and the initial production version had a maximum speed of 177 mph (284 km/h).

The greatest single-day losses suffered by the Luftwaffe during the Polish campaign were those of 3 September 1939, when 22 German aircraft were destroyed. These comprised 4 Dornier Do 17s, 2 Fieseler Fi 156s, 1 Heinkel He 59, 2 Heinkel He 111s, 1 Henschel Hs 123, 3 Henschel Hs 126s, 1 Junkers Ju 52, 3 Junkers Ju 87s, 2 Messerschmitt Bf 109s and 3 Messerschmitt Bf 110s. One of the Messerschmitt Bf 110s was shot down accidentally by German troops near Ostrolenka. Luftwaffe personnel casualties on this day amounted to 34 killed, one wounded and 17 missing.

The greatest single victory achieved by the Royal Netherlands Air Force during the German invasion of the Low Countries was gained at 06.45 h on 10 May 1940 when a force of Fokker D XXIs intercepted 55 Junkers Ju 52/3m transport aircraft of KGzbV9. The Dutch pilots claimed to have shot down 37 of the formation, but German records indicate a total loss of 39 aircraft, 6 occupants killed, 41 presumed dead, 15 wounded and 79 missing.

The greatest single loss of aircraft in any one day suffered by any nation involved in the Second World War occurred on 22 June 1941. On that day Germany began Operation Barbarossa, its invasion of the Soviet Union, and by nightfall Soviet aircraft losses amounted to 1811, of which 1489 were destroyed on the ground.

The Royal Air Force heavy bomber with the greatest number of operational missions to its credit was the Avro Lancaster B Mark III, ED888, PM-M², of No. 103 (Bomber) Squadron. Mike Squared, known alternatively as 'The Mother of Them All', made its first operational sortie in a raid on Dortmund on the night of 4–5 May 1943. By the time the aircraft was retired in December 1944 it had logged 140 missions. This number of missions was, however, exceeded by the de Havilland Mosquito B Mk IX light bomber LR503, GB-F, of No. 105 Squadron and later 109 Squadron. Between 28 May 1943 and the end of the war, this aircraft completed no fewer than 213 operational sorties.

The greatest amphibious assault in history, preceded by air drops and Allied air force operations amounting to some 5000 sorties, the Operation 'Overlord' landings on the Normandy coast began on D-Day, 6 June 1944.

One of the greatest technical achievements of the Second World War, and representing the shortest elapsed time for the development of an entirely new jet fighter (which achieved combat status) was 69 days for the Heinkel He 162 Salamander. Conceived in an RLM specification issued to the German aircraft industry on 8 September 1944, the He 162 was the subject of a contract issued on 29 September 1944 for an aircraft capable of being mass-produced by semi-skilled labour using non-strategic materials. Sixty-nine days later, on 6 December 1944, the first prototype He 162V-1 was flown by Heinkel's Chief Test Pilot, Kapitän Peter, at Vienna-Schwechat. On 10 December the prototype broke up in the air and crashed before a large gathering of officials, and Peter was killed. Notwithstanding this set-back, the aircraft entered production and joined I and II Gruppen of Jagdgeschwader I at Leck/Holstein during April 1945. III Gruppe of this Geschwader was under orders to receive the new fighter but was forestalled by the end of the war. Known also as the Volksjäger, or 'People's Fighter', it was intended that large numbers would be constructed, but only 116 A-series machines were completed. The Salamander was not a pleasant machine to fly, and as a result few of these aircraft

Heinkel He 162 Salamander jet fighter, captured at the close of the war and brought to Britain for testing.

were encountered in combat. Its single BMW 003 turbojet, rated at 1760 lb (800 kg) thrust, provided a maximum speed of 522 mph (840 km/h) at 19 685 ft (6000 m).

The greatest number of sorties flown in a period of 24 hours during the Berlin Airlift was recorded on 16 April 1949. This was a total of 1398 flown by the international fleet of aircraft supplying West Berlin, which ferried in a total 12 940 tons (13 147 tonnes) of supplies.

The greatest number of persons carried by a US Navy Martin Mars flying-boat totalling 308 (301 passengers and 7 crew). This was recorded on 19 May 1949 by the *Marshall Mars* flying from Alameda (Idaho) to San Diego (California).

The greatest bomb-load carried by an operational bomber was that of the Boeing B-52 Stratofortress at 70 000 lb (31 751 kg); with this warload on board the B-52 had a range of approximately 3000 miles (4928 km). Dubbed 'the big stick', the YB-52 prototype was first flown on 15 April 1952 by A. M. 'Tex' Johnson. The first of three production B-52As was delivered to the USAF's Strategic Air Command (SAC) on 27 November 1957. B-52s became subsequently the main flying deterrent of SAC and continue to have a significant strategic role in USAF planning.

The aircraft with the greatest operating weight ever to serve as standardized equipment on board aircraft carriers was the Douglas A3D Skywarrior carrier-based attack-bomber. The first of two XA3D-1 prototypes was flown on 28 October 1952, and initial production A3D-1s (later A-3A) were first delivered to VAH-1 (US Navy Heavy Attack Squadron One) on 31 March 1956. The definitive production version, ultimately designated A-3B, served on board carriers of the Essex and Midway classes. The A-3B Skywarrior had a span of 72 ft 6 in (22.10 m), maximum loaded weight of 82 000 lb (37 195 kg), and was powered by two 12 400 lb (5624 kg) thrust Pratt & Whitney J57-P-10 turbojets, providing a maximum level speed of 610 mph (982 km/h) at 10 000 ft (3050 m).

The greatest devastation to targets in North Vietnam was caused during the 'Linebacker II' operations from 18 to 29 December 1972. In this period USAF Boeing B-52s flew more than 700 sorties, concentrating on 24 targets in the Hanoi and Haiphong areas, with such effect that the North Vietnamese asked for the resumption of peace negotiations and bringing agreement to end the Vietnam War on 27 January 1973.

Operation 'Full Flow', the greatest exercise to involve the British Army and RAF since the Second World War, began on 3 September 1984. This involved the transfer from the UK to Germany of 57 000 troops and their equipment to take part in the Lionheart/Cold Fire exercises.

Most:

The most widely used aeroplane type in military service at the beginning of the war which was to become known as the First World War was the Etrich Taube. Designed in Austria–Hungary in 1909 it was a 'bird-winged' monoplane powered by a single engine of 85–120 hp. Maximum speed was 72 mph (116 km/h). In August 1914, about half of all the aircraft in German service were of this type and others were operated by the Austro-Hungarian air service. Intended mainly for reconnaissance and training duties, Taubes were often used for dropping light bombs. Germany alone licence-built some 500, examples of which remained in service until 1916.

Most effective single-engined day bomber of the First World War was considered to be the British Airco (de Havilland) DH4. The prototype first flew in August 1916, at Hendon, and production aircraft served with the RFC/RAF, RNAS and American Expeditionary Force. Various engines were fitted, including a 375 hp Rolls-Royce Eagle VIII, which gave a maximum speed of 143 mph (230 km/h); bomb load was up to 460 lb (209 kg).

The most disastrous month in terms of losses for the RFC was April 1917, 'Bloody April', when nearly 140 of the 365 RFC aircraft mustered for an offensive were lost in the first half of the month.

The most successful fighter aeroplane of the First World War was the Sopwith Camel, which achieved no fewer than 1294 victories over enemy aircraft. Production Camels were operated by the RFC and RNAS from July 1917; a total of 5490 was built. Possessing excellent manoeuvrability, the Camel had a maximum speed of 115 mph (185 km/h).

The most successful German fighter of the First World War was the Fokker D VII, which first became operational on the Western Front in April 1918, with Jagdgeschwader I. The type also served with several air forces after the war. Powered by a 185 hp BMW inline engine, it had a maximum speed of 124 mph (200 km/h) and excellent manoeuvrability. By the autumn of 1918, D VIIs equipped over 40 Jastas of the German air force.

The most significant unit of the RAF (in terms of presaging the pattern of future air warfare) was the Independent Force, established on 5 June 1918 to carry out strategic bombing raids on German industrial and military targets. It was this force which dropped the largest Allied bombs of the war, the 1650 lb (750 kg) 'block busters'. The first heavy bombers of the Force were the Handley Page O/100 and O/400, supplemented by the lighter Airco (de Havilland) DH4, DH9, DH9A and the Royal Aircraft Factory FE2b.

The most important aircraft to the early post-war RAF was the de Havilland DH9A which had equipped its first operational squadron (No. 110) in June 1918 and which unit arrived in France on 31 August 1918. Following their use in the closing stages of the First World War, 'Nine-Acks' saw

service in Russia in their designated role as day bombers. Thereafter the DH9A is best remembered as a general-purpose aircraft, operating in Iraq and India until replaced by Westland Wapitis in 1931.

Most widely used inter-war military aircraft produced by the Fokker company, which moved back to Holland in 1918, was the CV. Provisions for fitting wings of differing area, and various engines, enabled many combat and observation roles to be performed. Five main variants were produced, designated CV-A to CV-E, of which the last two were most extensively used. CVs served with many air forces, including those of Finland, Hungary, Italy, the Netherlands, Norway, Sweden and Switzerland. The prototype first flew in 1924 and some CVs were still in service during the early years of the Second World War.

One of the most successful French aircraft produced between the wars was the Potez 25 reconnaissance and light bombing biplane, first flown during 1925. About 4000 examples were produced, in 87 variants, operated in France and by the armed forces of some 20 countries. Engines from several French manufacturers were installed, ranging from 450 to 600 hp. Accommodation was for two, and the Potez 25 had a maximum speed of 136 mph (219 km/h) with a 450 hp engine.

The most extensively used Fleet Air Arm aircraft of the inter-war period was the Fairey IIIF. The prototype made its first flight on 19 March 1926. Production totalled about 620 aircraft, of which more than 230 were operated by the RAF for general-purpose duties and some 365 by the Fleet Air Arm as spotter-reconnaissance general-purpose biplanes. The last FAA version was the Mk IIIB, powered by a 570 hp Napier Lion XIA engine and with a maximum speed of 120 mph (193 km/h). Fairey IIIFs were operated from land bases, used as seaplanes and catapulted from naval vessels. The type was pronounced obsolete by the FAA in 1940.

One of the most important aircraft of the US Army Air Corps from 1927 to the mid-1930s and the mainstay of its bomber units were Huff-Daland/Keystone twin-engined biplane bombers, built in many small production versions. All were basically similar externally, differing mainly in engines, tail units and wing configurations. The largest production version was the Keystone B-

3A, of which 36 were built, each powered by two 525 hp Pratt & Whitney Hornet engines and having a maximum speed of 114 mph (183 km/h). Bomb load was 2500 lb (1134 kg).

Most extensively used fighter aircraft of the French Air Force in 1932 were Nieuport-Delage 62s. Three main versions were produced: the ND62 powered by a 500 hp Hispano-Suiza 12 Mb engine (345 built), the ND622 with a 500 hp H-S 12 Md engine (330 built) and the ND629 with a 500 hp H-S 12 Mdsh supercharged engine (50 built). Others were exported. Maximum speed of the initial production version was 150 mph (241 km/h).

One of the most effective biplanes to equip the US Navy, the Curtiss SOC Seagull (which had flown initially in April 1934) served on every one of its aircraft carriers, battleships and cruisers from 1935 to 1945. Designed as a scouting-observation biplane, the first production version was the SOC-1, armed with one 0.30 in forward-firing Browning machine-gun and with a similar gun in the rear cockpit. Two 116 lb bombs could also be carried. Following the original order for 135 SOC-1s, 40 SOC-2s and 130 SOC-3/SON-1s were built. Powered by a 600 hp Pratt & Whitney Wasp engine, the SOC-1 had a maximum speed of 165 mph (265 km/h). Like the Fairey Swordfish biplane of the Royal Navy, the US Navy's Seagull remained in service longer than two types of aircraft built to replace it.

The most famous torpedo-bomber/reconnaissance aircraft ever built, the Fairey Swordfish (nicknamed 'Stringbag' because of its profusion of bracing struts and wires) was a 138 mph (222 km/h) biplane in a world of fast low-wing monoplanes. The prototype first flew on 17 April 1934 (as the TSR 2) and production Mk Is entered service with the FAA in July 1935. By the beginning of the Second World War, 13 squadrons were equipped with the type, 12 more being formed during the war. Among its epic victories were the attack on the Italian fleet at Taranto on 11 November 1940, and the crippling of the German battleship *Bismarck*. A total of 2391 Swordfish was built, the Mk I version being powered by a 690 hp Bristol Pegasus III M3 engine.

Most advanced British biplane fighter to serve with the RAF and FAA was the Gloster Gladia-tor which was flown as the Gloster SS.37 prototype on 12 September 1934. Entering service from February 1937 the RAF received 444 and the FAA 60 as Sea Gladiators before production ended in 1940. Only a few squadrons remained in service at the outbreak of the Second World War, but their classic exploits include operations from a frozen lake during the Norwegian campaign, participation in the surrender and capture of the Italian submarine *Galileo Galilei* on 18 June 1940, and the part played in the defence of Malta by the Sea Gladiators *Faith, Hope* and *Charity*.

The most unequal conflict of the 'between-wars' years began on 3 October 1935 when Italy declared war on Abyssinia, starting a campaign which was to last until 5 May 1936. The main Italian aircraft used in this conflict were the Caproni Ca 74, Ca 101, Ca 111 and Ca 133 bombers, and the Fiat CR20, CR30 and IMAM Ro 37 fighters.

The RAF's most famous and now legendary single-seat fighter of the Second World War was the Supermarine Spitfire, first flown as the Supermarine Type 300 prototype (K5054) on 5 March 1936. Its superb lines benefited from the experience which its designer, R. J. Mitchell, had gained during the development of racing seaplanes to compete in the Schneider Trophy Contests; its power plant derived also from the Schneider Contests, its Merlin engine a direct descendant of the Rolls-Royce 'R' that had brought Great Britain permanent possession of the coveted Trophy in 1931. The Spitfire also remained in service far longer than most of its contemporaries, the last operational sortie by the type being made in Malaya on 1 April 1954 by a photo-reconnaissance Spitfire P.R.19 (PS888) of No. 81 Squadron.

The most significant 'between wars' use of air power was during the Spanish Civil War which effectively began on 18 July 1936. The Spanish Republican Air Force mustered 214 obsolete aircraft at the outbreak of the Civil War. Additionally, the government had at its disposal 40 civil types of various designs. Between 1937 and 1939, 55 aircraft were built in the Republican zone. Aircraft despatched to Spain by friendly nations totalled 1947, of which 1409 came from Russia. The others included 70 Dewoitine D371, D500 and D510 fighters, Loire-Nieuport 46s and 15 S510 fighters from France; 72 aircraft, not including any fighters, from the USA; 72 aircraft from

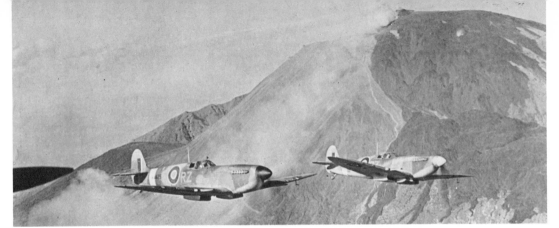

Above *RAF Spitfires fly by Mount Vesuvius during Italian operations.*

Right *Soviet Polikarpov I-15, the most numerous fighter of the Spanish Republicans.*

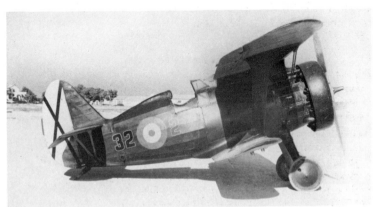

the Netherlands; 57 from Britain; and 47 from Czechoslovakia. Of these, some 400 are thought to have been destroyed other than in aerial combat, and 1520 were claimed shot down by Nationalist, German and Italian pilots.

The first Russian aircraft to enter combat in Spain in support of the Republican forces were the Polikarpov I-16 Type 6 fighters of General Kamanin's expeditionary command based at Santander. By September 1936, 105 of these aircraft had arrived in Spain and some 200 pilots and 2000 other personnel had also reached there from the Soviet Union. The I-16 first entered combat on 5 November 1936 and eventually a total of 475 was supplied. From March 1937 they were gathered in one formation designated Fighter Group 31, comprising seven squadrons of 15 aircraft each. More numerous was the I-15 biplane fighter, inferior to both the Fiat CR32 and Messerschmitt Bf 109, and no fewer than 415 were believed to have been lost in combat or on the ground. The most numerous Republican bomber type, the Soviet Tupolev SB-2, also fared badly; of 210 supplied, 178 were lost.

German intervention in the Spanish Civil War began in late July 1936 with the arrival of 20 Ju 52/3m bomber/transports, six Heinkel He 51 fighter biplanes and 85 volunteer air and ground crew. From this small beginning originated the Legion Condor, a balanced force of between 40 and 50-fighters, about the same number of multi-engined bombers,and about 100 miscellaneous ground-attack, reconnaissance and liaison aircraft, whose first C-in-C was Gen-Maj Sperrle. Volunteers from the ranks of the Luftwaffe served in rotation, to ensure the maximum dissemination of combat experience. Many of the major combat designs upon which Germany was to rely in the first half of the Second World War were first evaluated under combat conditions in Spain; the Heinkel He 111 bomber, Dornier Do 17 reconnaissance-bomber, Messerschmitt Bf 109 fighter, and the Henschel Hs 123 and Junkers Ju 87 ground attack aircraft were prominent. The contribution of the Legion Condor to the eventual Nationalist victory was considerable, but more important were the inferences drawn by Luftwaffe Staff planners. Valid lessons learned in Spain included the value of the dive-bomber in hampering enemy communications, and the effects of ground-strafing by fighters in the exploitation of a breakthrough by land forces. Less realistic was the impression gained of the relative invulnerability of unescorted bombers and dive-bombers, an impression based on the lack of sophisticated fighter resistance. In the field of fighter tactics, and in terms of combat experience by her fighter pilots, the Spanish Civil War put Germany at least a year ahead of her international rivals.

Italian intervention in the Spanish Civil War began in August 1936 with the arrival of 12 Fiat CR32 biplane fighters. CR32s were later to become the Nationalists' main fighters, superseding the slower Heinkel He 51s. The eventual strength of the Italian Aviacion del Tercio in Spain was some 730 aircraft, all supplied by Italy and including Fiat CR32s, SM81s, SM79s, BR20s, Ro37s, Ba65s and a squadron of Fiat G50s. Of these, 86 aircraft were lost on operations and 100 from other causes, and 175 flying personnel were killed. A total of 903 enemy aircraft was claimed destroyed in aerial combat, and a further 40 on the ground.

One of the most unusual fighter aircraft to serve with the US Army Air Force during the Second World War was Lockheed's P-38 Lightning. Of distinctive twin-boom configuration, it was first flown in XP-38 prototype form on 27 January 1939.

One of the Soviet Union's most outstanding combat aircraft of the Second World War was the Petlyakov Pe-2, the VI-100 prototype of which was first flown on 7 May 1939. In production form more than 11 000 were built; they formed the backbone of Soviet tactical operations on the Eastern Front, but were used also in fighter, reconnaissance and trainer roles.

The Polish fighter most widely used at the time of the German invasion in September 1939 was the PZL P11, of which 128 were on strength on 1 September 1939. They equipped Nos 111, 112, 113 and 114 Squadrons of the 1st Air Regiment based at Warsaw, Nos 121 and 122 Squadrons of the 2nd Air Regiment based at Krakow, Nos 131 and 132 Squadrons of the 3rd Air Regiment at Poznan, Nos 141 and 142 Squadrons of the 4th Air Regiment at Torun, No. 152 Squadron of the 5th Air Regiment in the Wilno/Lida area, and No. 161 Squadron of the 6th Air Regiment

based at Lwow. The P11/I prototype was flown for the first time during August 1931, and the first production P11as entered service in 1934. Definitive version was the P11c, powered by a PZL-built Mercury VI S2 radial engine of 645 hp, giving it a maximum level speed of 242 mph (390 km/h) at 18 000 ft (5485 m). Armament consisted of four 7.7 mm machine-guns, and two 12 kg fragmentation bombs could be carried beneath the wings.

The most famous Japanese bomber aircraft of the Second World War, one of the outstanding aircraft of that war **and the most extensively-built Japanese bomber,** was the Mitsubishi G4M Navy Type 1 Attack Bomber. First flown on 23 October 1939, the G4M—known by the Allied codename *Betty*—was first used operationally in May 1941 in an attack on Chungking. In service throughout the entire Pacific War, the last operational flight of two G4M1s carried the Japanese surrender delegation to Ie-Shima on 19 Aug 1945.

The USAAF fighter with the most unusual power plant installation, flown in XP-39B prototype form on 25 November 1939, was the Bell P-39 Airacobra. This had its engine mounted in the rear fuselage, driving a conventional tractor propeller in the nose via a long extension shaft that passed beneath the pilot's seat.

The most extensively built American aircraft of the Second World War, the Consolidated B-24 Liberator of which more than 18 000 were produced, was flown for the first time in XB-24 prototype form on 29 December 1939.

The French military aeroplane most widely used at the beginning of the Battle of France on 10 May 1940 belonged to the Potez 630 series, of which a total of 1250 were built. The main variants were the 630 and 631 fighters and the 63/II reconnaissance aircraft. First flown in April 1936, the three-seat Potez 630 fighter, powered by two 640 hp Hispano-Suiza HS 14AB 10/11 engines, had a maximum speed of 280 mph (450 km/h) at 13 000 ft (3960 m). Standard armament comprised two nose-mounted Hispano 9 or 404 cannon, plus one MAC machine-gun for rear defence. Shortage of cannon made it necessary to arm many 630/631s with four machine-guns and when, in February 1940, it was decided to increase the fire power of these fighters, the cannon were supplemented by six machine-guns mounted beneath the wings.

One of the most outstanding US Army Air Force fighters of the Second World War made its first flight in XP-47B prototype form on 6 May 1941. This was to become known as the Republic P-47 Thunderbolt, which had been designed under the leadership of Alexander Kartveli, and of which more than 15 000 were built before production ended.

The most successful US Navy fighter aircraft of the Second World War was the Grumman F6F Hellcat, the prototype of which flew for the first time on 26 June 1942. US Navy statistics record that almost 75 per cent of all Navy wartime combat victories were achieved with Hellcats, of which 12 275 had been built when production ended in November 1945.

The most convincing proof of the sinking of a U-boat by an attack from the air was provided by the aircraft which sank it, a Consolidated Liberator IIIA of RAF Coastal Command which, captained by Sqn Ldr D. M. Sleep, was engaged in an anti-submarine patrol on 20 October 1942. Attacking the U-boat from low level, the explosion from the aircraft's bombs damaged the Liberator severely and it was a major feat for the crew to fly it some 800 miles (1287 km) back to base where it crashed on landing. It was discovered subsequently that a small piece of the submarine, identified by the Admiralty, had imbedded itself in the Liberator's tailplane.

Perhaps the most unusual aircraft to enter Luftwaffe service, in late 1942, was the Heinkel He 111Z. It consisted of two conventional He 111s, linked together by a new wing centre-section which carried a fifth engine. Intended to tow the Messerschmitt Me 321 Gigant glider, the He 111Z saw very limited service in this role and as a transport aircraft.

The most successful destroyer of V1 flying-bombs in flight was Sqn Ldr Joseph Berry, RAF, who shot down 60 of these weapons during 1944.

Most important fighter aircraft of the FAA at the outbreak of the Korean War was the Hawker Sea Fury, which also proved to be the last piston-engined fighter in FAA squadrons. First flown on 21 February 1945, the type entered service with No. 807 Squadron in August 1947 and operated with distinction throughout the Korean War. The Sea Fury flown by Lt P. Carmichael of

No. 802 Squadron destroyed the squadron's first MiG-15 on 9 August 1952.

Most unusual design, that of the only combat aircraft of canard configuration to be the subject of a production contract during the Second World War, applies to the Japanese Kyushu J7W Shinden which was intended as a heavily armed high-performance interceptor for use by the Navy. Powered by a 2130 hp Mitsubishi MK9D 18-cylinder supercharged radial engine, driving a six-blade pusher propeller, the prototype made its first flight on 3 August 1945. Only two more short flights were made before the Japanese surrender.

The most unusual bomber programme initiated after the Second World War involved the series of Northrop flying wings. The first full-size prototype XB-35 flew on 25 June 1946. Designed as a long-range bomber, it comprised a cantilever aluminium sweptback wing, constructed in one piece. Directional control was via drag-inducing double-split flaps at the wingtips, and elevons and leading-edge fixed wingtip slots were fitted. The crew of seven were situated in a centre-section nacelle; six electrically operated gun turrets (four remotely controlled at outer wing stations) provided defensive armament. Powered by four turbo-supercharged Pratt & Whitney Wasp Major piston engines of 3000 hp each, the XB-35 had an all-up weight of 209 000 lb (94 800 kg) and a wing span of 172 ft (52.43 m). Its design had been started in 1942, followed by testing of four twin-engined scale models designated N-9M. Following the first flight of the prototype XB-35, 14 development aircraft were ordered by the USAF as YB-35s; two of these were converted into YB-49s, each with eight jet engines, and one into the YRB-49A with six jet engines. Although 30 RB-49s were ordered subsequently for operational service with the USAF, these were cancelled in 1949.

Britain's most successful military aircraft to be designed and built after the Second World War was undoubtedly the Hawker Hunter jet fighter, the first flight of the first of three prototypes (WB188) being made on 20 July 1951.

The US Navy's most effective 'dogfighter' during the Vietnam War, and the type with the best 'kill' record over Soviet-built MiG fighters was the Vought F8U Crusader. It had entered US Navy service almost a decade earlier, the first of them delivered to Squadron VF-32 at Cecil Field (Florida) on 25 March 1957.

Regarded as the USAF's 'most effective fighter of the Sixties' and as one of the US Navy's 'finest air weapons', the McDonnell Douglas F-4C Phantom II tactical fighter for the USAF was flown for the first time on 27 May 1963. Current versions of this well armed and equipped aircraft, which remains in large-scale service in 1988 and is the subject of many update programmes, have a maximum speed of Mach 2.25 at optimum altitude.

The US Navy's most sophisticated electronic warfare aircraft, the Grumman EA-6B Prowler, entered service with squadron VAQ-129 at NAS Whidbey Island on 29 January 1971.

A most important and large repatriation task, carried out by two RAF Britannia transport aircraft, ended on 22 December 1973 with the return of these aircraft to their base at Brize Norton, Oxfordshire. Between 30 October and 20 December 1973 they had in 90 sorties ferried a total of 16 300 refugees between Karachi and Dacca and Chittagong and Karachi. The task was continued by two more Britannias at the beginning of 1974.

Regarded as a most important navigation aid, the British Aerospace Terprom system which completed a period of technology demonstration trials on 26 March 1986 can provide navigational accuracy within 150–300 ft (45–91 m) of intended track, irrespective of flight duration. Even more important in modern combat scenarios is the fact that this is achieved without external communications or forward-projected radar emissions.

Formation Dates of Air Arms

ABU DHABI
Air Wing, Abu Dhabi Defence Forces, 1968
Abu Dhabi Air Force, 1972. Joined with Dubai Police Air Wing in 1976 to form United Arab Emirates Air Force

AFGHANISTAN
Afghan Military Air Arm, 1924
Afghan Air Force, 1937
Royal Afghan Air Force, 1948
Afghan Republican Air Force, 1973

ALBANIA
Albanian People's Army Air Force, 1947

ALGERIA
Armée de l'Air Algérienne, 1962

ANGOLA
Fôrça Aérea Populare de Angola, 1976

ARGENTINA
Air Force
Servicio Aeronautico del Ejercito, 10 August 1912
Fuerza Aérea Argentina, 4 January 1945
Army Aviation
Comando de Aviación del Ejercito, 3 November 1959
Naval Aviation
Comando de Aviación Naval Argentina, 17 October 1919

AUSTRALIA
Air Force
Army Aviation Corps, September 1912
Australian Flying Corps, January 1913
Australian Air Corps, 1920
Australian Air Force, 31 March 1921
Royal Australian Air Force, June 1921
Army Aviation
16 Army Light Aircraft Squadron, RAAF, 1960
1st Aviation Regiment (Divisional), 1966
Australian Army Aviation Corps, 1 July 1968
Naval Aviation
Fleet Air Arm, 1948

AUSTRIA
K.u.K. Militär-äronautische Anstalt, 1892
K.u.K. Luftschifferabteilung, 1909
Kommando der Luftstreitkräfte, 1928
Fliegertruppen des Österreichischen Bundesheeres, 1 June 1935
Österreichische Heeresfliegerkräfte, 1955

BAHRAIN
Bahrain Defence Force, Air Wing, 1977

BANGLADESH
Mukti Bahini Air Wing, 1971
Bangladesh Defence Force, Air Wing, 1972

BELGIUM
Compagnie des Ouvriers et Aérostiers, 5 March 1911
Compagnie des Aviators, 16 April 1913
Aviation Militaire, 20 March 1915
Aéronautique Militaire, 1925
Force Aérienne Belge, 1 October 1946

BELIZE
Belize Defence Force, Air Wing, 1983

BENIN
Force Aérienne de Dahomey, 1961
Force Aérienne du Benin, 1975

BOLIVIA
Cuerpo de Aviación, August 1924
Fuerza Aérea Boliviana, 1940

BOTSWANA
Botswana Defence Force, Air Wing, 1977

BRAZIL
Air Force
Brazilian Army Balloon Corps, 1908
Brazilian Army Air Service, 1918
Fôrça Aérea Brasileira, 20 January 1940
Naval Aviation
Naval Aviation School, 26 August 1916
Brazilian Naval Air Service, 1922
Absorbed into Air Force, 20 January 1941 until
   formation of Fôrça Aeronaval de Marinha do
   Brasil, 26 January 1965

BRUNEI
Royal Brunei Armed Forces, Air Wing, 1965

BULGARIA
Bulgarian Army Aviation Corps, 1912
Royal Bulgarian Air Force, 1937
Bulgarian People's Air Force, 1946

BURKINA FASO (formerly Upper Volta)
Force Aérienne de Burkina Faso, 4 August 1984

BURMA
Union of Burma Air Force, 1955

BURUNDI
Force Armée du Burundi, 1966

CAMEROUN
L'Armée de l'Air du Cameroun, 1960

CANADA
Canadian Aviation Corps, 1914 until February
   1915
Canadian Naval Air Service, 1918–19
Canadian Air Force, November 1918 until
   February 1920
Royal Canadian Air Force, 1 April 1924
Canadian Armed Forces—Air Command, 1968

CENTRAL AFRICAN REPUBLIC
Force Aérienne Centrafricaine, 1961

CHAD REPUBLIC
Escadrille Nationale Tchadienne, 1961

CHILE
Air Force
Escuela de Aeronautica Militar, 11 February
   1913
Chilean Army Aviation Company, 1918
Fuerza Aérea Chilena, 21 March 1930
Army Aviation
Comando de Aviación, Ejercito de Chile, 1948
Naval Aviation
Naval Aviation Service, 1919; united with
   Fuerza Aérea Chilena, 21 March 1930
Servicio Aviación de la Armada de Chile, 1948

CHINA (Chinese People's Republic)
Air Force
Air Force of the People's Liberation Army, 1950
Naval Aviation
Aviation of the People's Navy, 1950

COLOMBIA
Colombian Army Air Arm, April 1922
Fuerza Aérea Colombiana, 1943

COMORES
Comores Military Aviation, 1976

CONGO
Force Aérienne Congolaise, 1961

COSTA RICA
Guardia Civil Seccion Aérea, 1949

CUBA
Cuerpo de Aviación, 1917
Fuerza Aérea Ejercito de Cuba, 1955
Fuerza Aérea Revolucionaria, 1959

CZECHOSLOVAKIA
Czechoslovak Army Air Force, 29 October 1918
Slovak Air Force, 1939
Ceskoslovenské Letectvo, 1945

DENMARK
Air Force
Army Flying School, 2 July 1912
Army Flying Corps, 1 February 1923
Haerens Flyvertropper, 1932
Kongelige Danske Flyvevåbnet, 1 October 1950
Army Aviation
Haerens Flyvetjaeneste, July 1971
Naval Aviation
Navy Flying School, 1912
Sovaernets Flyvetjaeneste, 1971

DJIBOUTI
Force Aérienne Djiboutienne, 1978

DOMINICAN REPUBLIC
Dominican Army Aviation Company, 1939
El Cuerpo de Aviación Militar, 1948
Fuerza Aérea Dominicana, 1955

DUBAI
Air Wing, Union Defence Force, 1971
Dubai Police Air Wing, 1973. Joined with Abu
   Dhabi Air Force in 1976 to form United Arab
   Emirates Air Force

ECUADOR
Cuerpo de Aviadores Militares, 1920
Fuerza Aérea Ecuatoriana, 1935

EGYPT
Egyptian Army Air Force, May 1932
Royal Egyptian Air Force, 1939
Al Quwwat al-Jawwiya Ilmisriya, 1953

EL SALVADOR
Army Aviation Service, 1923
Fuerza Aérea Salvadorena, 1948

ETHIOPIA
Imperial Ethiopian Aviation, 1924
Imperial Ethiopian Air Force, 1946
Ye Ethiopia Ayer Hail, 1974

FINLAND
Ilmailuvoimat, March 1918
Ilmavoimat, 1920

FRANCE
Air Force
Service Aéronautique, April 1910
Aviation Militaire, October 1910
L'Armée de l'Air, August 1933
French Vichy Air Force, 1940
Forces Aériennes Françaises Libres, 1941
L'Armee de l'Air, 1943
Army Aviation
Aviation Légère de l'Armée de Terre, November
   1952
Naval Aviation
Service de l'Aéronautique de la Marine,
   12 March 1912
Aéronautique Maritime, 1925
Aéronautique Navale, 1945

GABON REPUBLIC
Force Aérienne Gabonaise, 1961

GERMANY, DEMOCRATIC REPUBLIC
Volkspolizei-Luft, March 1950
Luftstreitkräfte und Luftverteidigung, 1955

GERMANY, FEDERAL REPUBLIC
Air Force
Military Aviation Service, 1 October 1912
Luftwaffe, March 1935
Luftwaffe der Deutschen Bundesrepublik,
   24 September 1956
Army Aviation
Heeresfliegertruppen, 1957
Naval Aviation
Marineflieger, 1957

GHANA
Ghana Air Force, 1959

GREECE
Air Squadron of Royal Hellenic Army,
   September 1912
Hellenic Army Air Force, 1917
Hellenic Combat Air Force, December 1929
Royal Hellenic Air Force, November 1935
Hellenic Air Force, 1973

GUATEMALA
Cuerpo de Aéronautica Militar, 1929
Fuerza Aérea Guatemalteca, 1945

GUINEA-BISSAU
Force Aérienne de Guinea-Bissau, 1978

GUINEA REPUBLIC
Force Aérienne de Guineé, 1959

GUYANA
Air Wing, Guyana Defence Force, 1968
Air Command, Guyana Defence Force, 1970

HAITI
Corps d'Aviatión d'Haiti, 1943

HONDURAS
Aviación Militar Hondureña, 1933
Fuerza Aérea Hondureña, 1954

HONG KONG
Air Arm, Hong Kong Defence Force, 1 May
   1949
Air Arm, Royal Hong Kong Defence Force,
   1951
Royal Hong Kong Auxiliary Air Force, 1970

HUNGARY
Hungarian Air Arm, 1936
Magyar Királyi Légierö, 1938

INDIA
Air Force
Bharatiya Vayu Sena, 1 April 1933
Naval Aviation
Indian Naval Aviation, 1950

INDONESIA
Air Force
Netherlands East Indies Army Air Corps, 1940
Netherlands East Indies Air Arm, 1945
Tentara Nasional Indonesia—Angkatan Udara, 1950
Army Aviation
Tentara Nasional Indonesia—Angkatan Darat, 1959
Naval Aviation
Tentara Nasional Indonesia—Angkatan Laut, 1958

IRAN
Air Office of the Imperial Iranian Army, 1924
Imperial Iranian Air Force, 1932
Islamic Republic of Iran Air Force, 1979

IRAQ
Royal Iraqi Air Force, 1931
Al Quwwat al-Jawwiya al-Iraqiya, 1958

IRISH REPUBLIC (Eire)
Irish Air Corps, 1922

ISRAEL
Sherut Avir, November 1947
Chel Ha'Avir, 27 May 1948
Heyl Ha'Avir, 1951

ITALY
Air Force
Battaglione Aviatori, 27 June 1912
Servizio d'Aviazione Coloniale, 19 November 1912
Flotta Aerea d'Italia, 28 November 1912
Corpo Aeronautico Militare, 7 January 1915
Regia Aeronautica, 23 March 1923
Aeronautica Militare Italiana, 13 October 1943
Army Aviation
Aviazione Leggera dell'Esercito, 1951
Naval Aviation
Aviazione per la Marina Militare, 1943

IVORY COAST
Force Aérienne de la Côte d'Ivoire, 1962

JAMAICA
Air Wing, Jamaica Defence Force, July 1963

JAPAN
Air Force
Provisional Committee for Military Balloon Research, 30 July 1909
Air Battalion of the Army Transport Command, December 1915
Army Aviation Department, April 1919
Army Air Corps, 1 May 1925
Japan Air Self-Defence Force (Koku Jiei-tai), 1 July 1954
Army Aviation
Japanese Army Air Force, 1911
Japan Ground Self-Defence Force (Rikujye Jiei-tai), 1 July 1954
Naval Aviation
Naval Committee for Aeronautical Research, 26 June 1912
Japanese Naval Air Service, 1912
Naval Air Corps, April 1916
Japan Maritime Self-Defence Force (Kaijoh Jiei-tai), 1 July 1954

JORDAN
Arab Legion Air Force, 1949
Al Quwwat al-Jawwiya Almalakiya al-Urduniya, 1956

KAMPUCHEA
Royal Khmer Aviation, 1953
Aviation Nationale Khmere, 1954
Air Force of Kampuchea Liberation Army, 1975

KENYA
Kenya Air Force, 1 June 1964
The '82 Air Force, August 1982

KOREA, NORTH
North Korean Aviation Society, September 1945
North Korean Army's Aviation Division, 1946
Korean People's Armed Forces Air Corps, 1948
Korean People's Army Air Force, May 1955

KOREA, SOUTH
Republic of Korea Air Force (Hankook Kong Goon), May 1949

KUWAIT
Kuwait Air Force, 1960

LAOS
Laotian Army Aviation Service, 1955
Royal Lao Air Force, August 1960
Air Force of the People's Liberation Army, April 1975

LEBANON
Al Quwwat al-Jiwwiya al-Lubnania, 1949

LESOTHO
Police Mobile Unit (Air Wing), 1978
Lesotho Royal Defence Force—Air Squadron,
  20 June 1986

LIBERIA
Liberian Army Air Reconnaissance Unit, 1976

LIBYA
Air Force
Royal Libyan Air Force, 1959
Al Quwwat al-Jawwiya al-Libiyya, 1970
Army Aviation
Aviation Section of Army, 1970

MADAGASCAR
Armée de l'Air Malagache, 24 April 1961

MALAWI
Malawi Army Air Wing, 1966

MALAYSIA
Malayan Volunteer Air Force, September 1940
Malayan Auxiliary Air Force, 1 October 1950
Royal Malayan Air Force, 1 June 1958
Royal Malaysian Air Force, 16 September 1963

MALI REPUBLIC
Force Aérienne de la République de Mali, 1962

MALTA
Armed Forces of Malta, Helicopter Flight, 1971

MAURITANIA
Force Aérienne Islamique de Mauritanie, 1961

MEXICO
Air Force
Mexican Aviation Corps, 1915
Fuerza Aérea Mexicana, 1924
Naval Aviation
Aviación de la Armada de Mexico, 1944

MONGOLIA
Air Force of the Mongolian People's Republic,
  1966

MOROCCO
Aviation Royale Chérifienne, 19 November
  1956
Force Aérienne Royale Marocaine, 1961

MOZAMBIQUE
Fôrça Populare Aérea de Libertação de
  Moçambique, 1975

NEPAL
Royal Nepalese Army Air Wing, early 1960s
Royal Nepal Air Force, 1979

NETHERLANDS
Air Force
Army Balloon Unit, 1886
Luchtvaartafdeling, 1 July 1913
Wapen der Militaire Luchtvaart, 1 November
  1938
Koninklijke Luchtmacht, 27 March 1953
Naval Aviation
Marine Luchtvaartdienst, 18 August 1917

NEW ZEALAND
New Zealand Permanent Air Force, June 1923
Royal New Zealand Air Force, 1 April 1937

NICARAGUA
Army Air Arm, 1923
Fuerza Aérea de la Guardia Nacional, 9 June
  1938
Fuerza Aérea Guardia de Nicaragua, 1947
Fuerza Aérea Sandinista, 19 July 1979

NIGER
Force Aérienne de Niger, 1961

NIGERIA
Federal Nigerian Air Force, January 1964

NORWAY
Air Force
Haerens Flyvåpen, 1915
Kongelige Norske Luftforsvaret, early 1944
Naval Aviation
Marinens Flevevaesen, 1915, but combined with
  Haerens Flyvåpen in early 1944 to form
  Kongelige Norske Luftforsvaret

OMAN
Al Quwwat al-Jawwiya al-Sultanat Oman, 1958

PAKISTAN
Air Force
Royal Pakistan Air Force, 14 August 1947
Pakistan Air Force, 23 March 1956
Army Aviation
Air Observation Flight of RPAF, 1947
Pakistan Army Aviation Wing, 1958
Naval Aviation
Pakistan Navy Air Arm, 1973

PANAMA
Fuerza Aérea Panamena, January 1969

PAPUA NEW GUINEA
Papua New Guinea Defence Force, Air
    Transport Squadron, 14 November 1974

PARAGUAY
Fuerzas Aéreas Nacionales, 1935
Fuerza Aérea Paraguaya, 1949

PERU
Air Force
Peruvian Army Aviation Service, 1919
Cuerpo de Aeronautica del Perú, 20 May 1929
Fuerza Aérea Peruana, July 1950
Army Aviation
Aviación del Ejercito Peruano, 1965
Naval Aviation
Peruvian Naval Air Service, 1924, but combined
    into Cuerpo de Aeronautica del Perú on 20
    May 1929
Servicio Aeronaval de la Marina Peruana, 1965

PHILIPPINES
Air Force
Philippine Army Air Corps, 2 May 1935
Philippine Air Force, 3 July 1947
Army Aviation
Air Battalion, Philippine Army, 1980
Naval Aviation
Philippine Naval Aviation, 1975

POLAND
Air Force
1st Polish Aviation Unit, 19 August 1917
Aviation of the 1st Polish Corps, March 1918
1st Aviation Unit of the Polish Forces,
    15 October 1918
Polskie Wojska Lotnicze, 29 September 1919
Pulk Lotnictwa Mysliwskiego Warszawa,
    10 August 1944
Polskie Wojska Lotnicze, 1945
Naval Aviation
Morskie Lotnictwo Wojskowe, 1945

PORTUGAL
Air Force
Campo de Seixcal, 1912
Arma da Aeronáutica, 1917
Fôrça Aérea Portuguesa, 1 July 1952
Naval Aviation
Aviaçao Maritima, 1917, but merged into Fôrça
    Aérea Portuguesa on 1 July 1952

QATAR
Qatar Public Security Forces Air Wing, March
    1968

Qatar Emiri Air Force, 1974

ROMANIA
Corpul Aerian Româna, 1915
Divisia I-a Aerianá, 1919
Fortelor Regal ale Aeriene Româna, 1936
Fortele Aeriene ale Republicii Populare
    Român̂ia, 1947
Fortele Aeriene ale Republicii Socialiste
    Românîa, 1966

RWANDA
Force Aérienne Rwandaise, 1972

SAUDI ARABIA
Al Quwwat al-Jawwiya Assa'udiya, 1950

SENEGAMBIA
Armée de l'Air du Sénégal, 1960
Armée de l'Air du Sénégambia, December 1981

SEYCHELLES
Seychelles Defence Force Air Wing, 1980

SHARJAH
Amiri Guard Air Wing, 20 December 1984

SIERRA LEONE
Defence Force Air Arm, 1973

SINGAPORE
Singapore Air Defence Command, September
    1971
Republic of Singapore Air Force, 1 April 1975

SOMALIA
Somalian Aeronautical Corps, 1961

SOUTH AFRICA
South African Aviation Corps, early 1915
No. 26 (South African) Squadron, Royal Flying
    Corps, 1915–18
Suid Afrikaanse Lugmag, 1 February 1920

SPAIN
Air Force
Servicio Militar de Aerostación, 1896
Aeronáutica Militar Española, March 1911
Servicio de Aeronáutica Militar Española,
    February 1913
Ejército del Aire Español, 9 November 1939
Fuerza Aérea Española, 1980
Army Aviation
Aviación Ligera del Ejército de Tierra, July 1965
Fuerzas Aeromoviles del Ejército de Tierra,
    March 1973

Naval Aviation
Aeronáutica Naval, 1917, but integrated into
    Ejército del Air Español on 9 November 1939
Arma Aérea de la Armada, June 1954

SRI LANKA
Royal Ceylon Air Force, 10 October 1950
Sri Lanka Air Force, 1971

SUDAN
Silakh al-Jawwiya as-Sudaniya, 1955

SURINAME
Suriname Air Force, 1982

SWAZILAND
Umbutfo Swaziland Defence Force, Air Wing,
    June 1979

SWEDEN
Air Force
Kungliga Svenska Flygvapnet, 1 July 1926
Army Aviation
Armen, 1954
Naval Aviation
Svenska Marinen, 1957

SWITZERLAND
Fliegertruppe, 31 July 1914
Militär-Flugwesen, 1919
Schweizerische Flugwaffe, a component of the
    Kommando der Flieger- und Flieger-
    abwehrtruppen, 19 October 1936

SYRIA
Al Quwwat al-Jawwiya al Arabia as-Suriya, 1946

TAIWAN
Army Air Arm, 1914
Chinese Aviation Service, 1919
Central Government Air Force, 1934
Chinese Air Force, 1946
Chinese Nationalist Air Force (Chung-Kuo
    Kung Chuan), 1949

TANZANIA
Tanzanian People's Defence Force, Air Wing,
    1964

THAILAND
Air Force
Royal Siamese Flying Corps, 23 March 1914
Royal Aeronautical Service, 1919
Royal Siamese Air Force, April 1937
Royal Thai Air Force, 1939
Army Aviation
Royal Thai Army, Air Arm, early 1950s

Naval Aviation
Royal Thai Navy, Air Arm, early 1950s

TOGO
Force Aérienne Togolaise, 1964

TONGA
Tonga Air Arm, mid-1986

TRANSKEI
Transkei Defence Force, Air Arm, late 1986

TRINIDAD & TOBAGO
Trinidad & Tobago Defence Force, Air Arm,
    1974

TUNISIA
Al Quwwat al-Jawwiya al-Djoumhouria al-
    Tunisia, 1960

TURKEY
Air Force
Army Aviation Section, 1912
Turkish Flying Corps, 1914
Turkish Army Air Service, 1917
Turkish Air Force (Türk Hava Kuvvetleri),
    1928
Army Aviation
Kara Ordusu Havaciligi, 1950
Naval Aviation
Cumhuriyet Bahrya, 1971

UGANDA
Uganda Army Air Force, 1964

UNITED ARAB EMIRATES
United Arab Emirates Air Force, May 1976

UNION OF SOVIET SOCIALIST REPUBLICS
Air Force
Imperial Russian Flying Corps, 1910
Chief Directorate, Workers' and Peasants' Red
    Air Fleet, 24 May 1918
Sovietskaya Voenno-vozdushniye Sily, 1924
Naval Aviation
Naval Aviation School, 1910
Volga Military Flotille, 1918
Aviatsiya-Voenno-Morskovo Flota, 1924

UNITED KINGDOM
Air Force
Air Battalion of the Royal Engineers, 1 April
    1911
Royal Flying Corps, 13 May 1912
Royal Air Force, 1 April 1918
Army Aviation
Army Air Corps, 1 September 1957

Army Aviation, 1 August 1965
Naval Aviation
Royal Flying Corps Naval Wing, 13 May 1912
Royal Naval Air Service, 1 July 1914, but
    integrated into Royal Air Force on 1 April
    1918
Fleet Air Arm of RAF, April 1924
Naval Aviation (Air Branch of the Royal Navy),
    May 1939
Fleet Air Arm of Royal Navy, 1953

UNITED STATES OF AMERICA
Air Force
Aeronautical Division, US Signals Corps,
    1 August 1907
Aviation Section, US Signals Corps, 18 July
    1914
United States Air Service, 24 May 1918
United States Army Air Service, 4 June 1920
United States Army Air Corps, 2 July 1926
United States Army Air Force, 20 June 1941
United States Air Force, 18 September 1947
Army Aviation
US Army Air Forces, 1948
Naval Aviation
Naval Flying Corps, 29 August 1916, with naval
    aviation subsequently being carried out by US
    Navy and US Marine Corps air arms

URUGUAY
Air Force
Escuela Militar de Aéronautica, 20 November
    1916
Aéronautica Militar, 1919

Grumman Ea-6B Prowler, serving with VAQ-129.

Fuerza Aérea Uruguaya, 4 December 1953
Naval Aviation
Aviación Naval Uruguya, 1965

VENEZUELA
Air Force
Venezuelan Military Air Service, 17 April 1920
Regimiento de Aviatión Militar, January 1936
Fuerza Aérea Venezolana, 1949
Army Aviation
Aviación del Ejercito Venezolana, 1974
Naval Aviation
Naval Aviation Centre, early 1920s
Servicio de Aviación Naval Venezolana, 1974

VIETNAM
Observation, Communications, and Liaison
    Squadrons of the Vietnam Armed Forces
    (South Vietnam), 1951
Vietnam Democratic Republic Air Force (North
    Vietnam), 1954–5
Vietnam Air Force (South Vietnam), July 1955
Vietnamese People's Air Force, July 1976

YEMEN, NORTH
Yemen Arab Republic Air Force, 1962

YEMEN, SOUTH
Air Force of the People's Democratic Republic
    of Yemen, 1969

YUGOSLAVIA
Serbian Military Air Service, 1913
Aviation Department, Yugoslav Army, 1918
Jugoslovensko Ratno Vazduhoplovstvo, 1930,
    but disbanded 1941
Croatian Air Force, 1941–4
Jugoslovensko Ratno Vazduhoplovstvo,
    5 January 1945

ZAIRE
Force Aérienne Katangaise, 1961
Force Aériennes Congolaises, 1962
Force Aérienne Zaïroise, 1973

ZAMBIA
Zambian Air Wing, 1964
Zambian National Defence Forces, 1968

ZIMBABWE
Southern Rhodesia Air Section, 1936
Southern Rhodesian Air Force, 1939
Royal Rhodesian Air Force, October 1954
Rhodesian Air Force, 1969
Zimbabwe–Rhodesia Air Force, 1979
Zimbabwe Air Force, 1980

Research and Experimentation

Research has been fundamental to progress and achievement in aviation from the outset, whether the outcome of such work led to initial failure or established the foundations for subsequent demonstrable, commercial production or military successes. It is ironic that the names of many enlightened scientists, inventors and forward-thinkers who contributed to man's understanding of flight during the 16th–19th centuries, without themselves having demonstrated any form of workable flying machine, have largely been forgotten. Yet, without their contributions, both theoretical and practicable, the Wright Brothers, Santos-Dumont, Blériot and many others would have found their own research so much the harder. And once manned and powered flying was a reality, so the amount of research only increased, not least to meet the demands of war.

The United States of America can be said to have enjoyed the first lengthy period of technological superiority in manned heavier-than-air flying, through the research and experiments of pioneers like the Wright Brothers. However, by the close of the first decade of the 20th century, Europe, and especially France, had regained the initiative it had enjoyed in the previous two centuries, having more or less moved away from lighter-than-air experimentation and forged ahead in aeroplane design at a time of US complacency.

For a time after the First World War, there was still talk of the 'war to end wars'; but it did no such thing. Rather, the manner of its victories, and the conditions imposed upon the vanquished under the peace agreements which followed, made a

Gloster E.28/39 in developed form.

Second World War inevitable, and Germany brilliantly forged ahead of the rest of the world in rocketry, jet propulsion and other military orientated technologies during the 1930s through huge research programmes.

In the early post-Second World War years, when inventiveness and engineering skill held the key to progress, Britain set the pace in many ways. The United States was first to prove that the 'sound barrier' could be penetrated by the brute force of rocket power allied to human courage; it was the Fairey Delta 2 which combined British leadership in jet propulsion with design genius that demonstrated that passing the speed of sound, Mach 1, need result in nothing more alarming than the flicker of a needle or two on the instrument panel. British money began to run out by the time the Fairey Rotodyne pioneered the whole new field of vertical take-off and landing (VTOL) for commercial operations. It dried up completely before the British Aircraft Corporation's TSR.2 could keep Britain in the military 'big league' with its supersonic bombing capabilities.

The United States, on the other hand, launched into new generations of aviation research which investigated every kind of technique for achieving VTOL, without producing anything better than the relatively simple helicopter; and poured countless millions of dollars into a giant Mach 3 bomber that remained but a prototype. In a last fling at more reasonable economic levels, Britain produced the first thoroughly practical VTOL combat aircraft in the Harrier, which America decided it had to buy. With its French neighbours, it then evolved the Concorde supersonic airliner, unbeaten as a technological triumph.

Meanwhile, the United States has progressed relentlessly from the Mach 1.015 of 'Chuck' Yeager's little Bell X-1 of 1947 to Mach 6.72 with the North American X-15A-2, and then to 17 600 mph (28 325 km/h) orbital speed with its Shuttle spacecraft reusable transportation system. The Shuttle is included as a manned aircraft by virtue of making a conventional runway landing after a space mission. In this respect, it has the greatest variation in speeds of any manned aircraft, touching down at just 208 mph (334 km/h) EAS while unpowered. While spaceflight is covered in a companion volume to this publication, a small number of the most significant manned spaceflights are included here as they represent the culmination of earlier aviation research and experimentation.

Firsts:

The first gyroscopic automatic stabilizer was successfully demonstrated by the Americans, Lawrence B. Sperry and Lt Patrick Nelson Lynch Bellinger, in a Curtiss F flying-boat in 1913. The aircraft was longitudinally and laterally stabilized.

The first experiments with a pressurized cabin were made on a de Havilland DH4 at Wright Field in the USA during 1922.

The first full-size rocket-powered aeroplane in the world was the sailplane *Ente* (Duck), powered by two Sander slow-burning rocket motors and built by the Rhön-Rossitten Gesellschaft of Germany. Piloted by Friedrich Stamer, it made a flight of just over 0.75 mile (1.2 km) near the Wasserkuppe Mountain in about 1 min on 11 June 1928. The rocket-powered glider flown by Fritz von Opel at Rebstock, near Frankfurt, is often stated as being the world's first rocket aeroplane, but this did not fly until 30 September 1929. Known as the Opel-Hatry Rak-1, it however flew for more than 1.1 miles (1.8 km) and attained a speed of 100 mph (160 km/h). (It is worth noting here that Max Valier had demonstrated rocket propulsion in Germany in 1928 and had received backing from Fritz von Opel for his work. Further, in 1929 Prof Hermann Oberth built a liquid-fuelled rocket while in Berlin.)

The first work in Germany on the development of an aircraft turbojet engine began at Heinkel's Marienehe plant on 15 April 1936, when the German engineer Dr Hans Joachim Pabst von Ohain and Dipl Ing Max Hahn began work on such a power plant at the instigation of Ernst Heinkel.

The first aircraft turbojet engine in the world was bench-tested for the first time on 12 April 1937. This was the W/U Type with centrifugal compressor, designed by Briton Frank Whittle (later Sir Frank) for Power Jets and built by the British Thomson-Houston Company at Rugby. In March 1938 Whittle received an Air Ministry contract for a production engine, and on 15 May 1941 the Gloster E.28/39, powered by this W1 engine, took off at Cranwell on a 17 minute flight, flown by Flt Lt P. E. G. Sayer. **This was the first British turbojet powered aeroplane.** Interestingly, a non-airworthy version of the W1 engine that had been built simultaneously using spare parts and rejected components, known as the W1X, had been fitted to the E.28/39 for taxiing trials, during which (on 8 April 1941) the aircraft had made a few 'hop' flights.

The first aircraft with a completely successful pressurized cabin was the Lockheed XC-35. Built for research at high altitude, it was flown for the first time on 7 May 1937.

The first known project to develop a specifically designed rocket-powered manned aeroplane was begun in Germany as *Projekt X* by Dr Alexander Lippisch at the German DFS in July 1937. Though experimental, the resulting aircraft was the DFS 194, forerunner of the operational Messerschmitt Me 163 Komet rocket plane (see below).

The Heinkel HeS 3b turbojet engine designed by Pabst von Ohain was flown for the first time during June 1938, a Heinkel He 118 serving as a testbed aircraft.

The first specifically designed rocket-powered and piloted aeroplane was the Heinkel He 176, which made its maiden flight at the secret German research establishment at Peenemünde on 20 June 1939. Piloted by Erich Warsitz, the He 176 was powered by a single Walter HWK R.I-203 motor.

The first aircraft in the world to fly solely on the power of a turbojet engine was the German Heinkel He 178, which made its first true flight at Heinkel's Marienehe airfield on 27 August 1939. It was powered by a Heinkel HeS 3b engine designed by Dr Pabst von Ohain.

The first successful liquid-fuel rocket aircraft in the world was the German DFS 194 which,

having been conceived by a team under Dr Alexander Lippisch, was taken over by Messerschmitt A.G. at Augsburg and flown in August 1940 by Heini Dittmar. It was powered by a 600 lb (272 kg) thrust Walter rocket motor.

The first research aircraft to be designed for flight at 1000 mph (1600 km/h) was the Miles M-52. Development began in 1943, and by February 1946 the detail design was virtually completed. Construction was underway when the project was cancelled due to economic problems and the belief that it should have been designed with swept instead of very thin bi-convex wings. However, models of the M-52 flown during 1947–8 showed that the aircraft could have achieved its aim. Power for the M-52 was to have been provided by one Power Jets W2/700 turbojet engine, with augmentor and afterburner, developing up to 4100 lb (1860 kg) thrust.

The first American rocket-powered military aircraft was the Northrop MX-324, which was first flown under rocket power by Harry Crosby on 5 July 1944. It was powered by an Aerojet XCAL-200 motor, fuelled by monoethylaniline. It had originally flown as a glider in October 1943.

The world's first flying-wing jet fighter to fly was the Northrop XP-79B, which made its one and only test flight of 15 minutes' duration (before going out of control) on 12 September 1945. Powered by two 1150 lb (522 kg) thrust Westinghouse J30 turbojet engines, it was thought to be capable of 510 mph (821 km/h) and was intended to cut off the tails of enemy bombers using its welded magnesium wing. The pilot lay prone in the cockpit so as to withstand the impact.

The first British jet-powered aircraft to exceed a speed of Mach 1 was the de Havilland DH108, three examples of which were built to investigate the stability and control problems of swept wings, so providing information for the design of the de Havilland Comet I airliner. The first DH108 made its maiden flight on 15 May 1946, using a standard de Havilland Vampire fighter fuselage and powered by one 3750 lb (1700 kg) thrust Goblin 4 turbojet engine. This first aircraft was used to provide data on the slow-flying characteristics of the swept wings; the second and third were used for high-speed flying. The last aircraft recorded a speed between Mach 1.0 and 1.1 on 6 September 1948 while in a dive from 40 000 ft (12 200 m).

The first French aircraft to be designed specifically for stratospheric flight research was the Aérocentre Belphégor, which flew for the first time on 6 June 1946. Powered by a single Daimler-Benz DB 610 engine, developing 3000 hp, it had pressurized accommodation for five persons in its bulbous fuselage, including two research members; the pilot was situated in a cupola above the main cabin. With an all-up weight of 22 050 lb (10 000 kg), the Belphégor could fly to an altitude of 42 000 ft (12 800 m).

The first flying-boat in the world capable of a maximum level speed of over 500 mph (805 km/h) was the British Saunders-Roe SR A/1 jet fighter flying-boat which first flew on 16 July 1947. Powered by two Metrovick Beryl axial-flow turbojets, the SR A/1, which was also the world's first jet-powered flying-boat, had a top speed of 512 mph (824 km/h) and had an armament of four 20 mm guns. Three prototypes were built, but the project was abandoned when flight tests showed that the large flying-boat hull compromised both speed and manoeuvrability.

The first manned supersonic aeroplane in the world was the rocket-powered American Bell X-1. The second prototype made its first powered flight on 9 December 1946, piloted by Chalmers Goodlin, after being air-launched from a Boeing B-29 Superfortress. Flown by Capt Charles 'Chuck' Yeager, USAF, the X-1 was taken progressively nearer to 'the speed of sound' and finally, on 14 October 1947, escaped from the buffeting of near-sonic compressibility into the smooth airflow of supersonic flight. The speed recorded on that historic occasion was 700 mph

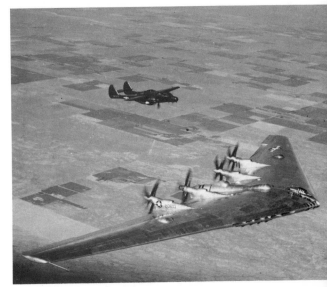

Above   Northrop XB-35 flying-wing bomber with P-61 Black Widow escort. (Northrop)

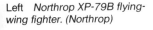

Left   Northrop XP-79B flying-wing fighter. (Northrop)

Right   The world's first jet flying-boat was the Saunders-Roe SR A/1.

(1126 km/h) at a height of 45 000 ft (13 715 m), the equivalent Mach* number being 1.06.

The first, and so far only, completely successful flying wing bombers were those of the Northrop B-35 and YB-49 series, with Pratt & Whitney Wasp-Major R-4360 piston engines and Allison J-35 turbojet engines respectively. The first of these to fly, the 172 ft (52.43 m)-span XB-35 prototype, took to the air on 25 June 1946. The first YB-49 jet bomber flew initially on 21 October 1947 and thirty B-49s were ordered for the USAF in 1948, later being cancelled.

The first piloted aircraft to be flown at twice the speed of sound was the Douglas Skyrocket, which flew for the first time on 4 February 1948. Designed to investigate sweptback wings, it was powered by one Reaction Motors XLR-8 rocket motor of 6000 lb (2720 kg) thrust and one Westinghouse J34 turbojet engine of 3000 lb (1360 kg) thrust. The wings were of conventional subsonic configuration with a 35° sweepback. Altogether three Skyrockets were built, and on 31

August 1953 one reached an altitude of 83 235 ft (25 370 m). However, the most memorable flight of a Skyrocket was made on 20 November of the same year when the aircraft attained a speed of Mach 2.005 after being launched from a Boeing 'motherplane' at 32 000 ft (9750 m).

The first jet-powered fighter to be designed specifically as a parasite aircraft was the McDonnell XF-85 Goblin, which made its first flight on 23 August 1948. Designed to be carried inside the forward bomb-bay of the Consolidated Vultee B-36 long-range bomber, the Goblin had an extremely short and stubby fuselage, with swept short-span wings and multiple tail surfaces. It was launched and picked up via a retractable 'skyhook' on the Goblin which hooked on to a retractable trapeze on the bomber. Following one abortive attempt to hook back on to the B-36, which nearly ended in disaster, the first successful hook-on was made on 14 October 1948. Although several more hook-ons were achieved, and the Goblin demonstrated a speed of 520 mph (837 km/h), the project was cancelled after only two Goblins had been built. One of them remains on view at the USAF Museum at Dayton, Ohio. The length of the Goblin was only 14 ft 10½ in (4.53 m); power was provided by a Westinghouse J34 engine of 3000 lb (1360 kg) thrust.

The Northrop X-4 Bantam was designed to investigate the subsonic flight characteristics of aircraft with swept wings but without a tailplane. Two X-4s were produced, the first flying on 15

*The use of the Mach scale for aircraft speeds was introduced by Prof Ackeret of Zürich, Switzerland. The Mach number is the ratio of the velocity of a moving body to the local velocity of sound. This ratio was first employed by Dr Ernst Mach (1838–1916) of Vienna, Austria, in 1887. Thus Mach 1.0 equals 760.98 mph (1224.67 km/h) at sea-level at 15°C, and is assumed, for convenience, to fall to a constant 659.78 mph (1061.81 km/h) in the stratosphere, i.e. above 36 089 ft (11 000 m).

McDonnell Goblin parasite fighter approaches the lowered trapeze on the Boeing B-29 Superfortress used for the experiments.

December 1948. The programme was completed successfully in April 1954, after some 60 flights had been made.

The first British delta-wing research aircraft was the Avro 707, which made its first flight on 4 September 1949. Designed to gain data on the flight characteristics of delta wings at low speeds, the Type 707 was basically a scale model of the then-projected Vulcan bomber. Following its destruction in an accident, the Type 707B was produced to continue low-speed research, first flying in September 1950. Two Type 707As then followed for research into high-speed flight; and the series was completed by a single Type 707C, a two-seat version built to give pilots training in flying delta-wing aircraft. The 707C first flew in mid-1953, powered by a Rolls-Royce Derwent engine of 3600 lb (1635 kg) thrust.

The first jet aircraft flown with variable-geometry wings was the Bell X-5, which flew for the first time on 20 June 1951. Design of the X-5 began in 1948, based on the seized German Messerschmitt P.1101 jet fighter that had been under construction as a prototype since July 1944 and was taken back to the USA in incompleted form. Two X-5s were built, the first crashing on 13 October 1953. The X-5 was powered by a single Allison J35-A-17 turbojet engine; its wing span varied from 30 ft 10 in (9.39 m) to 18 ft 7 in (5.66 m) in both unswept and swept positions respectively.

The first of three giant Saunders-Roe SR45 Princess flying-boats, and the only one to fly, made its maiden flight on 20 August 1952, piloted by Geoffrey Tyson. The largest British flying-boat ever built, though still dwarfed by the US Hughes H4 Hercules that flew once only (on 2 November 1947), it featured ten 3780 shp Bristol Proteus 600 turboprop engines. However, because of the growing capability of landplanes for long-range intercontinental services, the three Princess flying-boats were scrapped. Wing span was 219 ft 6 in (66.9 m), length 148 ft (45.11 m) and gross weight 330 000 lb (149 685 kg).

The Douglas X-3 was built to investigate the effectiveness of turbojet engines and short-span double-wedge wing and tail surfaces at very high altitudes, and to study thermodynamic heating at speeds up to Mach 2. Construction of the aircraft caused many problems, as it was built primarily of

From the Leduc 0.10 was developed the Leduc 0.21, seen above the Languedoc motherplane. First flown on 16 May 1953, it was completely successful and tested components for the proposed 0.22 interceptor.

Sud-Ouest SO 9000 Trident mixed-power research aircraft.

Convair Sea Dart using skis to gain hydrodynamic lift. (General Dynamics)

then little used titanium. To measure the pressure on the airframe during flight, a huge number of pin-hole orifices were positioned strategically over the airframe, and temperature and stress were also measured at many locations. Powered by two Westinghouse J34 turbojets, the X-3 made its unofficial maiden flight on 15 October 1952 and its official first flight on the 20th. Unfortunately, the X-3 proved barely capable of supersonic flight, managing Mach 1.21 in a dive during the manufacturer's tests but Mach 0.95 being the normal maximum level speed. The programme was terminated in May 1956, after 20 flights had been made by NASA.

Built as an experimental ramjet-powered aircraft, the French Leduc 0.10 made its first powered flight on 21 April 1949 after being released over Toulouse from a Languedoc motherplane. This carried the 0.10 above its fuselage on special mounting struts, providing the stream of air to flow into the engine which was necessary for the ramjet to work. On this occasion the 0.10 reached a speed of 422 mph (680 km/h) on 50 per cent power. Maximum speed achieved during a later flight was Mach 0.84. Three 0.10s were produced; each had a tubular double-skinned fuselage, the outer shell forming the annular ramjet duct and the inner shell accommodating the cockpit for the crew of two.

The first French supersonic aircraft and the first French rocket/turbojet mixed power research aircraft, designed to provide data for future interceptors of similar concept, was the Sud-Ouest SO 9000 Trident, which first flew on 2 March 1953. Power was provided initially by two wingtip-mounted Turboméca Marboré II turbojet engines. These were replaced later by Dassault Viper turbojet engines of nearly double the power, and an SEPR 481 rocket motor of 9920 lb (4500 kg) thrust was installed subsequently in the rear fuselage. Testing of the rocket power unit began in April 1955, and the Trident eventually attained a speed of 1055 mph (1700 km/h).

The Convair Sea Dart was an experimental seaplane fighter fitted with delta wings and hydroskis. It set several 'firsts', being **the first delta-winged seaplane** and **the first seaplane to exceed the speed of sound**. The original aircraft was designated XF2Y-1 and made its first flight on 9 April 1953. It was joined subsequently by the

development version, designated YF2Y-1, which exceeded Mach 1 on 3 August 1954 in a dive, shortly before being destroyed in an accident. Whereas the XF2Y-1 was powered by two Westinghouse J34 turbojet engines, each of 3400 lb (1542 kg) thrust, the later aircraft had two J46 engines of 6000 lb (2720 kg) thrust each, both with afterburning. The YF2Y-1 proved sufficiently promising for the US Navy to order three more similar aircraft, but the whole concept of a seaplane fighter was soon abandoned.

The first aircraft to test the practicability of the aero-isoclinic wing was the Short SB4 Sherpa, which made its maiden flight on 4 October 1953. The wing was designed as a partially flexible structure, with all-moving tips which were used as both ailerons and elevators. Flight testing showed that the handling characteristics of the aircraft were very satisfactory.

The two most unusual experimental VTOL fighters built in America were the Lockheed XFV-1 and Convair XFY-1 'tailsitters'. Designed to the same specification, both had a maximum speed of about 500 mph (805 km/h) and were powered by Allison YT-40A turboprops driving coaxial contra-rotating propellers. The Lockheed XFV-1 was the first to fly, in March 1954; it had straight wings and a cruciform tail unit onto which castoring wheels were fitted as the landing gear. The Convair XFY-1 made its maiden flight on 2 August 1954, and differed from its competitor mainly in having delta wings, with large delta tail surfaces above and below the fuselage forming a cruciform with the wings. Castoring wheels were positioned at the tips of these wings and tail surfaces, to form the vertical landing gear. The pilots of both aircraft sat on gimballed seats, enabling them to be in a near-upright position irrespective of whether the aircraft was in a horizontal or vertical attitude. The XFV-1 made only conventional take-offs; but many VTOL flights were made by the XFY-1 before the concept of a tail-sitting VTOL fighter was abandoned. The Convair XFY-1 made its first transition from vertical to horizontal flight, and vice versa, on 2 November 1954, making this **the first full transition by an aeroplane**.

Built to test the flight characteristics of swept wings at low speed, the Short SB5 produced data that was used in the design of the English Electric

P1 prototype and, subsequently, the production Lightning fighter. The wings on the SB5 were tested at four different angles of sweepback, ranging from 50° to 69°, with combinations of a high or low mounted tailplane with various angles of incidence. After making its maiden flight on 2 December 1952, the aircraft was still flying experimentally in the early 1960s.

The first French, and European, aircraft to exceed Mach 1 in level flight without the use of an afterburner or rocket power was the Nord Gerfaut 1A, a small delta-winged research aircraft intended to gather information on high-speed flight useful to future fighter design. It first flew on 3 August 1954. The improved Gerfaut II, of 1956 appearance, attained Mach 1.3 on the power of a 9700 lb (4400 kg) thrust SNECMA Atar 101G turbojet engine.

The first aircraft to set a world speed record of over 1000 mph (1600 km/h) was the Fairey Delta 2, the first example of which made its maiden flight on 6 October 1954. Built originally to investigate the problems encountered during transition from subsonic to supersonic speeds, each Delta 2 was powered by a Rolls-Royce Avon turbojet engine. The first aircraft had an Avon RA5 which gave 12 000 lb (5445 kg) thrust, the second an RA28 which developed 1000 lb (450 kg) more thrust. The record was set on 10 March 1956, off the Sussex coast between Ford and Chichester, Lt Cdr L. Peter Twiss flying the first aircraft (WG774) at an FAI accredited speed of 1131.76 mph (1821.39 km/h), the fastest of two runs made at 1147 mph (1846 km/h). Subsequently, this aircraft was converted into the BAC 221, with new delta wings and control surfaces, new landing gear, longer fuselage and a hydraulically actuated drooping nose. Data gained with it were used in the development of the Concorde SST airliner.

The first aircraft to carry an airborne nuclear reactor was the Convair NB-36H, a modified B-36H strategic bomber that first flew with the reactor operating in September 1955. In total, this aircraft completed 47 flights with the reactor in the aft bomb bay, intended not to power the engines but to test shielding in preparation for the

Above   *Fairey Delta 2, the first aircraft to fly at over 1,000 mph. (Shell)*
Below   *Convair NB-36H with a nuclear reactor on board.*

two actual X-6 aircraft (again modified B-36Hs) that would have General Electric P-1 nuclear turbojet engines fitted. In the event, the X-6s were never completed.

The first aircraft to fly at over Mach 3 in level flight was the Bell X-2, two examples of which were built for continued research at transonic and supersonic speeds. Built with a K-monel metal fuselage, and stainless steel swept wings and tail unit, the first X-2 was destroyed after an explosion in its B-50 motherplane which resulted in the research aircraft being jettisoned. The second X-2 made its maiden flight on 18 November 1955, but after several successful flights this too was destroyed, on 27 September 1956, at the end of a test in which it recorded Mach 3.2.

The Ryan X-13 Vertijet first flew on 10 December 1955 as a turbojet-powered vertical take-off and landing aircraft, although on this occasion it flew in conventional aeroplane mode. Vertical flights, with the aircraft resting on its tail and pointing upward, began on 28 May 1956. On 28 November 1956, an X-13 (two built) completed **the world's first transition by a pure jet aircraft from horizontal to vertical flight and vice versa**, and then on 11 April 1957 **the first full transition from vertical to horizontal flight and back again for a vertical descent** and hook-on landing to its special trailer.

Built to test a turbo-ramjet engine, which was designed to form the bulk of the aircraft's airframe, the French Nord 1500-02 Griffon II was a direct development of the earlier Griffon I, which had been powered by a conventional turbojet only. The Griffon had a turbojet mounted inside the ramjet, to propel it to the speed at which the ramjet could ignite and provide power. It flew for the first time on 23 January 1957, and exceeded Mach 1 on 17 May, with its ramjet power on. Over 200 flights were made by the aircraft, culminating in a flight during which Mach 2.19 was attained on 13 October 1959, at which speed the ramjet developed four-fifths of the aircraft's total thrust.

One of the first French research aircraft to give an effective STOL demonstration of the 'blown-wing' or 'deflected-slipstream' technique, the Breguet 940 Integral research aircraft, was flown for the first time on 21 May 1958. It led to production of the similar Breguet 941S, four of which served with the Armée de l'Air.

Short SC.1 making a transition from hovering to forward flight.

The first full transitions from vertical to horizontal flight, and vice versa, by a British jet aeroplane, and the world's first transitions with the aeroplane itself remaining in flat horizontal attitude, were made by the Short SC.1 VTOL research aircraft on 6 April 1960. The aircraft was powered by four Rolls-Royce RB.108 turbojet engines mounted to give vertical jet lift, and a fifth engine mounted horizontally to give forward flight.

The world's first fully successful experimental V/STOL fighter was the Hawker Siddeley P1127. The first of two prototypes made its initial tethered hovering flight on 21 October 1960. In September 1961 the first transition flights from vertical to horizontal were made, and in 1963 the type was tested on board HMS *Ark Royal*. Several other development and evaluation models were built, with the name Kestrel, leading subsequently to the production Harrier. Power for the Kestrel was provided by one Bristol Siddeley Pegasus 5 vectored-thrust turbofan engine of 15 200 lb (6895 kg) thrust.

The first human to enter space was the Soviet cosmonaut Flt Maj Yuriy Alexeyevich Gagarin (aged 27, born Friday 9 March 1934 near Gzatsk, died in a jet crash on Wednesday, 27 March 1968). Launched at 09.07 h, Moscow time, on 12 April 1961, from Baikonur, East Kazakhstan, in the 10 417 lb (4725 kg) *Vostok 1* spacecraft, Gagarin completed a single orbit of the Earth, landing safely in the USSR 1 h 48 min later.

Above *North American XB-70A Valkyrie Mach 3 research bomber.*

Left *Alan B. Shepard in the Mercury capsule just before his 5 May 1961 sub-orbital spaceflight. (NASA)*

The first full-throttle test flight of the North American X-15A was made on 21 April 1961, piloted by Maj Robert White, USAF, when a speed of 3074 mph (4947 km/h) was attained. (See also Fastest.)

The first American to enter space was Alan B. Shepard who, on 5 May 1961, was launched in a sub-orbital trajectory of 297 miles (478 km). In his 15 min 22 s journey in the *Mercury* capsule *Freedom 7*, Shepard had attained a height of 118 miles (190 km) and travelled at a speed of 5188 mph (8350 km/h). (The third man into space was also an American, Virgil Grissom, who travelled in sub-orbital flight on 21 July 1961.)

The first American astronaut to go into Earth orbit was Lt Col John H. Glenn who, on 20 February 1962, completed three orbits in *Mercury* capsule 6 *Friendship 7*. The flight lasted 4 h 55 min 23 s.

First pilot of a fixed-wing aircraft to gain 'astronaut's wings', for having attained an altitude of more than 50 miles (80 km) above the Earth's surface, was NASA test pilot Joe Walker. They were awarded after he had flown the North American X-15A to a height of 271 000 ft (82 600 m) on 17 January 1963.

The first woman to enter space was the Soviet cosmonaut Jr Lt Valentina Vladimirovna Tereshkova, aged 26, who, in *Vostok 6*, was placed in Earth orbit on 16 June 1963 and completed 48 orbits in 70 h 41 min.

The largest research aircraft ever built was the North American XB-70A Valkyrie, which was designed originally as a Mach 3 strategic bomber for the USAF, but modified subsequently into an aerodynamic test vehicle. Two Valkyries were built, the first flying on 21 September 1964. Each had large delta wings, with hydraulically drooping wingtips and 12 elevons and canard foreplanes. Power was provided by six General Electric YJ93 turbojet engines, each giving a thrust of 31 000 lb (14 050 kg) with afterburning. Mach 3 was achieved for the first time on 14 October 1965. One of the Valkyries was destroyed at a later date after colliding with its accompanying chase aircraft, and the programme was completed in 1969 after the surviving aircraft had made more than 70 flights.

The first multi-crew space mission was achieved by the Soviet Union, following the launch of the three-man *Voskhod 1* on 12 October 1964. Crewed by cosmonauts Vladimir Komarov, Konstantin Feoktistov and Boris Yegorov, the mission (without use of spacesuits) lasted 1 d 17 min and covered 16 Earth orbits.

The first ever EVA (Extravehicular Activity) or 'spacewalk' was accomplished by Soviet cosmonaut Alexei Leonov who, with Pavel Belyayev, crewed *Voskhod 2*. Launched on 18 March 1965, the flight lasted 1 d 2 h 2 min, during which Leonov spent 23 min 41 s in a spacesuit outside the craft but tethered to it by a 16 ft (5 m) line.

The **first American multi-crew mission and the first mission to perform manned orbital manoeuvres** was *Gemini 3*, a two-man spacecraft, with astronauts Virgil Grissom and John Young on board. The first mission to begin with a launch using a huge Titan II booster, it was made on 23 March 1965 and lasted 4 h 53 min.

The **first American 'spacewalk'** was performed by Edward White who, with James McDivitt, crewed *Gemini 4*. Launched on 3 June 1965, the mission lasted 4 d 1 h 56 min, during which White made a 21 minute 'spacewalk'.

The **first recognized manoeuvred rendezvous in space** was achieved by American spacecraft *Gemini 6* and *Gemini 7*, launched on 15 December and 4 December 1965 respectively. During the mission, which lasted 13 d 18 h 35 min for *Gemini 7*, *Gemini 6* was manoeuvred to within 6 ft (1.8 m) of *Gemini 7*. *Gemini 6* and 7 were crewed by Walter Schirra and Thomas Stafford and Frank Borman and James Lovell respectively.

The **first docking of spacecraft in space** was achieved by America's *Gemini 8* and an Agena docking target. Launched on 16 March 1966, *Gemini 8* was crewed by Neil Armstrong and David Scott. The docking, however, had to be terminated almost immediately as the spacecraft began spinning uncontrollably.

The **first unpowered flight of the Northrop/ NASA M2-F2 lifting-body re-entry research vehicle** was made on 12 July 1966, following launch at 45 000 ft (13 710 m) from a B-52 'motherplane'. Representing one of the stages in development of NASA's Space Shuttle, it had a fuselage structure D-shaped in cross-section with the straight side of the 'D' forming the upper surface. After five unpowered flights it was dismantled for examination and then rebuilt, as the M2-F3, with power provided by an 8000 lb (3629 kg) thrust Thiokol XLR-11 rocket engine. The M2-F3 made its first powered flight on 25 November 1970, achieving a speed of Mach 0.8 at 53 000 ft (16 150 m). When the programme terminated in December 1972, a total of 20 powered flights had been made.

The **world's first experimental space bomb** was launched on 25 January 1967 as Cosmos K-139 by the Soviet Union. A version of the SS-9 *Scarp* intercontinental ballistic missile, it became known as FOBS (Fractional Orbital Bombardment System). It is believed that this system did not become operational.

The **first spaceflight fatality** was Soviet cosmonaut Col Vladimir Mikhailovich Komarov. Launched on board *Soyuz 1* on 23 April 1967, he met his death after being in orbit for more than 25 h, when his craft impacted on the final descent due to parachute failure.

The **first variable-geometry ('swing-wing') aircraft of European design to fly** was the Dassault Mirage G strike fighter prototype, which made its maiden flight at Istres, France, on 18 November 1967. This aircraft was lost in an accident on 13 January 1971, by which time it had accumulated some 400 hours of flight testing, and had demonstrated a maximum speed in excess of Mach 2. (See also General Dynamics F-111 in Air Warfare and Military Aviation.)

The **first manned flight around the Moon** was performed by American spacecraft *Apollo 8*, launched on 21 December 1968 with astronauts Frank Borman, James Lovell and William Anders on board. Flying around the Moon on 24 December, they returned to Earth on the 27th. Mission time was 6 d 3 h 1 min.

The **first manned spacecraft to go into lunar orbit** was *Apollo 10*. Launched on 18 May 1969 with astronauts Thomas Stafford, Eugene Cernan and John Young on board, this was a Moon landing rehearsal, during which Stafford and Cernan made two descents to within 8.7 miles (14 km) of the Moon's surface in the Lunar Module. The mission lasted for 8 d 3 min.

The **first human to set foot on the Moon** was the American astronaut Neil A. Armstrong, aged 38 (born on Tuesday 5 August 1930 at Wapakoneta, Ohio). At 02.56 h 20 s GMT on Monday 21 July 1969 Armstrong stepped on to the Moon's surface from the lunar module *Eagle*, an event watched through television by 600 million viewers 232 000 miles away on Earth. Shortly afterwards his colleague Edwin E. A. Aldrin joined him on the Moon, while Michael Collins remained in Moon orbit in the command module *Columbia*. The entire flight to the Moon by *Apollo 11* had been a complete success, having begun on 16 July, and the safe return to Earth was terminated with splash-down at 16.49 h GMT on 24

July, 940 miles (1510 km) south-west of Honolulu in the Pacific Ocean.

In his Special State of the Union Message of 25 May 1961, eight years earlier, the late President John F. Kennedy had addressed to Congress a request for additional funds to accelerate space research:

"I believe this nation should commit itself to achieving the goal before this decade is out, of landing a man on the Moon and returning him to Earth. No single space project in this period will be more exciting, or more impressive, or more important for the long-range exploration of space; and none will be so difficult or expensive to accomplish. Including necessary supporting research, this objective will require an additional $531 000 000 this year and still higher sums in the future. We propose to accelerate development of the appropriate lunar space craft. We propose to develop liquid and solid boosters much larger than any now being developed. . . . We propose additional funds for other engine development and for unmanned explorations, which are particularly important for one purpose which this nation will never overlook—the survival of the man who first makes this daring flight. But in a very real sense, it will not be one man going to the Moon—it will be an entire nation. For all of us must work to put him there."

After the expenditure of $24 000 000 000 Neil Armstrong brought success to the President's proposal.

The first powered flight of the Martin Marietta SV-5P Pilot (X-24A) was made on 19 March 1970. A lifting-body research aircraft to expand and complement the work of the Northrop/NASA HL-10 and M2-F2, it was designed for use to prove that NASA's planned Space Shuttle would be able to re-enter the Earth's atmosphere, fly under control like any other fixed-wing aircraft, and land on a conventional runway for subsequent re-use. Powered by an 8000 lb (3629 kg) thrust Thiokol XLR11 rocket engine and two Bell rockets each of 500 lb (227 kg) thrust, it completed a successful 28-flight programme as the X-24A, before being rebuilt as the X-24B. First flown in this latter form on 1 August 1973, it made its final powered flight on 23 September 1975.

The first two-crew man-powered aircraft to

Edwin Aldrin stands by the deployed Solar Wind Composition during the first mission to the Moon. (NASA)

fly, on 23 December 1972 at Radlett, Herts, was the Hertfordshire Pedal Aeronauts Toucan. Its best flight, of 2100 ft (640 m), was made on 3 July 1973. It was superseded by the modified Toucan 2 which, with a wing span of 139 ft (42.37 m), was **the largest man-powered aircraft built**.

The first electrically powered manned aircraft to fly was the Austrian Militky MB-E1. Derived from the airframe of a Brditschka HB-3 sailplane, and powered by a Bosch electric motor driven by rechargeable batteries, it was flown for the first time at Linz on 21 October 1973.

The first large aircraft with an air cushion landing system (ACLS) was the de Havilland Canada XC-8A Buffalo, a specially modified STOL transport developed with joint Canadian and United States funding. The first ACLS take-off was made on 31 March 1975. It was used in a programme to evaluate an ACLS for operation from such diverse surfaces as ice, rough fields, sand, snow, swamps and water. Prior to the XC-8A, Bell had flown a modified small Lake LA-4 with such a landing system, from September 1967, but even this was not the first aircraft with an ACLS. Earlier experiments included those in the Soviet Union before 1941, using a UT-2 monoplane trainer and a Pe-2.

The first combined US and USSR space mission was the ASTP (Apollo-Soyuz Test Project), during which the crews of Soyuz 19 and the Apollo

ASTP docked in orbit for astronaut/cosmonaut exchanges and combined experiments. *Soyuz* was launched on 15 July 1975 with Alexei Leonov and Valeri Kubasov on board, and the same day America launched the *Apollo* with astronauts Thomas Stafford, Vance Brand and Donald Slayton. The mission ended on the 24th.

NASA's Space Shuttle carrier, a specially modified Boeing 747-123 operated formerly by American Airlines, flew for the first time following modification on 2 December 1976. Its first flight with the Space Shuttle Orbiter *Enterprise* carried 'piggy-back' above the fuselage was made on 18 February 1977. The first free flight, when the Space Shuttle was launched from the carrier at a height of 22 800 ft (6950 m) to glide in unpowered flight and make a successful landing at Edwards AFB, was achieved on 13 August 1977. The Space Shuttle carrier is **the first modern aircraft to be used for piggy-back transportation.**

The first 1-mile (1.6-km) figure-of-eight flight by a man-powered aircraft was achieved on 23 August 1977. This was accomplished in the *Gossamer Condor* aircraft, designed by a team in the United States under the leadership of Dr Paul MacCready. Spanning 96 ft 0 in (29.26 m) and having a gross weight of 207 lb (94 kg) including its pilot/power unit racing cyclist Bryan Allen, the 7 min 27.5 s flight between and around two pylons half a mile apart was made at Shafter, California, winning the £50 000 Kremer Prize.

Claimed to be the first flight by a solar-powered aircraft, the Solar One designed by Freddie To made its first brief hop in the UK on 19

December 1978. A flight covering a distance of almost three-quarters of a mile (1200 m) was made from Lasham Airfield, Hampshire, on 13 June 1979. In this aircraft batteries were used to store the electricity generated by 750 solar cells, and as a result purists have argued that this was an electric- rather than solar-powered aircraft.

The MacCready Gossamer Penguin, an interim solar-powered aircraft converted from a three-quarter scale version of the *Gossamer Albatross*, made its first purely solar-powered flight on 7 August 1980. Piloted by Janice Brown, weighing 99 lb (45 kg), a straight flight of about 2 miles (3 km) was recorded. The *Gossamer Penguin* had flown earlier under solar power, on 18 May 1980, when a short climbing flight was made following an assisted take-off.

A first short-duration pure solar-powered test flight was made by the MacCready *Solar Challenger* on 20 November 1980. On 7 July 1981, piloted by Steve Ptacek (USA), the *Solar Challenger* became the first aircraft of this category to achieve a crossing of the English Channel. Taking off from Cormeilles-en-Vexin, near Paris, the aircraft was flown a distance of 163 miles (262 km) to make a landing at Manston aerodrome, Kent, 5 h 23 min later. Power for the *Challenger* was provided by no fewer than 16 128 solar cells on the upper surfaces of the wings and tailplane, providing maximum power of 3 hp to the electric motor power unit.

The world's first reusable spacecraft was America's NASA Space Shuttle Orbiter *Columbia*, which was launched on its first mission (STS-1) on 12 April 1981. Crewed by John Young and Robert Crippen, *Columbia* took off under the power of its own engines and those of two jettisonable boosters and made 37 orbits before landing 2 d 6 h 21 min later as an unpowered aircraft on the dry bed of Rogers Lake, Edwards Air Force Base, California, on the 14th.

Largest:

The largest flying-boat in the world, the largest aeroplane ever flown, and the aircraft with the greatest wing span ever built was the Hughes H4 Hercules. The 180 ton (183 tonne) flying-boat was powered by eight 3000 hp Pratt & Whitney R-4360 piston engines, had a wing span of 320 ft (97.54 m), and an overall length of

Solar One, claimed to be the first solar-powered aircraft to fly.

219 ft (66.75 m). Big enough to accommodate up to 700 passengers, it was intended primarily as a freighter and no cabin windows were provided. Piloted by its sponsor, the American millionaire Howard Hughes, it flew on only one occasion, covering a distance of about a mile, at a height of approximately 80 ft (24 m) over Los Angeles Harbor, California, on 2 November 1947. No production followed.

The largest landplane ever built in Britain was the Bristol Brabazon I, which had a wing span of 230 ft (70.10 m), length of 177 ft (53.95 m) and maximum take-off weight of 290 000 lb (131 542 kg). It was first flown as a prototype (G-AGPW) on 4 September 1949. No production followed.

North American X-15 powers away from its B-52 motherplane.

Fastest:

The fastest aeroplane ever flown is the rocket-powered North American X-15A-2 research aircraft. Three X-15s were built during the late 1950s and the first free flight was made on 8 June 1959. Just over three months later, on 17 September, the second craft made the first powered flight. Because the 60 000 lb (26 215 kg) thrust Thiokol XLR99-RM-2 rocket engine was not ready, two XLR11-RM-5 engines powered X-15 No. 2. Despite the fact that these gave a combined thrust of only 33 000 lb (15 000 kg), a speed of Mach 2.3 was recorded. By December 1963, then powered by the XLR99, speed had climbed to Mach 6.06, and a surface skin temperature of 1320°F (715.6°C) had confirmed yet another problem associated with very high-speed flight. Following a landing accident to No. 2, it was rebuilt and various modifications introduced, becoming the X-15A-2. The highest altitude the X-15 attained was 354 200 ft (67.08 miles) on a flight by J. A. Walker on 22 August 1963, and the highest speed was 4534 mph (Mach 6.72) by W. J. Knight on 3 October 1967. A list of the progressive speeds achieved by these aircraft is given at the end of the book.

First aircraft to fly faster than Mach 1. See Firsts, Bell X-1; 14 October 1947.

First aircraft to fly faster than Mach 2. See Firsts, Douglas Skyrocket; 20 November 1953.

First aircraft to fly faster than Mach 3. See Firsts, Bell X-2; 18 November 1955.

Longest:

The world distance in a straight line record for human-powered flight was set on 12 June 1979 in the man-powered *Gossamer Albatross*, designed by Dr Paul MacCready. Piloted and pedalled by Bryan Allen, the *Albatross* took off from Folkestone, Kent, at 05.51 h and landed 22.26 miles (35.82 km) distant at Cap Gris Nez, France, at 08.40 h. The duration was 2 h 49 min, and this achievement won the £100 000 Kremer Prize for **the first man-powered crossing of the English Channel**. This flight also established **the current world duration record for human-powered aircraft**, at 2 h 49 min.

The current women's world distance in a straight line record for human-powered aircraft stands at 4.255 miles (6.83 km), set by American Lois McCallin in the Massachusetts Institute of Technology (MIT) *Michelob Light Eagle* on 21 January 1987.

The current women's world distance in a closed circuit record for human-powered flight stands at 9.59 miles (15.44 km), set by American Lois McCallin in the MIT *Michelob Light Eagle* on 21 January 1987.

The current women's world duration record for human-powered aircraft stands at 37 min 38 s, set by American Lois McCallin in the MIT *Michelob Light Eagle* on 21 January 1987.

The current world distance in a closed circuit record for human-powered aircraft stands at 36.452 miles (58.664 km), set on 22 January 1987 by American pilot Glenn Tremml in the MIT *Michelob Light Eagle*.

Valour and Achievement

Valour is described by the Oxford English Dictionary as 'the quality of mind which enables a person to face danger with boldness or firmness' and achievement as something which is 'finished, carried out successfully, or brought to an end'. They are clearly closely related, bound together by the words of John Milton: 'And courage never to submit or yield: And what is else not to be overcome?'

It is easy to assume that the award of a decoration for gallantry is as the result of a valorous action in battle. But sometimes the mind questions which is the greatest or most meritorious aspect of valour. Is it one of sacrifice in the heat of battle, when death seems inevitable, and if that is the case there is nothing left to lose? Or is it one of cold courage, that takes a man again and again in combat with a ruthless enemy?

The pages which follow provide many instances of the bravery of men and women of all nations in both war and peace. Inevitably courage abounds in plenty during times of conflict, but it is also an essential ingredient of so many tasks that are faced frequently by those engaged in the world of aviation, whether it be a military, civil or competitive aspect. Courage is needed not only by the military pilot and his crew, but is equally essential for those who have the responsibility of carrying passengers by airline in all weathers. Though the performance of new aircraft is now far more predictable than in the past, test pilots still face many hazards as routine. And for those who set out to establish new records, whether for speed, altitude or distance, great courage is almost invariably an essential ingredient for achievement. Imagine, if you can, the new great distance record established by Dick Rutan and Jeana Yeager, namely the non-stop and unrefuelled round-the-world flight of the aircraft Voyager during 14–23 December 1986. For 9 days, 3 minutes and 44 seconds this remarkable aircraft was airborne on its non-stop flight, the two pilots confined in a cockpit 5 ft 7 in (1.70 m) in length and just 1 ft 9.5 in (0.55 m) in width, a 'rest' cabin 7 ft 6 in (2.29 m) long and only 2 ft (0.61 m) wide and with little real chance of both surviving a serious emergency.

Happily, humans are still capable of great courage and achievements and it is good to know that the world of aviation still has more than its fair share of such people. The following section of this book records just some of their entries on the pages of aviation history.

The first hero of spaceflight, Major Yuriy Gagarin. (Soviet Weekly)

The first men to reach the moon, Neil Armstrong, Michael Collins and Edwin Aldrin. (NASA)

Svetlana Savitskaya, who holds the current record for extra-vehicular duration in space, set on 25 July 1984 at 3 hours 33 min 4 secs while at Salyut-7 (Novosti)

Firsts:

The first serving officer of the British Army to be awarded a Pilot's Certificate in England was Capt George William Patrick Dawes who was awarded Certificate No. 17 for qualification on a Humber monoplane at Wolverhampton on 26 July 1910.

Dawes died on 17 March 1960 aged 80. He had served in South Africa between 1900 and 1902 when he was awarded the Queen's Medal with three clasps, and the King's Medal with two clasps. He took up flying privately in 1909 and was posted to the RFC on its formation in 1912. He commanded the Corps in the Balkans from 1916 to 1918 as Acting General but used his permanent rank of Lt Col, during which time he was awarded the DSO and the AFC, was mentioned in despatches seven times, and awarded the Croix de Guerre with three palms, the Serbian Order of the White Eagle, the Order of the Redeemer of Greece and created Officer of the Légion d'honneur. He served with the Royal Air Force in the Second World War as a Wing Commander, retiring in 1946 with the MBE. He thus was one of the very few officers who served actively in the Boer War and both world wars. Dawes is also credited with having made the first flight in the Indian sub-continent.

The first gallantry decoration to be 'earned' by a marine aviator was the Distinguished Flying Cross awarded posthumously to Eugene B. Ely, who was killed while flying on 14 October 1911. The award of the DFC was made 25 years later in recognition of his outstanding contributions to marine aviation during 1910 and 1911. His sole reward during his life was an award of $500 made by the US Aeronautical Reserve during 1911.

The first true fighter leader of the First World War was Hauptmann Oswald Boelcke. He became interested in aviation during army manoeuvres, and gained his Pilot's Certificate at the Halberstadt Flying School on 15 August 1914. He was posted to La Ferte to join Feldfliegerabteilung Nr 13 in September and, with his brother Wilhelm as observer, soon amassed a considerable number of sorties in Army Co-operation Albatros B II biplanes. By early 1915 he had 42 missions in his log-book, and had been awarded the Iron Cross, Second Class. The visit of Leutnant Parschau to his unit to demonstrate the Fokker M8 monoplane scout fired him with enthusiasm; and in April, having received the Iron Cross, First Class, he secured a posting to Hauptmann Kastner's Feldfliegerabteilung Nr 62, where he flew an armed machine for the first time—an Albatros C I, number 162/15. Before long, he was selected to fly early examples of Fokker's E-series armed monoplane scouts; few were available, and Boelcke, Kastner and Leutnant Max Immelmann at first took turns to fly them. After a tour of other fronts in early 1916, Boelcke returned to the West and was given command of the new Jagdstaffel Nr 2 (Jasta 2) which was equipped with Albatros D I and D II scouts. Boelcke was killed on 28 October 1916 during an engagement in which one of his colleagues, Leutnant Boehme, who was flying close to him, banked sharply. Boehme's undercarriage struck the wing of his Albatros, which spiralled to the ground. He was 25 years old, a holder of the Ordre Pour le Mérite and numerous other decorations, the victor of 40 aerial combats, and the idol of his country.

The first air Victoria Cross was awarded posthumously to Lt W. B. Rhodes Moorhouse, pilot of a BE2c of No. 2 Squadron, RFC, for gallantry in a low-level bombing attack on Courtrai railway station on 26 April 1915.

One of Germany's first two great fighter aces was Leutnant Max Immelmann, 'The Eagle of Lille'. He was serving with Feldfliegerabteilung No. 62 at Douai when the first Fokker monoplane scouts became available. Hauptmann Kastner instructed Boelcke in the subtleties of the new machine, and Boelcke taught Immelmann. On 1 August 1915 Immelmann was responsible for the first victory by a Fokker E.I fighter with synchronized machine-gun, but he met his death on 18 June 1916 when an FE2b of No. 25 Squadron, RFC, shot him down near Lens. Immelmann had, by then, gained 15 'air victories'.

Max Immelmann, 'The Eagle of Lille'.

Albert Ball in a Royal Aircraft Factory SE5, his final mount. (Imperial War Museum)

The first great British ace, Capt Albert Ball, joined No. 13 Squadron, RFC, in France on 15 February 1916, his first operational squadron. His first mount was a BE2c used on artillery-spotting flights. In May he was posted to No. 11 Squadron, equipped with Nieuport scouts. His first two air victories came on 22 May, when he drove down an Albatros D I and forced an LVG two-seater to land. Only the latter was confirmed. His last squadron was No. 56, which flew the new SE5 fighter and the Nieuport Ball loved to fly. As Flt Cdr, Ball gained his 47th and last victory on 6 May 1917. The following evening he dived an SE5 into dense cloud while chasing a German two-seater near Lens and was never seen alive again. His wrecked aircraft and his body were found by the Germans. His Victoria Cross was gazetted on 3 June 1917.

The first British gallantry decorations to be gazetted in the Second World War, on 10 September 1939, were two Distinguished Flying Crosses awarded to Flying Officer A. McPherson and Flt Lt K. C. Doran. McPherson, from the RAF's No. 139 Squadron, had been captain of the first British aircraft to cross the German frontier, on 3 September 1939; and Doran, from No. 110 Squadron, had led a formation of five aircraft which were the first British aircraft to drop bombs on enemy targets during the Second World War.

One of the first members of the Royal Air Force to be awarded the George Cross was Aircraftsman Vivian ('Bob') Holloway who, in July 1940, at Cranfield, Bedfordshire, entered a crashed and blazing bomber and extricated the pilot, and in so doing suffered severe burns to his hands. One month later, at the moment of returning from hospital, he again dashed into a blazing aircraft three times amongst exploding ammunition, and brought out three crew members. He survived his near-fatal burns despite having been on the danger list for 27 days.

The first Victoria Cross to be won during the Battle of Britain was awarded posthumously to Acting Seaman J. F. (Jack) Mantle, RN, who was operating an anti-aircraft gun aboard HMS *Foyle Bank* in Portland Harbour, Dorset, on 4 July 1940. The ship, the only one in port with an anti-aircraft gun, became the focus of an enemy raid and was hit by a bomb which cut the power supply. Jack Mantle, though severely wounded, continued to fire the gun, operating it manually; despite another direct hit upon the ship, which severed his left leg, he remained at his post until the end of the raid but succumbed to his terrible wounds almost immediately afterwards. His Victoria Cross was only the second to be awarded for an action in or over Great Britain, the first having been awarded to Lt W. Leefe Robinson of No. 39 Home Defence Squadron, RFC, for his destruction of a Schütte-Lanz airship on the night of 2–3 September 1916 at Cuffley, Hertfordshire.

The first Victoria Cross awarded to a pilot of RAF Bomber Command was that won by Flt Lt R. A. B. Learoyd. The award was made for gallantry when, on the night of 12–13 August 1940, Flt Lt Learoyd was flying Hampden P4403, as one of a force of five from Nos 49 and 83 Squadrons which dropped delayed action bombs on an aqueduct of the Dortmund–Ems Canal.

The first jet fighter pilot to achieve five confirmed aerial victories over jet aircraft was Capt James Jabara, an F-86 Sabre pilot of the 4th Fighter Interceptor Wing, USAF, who shot down his fifth MiG-15 on 20 May 1951. Capt Jabara later went on to destroy a total of 15 MiG-15s, thereby becoming the second most successful Allied pilot of the Korean War.

The first US Navy pilot to achieve five air victories over Korea was Lt Guy Bordelon who, flying a piston-engined Vought F4U Corsair, shot down his fifth victim on 17 July 1953.

The first US aces of the Vietnam war were the two-man team of Lt Randy Cunningham and his RIO (Radio Intercept Officer) Lt (Jg) William Driscoll of the US Navy's Squadron VF-96 flying off the USS *Constellation*. In a dramatic action on 10 May 1972 they destroyed their third, fourth and fifth North Vietnamese MiG fighters to achieve their ace status, an action which terminated in Cunningham and Driscoll ejecting from their battle-damaged F-4J Phantom II over the Gulf of Tonkin and their rescue by a US Marine Corps Boeing Vertol HH-46A Sea Knight.

The US Air Force's first aces of the Vietnam War were Capt Richard S. Richie and Lt Charles DeBellevue (RIO) of the 555th Tactical Fighter Squadron, who recorded their fifth 'kill' on 28 August 1972 while flying a combat patrol in their McDonnell Douglas F-4C Phantom II.

Highest:

The highest-scoring Allied pilot during the Battle of Britain was Sergeant Josef Frantisek, a Czech pilot who served with No. 303 (Polish) Squadron, RAF. His confirmed score of 17 enemy aircraft shot down was achieved entirely during September 1940; he was killed on 9 October 1940. The only British gallantry decoration awarded to Frantisek was the Distinguished Flying Medal, but he had been awarded previously the Czech War Cross and the Polish Virtuti Militari.

Greatest:

The greatest 'balloon buster' of the First World War in terms of numbers was French Sous-Lieutenant Michel Coiffard, whose 34 air 'victories' included the destruction of 28 observation balloons.

The second greatest 'balloon buster' of the First World War in terms of numbers was the Belgian ace of aces Willy Coppens, who included 26 balloons within his total of 37 war victories.

The German pilot responsible for the destruction of the greatest number of enemy balloons during the First World War was Leutnant Heinrich Gontermann, who destroyed 18, including three confirmed in one day.

The British and Empire pilot credited with the destruction of the greatest number of balloons during the First World War was Capt Andrew Wetherby Beauchamp-Proctor, a South African pilot serving with the RFC/RAF. His war total of 54 air victories included 16 balloons. Beauchamp-Proctor was the fifth highest-ranking British and Empire pilot of the war and he received the Victoria Cross.

The greatest Allied ace of the First World War was Capitaine René Paul Fonck, who served with Escadrille SPA103, one of the units of the famous Groupe de Combat No. 12 'Les Cigognes'. Officially Fonck is credited with 75 victories; his own personal estimate, including aircraft destroyed but not confirmed by Allied ground observers, was 127. His first victory came on 6 August 1916, when he forced down a Rumpler while flying a Caudron G IV reconnaissance and bombing biplane. His second victory, gained on 17 March 1917, was against one of five attacking Albatros

fighters. This second confirmed victory led to his transfer to the 'Cigognes' group a month later. On 9 May 1918 he achieved no fewer than six confirmed 'kills'—including three two-seaters destroyed in 45 s, the three wrecks being found in a radius of 1200 ft (365 m). On 26 September he again shot down six aircraft, comprising a two-seater, four Fokker D VIIs, and an Albatros D V. Fonck's last victory was over a leaflet-dropping two-seater on 1 November 1918. Fonck died peacefully in his sleep at his Paris home on 18 June 1953.

The greatest ace of the First World War, in terms of confirmed aerial victories, was Rittmeister (Cavalry Captain) Manfred, Freiherr von Richthofen—the so-called 'Red Baron'. The eldest son of an aristocratic Silesian family, he was born on 2 May 1892 and was killed in action on 21 April 1918, by which time he had been credited with 80 victories, had been awarded his country's highest decoration, commanded the élite unit of the Imperial German Air Service (Luftstreitkräfte), and was the object of great adulation in his homeland and an ungrudging respect among his enemies. Early in the war, Richthofen served on the Eastern Front as an officer in Uhlan Regiment Nr 1 'Kaiser Alexander III, and transferred to the Air Service in May 1915. His first operational posting was to Feldfliegerabteilung Nr 69; with this unit he flew two-seater reconnaissance machines in the East—without apparently any unusual skill. In September 1916 he was selected for Jagdstaffel 2, the scout squadron led by Oswald Boelcke (q.v.). His first officially recognized victory was over an FE2b of No. 11 Squadron, RFC; Richthofen, flying an Albatros D II scout, shot down this aircraft on 17 September 1916; the crew, 2nd Lt L. B. F. Morris and Lt T. Rees, lost their lives. Richthofen continued to score steadily, and in January 1917 was awarded the coveted 'Blue Max', the Ordre pour le Mérite. He was given command of Jagdstaffel 11, and characteristically maintained a collection of silver cups, each engraved with the particulars of a victim. The silversmith's most lucrative month was 'Bloody April' of 1917, when Richthofen shot down 21 aircraft. In June 1917 he was given command of a new formation, Jagdgeschwader Nr 1, comprising Jastas 4, 6, 10 and 11; this group of squadrons became known to the Allies as 'Richthofen's Flying Circus', because of the bright colours of their aircraft. Contrary to popular legend Richthofen did not invariably fly a personal all-red aircraft but a variety of Albatros D IIIs and Fokker Dr Is, some of which were painted blood-red all over and some only partially red. Richthofen's death on 21 April 1918 has been the subject of controversy ever since. He was flying Fokker Dr I number 425/17 when he became engaged in combat with Sopwith Camels of No. 209 Squadron, RAF, over Sailly-le-Sec. At one point, 2nd Lt W. R. May was flying at low altitude with Richthofen in pursuit and the aircraft of Capt A. Roy Brown, DSC, diving to attack the German. Brown opened fire in an attempt to save the inexperienced May from the enemy ace, and Richthofen's triplane was then seen to break away and crash-land. Richthofen was found dead in his cockpit with a bullet wound in the chest. At about the same time as Brown attacked, machine-gunners of an Australian Field Artillery battery fired at Richthofen's aircraft. Although Brown was officially credited with the 'kill', it has never been established who fired the fatal shot.

The greatest American 'balloon buster' of the First World War and arguably the greatest of all 'balloon busters' was 2nd Lt Frank Luke, a fighter pilot of the 27th Aero (Pursuit) Squadron who gained all his 15 balloon and 6 aeroplane 'victories' in a space of just 16 days. Born in 1897, Luke enlisted in the US Signal Corps (Aviation Section) in September 1917 and was commissioned in January 1918. He was sent to France in March 1918, where, after completing advanced flying and aerial gunnery training, he initially ferried aircraft. However, he was posted to the 27th Aero (Pursuit) Squadron in late July. On 16 August he broke formation against orders and scored his first aerial victory. This was only the first of many brushes with authority. Luke formed a close friendship with Lt Wehner and together they became balloon busters of great skill. The first balloon to fall to Luke's guns was destroyed on 12 September, near Marrieulle. Between this date and his death while on an unauthorized balloon busting mission, on 28 September, Luke shot down a further 14 balloons. With aeroplanes destroyed, his total of air victories was 21, making him America's second ranking ace of the war. He was awarded a posthumous Congressional Medal of Honor.

During the Second World War the greatest

altitude from which anyone jumped without a parachute and survived was 22 000 ft (6705 m). In January 1942 Lt I. M. Chisov of the USSR fell from an Ilyushin Il-4 which had been badly damaged. He struck the ground a glancing blow on the edge of a snow-covered ravine and slid to the bottom, sustaining a fractured pelvis and severe spinal damage. It is estimated that the human body reaches 99 per cent of its low-level terminal velocity after falling 1880 ft (573 m); this is 117–125 mph (188–201 km/h) at normal atmospheric pressure in a random posture, but up to 185 mph (298 km/h) in a head-down position. **The British record** stands at 18 000 ft (5490 m) set by Flt Sgt Nicholas Stephen Alkemade, RAF, who jumped from a blazing Lancaster bomber over Germany on 23 March 1944. His headlong fall was broken by a fir tree, and he landed without a broken bone in an 18 in (46 cm) snow-bank.

The greatest number of enemy aircraft destroyed by a US Navy pilot in the course of a single sortie was achieved on 24 October 1944, when Cdr David McCampbell, accompanied by one other aircraft, attacked a formation of 60 land-based Japanese aircraft approaching the US Fleet. Cdr McCampbell destroyed nine enemy aircraft and for this action, the destruction of seven enemy aircraft on 19 June 1944 and his inspired leadership of Air Group 15, he was awarded the Congressional Medal of Honor.

The greatest decoration for gallantry to be given to a member of the Royal Canadian Navy during the Second World War was the Victoria Cross awarded posthumously to Lt Robert Hampton Gray of the RCN Volunteer Reserve. Attached to the Fleet Air Arm, and as the pilot of a Vought Corsair fighter-bomber, he was killed on 9 August 1945 while making an attack on a Japanese destroyer in the bay of Onagawa Wan. This occurred after the two atomic bomb attacks on Japan and only a few days before the Japanese surrender; Gray was thus the recipient of the last Victoria Cross to be won during the Second World War, and his was also the only one of the war awarded to a member of the RCN.

The greatest number of combat victories in the Korean War was achieved by Capt Joseph McConnell of the USAF's 39th Fighter Interceptor Squadron. On 18 May 1953 he destroyed three

North Korean Mikoyan MiG-15s, bringing his total score to 16 confirmed victories.

The greatest altitude from which anyone has fallen without a parachute and survived is 33 330 ft (10 160 m). This occurred on 26 January 1972 when a Douglas DC-9 airliner of Jugoslovenski Aerotransport exploded and was destroyed over the Czechoslovak village of Serbska Kamenice. Air hostess Vesna Vulovic survived the fall, suffering a 27 day coma and many broken bones which enforced a 16 month stay in hospital.

Georges Marie Ludovic Jules Guynemer at Verdun in 1916.

Most:

France's second most successful pilot of the First World War was Capitaine Georges Marie Ludovic Jules Guynemer, who served in the 'Cigognes' group with Escadrille MS3/N3/SPA3 and achieved the first of his 54 confirmed victories on 19 July 1915 while in a Morane-Saulnier Parasol. He failed to return from a flight over Poelcapelle (Belgium) on 11 September 1917 and he has no known grave. However, although it is often asserted that no trace of his body or aircraft has ever been found, the records of the 413th Württemberg Regiment, which held that section of the German line on the date in question, show that both were indeed found and identified and that various papers on Guynemer at the time were removed. There is some question as to the identity of the pilot who shot down Guynemer, although usually Leutnant Kurt Wisseman, Jagdstaffel 3, is credited. Wisseman himself was shot down and killed on 28 September 1917.

Britain's most successful fighter pilot in the First World War was Major Edward 'Mick' Mannock. His score of combat victories stands at 73, but he is known to have insisted that several additional victories justly attributable to him should be credited to other pilots. Born on 24 May 1887, the son of a soldier, Mannock was working in Constantinople when the war broke out, and was interned by the Turks. He was repatriated in April 1915 on health grounds and rejoined the Territorial Army medical unit to which he had belonged before leaving the country. He was commissioned in the Royal Engineers on 1 April 1916 and finally transferred to the Royal Flying Corps in August 1916. His acceptance for flying duties was remarkable as he suffered from astigmatism in the

left eye, and must have passed his medical by a ruse. He gained his Pilot's Certificate on 28 November 1916, and was posted to No. 40 Squadron, France, on 6 April 1917, the unit being equipped at that time with Nieuport scouts. He shot down a balloon on 7 May, and on 7 June scored his first victory over an aeroplane. Returning from leave in July he shot down two-seaters on the 12th and 13th of that month, and his Military Cross was gazetted. He was promoted Captain, and took command of a flight. His score grew rapidly, as he was possessed by a bitter and ruthless hatred of the enemy, uncommon among his contemporaries. His care of the pilots under his command, however, was irreproachable, and he has been judged the greatest patrol leader of any combatant air force. In January 1918 he returned to England to take enforced leave, by which time his score stood at 23. He returned to France in March as a Flt Cdr in the newly formed No. 74 ('Tiger') Squadron, equipped with the SE5a, and in his three months with the unit added 39 to his score. He was promoted Major in mid-June, and was given leave before taking command of No. 85 Squadron. With No. 85 he raised his score to 73 before being shot down on 26 July by German ground fire that hit his petrol tank. His grave has never been found and it was nearly a year later that he was awarded a posthumous Victoria Cross.

The second most successful British and Empire pilot of the war was a Canadian, William Avery Bishop, born on 8 February 1894 in Ontario. While in England as a cavalry subaltern in the Canadian Mounted Rifles in 1915, Bishop decided he would see more action as a pilot, and transferred to the Royal Flying Corps in July of that year. He flew in France as an observer with

No. 21 Squadron for several months, and was hospitalized as the result of a crash-landing and frostbite. He trained subsequently as a pilot and joined No. 60 Squadron in March 1917. The squadron was at that time equipped with Nieuport 17 scouts, an aircraft which Bishop was to handle brilliantly. On 25 March he scored his first victory over an Albatros and subsequently gained many honours including the Victoria Cross for his action over an enemy airfield on 2 June. When his score reached 45, Bishop was promoted Major and awarded a Bar to his DSO. Late in 1917 and early in 1918 he carried out a number of non-combat duties, including recruiting drives in Canada and instructing at an aerial gunnery school. He was subsequently given command of No.85 Squadron, flying SE5as, and went back to France on 22 May 1918. After gaining 27 more victories, he was recalled to England, and never flew operationally again. His DFC was gazetted on 2 July. Bishop remained in the service, rising to the rank of Honorary Air Marshal in the Royal Canadian Air Force. He died in Florida, USA, in September 1956.

The most successful fighter pilot of the Royal Naval Air Service during the First World War, and, with 60 confirmed victories, third in the overall British and Empire aces' list, was Raymond Collishaw. A member of No. 3 Wing, RNAS, he gained his first air victory on 12 October 1916. In February 1917 he joined a scout unit, No. 3 (Naval) Squadron, and in April was posted to No. 10 (Naval) Squadron as commander of 'B' Flight. Equipped with Sopwith Triplanes, the 'Black Flight' of 'Naval Ten' earned a reputation as one of the most formidable Allied units of the war. The Flight was composed entirely of Canadians; their aircraft were decorated with black paint, and named *Black Maria* (Collishaw), *Black Prince*, *Black Sheep*, *Black Roger* and *Black Death*. Between May and July 1917 the Flight destroyed 87 enemy aircraft, and during June Collishaw himself shot down 16 in 27 days. After the Armistice, Collishaw commanded No. 47 Squadron in the Russian campaign of 1919–20, where he destroyed two more aircraft. He remained in the Royal Air Force, serving in the Second World War and reaching the rank of Air Vice-Marshal, CB, with the DSO and Bar, DSC, DFC and Croix de Guerre, as well as both military and civil grades of the OBE.

The most successful American pilot of the First World War was Capt Edward Vernon Rickenbacker, with 26 confirmed aerial victories. Born on 8 October 1890 in Columbus, Ohio, Rickenbacker made a considerable name for himself between 1910 and 1917 as one of America's leading racing motorists. While in England in 1917, he became interested in flying and when America entered the war he returned home and advanced the idea of a squadron composed entirely of racing drivers. The idea did not arouse official interest, but a meeting with Gen Pershing in Washington led to Rickenbacker's enlistment and sent him to France as the General's chauffeur. In August 1917 he transferred to the Aviation Section, and his mechanical expertise led to a posting to the 3rd Aviation Instruction Center at Issoudun as Chief Engineering Officer. In his own time he completed advanced flying and gunnery courses, and on 4 March 1918 finally secured a transfer to the 94th Aero Squadron—the 'Hat-in-the-Ring' squadron commanded by Raoul Lufbery, the Escadrille Lafayette ace. With Lufbery and Douglas Campbell, Rickenbacker flew **the first American patrol over enemy lines** on 19 March, and on 29 April he shot down his first victim, an Albatros scout. On 30 May his fifth victory qualified him as an ace, but it was to be his last for four months. An ear infection put him in hospital and convalescence until mid-September, when he returned to the squadron as a Captain and Flight Commander. He took over command of the 94th on 25 September, and continued to score heavily until the Armistice. Capt Rickenbacker was active in the automobile and airline industries between the wars, and was largely responsible for building up Eastern Air Lines, of which corporation he became Chairman in 1953. During the Second World War he toured widely, visiting Air Force units abroad and undertaking various missions for his Government. In the course of a flight over the Pacific his aircraft was forced to ditch, and Rickenbacker survived 21 days on a life-raft before being picked up. He remained active in various public fields until his death on 23 July 1973, at the age of 82. His many American and foreign decorations included his country's highest award for gallantry, the Congressional Medal of Honor.

Following a most courageous action on 16 August 1940, Flt Lt James Brindley Nicholson, RAF, became the recipient of the only Victoria

Cross awarded to a member of RAF Fighter Command. A flight commander of No. 249 (Hurricane) Squadron, Nicholson was leading a section of three fighters on patrol near Southampton, Hampshire, when he sighted enemy aircraft ahead. Before he could complete the attack his section was 'bounced' from above and behind by German fighters which shot down one Hurricane and set Nicholson's aircraft ablaze. With flames sweeping up through his cockpit, the British pilot remained at his controls long enough to complete an attack on an enemy aircraft which had flown into his sights, and then baled out. Meanwhile, a detachment of soldiers on the ground, seeing Nicholson and his wingman descending on parachutes and believing them to be enemy paratroops, opened fire with rifles. Nicholson was hit but survived his wounds and burns; but his colleague was dead when he reached the ground (whether or not he was killed by rifle-fire has never been established).

One of the most gallant torpedo attacks made by aircraft during the Second World War, and also the last torpedo attack launched by the Fairey Swordfish, was on 12 February 1942, when six unescorted aircraft of No. 825 Squadron, led by Lt Cdr Eugene Esmonde, FAA, attempted to torpedo the German battleships *Gneisenau* and *Scharnhorst* and the heavy cruiser *Prinz Eugen*. This was in an attempt to prevent these warships from escaping through the English Channel, but without fighter escort the Swordfish faced a hopeless task, and all six were shot down by the protective umbrella of German fighter aircraft. Only five of the 18 crew members survived: all were decorated and a posthumous Victoria Cross was awarded to Lt Cdr Esmonde, the first to be won by a member of the Fleet Air Arm.

Almost certainly the most unusual response to a valorous action was that given to Lt Michael Devyatayev, a Soviet fighter pilot shot down by the Luftwaffe over Lvov on 13 July 1944, who is the only known pilot who has been both gaoled and awarded his country's highest gallantry decoration for the same exploit. Taken prisoner by the Germans, Devyatayev escaped, seized a Heinkel He 111 bomber and flew nine other escapees back to Soviet-held territory. On regaining his freedom, the 23-year-old pilot was gaoled under the USSR criminal code which labelled him a traitor for having been taken prisoner. Nine years later, in 1953,

he was freed under an amnesty prevailing at the time, and in 1958 was made Hero of the Soviet Union and awarded the Order of Lenin and Gold Star Medal.

The most successful fighter pilot in the world, and Germany's leading ace in the Second World War, was Maj Erich Hartmann of Jagdschwader 52. The first of only two fighter pilots in the world to score 300 victories, the achievement brought him into a select band of men—numbering 27 only—who wore the Diamonds to the Knight's Cross, the award being made on 25 July 1944. Hartmann eventually surrendered to American forces in Czechoslovakia during May 1945, by which time he had scored a total of 352 victories.

The most successful German fighter pilot in combat against the Western Allies during the Second World War was Hauptmann Hans-Joachim Marseille. In April 1941 he was posted to I Gruppe Jagdgeschwader 27 in Libya, and it was in desert warfare that he became a master. On 2 September 1942 he received the Diamonds to his Knight's Cross. Known as the 'Star of Africa', he died on 30 September 1942 when he baled out of his Messerschmitt Bf 109G but his parachute failed to open. Then only 22 years old, he had been credited with 158 victories, all of them gained in combat against the RAF and Commonwealth air forces.

The most successful English fighter pilot of the Second World War was Gp Capt James Edgar 'Johnnie' Johnson, credited with 38 confirmed aerial victories over German aircraft. Johnson remained in the RAF after the war, retiring finally with the rank of Air Vice-Marshal in 1966.

The most successful American fighter pilot of the Second World War was Maj Richard Ira Bong, whose 40 confirmed aerial victories are unsurpassed by any American military pilot of any war. Born at Superior, Wisconsin, on 24 September 1920, Bong enlisted as a Flying Cadet on 29 May 1941. After flying training at Tulare and Gardner Fields, California, and Luke Field, Arizona, he received his 'wings' and a commission (all American military pilots were automatically commissioned) on 9 January 1942. In May he was posted to Hamilton Field, California, for combat training on the Lockheed P-38 Lightning twin-engined fighter, and subsequently joined the 9th

Maj Richard Ira Bong. (US Air Force)

Fighter Squadron of the 49th Fighter Group, then based in Australia. All of his 40 victories had been scored by late 1944, in the Pacific theatre of war. General George C. Kenney, his commanding officer, ordered him back to the United States in December 1944, with a recommendation for the Congressional Medal of Honor—which award was subsequently granted. Bong became a test pilot for Lockheed at Burbank, California; on 6 August 1945, the day the world's first atomic bomb was dropped on Hiroshima, he died when the engine of his P-80 jet failed. Many of his victories were gained while flying the P-38J *Marge* named after his fiancée.

The most successful Soviet woman fighter pilot of the Second World War,* and thus presumably the most successful woman fighter pilot in the world, served with the mixed-sex 73rd Guards Fighter Regiment. She was Jr Lt Lydia

*During the Second World War, most Russian women combat pilots served with the 122nd Air Group of the Soviet Air Force. This all-female unit comprised the 586th Fighter Air Regiment, the 587th Bomber Air Regiment and the 588th Night Bomber Air Regiment. The 586th IAP (Istebitelnyi aviatsionnyi polk=fighter air regiment) was formed at Engels, on the Volga River, in October 1941; it was commanded by Maj Tamara Aleksandrovna Kazarinova. The pilots of this unit flew a total of 4419 operational sorties, took part in 125 air combats, and were credited with 38 confirmed victories. The unit flew Yak-1, -7B and -9 fighters. During the Second World War, 30 Russian airwoman received the gold star of a Hero of the Soviet Union. It is believed that 22 of them served with the 588th/46th Guards Night Bomber Air Regiment, which was equipped with Po-2 biplanes.

Lityvak, who was killed in action on 1 August 1943 at the age of 22, with a total of 12 confirmed victories while flying Yak fighters.

During the Korean War one of the most courageous and self-sacrificing actions was that of Maj George A. Davis Jr of the USAF. On 10 February 1952 Davis was flying a North American F-86 Sabre, in company with a wingman, when he spotted a formation of 12 Mikoyan MiG-15s preparing to 'jump' a force of USAF fighter-bombers at lower level. Without hesitation he attacked the enemy formation, destroying two of their number before being hit and crashing to his death. This courageous action proved sufficient to prevent the MiGs from attacking the fighter-bombers, which completed their mission successfully, and the self-sacrifice of Davis was recognized by the posthumous award of the Medal of Honor.

The most successful US Marine Corps pilot of the Korean War was Maj John Bolt who on 11 July 1953, while flying a North American F-86 Sabre of the USAF's 39th Fighter Interceptor Squadron, destroyed two MiG-15s to bring his total score to six. He thus became the Marine Corps' only ace of the Korean War. The US Navy's only ace of this war was Lt Guy P. Bordelon who gained his 'ace' status by the destruction of his fifth enemy aircraft, a Yakovlev Yak-18, on 27 July 1953.

The Great Air Fighters of the First World War

The six most successful British and Empire pilots of the First World War
* Bar to award

Maj Edward Mannock, VC, DSO**, MC ..	73
Maj W. A. Bishop, VC, DSO*, MC, DFC, LD'H, CDEG	72
Maj R. Collishaw, DSO*, DSC, DFC, CDEG..........................	60
Maj J. T. B. McCudden, VC, DSO*, MC*, MM, CDEG.....................	57
Capt A. W. Beauchamp-Proctor, VC, DSO, MC*, DFC	54
Capt D. R. MacLaren, DSO, MC*, DFC, LD'H, CDEG	54

In addition to the above
  8 pilots gained between 40 and 52 victories
 11 pilots gained between 30 and 39 victories
 57 pilots gained between 20 and 29 victories
226 pilots gained between 10 and 19 victories

With his head in bandages, Rittmeister Manfred Freiherr von Richthofen is honoured by the Kaiser.

476 pilots gained between 5 and 9 victories
Thus by the 'five victory' convention, the British and Empire air forces of the First World War produced 784 aces.

The six most successful German pilots of the First World War

Rittmeister Manfred, Freiherr von
   Richthofen 80
Oberleutnant Ernst Udet................ 62
Oberleutnant Erich Loewenhardt 53
Leutnant Werner Voss 48
Leutnant Fritz Rumey 45
Hauptmann Rudolph Berthold 44
All of these pilots were decorated with the Ordre Pour le Mérite.

In addition to the above
  6 pilots gained between 40 and 43 victories
 21 pilots gained between 30 and 39 victories
 38 pilots gained between 20 and 29 victories
 96 pilots gained between 10 and 19 victories
196 pilots gained between 5 and 9 victories
Thus by the 'five victory' convention, the Imperial German air force of the First World War produced 363 aces.

The four most successful French pilots of the First World War

Capitaine René P. Fonck 75
Capitaine Georges M. L. J. Guynemer 54
Lieutenant Charles E. J. M. Nungesser 45
Capitaine Georges F. Madon 41

In addition to the above
  2 pilots gained between 30 and 39 victories
  8 pilots gained between 20 and 29 victories
 39 pilots gained between 10 and 19 victories
105 pilots gained between 5 and 9 victories
Thus the French air forces of the First World War produced 158 aces.

The four most successful American pilots of the First World War

Capt Edward V. Rickenbacker, CMH, DSC,
  L D'H, C D E G 26
2nd Lt Frank Luke Jr, CMH, DSC, C D E G   21
Maj G. Raoul Lufbery, L D'H, MM, C D E G,
  MC 17
Lt G. A. Vaughn Jr, DSC, DFC 13

In addition to the above
84 pilots gained between 5 and 12 victories; thus America produced 88 aces during the First World War. (It should be noted that the above figures include pilots who served with foreign air forces only, pilots who served with the American forces only, and pilots with mixed service, and all victories gained by these pilots irrespective of service.)

The four most successful Italian pilots of the First World War

Maggiore Francesco Baracca 34
Tenente Silvio Scaroni 26
Tenente-Colonnello Pier Ruggiero Piccio.. 24
Tenente Flavio Torello Baracchini 21

In addition to the above
39 pilots gained between 5 and 20 victories; thus Italy produced 43 aces during World War I.

The four most successful Austro–Hungarian pilots of the First world War

Hauptmann Godwin Brumowski 35–40
Offizierstellvertreter Julius Arigi 26–32
Oberleutnant Frank Linke-Crawford .. 27–30
Oberleutnant Benno Fiala, Ritter von
  Fernbrugg 27–29

(It should be noted that Austrian, Hungarian and Italian sources disagree as to the absolute accuracy of these pilots' scores.)

In addition to the above
Approximately 26 pilots gained between 5 and 19 victories. Thus it can be stated with reasonable certainty that the Austro–Hungarian Imperial air forces produced between 25 and 30 aces during the First World War.

The four most successful Imperial Russian pilots of the First World War

Staff Capt A. A. Kazakov, DSO, MC, DFC, LD'H.	17
Capt P. V. d'Argueeff	15
Lt Cdr A. P. Seversky	13
Lt I. W. Smirnoff	12

In addition to the above
Either 14 or 15 pilots gained between 5 and 11 victories; thus the Imperial Russian air forces produced either 18 or 19 known aces during the First World War. Other Russian pilots became aces, but the records are incomplete.

The four most successful Belgian pilots of the First World War

2nd Lt Willy Coppens, DSO	37
Adj André de Meulemeester	11
2nd Lt Edmond Thieffry	10
Capt Fernand Jacquet, DFC	7

Confirmation of aerial victories during the First World War was subject to the most stringent regulations, and this has led to confusion over the actual number of victories achieved by various pilots. The figures quoted earlier are, with certain exceptions, those accepted officially as accurate in the countries of origin, and refer only to confirmed victories within the letter of the regulations. They are thus more liable to err on the side of under rather than overstatement.

The numbers of aircraft shot down by fighter pilots of the Second World War

varied much more widely than was the case in the First World War, due to the enormous differences in conditions and standards of equipment in the various combat areas. Comparison of the lists of national top-scoring fighter pilots reveals the almost incredible superiority of German pilots in terms of confirmed victories—i.e. Major Erich Hartmann, the Luftwaffe's leading ace, is credited with nearly nine times as many victories as the leading British and American pilots, and 35 Germans are credited with scores in excess of 150.

Since the end of the war there have been persistent attempts to discredit these scores; but by any reasonable criterion, the figures must now be accepted as accurate. The Luftwaffe's confirmation procedure was just as rigorous as that followed by Allied air forces, and the quoted figures are those prepared at unit level and were not subject to manipulation by the Propaganda Ministry. The main reasons for the gulf between German and Allied scores were the different conditions of service and the special circumstances which existed on the Russian Front in 1941 and 1942. In Allied air forces an operational tour by a fighter pilot was almost invariably followed by a posting to a second-line establishment for several months. This process of rotating pilots to areas where they could recover from the strain of prolonged combat operations was unknown in the Luftwaffe; apart from very short periods of leave, a German fighter pilot was effectively on combat operations from the day of his first posting until the day his career ended—in death, serious injury or capture. The Luftwaffe fighter pilot's career was thus, in real terms, about twice as long as his RAF or USAAF counterpart.

When Germany invaded the Soviet Union in June 1941, the Russian Air Forces were equipped with very large numbers of obsolescent aircraft. They had no fighter whose speed and armament approached the performance of the Messerschmitt Bf 109E and BF 109F, and their bombers in squadron service were markedly inferior to contemporary European designs. Thus, the Luftwaffe was presented with large numbers of easy targets—the perfect environment for the development of a fighter pilot's skill and confidence. The situation did not become significantly more challenging for many months, by which time many of the Jagdflieger had learned their trade so well that they retained the initiative. Despite this factor, one is left with the inescapable conclusion that Germany produced a group of officers who were fighter pilots of exceptional skill and determination.

The pilots who scored **100 or more victories against the Western Allies** in northern Europe, southern Europe, the Mediterranean area and North Africa were as follows (Western victories only, in cases of mixed service):

Hauptmann Hans-Joachim Marseille	158
Oberstleutnant Heinz Bär	124
Oberstleutnant Kurt Bühligen	112
Generalleutnant Adolf Galland	104

Major Joachim Müncheberg	102
Oberstleutnant Egon Mayer	102
Major Werner Schroer	102
Oberst Josef Priller.	101

These figures become even more impressive if one reflects on the fact that Marseille achieved 151 of his victories between April 1941 and September 1942; and that Galland did virtually no combat flying between November 1941 and the end of 1944, while he occupied the post of General of Fighters.

Two categories of victories in northern Europe are worthy of special attention; those scored over heavy bombers, and those scored while flying jet aircraft. The achievements of the world's first generation of jet combat pilots are described elsewhere in this chapter. The Luftwaffe placed great value on the destruction of the very heavily armed four-engined Boeing Fortress and Consolidated Liberator bombers which formed the United States 8th Air Force's main equipment in the massive daylight bombing offensive of 1943-5. Usually flying in dense formations protected by an enormous combined firepower—and, in the later months, by superb escort fighters—these large aircraft were obviously far more difficult to destroy than smaller ones. The leading 'heavy bomber specialists' among Germany's daylight home defence pilots included:

Oberleutnant Herbert Rollwage	44
Oberst Walther Dahl	36
Major Werner Schroer	26
Hauptmann Hugo Frey	26
Oberstleutnant Egon Mayer	25
Oberstleutnant Kurt Bühligen	24
Oberstleutnant Heinz Bär	21
Hauptmann Hans-Heinrich König	20
Hauptmann Heinz Knoke	19

The Great Air Fighters of the Second World War

The most successful fighter pilots of the Second World War, by nationality, are listed below: all scores are levelled down to the nearest unit: British Gallantry decorations are quoted:

(*Bar to award.)	*Aircraft*
Country of origin	*destroyed in*
	combat
Australia	Gp Capt Clive R. Caldwell,
	DSO, DFC* 28

Austria	Maj Walter Nowotny	258
Belgium	Flt Lt Vicki Ortmans, DFC. . .	11
Canada	Sqn Ldr George F. Buerling, DSO, DFC, DFM*	31
Czecho-slovakia	Sgt Josef Frantisek, DFM	28
Denmark	Gp Capt Kaj Birksted . . .	either 8 or 10
Finland	F/Mstr E. I. Juutualainen	94
France	Sqn Ldr Pierre H. Clostermann, DFC*	19
Germany	Maj Erich Hartmann	352
Hungary	2nd Lt Dezjö Szentgyörgyi . . .	43
Ireland	Wg Cdr Brendan E. Finucane, DSO, DFC**	32
Italy	Maj Adriano Vinconti	26
Japan	Sub-Officer Hiroyoshi Nishizawa	103
Netherlands	Lt Col van Arkel. . . . 12 V-1s and 5
New Zealand	Wg Cdr Colin F. Gray, DSO, DFC**	27
Norway	Flt Lt Svein Heglund . . . . either 14 or 16
Poland	Jan Poniatowski (rank unknown)	36
Romania	Capt Prince Constantine Cantacuzino.	60
South Africa	Sqn Ldr M. T. St J. Pattle, DFC*	41
United Kingdom	Gp Capt James E. Johnson, DSO**, DFC*	38
United States	Maj Richard I. Bong	40
USSR	Guards Col Ivan N. Kozhedub	62

Fighter pilots serving with the Royal Air force during the Second World War who achieved 25 or more confirmed aerial victories (*countries of origin indicated in parentheses*):

Sqn Ldr M. T. St J. Pattle, DFC*	41	(SA)
Gp Capt J. E. Johnson, DSO**, DFC*	38	(UK)
Gp Capt A. G. Malan, DSO*, DFC* . .	35	(SA)
Wg Cdr B. E. Finucane, DSO, DFC** .	32	(Ir)
Sqn Ldr G. F. Buerling, DSO, DFC, DFM*	31	(Ca)
Wg Cdr J. R. D. Braham, DSO** DFC**, AFC.	29	(UK)
Wg Cdr R. R. S. Tuck, DSO, DFC** . .	29	(UK)
Sqn Ldr N. F. Duke, DSO, DFC**, AFC	28	(UK)
Gp Capt C. R. Caldwell, DSO, DFC* .	28	(Au)

Gp Capt F. H. R. Carey, DFC**, AFC,
    DFM .... 28 (UK)
Sqn Ldr J. H. Lacey, DFM* .... 28 (UK)
Wg Cdr C. F. Gray, DSO, DFC** .... 27 (NZ)
Flt Lt E. S. Lock, DSO, DFC* .... 26 (UK)
Wg Cdr L. C. Wade, DSO, DFC** ... 25 (US)

Fighter pilots serving with the United States air forces during the Second World War who achieved 25 or more confirmed aerial victories:
USAAF:
Maj Richard I. Bong (CMH) 40
Maj T. B. McGuire (CMH) 38

Col F. S. Gabreski 31
Lt Col R. S. Johnson 28
Col C. H. MacDonald 27
Maj G. E. Preddy 26
USN:
Capt D. McCampbell 34
USMC:
Maj J. J. Foss 26
Lt R. M. Hanson 25
Lt Col G. Boyington 22
(Lt Col Boyington is known to have destroyed an additional six enemy aircraft while serving with the Air Volunteer Group under Chinese command.)

Luftwaffe fighter pilots with 150 or more confirmed victories during the Second World War and the Spanish Civil War

✠❦✖◆ =Knight's Cross with Oak Leaves, Swords and Diamonds
✠❦✖ =Knight's Cross with Oak Leaves and Swords
✠❦ =Knight's Cross with Oak Leaves
✠ =Knight's Cross of the Iron Cross

Name, rank, decorations	Units	Total score	Day/ Night	Fronts	Four engined	With jet a/c
Major Erich Hartmann ✠❦✖◆	JG 52	**352**	352/0	352 E	0	0
Major Gerhard Barkhorn ✠❦✖	JG 52, 6, JV 44	**302**	301/1	301 E	0	?
Major Günther Rall ✠❦✖	JG 52, 11, 300	**275**	275/0	3 W, 272 E	?	0
Oberleutnant Otto Kittel ✠❦✖	JG 54	***267**	267/0	267 E	0	0
Major Walter Nowotny ✠❦✖◆	JG 54, Kdo. Nowotny	**258**	258/0	255 E, 3 W	*1	3
Major Wilhelm Batz ✠❦✖	JG 52	**237**	237/0	232 E, 5 W	2	0
Major Erich Rudorffer ✠❦✖	JG 2, 54, 7	**222**	222/0	136 E, 60 W, 26 Afr	10	12
Oberstleutnant Heinz Bär ✠❦✖	JG 51, 77, 1, 3, JV 44	**220**	220/0	96 E, 79 W, 45 Afr	*21	16
Oberst Hermann Graf ✠❦✖◆	JG 51, 52, 50, 11, 52	**212**	212/0	202 E, 10 W	10	0
Major Theodor Weissenberger ✠❦	JG 77, 5, 7	**208**	208/0	175 E, 33 W	?	8
Oberstleutnant Hans Philipp ✠❦✖	JG 76, 54, 1	**206**	206/0	177 E, 29 W	1	0
Oberleutnant Walter Schuck ✠❦	JG 5, 7	**206**	206/0	198 E, 8 W	4	8
Major Heinrich Ehrler ✠❦	JG 5, 7	***204**	204/0	204 E?	?	?
Oberleutnant Anton Hafner ✠❦	JG 51	**204**	204/0	184 E, 20 Afr	5	0
Hauptmann Helmut Lipfert ✠❦	JG 52, 53	**203**	203/0	majority E, *4 W	2	0
Major Walter Krupinski ✠❦	JG 52, 5, 11, 26, JV 44	**197**	197/0	177 E, 20 W	1	?
Major Anton Hackl ✠❦✖	JG 77, 11, 26, 300, 11	**192**	192/0	105 E, 87 W	32	0
Hauptmann Joachim Brendel ✠❦	JG 51	**189**	189/0	189 E	0	0
Hauptmann Max Stotz ✠❦	JG 54	**189**	189/0	173 E, 16 W	0	0
Hauptmann Joachim Kirschner ✠❦	JG 3, 27	**188**	188/0	167 E, 13 Gr, 6 W, 2 Malta	*2	0
Major Kurt Brändle ✠❦	JG 53, 3	**180**	180/0	160 E, 20 W	0	0
Oberleutnant Günther Josten ✠❦	JG 51	**178**	178/0	majority E	1	0
Oberst Johannes Steinhoff ✠❦✖	JG 26, 52, 77, 7, JV 44	**176**	176/0	148 E, 28 W & Afr	4	6
Oberleutnant Ernst-Wilhelm Reinert ✠❦✖	JG 77, 27	**174**	174/0	103 E, 51 Afr, 20 W	2	0
Hauptmann Günther Schack ✠❦	JG 51, 3	**174**	174/0	174 E	0	0
Hauptmann Emil Lang ✠❦	JG 54, 26	**173**	173/0	148 E, 25 W	?	0
Hauptmann Heinz Schmidt ✠❦	JG 52	**173**	173/0	173 E	0	0
Major Horst Ademeit ✠❦	JG 54	**166**	166/0	165 E, 1 W	0	0
Oberst Wolf-Dietrich Wilcke ✠❦✖	JG 53, 3	**162**	162/0	137 E, 21 W, 4 Malta	4	0
Hauptmann Hans-Joachim Marseille ✠✖❦◆	JG 52, 27	**158**	158/0	151 Afr, 7 W	0	0
Hauptmann Heinrich Sturm ✠	JG 52	**157**	157/0	157 E	0	0
Oberleutnant Gerhard Thyben ✠❦	JG 3, 54	**157**	157/0	152 E, 5 W	?	0
Oberleutnant Hans Beisswenger ✠❦	JG 54	**152**	152/0	152 E	0	0
Leutnant Peter Düttmann ✠	JG 52	**150**	150/0	150 E	0	0
Oberst Gordon Gollob ✠❦✖◆	ZG 76, JG 3, 77	**150**	150/0	144 E, 6 W	0	0

Progressive world absolute speed records achieved by man in the atmosphere

Speed		Pilot	Nationality	Aircraft	Location of achievement	Date
mph	km/h					
34.03	54.77	Paul Tissandier	France	Wright biplane	Pau, France	20 May 1909
43.34	69.75	Glenn Curtiss	USA	Herring-Curtiss biplane	Reims, France	23 Aug 1909
46.17	74.30	Louis Blériot	France	Blériot monoplane	Reims, France	24 Aug 1909
47.84	76.99	Louis Blériot	France	Blériot monoplane	Reims, France	28 Aug 1909
48.20	77.57	Hubert Latham	France	Antoinette monoplane	Nice, France	23 Apr 1910
66.18	106.50	Léon Morane	France	Blériot monoplane	Reims, France	10 Jul 1910
68.18	109.73	Alfred Léblanc	France	Blériot monoplane	Belmont Park, Long Island, USA	29 Oct 1910
69.46	111.79	Alfred Léblanc	France	Blériot monoplane		12 Apr 1911
74.40	119.74	Édouard Nieuport	France	Nieuport biplane		11 May 1911
77.67	124.99	Alfred Léblanc	France	Blériot monoplane		12 Jun 1911
80.80	130.04	Édouard Nieuport	France	Nieuport biplane	Châlons, France	16 Jun 1911
82.71	133.11	Édouard Nieuport	France	Nieuport biplane	Châlons, France	21 Jun 1911
90.18	145.13	Jules Védrines	France	Deperdussin monoplane	Pau, France	13 Jan 1912
100.21	161.27	Jules Védrines	France	Deperdussin monoplane	Pau, France	22 Feb 1912
100.99	162.53	Jules Védrines	France	Deperdussin monoplane	Pau, France	29 Feb 1912
103.64	166.79	Jules Védrines	France	Deperdussin monoplane	Pau, France	1 Mar 1912
104.32	167.88	Jules Védrines	France	Deperdussin monoplane	Pau, France	2 Mar 1912
106.10	170.75	Jules Védrines	France	Deperdussin monoplane		13 Jul 1912
108.16	174.06	Jules Védrines	France	Deperdussin monoplane	Chicago, Illinois, USA	9 Sep 1912
111.72	179.79	Maurice Prévost	France	Deperdussin monoplane		17 Jun 1913
119.22	191.87	Maurice Prévost	France	Deperdussin monoplane	Reims, France	27 Sep 1913
126.666	203.85	Maurice Prévost	France	Deperdussin monoplane	Reims, France	29 Sep 1913

The final entry above was the last world absolute speed record to be ratified by the FAI until 1920, more than a year after the end of the First World War.

Louis Blériot. (Air Force)

Progressive world absolute speed records achieved by man in the atmosphere

mph	km/h	Pilot	Nationality	Aircraft	Location of achievement	Date
171.01	275.22	Sadi Lecointe	France	Nieuport-Delage 29	Villacoublay, France	7 Feb 1920
176.12	283.43	Jean Casale	France	Blériot monoplane	Villacoublay, France	28 Feb 1920
181.83	292.63	Baron de Romanet	France	Spad biplane	Buc, France	9 Oct 1920
184.51	296.94	Sadi Lecointe	France	Nieuport-Delage 29	Buc, France	10 Oct 1920
187.95	302.48	Sadi Lecointe	France	Nieuport-Delage 29	Villacoublay, France	20 Oct 1920
191.98	308.96	Baron de Romanet	France	Spad biplane	Buc, France	4 Nov 1920
194.49	313.00	Sadi Lecointe	France	Nieuport-Delage 29	Villacoublay, France	12 Dec 1920
205.20	330.23	Sadi Lecointe	France	Nieuport-Delage 29	Villesauvage, France	20 Sep 1922
211.89	341.00	Sadi Lecointe	France	Nieuport-Delage 29	Villesauvage, France	21 Sep 1922
222.93	358.77	Brig Gen W. A. Mitchell	USA	Curtiss HS D-12	Detroit, Michigan, USA	13 Oct 1922
233.00	374.95	Sadi Lecointe	France	Nieuport-Delage 29	Istres, France	15 Feb 1923
236.54	380.67	Lt R. L. Maughan	USA	Curtiss R-6	Wright Field, Ohio, USA	29 Mar 1923
255.40	411.04	Lt A. Brown	USA	Curtiss HS D-12	Mitchell Field, NY, USA	2 Nov 1923
267.16	429.96	Lt Alford J. Williams	USA	Curtiss R-2 C-1	Mitchell Field, NY, USA	4 Nov 1923
278.47	448.15	Adj Chef A. Bonnet	France	Ferbois V-2	Istres, France	11 Dec 1924
297.83	479.21	Maj Mario de Bernardi	Italy	Macchi M-52	Venice, Italy	4 Nov 1927
318.57	512.69	Maj Mario de Bernardi	Italy	Macchi M-52bis	Venice, Italy	30 Mar 1928
406.94	654.90	Flt Lt G. H. Stainforth AFC	GB	Supermarine S6B	Ryde, IoW, England	29 Sep 1931
423.76	681.97	Warrant Officer F. Agello	Italy	Macchi-Castoldi 72	Lago di Garda, Italy	10 Apr 1934
440.60	709.07	Lt F. Agello	Italy	Macchi-Castoldi 72	Lago di Garda, Italy	23 Oct 1934
463.82	746.45	Flugkapitän Hans Dieterle	Germany	Heinkel He 100V-8	Oranienburg, Germany	30 Mar 1939
469.22	755.138	Flugkapitän Fritz Wendel	Germany	Messerschmitt Bf 109R	Augsburg, Germany	26 Apr 1939

The final entry above was the last world absolute speed record to be ratified by the FAI until November 1945, more than six years later.

mph	km/h	Pilot	Nationality	Aircraft	Location of achievement	Date
606.25	975.67	Gp Capt H. J. Wilson, AFC	GB	Gloster Meteor F4	Herne Bay, Kent, England	7 Nov 1945
615.65	990.79	Gp Capt E. M. Donaldson, DSO, AFC	GB	Gloster Meteor F4	Rustington, Sussex, England	7 Sep 1946
623.61	1003.60	Col Albert Boyd	USA	Lockheed P-80R Shooting Star	Muroc, California, USA	19 Jun 1947
640.60	1030.95	Cdr T. F. Caldwell, USN	USA	Douglas D-558 Skystreak	Muroc, California, USA	20 Aug 1947
650.78	1047.33	Maj M. E. Carl, USMC	USA	Douglas D-558 Skystreak	Muroc, California, USA	25 Aug 1947
670.84	1079.61	Maj R. L. Johnson USAF	USA	North American F-86A Sabre	Muroc, California, USA	15 Sep 1948
698.35	1123.89	Capt J. Slade Nash, USAF	USA	North American F-86D Sabre	Salton Sea, California, USA	19 Nov 1952
715.60	1151.64	Lt Col W. F. Barnes, USAF	USA	North American F-86D Sabre	Salton Sea, California, USA	16 Jul 1953

mph	km/h	Pilot	Nationality	Aircraft	Location	Date
727.48	1170.76	Sqn Ldr Neville Duke, DSO, OBE, DFC, AFC	GB	Hawker Hunter 3	Littlehampton, Sussex, England	7 Sep 1953
735.54	1183.74	Lt Cdr M. Lithgow, OBE	GB	Supermarine Swift 4	Libya	25 Sep 1953
752.78	1211.48	Lt Cdr J. B. Verdin, USN	USA	Douglas F4D-1 Skyray	Salton Sea, California, USA	3 Oct 1953
754.99	1215.04	Lt Col F. K. Everest, USAF	USA	North American YF-100A Super Sabre	Salton Sea, California, USA	29 Oct 1953
822.09	1323.03	Col H. A. Hanes, USAF	USA	North American F-100C Super Sabre	Edwards Air Force Base, California, USA	20 Aug 1955
1131.76	1821.39	Lt P. Twiss, OBE, DSC	GB	Fairey Delta 2	Chichester, Sussex, England	10 Mar 1956
1207.34	1943.03	Maj Adrian Drew, USAF	USA	McDonnell F-101A Voodoo	Edwards Air Force Base, California, USA	12 Dec 1957
1403.79	2259.18	Capt W. W. Irvin, USAF	USA	Lockheed F-104A Starfighter	Edwards Air Force Base, California, USA	16 May 1958
1483.51	2387.48	Col G. Mosolov	USSR	Mikoyan Type E-66	Sidorovo, Tyumenskaya, USSR	31 Oct 1959
1525.93	2455.74	Maj J. W. Rogers, USAF	USA	Convair F-106A Delta Dart	Edwards Air Force Base, California, USA	15 Dec 1959
1606.51	2585.43	Lt Col R. B. Robinson	USA	McDonnell F4H-1F Phantom II	Edwards Air Force Base, California, USA	22 Nov 1961
1665.89	2681.00	Col G. Mosolov	USSR	Mikoyan Type E-166	Sidorovo, Tyumenskaya, USSR	7 Jul 1962
2070.10	3331.51	Col R. L. Stephens	USA	Lockheed YF-12A	Edwards Air Force Base	1 May 1965
2193.17	3529.56	Capt E. W. Joersz / Maj G. T. Morgan Jr	USA	Lockheed SR-71A	Edwards Air Force Base	28 Jul 1976

Progressive (selected) maximum speeds achieved by the American X-15 rocket-powered research aircraft

The record speed achieved by Captain Joersz and Major Morgan on 28 July 1976 represents the highest ratified speed record attained by an aeroplane which took off under its own power from the earth's surface. Between 1960 and 1967, however, the US Air Force conducted a substantial programme of manned flight trials with the North American X-15 and X-15A-2. Powered by a liquid oxygen and ammonia rocket engine, the X-15 was carried to altitude by a Boeing B-52 before embarking upon ultra-high-speed and high altitude flights, as summarized next.

mph	km/h	Mach No.	Pilot	Date
2111	3397	3.19	J. A. Walker	12 May 1960
2196	3534	3.31	J. A. Walker	4 Aug 1960
2275	3661	3.50	R. M. White	7 Feb 1961
2905	4675	4.43	R. M. White	7 Mar 1961
3074	4947	4.62	R. M. White	21 Apr 1961
3307	5322	4.95	J. A. Walker	25 May 1961

mph	km/h	Mach No.	Pilot	Date
3647	5869	5.21	R. M. White	11 Oct 1961
3900	6276	5.74	J. A. Walker	17 Oct 1961
4093	6587	6.04	R. M. White	9 Nov 1961
4104	6605	5.92	J. A. Walker	27 Jun 1962
3074	4947	6.33	W. J. Knight	18 Nov 1966
4250	6840	6.72	W. J. Knight	3 Oct 1967

Major Knight with the X-15A-2, the fastest aeroplane of all time.

Progressive world absolute height records achieved by man in the atmosphere

Height ft	m	Pilot	Nationality	Aircraft	Location	Date
508	155	H. Latham	GB	Antoinette	Reims, France	29 Aug 1909
984	300	Comte Charles de Lambert	France	Wright	Paris, France	18 Oct 1909
1486	453	H. Latham	GB	Antoinette	Châlons, France	1 Dec 1909
3281	1000	H. Latham	GB	Antoinette	France	7 Jan 1910
3966	1209	L. Paulhan	France	Henry Farman	Los Angeles, USA	12 Jan 1910
4380	1335	W. Brookins	USA	Wright	Indianapolis, USA	14 Jun 1910
4540	1384	H. Latham	GB	Antoinette	Reims, France	7 Jul 1910
6234	1900	W. Brookins	USA	Wright	Atlantic City, USA	10 Jul 1910
6601	2012	A. Drexel	USA	Blériot	Lanark, Scotland	11 Aug 1910
8471	2582	Léon Morane	France	Blériot	Deauville, France	3 Sep 1910
8488	2587	G. Chavez	France	Blériot	Issy-les-Moulineaux, France	8 Sep 1910
9120	2780	H. Wynmalen	France	Henry Farman	Mourmelon, France	1 Oct 1910
9449	2880	A. Drexel	USA	Blériot	Philadelphia, USA	Oct 1910
9711	2960	R. Johnston	USA	Wright	Belmont Park, USA	31 Oct 1910
10170	3100	G. Legagneux	France	Blériot	Pau, France	8 Dec 1910
10423	3177	M. Loridan	France	Henry Farman	Châlons, France	8 July 1911
10466	3190	Capt Félix	France	Blériot	Etampes, France	9 Aug 1911
12828	3910	Roland Garros	France	Blériot XI	St-Malo, France	4 Sep 1911
16076	4900	Roland Garros	France	Blériot XI	Houlgate, France	6 Sep 1912
17880	5450	G. Legagneux	France	Morane-Saulnier	Corbeaulieu, France	17 Sep 1912
18405	5610	Roland Garros	France	Morane-Saulnier	Tunis	11 Dec 1912
19291	5880	M. Perreyon	France	Blériot XI	Buc, France	11 Mar 1913
20079	6120	G. Legagneux	France	Nieuport	St-Raphael, France	28 Dec 1913

The final entry above was the last world absolute height record to be ratified by the FAI until 1920, more than a year after the end of the First World War.

Height ft	m	Pilot	Nationality	Aircraft	Location	Date
33 113	10 093	Maj R. W. Schroeder	USA	Lepere	Dayton, USA	27 Feb 1920
34 508	10 518	Lt J. A. MacReady	USA	Lepere	Dayton, USA	18 Sep 1921
35 242	10 742	Sadi Lecointe	France	Nieuport	Villacoublay, France	5 Sep 1923
36 565	11 145	Sadi Lecointe	France	Nieuport	Issy-les-Moulineaux, France	30 Oct 1923
38 418	11 710	Lt C. C. Champion	USA	Wright Apache	Washington, USA	25 Jul 1927
39 140	11 930	Lt Apollo Soucek	USA	Wright Apache	USA	8 May 1929
41 795	12 739	W. Neuenhofen	Germany	Junkers W34	Dessau	26 May 1929
43 166	13 157	Lt Apollo Soucek	USA	Wright Apache	Washington, USA	4 Jun 1930
43 976	13 404	Capt C. F. Uwins	GB	Vickers Vespa	Filton, England	16 Sep 1932
44 820	13 661	G. Lemoine	France	Potez 50	Villacoublay, France	28 Sep 1933
47 352	14 433	Cdr R. Donati	Italy	Caproni 161	Rome, Italy	11 Apr 1934
48 698	14 843	G. Détré	France	Potez 50	Villacoublay, France	14 Aug 1936
49 944	15 223	Sqn Ldr S. R. Swain	GB	Bristol 138	Farnborough, England	28 Sep 1936
51 362	15 655	Lt Col M. Pezzi	Italy	Caproni 161	Montecelio, Italy	8 May 1937
53 937	16 440	Flt Lt M. J. Adam	GB	Bristol 138	Farnborough, England	30 Jun 1937
56 046	17 083	Lt Col M. Pezzi	Italy	Caproni 161 bis	Montecelio, Italy	22 Oct 1938

The final entry above was the last world absolute height record to be ratified by the FAI until March 1948, more than nine years later.

Height ft	m	Pilot	Nationality	Aircraft	Location	Date
59 445	18 119	J. Cunningham	GB	de Havilland Vampire I	Hatfield, England	23 Mar 1948
63 668	19 406	W. F. Gibb	GB	English Electric Canberra	England	4 May 1953
65 889	20 083	W. F. Gibb	GB	English Electric Canberra	England	29 Aug 1955
70 308	21 430	M. Randrup	GB	English Electric Canberra	England	28 Aug 1957
76 932	23 449	Lt Cdr G. C. Watkins	USA	Grumman F11F-1 Tiger	USA	18 Apr 1958
79 452	24 217	R. Carpentier	France	SO9050 Trident (F-ZWUM)	France	2 May 1958
91 243	27 811	Maj H. C. Johnson	USA	Lockheed F-104A Starfighter	USA	7 May 1958
94 659	28 852	Maj V. Ilyushin	USSR	Sukhoi T431	USSR	14 Jul 1959
98 556	30 040	Cdr L. Flint	USA	McDonnell Douglas F-4 Phantom II	USA	6 Dec 1959
103 389	31 513	Capt J. B. Jordan	USA	Lockheed F-104C Starfighter	USA	14 Dec 1959
113 891	34 714	Col G. Mosolov	USSR	Mikoyan E-66A	USSR	28 Apr 1961
118 898	36 240	A. Fedotov	USSR	Mikoyan E-266	USSR	25 Jul 1973
123 524	37 650	A. Fedotov	USSR	Mikoyan E-266M	USSR	31 Aug 1977

Distance miles	km	Pilot	Nationality	Aircraft	Location of start	Date
722 ft	220 m	A. Santos-Dumont	Brazil	Santos-Dumont 14 bis	Bagatelle, France	12 Nov 1906
2530 ft	771 m	H. Farman	France	Voisin	Issy-les-Moulineaux, France	26 Oct 1907
0.62	1	H. Farman	France	Voisin	Issy-les-Moulineaux, France	13 Jan 1908
1.25	2.004	H. Farman	France	Voisin	Issy-les-Moulineaux, France	21 Mar 1908
2.44	3.925	L. Delagrange	France	Voisin	Issy-les-Moulineaux, France	11 Apr 1908
7.92	12.75	L. Delagrange	France	Voisin	Centocelle	30 May 1908
14.99	24.125	L. Delagrange	France	Voisin	Issy-les-Moulineaux, France	17 Sep 1908
41.38	66.60	Wilbur Wright	USA	Wright	Auvours, France	21 Sep 1908
62	99.8	Wilbur Wright	USA	Wright	Auvours, France	18 Dec 1908
77.48	124.7	Wilbur Wright	USA	Wright	Auvours, France	31 Dec 1908
83.26	134	Louis Paulhan	France	Voisin	Betheny	25 Aug 1909
96.08	154.62	H. Latham	GB	Antoinette	Betheny	26 Aug 1909
111.8	180	H. Farman	France	Farman	Betheny	27 Aug 1909
145.53	234.21	H. Farman	France	Farman	Mourmelon	4 Nov 1909
244	392.75	Jan Olieslagers	Belgium	Blériot	Mourmelon	20 July 1910
289.4	465.72	M. Tabuteau	France	Maurice Farman	Etampes, France	28 Oct 1910
320.6	515.9	G. Legagneux	France	Blériot	Pau, France	11 Dec 1910
363.35	584.75	M. Tabuteau	France	Maurice Farman	Buc, France	30 Dec 1910
388.4	625	Jan Olieslagers	Belgium	Nieuport monoplane	Kiewit	16 Jul 1911
449.21	722.94	Fourny	France	Maurice Farman	Buc, France	1 Sep 1911
460	740.3	Gobé	France	Nieuport monoplane	Pau, France	24 Dec 1911
628.1	1010.9	Fourny	France	Maurice Farman	Etampes, France	11 Sep 1912
634.5	1021.2	A. Seguin	France	Henry Farman	Buc, France	13 Oct 1913

The final entry above was the last world absolute distance record to be ratified by the FAI until 1925.

Distance miles	km	Pilot	Nationality	Aircraft	Location of start	Date
1967	3166	Capts L. Arrachart and H. Lemaître	France	Breguet 19	Etampes, France	3–4 Feb 1925
2675	4305	Capt L. Arrachart and Adj Arrachart	France	Potez 550	Le Bourget, France	26–7 Jun 1926
2930	4715.9	Capt L. Girier and Lt Dordilly	France	Breguet 19	Le Bourget, France	14–15 Jul 1926

Distance miles	km	Pilot	Nationality	Aircraft	Location of start	Date
3215	5174	Lt Challe and Capt Weiser	France	Breguet 19	Le Bourget, France	31 Aug–1 Sep 1926
3353	5396	Capts D. Costes and J. Rignot	France	Breguet 19	Le Bourget, France	28–9 Oct 1926
3609.5	5809	Charles Lindbergh	USA	Ryan monoplane	New York to Paris	20–1 May 1927
3911	6294	C. D. Chamberlin and A. Levine	USA	Bellanca	New York, USA	4–6 Jun 1927
4466.6	7188.25	A. Ferrarin and D. Prete	Italy	Savoia-Marchetti S64	Rome, Italy	3–5 Jul 1928
4912	7905	Capt D. Costes and M. Bellonte	France	Breguet 19	Le Bourget, France	27–9 Sep 1929
5011	8065	R. N. Boardman and J. Polando	USA	Wright J6	Brooklyn, USA	28–30 Jul 1931
5309	8544	Sqn Ldr O. Gayford and Flt Lt G. Nicholetts	GB	Fairey Special monoplane	Cranwell, England	6–8 Feb 1933
5657	9104	Rossi and P. Codes	France	Blériot Zapata	New York, USA	5–7 Aug 1933
6306	10148	Col M. Gromov, Ing S. Daniline and Cmdt A. Youmachev	USSR	ANT-25	Moscow to San Jacinto	12–14 Jul 1937
6658.3	10715.5	Flt Lts H. A. V. Hogan and Mosson	GB	Vickers Wellesley	Ismailia to Koepang	5–7 Nov 1938
7158.4	11 520.4	Sqn Ldr R. Kellett and Flt Lt Gething	GB	Vickers Wellesley	Ismailia to Darwin	5–7 Nov 1938
7158.4	11 520.4	Flt Lt A. N. Combe and Bornett	GB	Vickers Wellesley	Ismailia to Darwin	5–7 Nov 1938

The final entry above was the last world absolute distance record to be ratified by the FAI until 1945.

Distance miles	km	Pilot	Nationality	Aircraft	Location of start	Date
7916	12 739.6	Col Irving and Lt Col Stawley	USA	Boeing B-29 Superfortress	Northwest to Washington	12 Nov 1945
11 235.6	18 081.99	Cdr T. Davis and E. P. Rankin	USA	Lockheed P2V Neptune	Perth to Columbus, Ohio	29 Sep–1 Oct 1946
12 532.3	20 168.78	Maj Clyde P. Evely	USA	Boeing B-52H	Okinawa to Madrid, Spain	10–11 Jan 1962
24 986.664	40 212.139	Dick Rutan and Jeana Yeager	USA	Voyager	Round-the-world non-stop flight	14–23 Dec 1986

Index

The following space-saving abbreviations have been used in this Index:

A	aeroplane/aircraft	m-g machine-gun
AAM	air-to-air missile	mono monoplane
AC	aircraft carrier	N north
ASW	anti-submarine warfare	op operation/s/operational
AW	all-weather	pass passenger/s
dem	demonstrated/demonstration	RLG retractable landing gear
des	design/designed	RTW round the world
E	east	S south
Ex	experimental/experiments	SAM surface-to-air missile
F	flight/flown/fly/flying	SW sweptwing
f-b	flying-boat	TJ turbojet
H	helicopter	TP turboprop

UK signifies England, Scotland, Ulster &
Wales collectively or individually
VG variable-geometry
W west
WAR world altitude record
WDR world distance record
WSR world speed record
1WW First World War
2WW Second World War
X across/trans

IIIC (see Fairey)
IIID (see Fairey)
IIIF (see Fairey)
XIII (see SPAD)
XIX (see Breguet)
1MF1 (see Mitsubishi)
4-AT Trimotor (see Ford)
'14-bis': 81
17 (see Nieuport)
19 (see Breguet)
25 (see Potez)
28 (see Nieuport)
29 (see Nieuport-Delage)
62 (see Nieuport-Delage)
130 Clipper (see Martin)
146 CC.Mk 2 (see British
  Aerospace)
180 (see Cessna)
184 (see Short)
504 (see Avro)
534 Baby (see Avro)
581 Avian (see Avro)
600 (see Verville-Packard)
630 (see Potez)

A

A-1 (see Curtiss)
A3D Skywarrior (see Douglas)
A-4 (see Douglas)
A-4 (V-2) rocket: 154
A4N1 (see Nakajima)
A5M (see Mitsubishi)
A-6 Intruder (see Grumman)
A6M Zero (see Mitsubishi)
A-10A Thunderbolt II (see
  Fairchild)
A-11 (see Aero)
A 129 Mangusta (see Agusta)
AB (see Curtiss)
AB-2 (see Curtiss)
AB Aerotransport: 104
Abruzzo, B. L.: 22, 24
AC-130 (see Lockheed)
AD-1 Skyraider (see Douglas)
Adams, J.: 16
Ader, Clément: 73, 78, 133
AEG D.I.: 190
Aerial Carriage: 41
Aerial Experimental Assn: 84
Aerial Steam Carriage: 76
Aerial Steamer: 77
Aero A-11: 150
Aérocentre Belphégor: 211
Aero Club (UK): 20, 79, 83, 86, 88
Aéro Club de France: 78, 81
Aero Club of America: 81
Aero Club of California: 88
Aerodrome: 79
Aeroflot: 8, 120, 122
Aerolineas Argentinas: 121

Aeromarine West Indies Airways:
  100
Aeronautical Society (UK): 83
Aéronave: 77
Aeroplane: current
  WAR microlight: 129
  WAR piston-engined: 129
  WDR closed-circuit jet-powered:
    130, 131
  WDR straight-line microlights:
    130
  WDR straight-line seaplanes: 130
  WR payload to 2000 m: 131
  WSR closed-circuit TP-powered:
    128
  WSR RTW TJ-powered: 129
  WSR straight-line microlights:
    129
  WSR straight-line piston-engined:
    129
Aeroplane: Farthest travelling
  homebuilt: 130
Aeroplane: Fastest flexwing: 129
  RTW flight by 1931: 108, 109
Aeroplane/s: First
  1000-bomber raid RAF: 162
  12 000 lb bomb dropped op by
    RAF: 164
  acquired by US Navy: 136
  activities of Australian Flying
    Doctor Service: 106
  aerial combat between: 138
  aerial crop-dusting company: 102
  aeronautical exhibition: 77
  aeroplane meeting (USA): 88
  air attack with torpedo: 142
  air collision of two: 90
  air collision of two airliners: 101
  air-crossing Tasman Sea: 106, 107
  air disaster involving 100-plus: 176
  air-dropped torpedoes of Korean
    War: 174, 175
  airline F USA–Hawaii: 113
  airline passenger F Paris–London:
    96
  airliner F with propfan engine: 126
  airliner with pressurized cabin:
    116
  airline stewardess: 108
  airline providing food in F: 100
  airline to introduce inertial
    navigation: 124
  airmail F across Canadian
    Rockies: 99
  airmail/freight service USA–New
    Zealand: 115
  air raid on Germany by UK
    1WW: 140
  air victory (probably) with
    synchronized m-g: 142
  Allied to bomb Berlin 2WW: 159

all-metal (Soviet): 103
all-paper man-carrying: 124
American monoplane to F: 87
American woman killed in A
  accident: 92
American woman pass in: 86
American woman F solo in: 89
and only 2WW attack on USA by
  Japanese aeroplane: 162
and only Oxford/Cambridge air
  race: 101
attack by A on rocket research
  unit: 164
attack by Japanese A on US
  Pacific Fleet/Pearl Harbor: 161
attack by USA on Japanese
  mainland: 162
automatic approach and landing
  by Concorde: 124
automatic gyro stabilizer for: 209
aviation meeting in UK: 86
blind F, take-off, level F and
  landing: 151
blind solo F solely on
  instruments: 152
Boeing commercial: 100
Boeing commercial monoplane:
  108
bomb dropped on UK soil by
  enemy: 141
bomber with powered gun-turret
  (RAF): 154
bombing attack of 1WW: 140
bombs dropped from in war: 136
bombs dropped from on enemy
  city: 140
Briton to F all-UK A: 155
cantilever low-wing fighter of
  Armée de l'Air: 153
car ferry F of Silver City Airways:
  117
carriage of 11 pass: 131
carriage of 12 pass: 131
carriage of freight: 90
carriage of freight (UK): 91
carrier-based supersonic naval:
  177
Certificate of Airworthiness jet
  airliner: 119
charter flight: 106
Chinese National indigenous TP
  trainer: 183
cinematographer flown in: 84
circuit flight in Europe: 82
coast–coast airmail (USA): 98
coast–coast crossing USA in one
  day: 101
coast–coast F across USA: 91
combat in production (USA):
  147
combat mission of B-17: 161

combat op by Lancaster: 161
combat victory in Greek-Italian
  campaign: 159
commercial airmail F (USA): 104
commercial air route London–
  India: 107
commercial air route UK–central
  Africa: 108
commercial F over polar region:
  119
commercial to use UK FIDO fog
  dispersal system: 117
commercial transport to exceed
  Mach 2: 122
commercial use of composite A:
  116
company to deliver 1000 jet
  airliners: 122
completed F across Irish Sea: 92
completely automatic approach/
  landing by four-TJ airliner: 122
confirmation of lethality in naval
  battle: 162
contract for a military: 134
cross-country F solely on
  instruments: 83
crossing English Channel by
  powered hang-glider: 125
crossing English Channel with
  passenger: 89
crossing of Irish Sea: 90
daily air service India: 112
delta-wing seaplane: 213
des for jet fighter: 160
des as TJ tanker, transport: 180
des as troop transport: 149
des/built for air fighting: 142
des/built in Chinese People's
  Republic: 120
des by A. N. Tupolev: 101
des for jet-propelled: 77
des for powered, delta-winged: 77
des for supersonic tactical fighter-
  bomber: 178
des to fly at 1000 mph: 210
destroyed by ramming: 140
distance record FAI recognized:
  81
distribution of newspapers on
  daily basis: 97
Dutch national airline: 100
eight-gun fighter of FAA: 159
electric-powered manned to fly:
  219
enclosed-cockpit, RLG, mono
  fighter:
  French: 155
  German: 154
  Italian: 156
  Japanese: 156
  United Kingdom: 155
  United States: 154, 155

enclosed-cockpit, RLG, mono fighter in sqn service: 153
enemy night bomber destroyed over Germany: 147
enemy shot down by RAF on Western Front 2WW: 158
European VG: 218
European wide-body airliner: 124
E–W crossing N Atlantic: 106
E–W crossing N Atlantic by TJ-powered: 172
explosive bombs dropped: 135
exp with pressurized cabin: 209
FAA standardized jet fighter: 175
F above 1 mile high: 129
F across Andes: 95
F across Australia: 100
F across Canadian Rockies: 99
F across English Channel of pilot and 2 pass: 92
F across Mediterranean: 94
F across Mediterranean by microlight: 125
F across North Sea: 95
fatal accident, scheduled commercial F: 101
fatal accident, TJ airliner: 119
fatal accident, TJ airliner in scheduled service: 119
F at altitude of 1000 m: 129
fatality to occupant of powered: 134
F Australia–USA: 113
F by all-metal: 91
F by lightplane X-Sahara: 109
F by solar-powered: 220
F by woman South Africa–UK: 106
F Egypt–India: 95
F France–Egypt: 94
F in Australia: 87
F in Australia by Australian in indigenous A: 89
F in Austria: 84
F in Belgium: 82
F in Denmark: 86
F in Europe of about 30 min: 83
F in France of 1 hour: 84
F in Germany: 82
F in Ireland: 87
F in Italy: 82
F in New Zealand: 90
F in Spain: 88
F in Sweden: 86
F in Switzerland: 88
F lasting over 5 min: 80
F London–Cape Town: 104
F non-stop London–Paris: 91
F non-stop X-Atlantic: 98
F non-stop Rome–Paris: 99
F non-stop UK–Germany: 93
F of A with enclosed cabin: 92
F of Danish airliner to UK: 116
F of more than 100 km: 128
F of more than 1 mile (UK): 134
F of powered completely by TP engines: 116
F of revolutionary de Havilland DH60 Moth: 103
F of UK Empire Air Mail Programme: 115
F on single TP engine: 172
F over Alps: 90
F over Everest: 111
F over North Pole: 104
F over South Pole: 107, 108
F refuelling test Imperial Airways f-b: 115, 116
F solely on power of TJ engine: 210
F UK–Australia: 100
F UK–Egypt: 95
F UK–France & first two-way X-English Channel: 89
F UK–South Africa: 100
F with TJ engine: 210
fighter A for Luftwaffe: 153

firing of nuclear-tipped AAM: 179
first-line jet of USN/USMC: 171
flying-boat to exceed 500 mph: 211
flying day at Hendon: 91
flying-wing jet fighter: 210
formation f over N. Atlantic: 152
formation F over S. Atlantic: 152
four-engined attack bomber Japanese Navy: 158
four-engined bomber in service: 93
four-engined bomber on RAF operations: 160
four-engined monoplane heavy bomber in Soviet use: 152
four-engined to fly: 93
freight service by TP-powered: 119
French airmail service: 95
French fighter to exceed 250 mph: 155
French to exceed Mach 1 in level flight: 215
French for stratospheric F: 211
French reconnaissance F in: 135
French supersonic: 213
French to dem STOL 'blown wing': 216
French TJ-powered airliner: 120
full-size rocket-powered: 209
full-size triplane F: 83
full-size with ailerons: 80
fully automatic landing by: 115
fully automatic landing of F/A-18 Hornet: 185
German armoured: 146
German flown by German: 83
German in Spanish Civil War: 197
German shot down by RAF 2WW: 158
German shot down by UK-based RAF 2WW: 158
German shot down over UK 2WW: 158
German TJ-powered in op service: 163
German U-boat sunk by: 146
German work on TJ engine: 209
Gotha bomber shot down at night: 147
grounding of specific type: 136
'hop' F by seaplane: 79
important reconnaissance contribution to land battle: 140
indigenous French fighter: 172
intensive city bombardment, Spanish Civil War: 156
intentional attack by armed German against armed enemy: 142
intentional air victory at night: 145
interceptor des to be rocket powered, piloted & launched: 167, 168
internal airline services, Soviet Union: 100
Italian airmail service: 91
Italian in Spanish Civil War: 198
Japanese carrier-based fighter: 148
Japanese indigenous jet military transport: 183
Japanese indigenous supersonic: 183
jet built in Brazil: 183
jet fighter in RAF ops: 165
jet fighter to sustain supersonic level F: 176
jet fighter with variable-incidence wing: 178
jet lost in air combat: 165
jet night fighter sqn: 175
jet-powered airliner to reach 1000 sales total: 124

jet-powered parasite fighter: 212
jet V/STOL combat: 182
jet with VG wings: 214
jet X N. Atlantic non-stop & unrefuelled: 174
known air transportable hydrogen bomb: 178
land-based jet for ASW & maritime patrol: 182
landing on, taxi & take-off from water: 136
large air-cushion landing system: 219
large delta-wing bomber: 176
large-scale civil airlift: 151
large-scale military airlift: 156
launched by catapult on board ship: 143
lightplane competition (UK): 102
lightplane competition (two-seat) in UK: 103
lightplane F Equator–Equator via North Pole: 124
lightplane F London–Cape Town: 106
lightplane F London–Karachi: 105
Lockheed SR-71 for USAF: 182
low-level supersonic SW fighter of Royal Navy: 180
Luftwaffe attack on London 2WW: 159
Luftwaffe operational with tricycle RLG: 164
major air attack on Tokyo: 167
major UK seaplane contest: 93
major US air strikes on N. Vietnam: 181
man-carrying to 'hop' from level ground: 78
manned/powered to make sustained F in Europe: 81
manned supersonic: 211, 212
manned test of US ejection seat: 171
manned with petrol engine: 79
man-powered 1-mile figure-of-eight F: 220
man-powered to cross English Channel: 221
man to cross English Channel in: 85, 86
man to drop missiles from: 134
manufactured in series: 83
manufacturer to deliver 100 000 production A: 124
manufacturing company: 83
mass bombing raid on London 1WW: 146
mass bombing raid on UK at night (1WW): 147
mass Gotha bombing raid on UK (1WW): 146
military des/built in Czechoslovakia: 148
military firearm fired from: 135
military op by US: 138
military to land on ice at S. Pole: 179
military trials in UK: 137
mission by newly-formed RAF: 147, 148
model powered by steam engine: 76
modern design for: 76
monoplane airliner of Imperial Airways: 108
monoplane fighter of US Navy: 156, 157
monoplane heavy bomber in RAF service: 152
monoplane in FAA service: 156
multi-engine airliner with engines in rear fuselage pods: 120
multi-engine bomber of Luftwaffe: 156
national airline of Czechoslovakia: 102

naval vessel converted under construction to operate A: 142
night attack on U-boat using Leigh light: 162
night bombing attack from US AC: 164
night flights in: 88
N. Korean jet shot down at night: 176
no-booking guaranteed-seat shuttle in Europe: 124
non-stop airliner F London–Vancouver: 120
non-stop F Canada–UK: 113
non-stop F Hawaii–Egypt over N. Pole: 117
non-stop F Japan–USA: 109
non-stop F London–Bombay: 121
non-stop F UK–Australia: 181
non-stop F UK–Cape Town: 180
non-stop F UK–India: 107
non-stop F UK–South Africa: 107
non-stop F USA–Hawaii: 106
non-stop RTW flight: 172, 173
non-stop RTW flight by TJ: 180
non-stop RTW unrefuelled F: 7, 126, 222
non-stop solo X-N. Atlantic: 105
non-stop transatlantic F by executive jet: 122
non-stop US transcontinental F by woman: 110
non-stop X-N. Atlantic by jet fighter: 174
non-stop X-S. Atlantic: 106
non-stop X-USA: 102
official airmail F in UK: 95
official airmail F in Canada: 95
official airmail F in US: 91
official airmail in Italy: 95
official government airmail F: 90
official test of US Army's first: 134
officially recognized air meeting in UK: 86
officially recognized F in UK: 134
of Japanese Navy for ASW patrol: 164
of RAF Coastal Command with ASV radar: 161
of RAF with H2S blind bombing radar: 161, 162
of RFC to be brought down in action: 140
of US Navy to destroy German U-boats: 161
of US Navy with RLG: 153
of variable-incidence VG des: 95
one-mile F by Briton in UK A: 87
one of several manned and powered 'hops': 78
op carrier-based with tricycle RLG: 164
op four-engined bomber/reconnaissance: 141
op inflight refuelling of combat A: 176
op jet bomber: 166
op of US origin used by RAF during 2WW: 157
op rocket-powered fighter: 164
op seaplane unit of Imperial German Navy: 141
op use by A of rocket-powered remotely-controlled missiles: 164
op use of Albatros D.I.: 144
op use of composite combat A: 165
op use of Mitsubishi A6M2 Zero-Sen: 159
organized X-N. Atlantic ferry flights of US-built to Allies (WW2): 159
ornithopter to fly successfully: 77
outsize transport conversion of Boeing Stratocruiser: 121

over 200 km/h speed record: 128
over 200 mph fighter of RAF: 152
over 200 mph WSR: 149
over 400 mph WSR: 152
over 500 km/h WSR: 150
over 700 mph WSR: 176
over 2000 km/h WSR: 180
Pan American Airways service: 106
pass carried in Australia: 87
pass carried in Canada: 86
pass carried in Europe: 82
pass-carrying service from London City Airport: 187
passenger in: 82
pass/mail services London–Paris: 95
patent for m-g to be fired from: 135
piglet to fly in: 87
piloted flight over Mach 2: 212
piston-engined to exceed 500 mph: 165
post-1WW aviation event in UK: 98
post-1WW fighter for Italian air force: 150
post-1WW fighter for RAF: 150
post-1WW WSR: 148
post-2WW landing of German civil A in UK: 120
post-2WW long-distance record: 171
post-2WW SW jet fighter in European service: 172
powered flight in UK (almost certainly): 81
powered man-carrying to make a brief 'hop': 77
powered model to fly (presumed): 76
powered model to fly successfully: 76, 77
practical UK lightplane after 1WW: 97
procured for US Army use: 134
produced by Junkers & also 1st all-metal monoplane 143, 144
prosecution in UK for smoking in airliner: 114
pure jet op from AC: 170
purely commercial built in UK post-1WW: 96
purpose-built all-metal commercial: 99
purpose-designed suicide: 168
radar-controlled interception by: 151
RAF des to air-drop heavy loads: 176
RAF fighter to exceed 300 mph: 155
RAF fighter to exceed 400 mph: 161
RAF jet night fighter: 174
RAF leaflet raid over Germany 2WW: 157
RAF supersonic single-seat fighter: 177
RAF SW jet interceptor: 175
RAF to bomb targets on German soil 2WW: 159
RAF two-seat fighter with powered gun-turret: 156
raid on UK by: 141
raid on UK by German 'R' type bombers: 147
recorded ex use of ejection seat: 171
recorded night F in UK: 88
regular airmail service X-Atlantic: 116
regular civil air service in UK: 98
regular internal airmail service in UK: 113

regular supersonic F by civil transport A: 122
regular UK air service to South America: 117
regular US air freight service: 103
regular weekly airmail service UK–Australia: 113
resident Briton to fly as pass: 83
resident Briton to make officially recorded F in UK: 84
RFC air victory: 140
rocket-powered manned des: 210
Romanian to fly: 89
Royal Navy pilot to fly from ship: 136
RTW F air cargo service: 124
RTW F by homebuilt: 124
RTW F by microlight: 126
RTW F non-stop/unrefuelled: 7, 126, 222
RTW pass service by jet airliner: 121
Russian designed for air fighting: 141, 142
Russian in Spanish Civil War: 197
Russian with m-g: 138
scheduled airline: 94
scheduled air service London–Berlin: 102
scheduled daily international commercial airline: 99
scheduled jet service within Arctic Circle: 123
scheduled regular Australian air services: 101
scheduled regular international airmail service: 95
scheduled pass service by turbine-powered airliner: 118
Schneider Trophy Contest: 93
Sea Harrier combat victory: 185
seaplane competition: 91
seaplane F in New Zealand: 90
series-built fighter of Soviet Union: 159
Short C-class Empire f-b: 114
shot down & destroyed by another: 140
shot down by missile of Soviet Union: 180
significant gunship: 183
single-seat fighter in RFC service: 142
single-seat fighter to destroy enemy A by m-g fired through prop: 142
single-seat scout: 136
single-seat scout in production for military use: 138
six-TJ bomber to F in USA: 171
solar-powered to cross English Channel: 220
solo coast–coast X-USA: 101
solo F Australia–UK in homebuilt: 124
solo F by woman X-Atlantic: 113
solo F by woman Australia–Cape Town: 114
solo F by woman Australia–UK: 108
solo F by woman UK–Australia: 108
solo F Cape Town–Cairo: 106
solo F E–W X-N. Atlantic: 110
solo F South Africa–UK: 106
solo F UK–Australia: 106
solo return F UK–South Africa: 106
solo RTW F: 111, 112
solo RTW F by a woman: 121
solo RTW F by UK woman: 122
solo trans-Polar F: 118, 119
solo X-N. Atlantic by woman: 110
South Atlantic F attempt: 101
Soviet jet-bomber to F: 171
Soviet production jet-bomber: 171

Soviet pure-jet: 170
specially des low-level strike: 181
specifically des rocket-powered manned: 210
specification for military: 133
staged X-N. Atlantic (E–W): 103
staged X-N. Atlantic (E–W) by f-b: 108
staged X-Pacific: 103
staged X-S. Atlantic: 104
stage of planned US transcontinental air service inaugurated: 98
standard naval torpedo launched by naval A: 139
state airline of Soviet Union: 102
strategic bombing raid by: 141
submarine sunk by: 144
successful air raid on Germany by UK: 140
successful artillery spotting F: 136
successful ex V/STOL fighter: 216
successful flying-wing bomber: 212
successful inflight refuelling of: 150
successful liquid fuel rocket-powered: 210
successful passenger-carrying built in US: 104
successful pressurized cabin: 210
successful Russian: 83
successful still photos from: 87
successful use of air-to-air rockets against: 157
successful suicide attack: 167
successfully catapult-launched from boat: 138
supersonic bomber USAF: 179, 181
supersonic carrier-based interceptor Royal Navy: 182
supersonic commercial airliner operating regular scheduled pass services: 122
supersonic transport to fly: 12
sustained commercial daily pass services: 96
sustained pass service op by TP-powered airliners: 119
sustained/powered F in British Empire: 83, 84
sustained regular international pass service: 96, 97
sustained strategic bombing offensive by: 143
take-off from ship under way: 137
take-off from US AC: 150
take-off from water: 88
take-off/landing Japan's AC Hosho: 150
tenders for accepted by US Army: 134
tethered sustained F in Europe: 80
three-engine all-metal mono transport in commercial service: 103
through pass air service UK–Australia: 113
TJ airliner: 118
TJ airliner in Aeroflot service: 120
TJ airliner in commercial service: 119
TJ airliner service South America–UK: 121
TJ AW fighter of Royal Navy: 177
TJ AW interceptor of USAF: 172
TJ AW interceptor of USAF ADC: 173
TJ engine for: 209, 210
TJ fighter in US service: 164
TJ flight non-stop X-Pacific: 176
TJ military transport: 179
TJ-powered to exceed Mach 1: 172

to be 'forced down' by another: 88
to carry airborne nuclear reactor: 215, 216
to carry more than 100 pass X-N. Atlantic: 173
to carry pilot & two pass: 84
to decide issue of naval battle: 162
to drop bombs on enemy ship: 138
to drop bombs on London (1WW): 144, 145
to exceed Mach 3 in level F: 216
to F with cantilever wings: 81
to land in Fiji: 106
to land on a ship: 135, 136
to land on a ship under way: 146, 147
to land/take-off from Mount Washington: 117
to record four X-Atlantic crossings in one day: 123
torpedo dropped from: 135
to take-off from ship: 135
to test-drop 22 000 lb 'Grand Slam' bomb: 168
TP civil transport service: 117
TP-powered to fly in USA: 167
tractor-engined biplane: 83
transatlantic arrivals at Heathrow Airport: 117
'Trans-world' air race: 113
trials of depot ships on N. Atlantic route: 115
triplane fighter in service: 144
true ancestor of modern airliners: 111
true transPacific F: 106
turbine airliner to gain Airworthiness Certificate: 118
turbine-powered airliner with 25 years' service: 125
twin-engine bomber des for Luftwaffe: 152, 153
twin-engined jet: 160
twin-engined single-seat fighter to op from Royal Navy AC: 168
twin-engined strike for Royal Navy AC: 170, 171
twin-jet delta-wing fighter: 175, 176
two-crew man-powered F: 219
two women pass to F on UK–France airline service: 99
U-boat damaged by RAF: 157
UK airline company to be registered: 95
UK armed A flown into action: 139
UK bombers over Berlin 2WW: 158
UK bombs on German mainland 2WW: 159
UK Certificate of Airworthiness: 97
UK combat victory of 2WW recorded on gun-camera: 158
UK commercial A with auto pilot: 100
UK delta-wing research: 214
UK des as military transport: 181
UK des/built as armed fighting machine: 138
UK F across Sahara: 109
UK jet-bomber in RAF: 174
UK jet-powered to exceed Mach 1: 211
UK military insignia for: 141
UK national airline: 102
UK naval with powered gun-turret: 158
UK post-2WW survey F to South America: 116, 117
UK powered to fly tethered: 78
UK reconnaissance F over German territory: 140

UK registered civil: 97
UK single-seat monoplane to serve on Royal Navy AC: 159
UK sqns to fly to France 1WW: 139
UK TJ-powered: 209, 210
UK to attack U-boat 2WW: 158
UK to carry civil markings: 97
UK to cross German frontier 2WW: 157
UK to drop bombs on enemy targets 2WW: 157
UK to win major international event: 94
UK twin-engined to land on AC: 164
UK V-bomber: 175
UK woman to F solo in: 88
under 9-day F UK–Japan: 109
unit formed for suicide op: 166
unit of RFC to bomb strategic targets in Germany 1WW: 147
unit of US Army with A: 138
unmanned models to sustain powered flight: 78
unmanned to fly from level ground: 77
unofficial carriage of mail in UK: 89
US aerial mining of Vietnam: 182
US airmail carried by TJ-powered: 117
US all-jet to land on AC: 169
US armed with m-g: 137
US Army armoured production A: 149
US Army coast–coast F across USA: 95
US bomber sqn 1WW: 148
US-built in UK service to destroy German A 2WW: 159
US coast–coast all-air pass service: 108
US des/built jet fighter: 165
US des fighter built extensively: 148
US des for COIN ops: 183
US emergency use of ejection seat: 173
US ex airmail service: 95
US fighter sqn in France 1WW: 147
US forest fire observed from: 95
US four-jet bomber: 172
US in RAF service post-2WW: 173
US international airmail service: 96
US international scheduled pass air service: 100
US manufacturing company: 82
US military hit by fire on active service: 138
US Navy jet fighter in combat: 173, 174
US Navy single-seat carrier-based dive-bomber/torpedo carrier: 168
US Navy with hydraulic wing fold: 154
US night fighter patrol 1WW: 148
US observation over enemy lines: 148
US rocket-powered military: 210
US single-seat with powered gun-turret: 161
US six-engined: 150
US TJ-powered transport: 119
US to land by jet power on ship: 168, 169
US trials of for ASW use: 138
US with fly-by-wire control: 183
US woman pilot on regular airmail service: 113
USAF op delta-winged: 178
USAF SW fighter: 171

used in parasite fighter ex: 144
use in major fleet battle: 144
use of for violence in civil crime: 104
use of in war: 136
use of large fighter formations: 144
use of RAF Pathfinder Force: 163
use of Sea Harrier in combat: 184
use of wireless to transmit message to ground: 89
use on military ops in South America: 142
use on manoeuvres by US Army: 137
variable-pitch propeller: 102
vertical/horizontal/vertical transitions by pure jet: 216
vertical/horizontal/vertical transitions by UK jet: 216
victories in 'Continuation War': 163
victory against Soviet A during 'Winter War': 158
victory by jet pilot v. jet fighter: 174
VTOL fixed-wing combat in US service: 183
warship sunk by: 140
W–E crossing of Arctic: 106
W. European in Mach 2 level F: 180
W. European to dive supersonically: 174
wide-body commercial transport: 122
wide-body transport op by two-man crew: 124
wide-body transport to fly in Soviet Union: 124
with coupled twin-turbine engine: 173
with ejection seats as standard: 163, 164
with practical RLG: 100
with swing-tail for rear loading: 121
woman passenger in: 82, 83
woman passenger to F in UK: 86
woman (probably) to fly TJ fighter: 170
woman to fly across English Channel: 91
woman to fly faster than speed of sound: 119
WSR over 1000 mph: 215
X-Atlantic crossing by air: 97
X-Atlantic deployment of USAF jet fighters: 172
X-Atlantic F by UK Prime Minister: 116
X-Atlantic pass service F by turbine-powered: 120
X-Atlantic pass service F by TJ-powered airliner: 120
X-Pacific airmail service: 114
X-Pacific pass service: 114
X-Pacific service with TJ-powered airliners: 121
X-Pacific solo F by woman: 121
Aeroplane: Fastest
  before 2WW: 190, 191
  ever flown: 221
  French/UK combat 1WW: 190
  German combat 1WW: 190
  German-developed 1WW: 190
  in military service: 191
  Italian combat 1WW: 190
  light bomber mid-1920s: 190
  non-stop air-refuelled RTW F: 191
  of RAF Bomber Command 1941–51: 191
  op twin-piston engined: 191
  piston-engined: 191
  piston-engined fighter des for Luftwaffe: 191

Aeroplane: Greatest
  air tragedy: 131
  bombload of op bomber: 194
  number carried in Martin Mars: 194
  number of ops, RAF 2WW: 193
  number of sorties in 24 h of Berlin Airlift: 194
  one-day loss of 2WW: 193
  one-day loss of Luftwaffe in Polish campaign: 193
  operating weight of carrier-based: 194
  producer of f-b: 193
  sales total of commercial: 131
  single victory of Netherlands AF during German invasion: 193
Aeroplane: Highest
  current WAR, air-breathing: 192
  known interception by unpressurized: 192
Aeroplane: Largest
  flying-boat: 220, 221
  f-b built between the wars: 127
  f-b of US Navy: 188
  force assembled 1WW for single op: 187
  French of between-wars years: 187
  German military f-b of 2WW: 189
  German op 1WW: 187
  in world currently: 127
  Japanese of between-wars years: 187
  losses in single day of ops: 187, 188
  Luftwaffe airborne assault 2WW: 188
  military f-b in current service: 189
  op f-b of 2WW: 188
  RAF transport op since Berlin Airlift: 189
  research A ever built: 217
  Russian Army bomber 1WW: 187
  single production programme: 184
  to lift off ground briefly in 19th century: 126
  UK landplane: 221
  UK military f-b: 188
  UK operational 1WW: 187
  USAF bomber: 189
  US landplane: 189
Aeroplane: Last
  biplane heavy bomber of RAF: 151
  biplane to serve with FAA: 157
  carrier-based biplane fighter of Japanese Navy: 156
  of wooden basic structure for RAF: 150
  op biplane in US service: 153
  open cockpit biplane of RAF: 151
  revenue F of Comet 4: 125
  revenue F of Boeing 707 with PanAm: 125
  scheduled op by piston-engined airliner from Heathrow: 121
  sporting events before 1WW: 95
Aeroplane: Longest
  duration man-powered F by woman: 221
  F by end of 1908: 129, 130
  non-stop unrefuelled distance before 1WW: 192
  non-stop unrefuelled distance by military: 192
  point-to-point op combat sortie: 192, 193
  production run of US 2WW fighter: 192
  serving des of 1WW: 192
  WDR man-powered: 221
  WDR man-powered closed circuit: 221
  WDR man-powered closed circuit

by woman: 221
WDR man-powered straight line by woman: 221
Aeroplane: Most
  advanced UK biplane fighter: 196
  disastrous month for RFC 1WW: 195
  effective single-engine day bomber start 1WW: 195
  effective USAF fighter of 1960s: 200
  effective US Navy dogfighter in Vietnam: 199, 200
  extensively-built US 2WW: 198
  extensively used by FAA inter-war years: 195
  extensively-used French fighter in 1932: 196
  famous Japanese bomber 2WW: 198
  famous RAF single-seat fighter 2WW: 196
  famous torpedo-bomber/reconnaissance: 196
  gallant torpedo attacks by: 230
  important endurance F by 21/8/1908: 83
  important fighter early in Korean War: 199
  important to post-1WW RAF: 195
  significant unit of RAF 1WW: 195
  sophisticated US Navy electronic warfare A: 200
  successful fighter 1WW: 105
  successful French of inter-war years: 195
  successful German fighter 1WW: 195
  successful mono (probably) before 1WW: 83
  successful UK military post-2WW: 199
  successful US Navy fighter 2WW: 199
  unequal conflict of inter-war years: 196
  unusual in US service 2WW: 198
  unusual post-2WW bomber programme: 199
  widely used Fokker of inter-war years: 195
  widely used French at start of 2WW: 198
  widely used military start of 1WW: 194
  widely used Polish fighter start 2WW: 198
Aeroplane:
  new women's solo F record UK–Australia: 125
  new women's solo RTW flight record: 125
  oldest airworthy airliner: 131
  only mass hijacking of civil airliners: 131
  smallest in current use: 127, 128
  successful test of Travel Air biplane with steam powerplant: 111
Aero Spacelines B-377PG Pregnant Guppy: 121
Aérospatiale SA 315B Lama: 62
Aérospatiale/BAC Concorde: 73, 122, 123, 124, 209, 215
Aerovias Nacionales de Colombia SA (Avianca): 130
AF-WRI-1: 22
Agusta A 129 Mangusta: 57, 58
AH-1G HueyCobra (see Bell)
AIDC XH-C-1A: 183
Airacomet (see Bell)
Air Arms, formation dates: 200–7
Airbus (see Airbus Industrie)
Airbus Industrie Airbus: 121, 124
Airco DH2: 142

Aircraft: First
 occasion music played from: 14
 op fighters carried by dirigibles: 37
 powered by an internal
  combustion engine: 25
Aircraft carrier: First
 angled-deck of US Navy: 176, 177
 destroyed by US airmen: 162
 French: 150
 in world: 18
 night landing on: 150
 of flush deck des: 145
 of modern layout: 145, 146
 purpose-built for Japanese Navy:
  149
 to carry full sqn of landplanes:
  145
 US lost during 2WW: 162
 US to carry heavier-than-air craft:
  148
 world's longest lived: 145, 146
Aircraft Transport & Travel Ltd: 95,
 96, 99, 131
Air France: 123, 124, 159
Airgraph service, origin: 19
Air India: 121
Air League Challenge Cup Air Race:
 101
Airship (see Dirigible)
Airspeed Horsa: 68
Akagi: 162
Akitsu Maru: 47
Alabaster, Capt R. C.: 119
Albatros
 D.I: 144, 224, 225
 D.II: 224, 226
 D.III: 34, 227
 D.V: 148, 226
Alcock, Capt J.: 7, 98, 99, 100, 123
Aldrin, E. A. A.: 218, 223
Alfeurov, G. G.: 60
Alkemade, Flt Sgt N. S.: 227
Allen, B.: 220, 221
Allen, Brig-Gen J.: 133
Altair (see Lockheed)
Altmark: 157
America: 29
American Airlines: 114
American Overseas Airlines: 117
Amundsen, R.: 35
An-124 (see Antonov)
Anders, W.: 218
Anderson, Capt O.: 20
Anderson, Capt R. C.: 182
Anderson, M. L.: 22
Andreani, Chev. P.: 13
Andrée S. A.: 10, 20
Andreev, E.: 70
ANEC monoplane: 102
Ansaldo SVA 5 Primo: 190
Anson (see Avro)
ANT-1 (see Tupolev)
ANT-2 (see Tupolev)
Antoinette IV: 85
Antoinette VII: 129
Antonov An-124: 8, 127, 131
Aoki, R.: 24
Apollo 8: 218
Apollo 10: 218
Apollo 11: 218
Apollo ASTP: 219, 220
Appleby, J.: 66
Aquila Airways: 120
Ar 68 (see Arado)
Ar 234 Blitz (see Arado)
Arado Ar 68: 153
Arado Ar 234 Blitz : 166
Archdeacon, E.: 82
Archimedes of Syracuse: 9
Archytas of Tarentum: 77
Argosy (see Armstrong Whitworth)
Armstrong, N. A.: 218, 219, 223
Armstrong Whitworth
 Argosy: 107
 AW15 Atalanta: 108
 AW23: 116
 Meteor NF11: 174

Whitley: 157, 158, 159, 160, 161
Arnold, Lt L. P.: 103
Arrowsmith, Corp V.: 157
Astir CS (see Grob)
AS-W12 (see Schleicher)
Attacker (see Supermarine)
Aubrun, E.: 88
Australasian: 17
AV-8 Harrier (see Hawker Siddeley)
AV-8B Harrier II (see McDonnell
 Douglas/British Aerospace)
Aveline stabilizer: 100
Aviasud Sirocco: 125, 126
Avion III: 78
Avro
 504: 139, 140, 141
 581 Avian: 106
 Anson: 158
 Avian III: 106
 Lancaster: 161, 164, 168, 193
 Lancastrian: 117
 Rota Mk I: 44
 Type 707: 214
 Type F: 92
 Vulcan: 176, 181, 185, 192, 193
AW15 Atalanta (see Armstrong
 Whitworth)
AW23 (see Armstrong Whitworth)
Ayling, J. R.: 113
Aztec (see Piper)

B

B-1 (see Boeing)
B-1B (see Rockwell)
B-3A (see Huff-Daland/Keystone)
B-8 Gyro-Copter (see Bensen)
B-17 Flying Fortress (see Boeing)
B-24 Liberator (see Consolidated)
B-25 Mitchell (see North American)
B-26 (see Douglas)
B-29 Superfortress (see Boeing)
B-35 (see Northrop)
B-36 (see Convair)
B-45 Tornado (see North
 American)
B-47 Stratojet (see Boeing)
B-50 (see Boeing)
B-52 Stratofortress (see Boeing)
B-57 (see Martin)
B-58 Hustler (see Convair)
B-377PG Pregnant Guppy (see Aero
 Spacelines)
Ba 349 Natter (see Bachem)
Babington, Flt Cdr J. T.: 141
Baby Bird (see Stits)
BAC TSR.2: 209
Bachem Ba 349 Natter: 167
Bacon, Roger: 73
Baden-Powell, Maj B. F. S.: 83
Bager, R.: 101
Bailey, Lady: 106
Balbo, Gen I.: 152
Balchen, Bernt: 108
Baldwin, Capt T.: 134
Baldwin, F. W. ('Casey'): 86
Baldwin, Sgt I.: 20
Ball, Capt A.: 224, 225
Balloon: First
 application of a propeller to: 14
 ascent by Scots aeronaut: 14
 Englishman to record 100 flights:
  17
 Joint Stock Co associated with:
  17
 kite-balloon use in army
  manoeuvres: 20
 manned ascent in Austria: 14
 manned ascent in UK: 14
 proposal for winged surface to
  control F: 13
 recognized des for kite-balloon:
  17
 recorded des for: 11
 tethered ascent by woman: 14
 UK aeronautical magazine: 17
 UK army aeronaut: 18

UK army balloon: 20
Balloon: Greatest
 'balloon buster' of 1WW: 24
Balloon: Largest
 ever built: 23
 non-rigid kite-balloon: 23
 planned flight: 24
Balloon (gas): First
 aeronaut knighted for F attempt:
  15
 ascent by UK aeronaut: 14
 ascent by woman in UK: 15
 ascent unmanned: 12
 ascent in Australia: 17
 ascent of man on horse: 17
 ascent in Canada: 20
 attempt to cross Irish Sea: 15
 attempt to explore Arctic: 20
 crossing of English Channel: 14
 crossing of Irish Sea: 17
 crossing of North Sea: 19
 F into stratosphere: 20
 F over Alps: 17
 F over UK: 14
 Gordon Bennett Trophy race: 20
 International race: 20
 International race in UK: 21
 long-distance journey from UK:
  17
 long-distance F in USA: 18
 major military operation: 19
 manned ascent in
  Belgium: 16
  Germany: 16
  Netherlands: 16
  Switzerland: 16
  USA: 16
 men carried in free F: 13
 military use in UK: 20
 military use outside Europe: 19
 national race in USA: 21
 non-stop F across USA: 22
 official race in UK: 20
 op use of international bomb-
  carrying: 21, 167
 over 100 000 ft altitude record:
  21, 22
 photographs from: 18
 public demonstration in UK: 13
 ratified altitude record: 20
 telegraph message sent from: 18
 UK woman to travel by in UK: 15
 use of man-carrying in war: 16
 woman aeronaut killed in flying
  accident: 17
 X-Atlantic crossing: 22
 X-Atlantic F attempt: 19
 X-Pacific crossing: 22
Balloon (gas): Greatest
 most famous crossing of North
  Sea: 24
Balloon (gas): Highest
 altitude attained by woman: 23
 manned altitude attained: 23
Balloon (gas): Longest
 current WDR: 24
 distance F by woman: 24
 duration by a woman: 24
Balloon (hot-air): First
 altitude record ratified by FAI: 23
 ascent by UK aeronaut: 14
 ascent of living creatures: 12
 ascent of one capable of lifting a
  man: 11
 balloon bombing raid: 17
 crossing of Alps: 22
 free F by a woman: 14
 known award for an aviation feat:
  12
 man carried aloft in: 12
 manned ascent in Italy: 13
 man to survive destruction of in
  F: 17
 men carried in free F: 13
 model demonstrated by
  Montgolfiers: 11
 public demonstration by

Montgolfiers: 12
 successful demonstration: 11
 unmanned exp in Germany: 13
 unmanned F in UK: 13
 X-Atlantic crossing: 22
Balloon (hot-air): Fastest
 manned ever flown: 23
Balloon (hot-air): Highest
 current WAR: 24
 current women's WAR: 23
Balloon (hot-air): Largest
 built by Montgolfiers: 23
 ever flown: 23
Balloon (hot-air): Longest
 distance F by: 24
 distance F by woman: 24
 duration by a woman: 24
 duration by manned: 24
Balloon (mixed): First
 aeronauts killed in: 15
Balloon (mixed): Highest
 current WAR: 24
 current WDR: 24
Balloon (mixed): Longest
 world duration: 24
Balloon (pressurized):
 current WAR: 24
 current WDR: 24
 current world duration record: 24
Barber, Horatio: 91
Barling, XNBL-1: 150
Barnard, Capt F. F.: 101
Barnes, Lt-Col W. F.: 176
Barreswil, M.: 19
Batson, Lt J. E. D.: 181
Batten, Jean: 108, 114, 125
Battle (see Fairey)
Baumgarten, Herr: 26
BE1 (see Farnborough)
BE2 (see Farnborough)
BE2c (see Royal Aircraft Factory)
BE2e (see Royal Aircraft Factory)
BE8 (see Royal Aircraft Factory)
Beamont, Wg Cdr R. P.: 177
Beardmore Wee Bee: 103
Béam: 150
Beauchamp-Proctor, Capt A. W.:
 226
Beaumont, Capt F.: 20
Beetham, Wg Cdr M. J.: 180
'Beethoven-Gerät': 165
Belfast (see Short)
Belgica: 20
Bell
 Airacomet: 165
 AH-1G HueyCobra: 55, 56, 57
 GAM-63 Rascal: 180
 JetRanger III: 57
 Model 47: 50
 Model 206L LongRanger II: 56,
  60
 Model 209 HueyCobra: 55
 X-1: 209, 211
 X-2: 216
 X-5: 214
 XV-3: 53, 54
Bell, Gordon: 139
Bellinger, Lt P. N. L.: 138, 209
Belphégor (see Aérocentre)
Belyaev, P.: 217
Bennett, Capt D. C. T.: 130, 163
Bennett, F.: 104
Bennett, J. G.: 20
Bensen B-8 Gyro-Copter: 62
Bensen B-8B Gyro-Boat: 54
Bentley, R. R.: 106
Berlin Airlift, start: 172
Berry, Capt A.: 67
Berry, J.: 21
Berry, Sqn Ldr J.: 199
Berson, Professor: 20
Beta: 28
Bettingham, Lt C. A.: 137
Beverley (see Blackburn)
Bf 109 (see Messerschmitt)
Biard, H.: 99
Bienvenu, M.: 41

Biggin, G.: 15
Birch, Lt W. C.: 142
Bishop, W. A.: 228, 229
Bismarck: 196
Black, T. C.: 113
Blackburn
  Beverley: 176
  Buccaneer: 181
  Roc: 158
  Skua: 156, 158
Bladud: 73
Blair, C.: 119
Blanchard, J.-P.: 14, 16, 17, 65
Blanchard, Mme.: 17
Blenheim (see Bristol)
Blériot, L.: 73, 81, 82, 83, 85, 136,
  208, 236
Blériot
  Type VI: 81
  VII: 81
  XI: 83, 85, 86
  XII: 84, 86
  XIII: 86
Blohm und Voss
  Bv 222 Wiking: 188
  Bv 238: 189
  Ha 139: 115
BN-2 Islander (see Britten-Norman)
Bodensee: 33
Boeing
  B-1: 100
  B-17 Flying Fortress: 116, 161,
    162, 166, 167
  B-29 Superfortress: 117, 167, 173,
    211, 212
  B-47 Stratojet: 176
  B-50: 173, 216
  B-52 Stratofortress: 178, 180, 182,
    183, 186, 191, 193, 194
  DB-47: 180
  E-3A Sentry: 185
  EC-135: 181
  GA-1: 149
  IM-99 Bomarc: 176
  KB-29: 176
  KC-135: 180, 181
  Model CL-4S: 96
  Model 200 Monomail: 108, 109
  Model 247: 111
  Model 307 Stratoliner: 116
  Model 314: 116
  Model 367-80: 119, 120
  Model 707: 119, 120, 121, 122,
    125, 131
  Model 727: 8, 124, 126, 131
  Model 737: 8, 131
  Model 747: 8, 122, 123, 131, 220
  P-26: 152
  Stratocruiser: 121
  Y1B-9A: 153
Boeing Air Transport: 108
Boeing Vertol HH-46 Sea Knight:
  225
Boelcke, Haupt O.: 144, 224, 226
Bogan, B.: 22
Bolt, Maj J.: 231
Bong, Maj R. I.: 230, 231
Bonney, L.: 114
Boothman, Flt Lt J. N.: 152
Bordelon, Lt G. P.: 225, 231
Borelli, G.: 74
Borgward Kolibri 1: 54
Borman, F.: 218
Borton, Brig-Gen A. E.: 95
Bossoutrot, L.: 96, 97
Boulet, J.: 62
Boulton Paul
  Defiant: 186
  Overstrand: 154
  P.108 Balliol: 172
Bourgeois, D.: 13
Bournemouth: 38
Bowser, Lt Cdr R. S.: 39
Boyce, Flt Lt: 150
BR (see Fiat)
Brabazon I (see Bristol)
Brancker, Maj-Gen Sir S.: 36

Brand, Sqn Ldr C. Q.: 100
Brand, V.: 220
Brandt, Deck Off P.: 145
Brandon, 2nd Lt: 32
Branson, R.: 7, 22
Breguet, L.: 45, 131
Breguet
  XIX: 106
  19: 149
  Integral: 216
Breguet-Richet helicopter: 42
Brennan, L.: 43
Brewer, G.: 83
Brewster F2A Buffalo: 156, 157
Briggs, Sqn Cdr E. F.: 141
Bright, Capt W. J.: 124
Brink, H.: 24
Bristol
  Blenheim: 73, 113, 157, 158
  Brabazon I: 221
  Britannia: 120
  F2B Fighter: 148, 149, 192
  Freighter: 117
  Scout: 144
  Sycamore: 50
  Type 142: 73, 113
  Type 173: 52
Britannia (see Bristol)
British Aerospace
  146 CC. Mk 2: 186
  Hawk: 189
  Jetstream 31: 189
  Sea Harrier: 184, 193
British Airways: 114, 123, 124, 186
British Army Aeroplane No. 1: 86,
  134
British European Airways: 50, 51,
  119
British Marine Air Navigation Co:
  103
British Overseas Airways
  Corporation (BOAC): 116,
  119, 120
Britten-Norman BN-2 Islander: 124
Broadwick, G.: 67
Brock, W. L.: 95
Brookins, W.: 109
Brown, Capt A. R.: 227
Brown, J.: 220
Brown Jr, Lt R. J.: 174
Brown, Lt A. W.: 98, 123
Brown, Lt Cdr E. M.: 170
Brown, Mr: 7
BS1 (see Farnborough)
Buccaneer (see Blackburn)
Burattini, T. L.: 76
Butler, F. H.: 20, 83
Buxton, Capt F. L.: 124
Bv 222 Wiking (see Blohm und
  Voss)
Bv 238 (see Blohm und Voss)
Byrd, Lt Cdr R. E.: 104, 108

C

CI (see Hansa-Brandenburg)
CV (see DFW)
CV (see Fokker)
C-1 (see Kawasaki)
C-2 (see Fokker)
C.4 (see Cierva)
C-5 Galaxy (see Lockheed)
C.6 (see Cierva)
C.8L (see Cierva)
C11 (see LVG)
C.30A (see Cierva)
C-47 (see Douglas)
C-124 Globemaster II (see Douglas)
C-130 Hercules (see Lockheed)
C.160 (see Transall)
C200 Saetta (see Macchi)
Ca 2 (see Caproni)
Ca 161 (see Caproni)
Cabral, Capt S.: 101
Calder, Sqn Ldr C. C.: 168
Camel (see Sopwith)
Camerman, Lt: 135

Cameron, Capt J.: 50
Cameron, D.: 22, 24
Camm, S.: 103, 152
Campbell, Lt D.: 148, 229
Canadair CL-44: 121
Canadian Pacific Airlines: 119
Canberra (see English Electric)
Candelaria, Teniente L. C.: 95
Canning, C.: 124
Caplan, Ms: 24
Capper, Col J. C.: 20, 27
Capper, Mrs J. C.: 20
Caproni Ca 2: 143
Caproni Ca 161: 8, 129
Carmichael, Lt P.: 199
Carr, R. H.: 67
Carver, Lt L. V.: 159
Castoldi, Dr M.: 156
'Catafighter' scheme: 159, 160
Cathedral (see Cody)
Caudron G IV: 226
Cavallo, T.: 11
Cavendish, H.: 9, 11
Cayley, Sir G.: 41, 65, 66, 74, 76
C-Class (see Short)
Celebi, H.: 65
Centre NC 223.4: 159
Cernan, E.: 215
Césari, Lt: 140
Ceskoslovenske Statni Aerolinie:
  102
Cessna 180: 121
Cessna Turbo Centurion: 125
CG-4 (see Waco)
CH-53E Super Stallion (see
  Sikorsky)
Chambers, Capt W. I.: 138
Chandler, R. J.: 130
Chandler, Capt C. de F.: 137
Chanute, O.: 71, 72
Chapman, V. E.: 144
Charabanc (see Grahame-White)
Charles, J. A. C.: 12, 13
Chavez, G.: 90
Chisholm, J.: 125
Chisov, Lt I. M.: 227
Church, E.: 108, 109
Churchill, Rt Hon W. S.: 116
Cierva
  C.4: 44
  C.6C: 44
  C.6D: 44
  C.8L: 44
  C.30A: 44
City of Cardiff: 28
CL-44 (see Canadair)
Clark, Capt A. C.: 182
Clark, J.: 92
Clark, R.: 24
Clydesdale, Marquess of: 111
Cobham, A.: 104, 116
Coburn, J. W.: 57, 60
Cochran, J.: 119
Cocking, R.: 17, 63, 65
Cody, S. F.: 27, 66, 67, 86, 93, 134,
  137
Cody *Cathedral*: 137
Coiffard, Sous-Lt M.: 226
Collett, Flt Lt: 140
Collins, M.: 218, 223
Collishaw, R.: 229
Colmore, Lt G. C.: 135
Columbia: 220
Comanche 260 (see Piper)
Combe, Flt Lt A. N.: 192
Comet (see de Havilland)
Concorde (see Aérospatiale/BAC)
Coney, Lt W. D.: 101
Conran, Capt E. L.: 142
Consolidated
  B-24 Liberator: 167, 198, 199
  NY-2: 152
  PBY Catalina: 193
Constellation (see Lockheed)
Convair
  B-36: 189, 212, 215, 216

B-58 Hustler: 179, 181
CV-340: 120
F-102 Delta Dagger: 178
Sea Dart: 213
XFY-1: 214
Cook, Cadet E. R.: 180
Cook, D.: 125
Cook, Miss E. M.: 88
Coppens, W.: 226
Cordner, Mr: 66
Cornu, P.: 42
Corporal (see Firestone)
Costes, Capt D.: 106
Coutelle, Capt: 16
Coutinho, Capt G.: 101
Cover, C. A.: 114
Cowan, R.: 20
Coxwell, H. T.: 17, 19
C.R.1 (see Fiat)
Crippen, R.: 220
Crissy, Lt M. S.: 135
Crocco, G. A.: 42
Crooks, W. G.: 130
Crosbie, R.: 15
Crosby, H.: 210
Croy, Lt M.: 165
Crusader: 19
Cub (see Piper)
Cuckoo (see Sopwith)
Culley, Flt Sub-Lt S.: 148
Cunningham, Lt R.: 225
Curtiss, G. H.: 82, 130, 135, 136
Curtiss
  A-1: 136
  AB: 138
  AB-2: 143, 145
  F9C Sparrowhawk: 37
  F9C-2 Sparrowhawk: 37
  Jenny: 34, 99
  JN-4: 95
  Model F: 209
  SBC Helldiver: 153
  SOC Seagull: 196
CV-340 (see Convair)
Cygnet (see Hawker)

D

D.I (see A.E.G.)
D.I (see Albatros)
D.II (see Albatros)
D.III (see Albatros)
D.IIIa (see Pfalz)
D.V (see Albatros)
D.VI (see Siemens-Schuckert)
D.VII (see Fokker)
D.VIII (see Fokker)
D.XXI (see Fokker)
D500 (see Dewoitine)
Dacre, Flt Lt G. B.: 143
Daily Mail prizes: 81, 84, 86, 88, 89,
  102
Daily Mail Transatlantic Air Race:
  123, 124
Daimler Airways: 101, 102, 103
Dakota (see Douglas)
d'Arlandes, Marquis: 13
Dassault
  MD.450 Ouragan: 172
  MD.452 Mystère: 174
  Mirage III: 180
  Mirage 2000: 185, 186
  Mirage G: 218
Davey, C.: 24
da Vinci, L.: 40, 41, 64, 74
Da Vinci 2: 7, 58
Davis, Lt Cdr B: 123
Davis, Ms C.: 24
Davis Jr, Maj G. A.: 231
Dawes, Capt G. W. P.: 223
Dayton-Wright RB Racer: 100
DB-3 (see Ilyushin)
DB-47 (see Boeing)
DC-1 (see Douglas)
DC-2 (see Douglas)
DC-3 (see Douglas)
DC-4 (see Douglas)

DC-6B (see Douglas)
DC-8 (see Douglas)
Dean, Flg Off: 165
DeBellevue, Lt C.: 225
de Caxias, Marquis: 19
Defiant (see Boulton Paul)
Defries, C.: 87
Degen, J.: 41
de Havilland, Geoffrey: 136
de Havilland
    Comet: 119, 120, 121, 125, 179,
        182, 211
    DH4: 96, 98, 101, 147, 150, 190,
        195, 209
    DH6: 96
    DH9: 97, 101, 149, 195
    DH16: 96, 99, 131
    DH18: 101
    DH34: 103
    DH50: 104, 106
    DH60 Moth: 103, 105, 108, 112,
        114
    DH66 Hercules: 107
    DH80 Puss Moth: 109, 110, 111
    DH88 Comet: 113
    DH106 Comet 1: 117, 118, 119,
        125
    DH108: 211
    Dragon: 113
    Hornet: 191
    Mosquito: 191, 193
    Sea Hornet: 168
    Sea Mosquito: 164
    Sea Venom: 177
    Vampire: 170, 172, 175, 211
de Havilland Canada
    DHC-7 Dash 7: 187
    XC-8A Buffalo: 219
de la Cierva, J.: 44
de la Ferté, Capt P. J.: 140
Delag: 28, 30, 33
Delagrange, L.: 82, 83, 86, 130
de la Loubères, M.: 65
de la Meurthe, H. D.: 82
de Lana-Terzi, F.: 9, 11
de Laroche, Mme la Baronne: 88
de Louvrie, C.: 77
Delta 2 (see Fairey)
Delta Air Lines: 102
Delta Air Service: 102
de Montalembert, Countess: 14
de Montalembert, Marchioness: 14
Demuyter, Lt E.: 20
Denny helicopter: 43
de Pateras Pescara, Marquis: 44
de Podenas, Countess: 14
Derry, J.: 118
de Rozier, F. P.: 12, 13, 15, 23
Destroyer EFB 1 (see Vickers)
Deutsche Lufthansa: 115, 120
Deutsche Luft-Reederei: 96, 101
Deutschland: 26
Devyatayev, Lt M.: 230
Dewoitine D500: 153
DFS 194: 210
DFW CV: 145
DH2 (see Airco)
DH4 (see de Havilland)
DH6 (see de Havilland)
DH9 (see de Havilland)
DH16 (see de Havilland)
DH18 (see de Havilland)
DH34 (see de Havilland)
DH50 (see de Havilland)
DH60 Moth (see de Havilland)
DH66 Hercules (see de Havilland)
DH88 Comet (see de Havilland)
DH106 Comet 1 (see de Havilland)
DH108 (see de Havilland)
DHC-7 Dash 7 (see de Havilland
    Canada)
di Bernardi, Maj M.: 150
Dirigible
    Early dem of controlled F in: 26
    Fastest in the world: 36

Dirigible: First
    airmail carried in Germany by: 29
    air raid on London 1WW: 31
    all-metal: 26
    attempt to cross Atlantic by: 29
    bought for military service: 27
    built and F by Briton: 27
    built in UK post-2WW: 38
    commercial airline: 28
    dem of parasite fighter concept:
        34
    equipped with a ballonet: 25
    fighter-carrying for op use: 37
    floating hangar for: 26
    flown Europe–UK: 28
    flown London–Paris: 28
    flown UK–France: 28
    F of Zeppelin LZ 1: 26
    for Austrian Army: 28
    for French Navy: 31
    for Italian Army: 28
    for Japanese Army: 28
    for Japanese Navy: 34
    for Russian Army: 28
    for UK Army: 27
    for UK ASW use: 31
    for US Navy: 32
    fully-controllable, powered: 26
    German inflated with helium: 38
    German to be brought down on
        UK soil: 32, 144
    great German pioneer of: 26
    helium-filled rigid in US service:
        34
    International Airship Exhibition:
        28
    international commercial service
        by: 30
    military for Spain: 28
    military Zeppelin (LZ 3): 27
    multiple death accident: 28
    non-rigid fuelled with blaugas: 36
    non-rigid helium-filled: 34
    non-rigid to be mast-moored: 28
    of hot-air configuration: 38
    over North Pole: 35
    partially successful attack on a
        submarine: 31
    people killed in accident: 26
    post-1WW commercial F: 33
    powered & manned: 26
    powered by internal combustion
        engine: 25
    powered by electric motor: 26
    practical: 27
    published design for: 25
    raid by on UK: 30
    received by US as German war
        reparations: 34
    rigid for German Navy: 29
    rigid for US Navy: 34
    rigid lost by German Navy: 29
    rigid with wooden structure: 28
    RTW flight: 36
    series-built for US Navy: 32
    shot down by French infantry
        1WW: 30
    successful of US Navy: 33
    successful 'hook-on' parasite exp:
        34
    successful mission by German
        1WW: 30
    successful use of petrol engine in:
        26
    two-way crossing of Atlantic by
        any aircraft: 33
    UK rigid: 29
    UK with wireless telegraphy: 28
    used by commercial airline: 28
    used in French Army
        manoeuvres: 28
    used in parasite A exp: 27
    used politically: 28
    with volume exceeding one
        million cubic feet: 30
    with volume exceeding 2.5
        million cubic feet: 33

X-Atlantic crossing UK–USA: 33
Zeppelin des to attack UK: 30
Zeppelin destroyed in bad
    weather: 27
Zeppelin to be brought down by
    air attack: 31
Zeppelin to be destroyed over
    UK: 31, 32
Zeppelin to be set on fire in an
    attack: 31
Zeppelin with cruciform tail: 30
Dirigible: Greatest
    captain: 39
    designer: 39
    duration F of mid-1920s: 35
    German one-day losses: 33
    number of persons carried X-
        Atlantic by: 39
    number of persons carried by: 37,
        39
    number of rigids operated: 39
Dirigible: Largest
    bomb of 1914 dropped by: 38
    built in USA: 38
    completed before 1WW: 30
    ever built: 38
    non-rigid built: 38
    number built by one company: 38
Dirigible: Last
    commercial developed in UK: 36
    German attack on UK causing
        death & injury: 33
    major disaster to: 37
    to serve with French Navy: 37
Dirigible: Longest
    distance flown by rigid: 33
    duration by non-rigid: 39
    duration on a mission without
        refuelling: 39
    FAI-accredited straight-line
        distance record: 39
Dittmar, H.: 164, 210
Dixmude: 35
Doblhoff/WMF 342: 48
Dobrolet: 102
Do 11 (see Dornier)
Do 17 (see Dornier)
Do 18 (see Dornier)
Do 217 (see Dornier)
Do 335 Pfeil (see Dornier)
Donaldson, Gp Capt E. M.: 170
Doolittle, Lt J. H.: 101, 151, 162
Doran, Flt Lt K. C.: 158, 225
Dorand, R.: 45
Dornier
    Do X: 127
    Do 11: 153
    Do 17: 156, 158
    Do 18: 158
    Do 217: 164
    Do 335 Pfeil: 191
    Komet: 101
    Wal: 104, 108
Double Eagle II: 10, 22
Double Eagle V: 10, 22, 24
Douglas
    A3D Skywarrior: 178, 194
    A-4: 182
    AD-1 Skyraider: 168, 175
    B-26: 173
    C-47: 172
    C-124 Globemaster II: 176
    Dakota: 69
    DC-1: 111, 114
    DC-2: 111, 113, 114
    DC-3: 111, 114, 119, 121
    DC-4: 158
    DC-6B: 119
    DC-8: 131
    DWC: 103
    F3D-2 Skynight: 176
    R4D: 179
    Skyrocket: 212
    TBD Devastator: 154, 162
    X-3: 214
Do X (see Dornier)
Doyle, T.: 60

Dr I (see Fokker)
Dragon (see de Havilland)
Dragonfly (see Westland/Sikorsky)
Driscoll, Lt (Jg) W.: 225
Dryden, H. L.: 168
Dufek, Rear Adm G. L.: 179
Duigan, J. R.: 89
Duke, R.: 101
Duncan, H.: 70
Dunning, Sqn Ldr E. H.: 145, 146,
    147
Dupuy-de-Lôme: 30
Duroug, J.: 19
du Temple de la Croix, F.: 77
DWC (see Douglas)

E

E14Y1 Glen (see Yokosuka)
E.28/39 (see Gloster)
EA-6B Prowler (see Grumman)
Earhart, A.: 110
Eastern Air Lines: 46
EC-135 (see Boeing)
Eckener, Dr H.: 36, 39
Edgar, L. E.: 71
Edmonds, Ft Cdr C. H.: 142, 143
Effimov, M.: 88
Efremov, E.: 61
Egginton, T.: 60
Eielson, Lt C. B.: 106
Eindecker E.I (see Fokker)
Eindecker E.III (see Fokker)
Ellehammer, J. C. H.: 43, 80, 82
Elliott, A. B.: 104
Ellsworth, L.: 35
Ellyson, Lt T.: 138
Ely, E. B.: 135, 224
EMB-326 Xavante (see EMBRAER)
EMBRAER EMB-326 Xavante: 183
Emmott, B. W. G.: 104
Endeavour: 24
England–Australia Commemorative
    Air Race: 124
Englehardt, Capt: 88
English Electric
    Canberra: 70, 174, 191
    Lightning: 177, 215
    P1: 214
    Wren: 102
Enterprise: 18
Entreprenant: 16
Éole: 78
Erblön, O.: 28
Esmonde, Lt Cdr E.: 230
Esnault-Pelterie, R.: 80
España: 28
Etrich, I.: 84
Etrich Taube: 84, 194
Euler, A.: 135
Everett, Lt R. W. H.: 159
Ewen, Mr W. H.: 87

F

F.VII/3m (see Fokker)
F2A Buffalo (see Brewster)
F2B Fighter (see Bristol)
F2H-1 Banshee (see McDonnell)
F3D-2 Skynight (see Douglas)
F-4 Phantom II (see McDonnell
    Douglas)
F4U Corsair (see Vought)
F6F Hellcat (see Grumman)
F7F-1 Tigercat (see Grumman)
F-8 Crusader (see Vought)
F8U Crusader (see Ling-Temco-
    Vought)
F9C Sparrowhawk (see Curtiss)
F9C-2 Sparrowhawk (see Curtiss)
F9F Panther (see Grumman)
F11F Tiger (see Grumman)
F13 (see Junkers)
F-14 Tomcat (see Grumman)
F-15 Eagle (see McDonnell
    Douglas)

F-16 Fighting Falcon (see General Dynamics)
F60 Goliath (see Farman)
F-82 Twin Mustang (see North American)
F-84 Thunderjet (see Republic)
F-86 Sabre (see North American)
F-89 Scorpion (see Northrop)
F-94 Starfire (see Lockheed)
F-100 Super Sabre (see North American)
F-102 Delta Dagger (see Convair)
F-104 Starfighter (see Lockheed)
F-105 Thunderchief (see Republic)
F-111 (see General Dynamics)
F221 (see Farman)
F/A-18 Hornet (see McDonnell Douglas)
Fa 223 (see Focke-Achgelis)
Fa 226 Hornisse (see Focke-Achgelis)
Fa 330 (see Focke-Achgelis)
Fabre, H.: 88
Fairchild A-10A Thunderbolt II: 184
Fairey
  IIIC: 97, 101
  IIID: 101
  IIIF: 195
  Battle: 158
  Delta 2: 209, 215
  Fox: 190
  Fulmar: 159
  Gannet: 173
  Hendon: 152
  Long Range Monoplane: 107, 108
  Rotodyne: 8, 54, 62, 209
  Swordfish: 158, 196, 230
Falklands War: 184, 185
Farban, M. F.: 17
Farman, H.: 81, 82, 83, 130
Farman F60 Goliath: 96, 101
Farman F221: 187
Farman brothers: 96, 97
Farnborough
  BE1: 136, 137
  BE2: 137, 139, 140, 142
  BS1: 136
  FB5 Gunbus (see Vickers)
  FD-1 (FH-1) Phantom (see McDonnell)
  FE2b (see Royal Aircraft Factory)
Fedotov, A.: 192
Feoktistov, K.: 217
Féquant, Lt: 135
Ferber, Capt: 86
Ferguson, H. G.: 87
Ferry, R. G.: 32
FF-1 (see Grumman)
Fiat BR: 99
Fiat C.R.1: 150
Fickel, Lt J. E.: 135
Fifield, Sqn Ldr J. S.: 69, 178
Filomechkina: 70
Finnair: 124
Finter, 1st Lt C. V.: 35
Firestone Corporal: 175
First
  4000 lb bomb used on ops by RAF: 160
  aerial map of US Army: 138
  airborne op UK paratroops 2WW: 160
  airforce op exclusively with all-metal mono fighters: 151
  air ops by Royal Navy airmen 1WW: 139
  airport on Falklands for wide-body A: 186
  Air Service of US Army formed: 138
  American astronaut in Earth orbit: 217
  American in space: 217
  apprentice of aircraft manufacturing company: 85
  Aviation Certificate awarded by

Royal Aero Club: 88
ballistic missile in US service: 175
country attacked by ballistic rockets: 165, 166
customs examination of air pass: 97
dem of radar signatures: 149
electro-mechanical F simulator: 151
exp space bomb: 218
extensive use of air-to-air rockets against A: 167
F of unpowered lifting-body: 218
French airmen killed on active service: 138
French bomber Groupe of 1WW: 140
full-time air correspondent: 81
German Army rocket: 153
human to land on Moon: 218
International Aviation Meeting: 86
Japanese naval vessel to support seaplanes: 140
launch of Soviet ballistic missile: 171, 172
London airport with outward customs clearance: 99
Luftwaffe long-range anti-shipping squadron: 158
major daylight attack on Berlin by USAAF: 164
major warship sunk by air-launched missile: 164
man in space: 183, 216, 222
manned F around the Moon: 218
manned spacecraft in Moon orbit: 218
manoeuvred space rendezvous: 218
move to introduce UK Shadow Factories: 155, 156
multi-crew space mission: 217
op atomic bombs: 168
op use of napalm: 165
pilotless long-range ground-to-air interceptor: 176
powered flight of SV-5P lifting-body: 219
prepared aerodrome in UK: 83
radio-guided flying-bomb: 144
regular use of Croydon as London's air terminal: 101
reusable spacecraft: 220
spacecraft docking in space: 218
spacecraft fatality: 218
spacewalk (EVA): 217
stage of Soviet involvement in Afghanistan: 184
steps to creation of post-2WW Luftwaffe: 179
successful use of Walleye guided bomb: 182
tests by Wright brothers of wing warping: 67
true stand-off bomb: 180
two post-2WW WSRs: 169
UK airmen killed on active service 1WW: 139
UK atomic bomb dropped: 179
UK combined op against Europe 2WW: 161
UK hardened A shelters: 185
UK hydrogen bomb dropped: 180
UK squadron for night bombing: 146
US action leading to involvement in Vietnam War: 181
US airborne assault in Vietnam: 182
US air-to-surface radar-guided missile: 168
US intercontinental missile: 180
US multi-crew space mission: 218
US anti-aircraft SAM: 169
US spacewalk (EVA): 218
USAF air-to-air guided missile: 178

USAF surface-to-surface missile: 175
use of electric beacons for night flying: 102
USMC air op in Korea: 174
US/Soviet combined space mission: 219, 220
wind tunnel of 3000 mph capability: 172
woman in space: 217
Fiske, Pil Off M. L.: 159
Fitzmaurice, Capt J.: 106
Fl 282 Kolibri (see Flettner)
Flash (see Pegasus)
Flessebles: 23
Flettner Fl 282 Kolibri: 47
Fleurant, M.: 14
Flyer (see Wright)
Flyer II (see Wright)
Flyer III (see Wright)
Flynn, Rev J.: 106
Focke, Prof H.: 45, 54
Focke-Achgelis
  Fa 223: 46, 49, 50
  Fa 226 Hornisse: 46
  Fa 330: 47
Focke-Wulf
  Fw 61: 45, 46
  Fw 190: 157, 165
  Fw 200 Condor: 116, 158, 159
Fokker
  CV: 195
  C-2: 106
  D.VII: 195, 226
  D.VIII: 190
  D.XXI: 158, 163, 193
  Dr I: 144, 147, 227
  Eindecker E.I: 142, 224
  Eindecker E.III: 143
  F.VII/3m: 104, 106, 107, 131
  M5K: 142
  M8: 142, 224
  T-2: 102
Fomitcheva, E.: 70
Fonck, Capt R. P.: 226
Fontana, J.: 77
Ford, H.: 103
Ford 4-AT Trimotor: 104, 108
Formation dates of Air Arms: 200-7
Foucault: 21
Fournier, R.: 85
Fox (see Fairey)
Franceschi, P.: 126
Franco, Commandante: 104
Frantisek, Sgt J.: 226
Frantz, Sgt J.: 140
Frasee, Lt C.: 173
Freedom 7: 217
Freighter (see Bristol)
Fresson, E. E.: 113
Friendship 7: 217
Frohwein, Lt: 145
Fruin, Lt J. L.: 173
Fuji T-1: 186
Fulmar (see Fairey)
Furnas, C. W.: 82
Fury I (see Hawker)
Fw 61 (see Focke-Wulf)
Fw 190 (see Focke-Wulf)
Fw 200 Condor (see Focke-Wulf)

G

G IV (see Caudron)
G4M (see Mitsubishi)
G5N Shinzan (see Nakajima)
G 23 (see Junkers)
G-102 (see Grob)
GA-1 (see Boeing)
Gagarin, Flt Maj Y. A.: 183, 216
Gager, O. A.: 18
Gakkel, Yakov M.: 83
Gakkel-3: 83
Galitsky, B.: 60
Gallagher, Capt J.: 173
GAM-63 Rascal (see Bell)
Gamecock (see Gloster)

Gamma: 28
Gannet (see Fairey)
GAR-1 Falcon (see Hughes)
Garnerin, A. J.: 63, 65
Garros, R.: 93, 94, 142, 143
Garstin, Sqn Ldr J. H.: 192
Gatty, H.: 108
Gaudron, A. F.: 24
Gauntlet (see Gloster)
Gavotti, Lt G.: 136
Gayford, Sqn Ldr O. R.: 107
Gee Bee Super Sportster: 129
Gelber Hund: 29
Gellatly, Sqn Ldr W. R.: 62
Gemini 3: 218
Gemini 4: 218
Gemini 6: 218
Gemini 7: 218
Gemini 8: 218
General Aircraft Hamilcar: 68
General Dynamics F-16 Fighting Falcon: 183, 184, 186
General Dynamics F-111: 181
Gerfaut (see Nord)
Gerli, A.: 13
Gerli, C.: 13
Geysendorffer, Capt G. J.: 106
'Giant Voice' competition: 186
Giffard, H.: 25
Gilmore, L.: 74
Gladiator (see Gloster)
Glenn, Lt Col J. H.: 217
Glider: First
  competition for: 69
  cross-Channel F by: 69
  F by Wright brothers: 67
  F exceeding 1 hr duration: 69
  F from balloon: 67
  known model representing flying machine: 64
  man to be carried aloft in: 66
  man to identify/record parameters of heavier-than-air F: 65, 76
  person carried aloft in: 65, 66
  recorded case of structural failure in F: 64
  rotary man-carrying as pilot escape system: 69
  short free-F in one of bird form: 66
  sustained F by: 65
  to be towed across North Atlantic: 69
  'tower-jumper' to achieve gliding F: 64
  UK National Hang-Gliding Championships: 69
Glider: Greatest
  altitude by woman (single-seat): 70
  altitude by woman (two-seat): 70
  distance record by hang-glider: 71
  height record (single-seat): 71
  height record (two-seat): 71
  straight-line distance (single-seat): 70
  straight-line distance (two-seat): 70
Glider: Largest
  of 2WW: 68
Glider: Most
  outstanding pioneers of: 71
Gloster
  E.28/39: 208, 209
  Gamecock: 150
  Gauntlet: 113, 151
  Gladiator: 196
  Grebe: 150
  Javelin: 175, 176
  Meteor: 69, 116, 165, 169, 170, 171, 178
  Sea Gladiator: 196
Gneisenau: 157, 230
Gnu (see Sopwith)
Gobeil, Sqn Ldr F.: 69
Godard, E.: 19
Godard, L.: 17

Golubev, I. N.: 78
Gontermann, Leut H.: 226
Gooden, F. W.: 67
Goodlin, C.: 211
Gorrell, F.: 22
Gossamer Albatross: 220, 221
Gossamer Condor: 220
Gossamer Penguin: 220
Gotha heavy bomber: 146, 147
Goupy, A.: 83
Goupy I: 83
Goupy II: 83
Grade, H.: 82, 83
Graf Zeppelin: 36, 39
Graf Zeppelin II: 38
Graham, R.: 43
Grahame-White, C.: 88, 89
Grahame-White Charabanc: 67
Gran, T.: 95
Grands Express Aériens: 101
Gray, Lt R. H.: 227
Great air fighters of 1WW: 231, 232
Great air fighters of 2WW: 234
Greatest fall without parachute &
  survival: 228
Greatest fall without parachute &
  survival 2WW: 227
Great Nassau Balloon: 17, 63, 65
Grebe (see Gloster)
Green, C.: 17
Griffin, Lt V. C.: 150
Griffiths-Jones, Sqn Ldr: 160
Griffon (see Nord)
Grimley, C.: 20
Grissom, V.: 217, 218
Grob Astir CS: 70
Grob G-102: 71
Grosse, H. W.: 70
Grosvenor Challenge Cup: 102
Grover, Lt G. E.: 20
Grumman
  A-6 Intruder: 182
  EA-6B Prowler: 200
  F6F Hellcat: 199
  F7F-1 Tigercat: 164
  F9F Panther: 173
  F11F Tiger: 177
  F-14 Tomcat: 184
  FF-1: 153
  Gulfstream II: 122
  Gulfstream III: 129
  Martlet: 159
  TBF Avenger: 161, 164
Guidoni, Capt: 135
Guille, C.: 65
Gulfstream II (see Grumman)
Gulfstream III (see Grumman)
Gulf War, start of: 184
Gull (see Percival)
Gusmao, B. L. de: 9, 11
Guynemer, Capt G. M. L. J.: 228
G. W. Parke Custis: 19
Gyrodyne QH-50A: 55
Gyroplane Laboratoire: 45

H

H4 (see Hughes)
H-21 Workhorse (see Piasecki)
H-21C (see Vertol)
Ha 139 (see Blohm und Voss)
Hafner, R.: 69
Hahn, Dipl Ing M.: 209
Halifax (see Handley Page)
Hamel, G.: 87, 91, 93
Hamilcar (see General Aircraft)
Hampden (see Handley Page)
Handley Page
  Halifax: 68, 162
  Hampden: 159, 225
  Heyford: 151
  Hinadai: 151
  HP45: 114
  O/10: 100
  O/400: 95, 97, 101, 195
  Victor: 176
  W8b: 103

Handley Page Air Transport: 97, 99,
  100, 103
Haney, R.: 71
Han Hsin, Gen: 73, 132
Hänlein, P.: 26
Hanlon, Lt D. R.: 142
Hansa: 30
Hansa-Brandenburg C.I: 95
Harding Jr, Lt J.: 103
Hargrave, L.: 63, 66
Harper, H.: 81
Harris, Air Cdre A. H.: 157
Harris, Lt H. R.: 69
Harris, R. R.: 71
Hartmann, Maj E.: 230
Harvey, 1st Off I.: 130
Harvey-Kelly, Lt H. D.: 139, 140
Hastings, Col: 15, 16
Hawk (see British Aerospace)
Hawker, H.: 94
Hawker
  Cygnet: 103
  Fury I: 152
  Hunter: 178, 199
  Hurricane: 155, 158, 230
  Sea Fury: 199
  Sea Hurricane: 159
  Typhoon: 161
Hawker-Siddeley
  AV-8 Harrier: 183, 184
  Harrier: 182, 193, 209, 216
  Nimrod: 182, 183
  P1127 Kestrel: 216
  Trident I: 124
Hayser, Maj S.: 181
He 51 (see Heinkel)
He 111 (see Heinkel)
He 111Z (see Heinkel)
He 118 (see Heinkel)
He 162 Salamander (see Heinkel)
He 176 (see Heinkel)
He 178 (see Heinkel)
He 219 (see Heinkel)
He 280 (see Heinkel)
Heath, Lady: 106
Hegenberger, Lt A. F.: 106, 152
Heinkel, E.: 209
Heinkel
  He 51: 153
  He 111: 156, 158, 230
  He 111Z: 199
  He 118: 210
  He 162 Salamander: 193, 194
  He 176: 210
  He 178: 210
  He 219: 164, 171
  He 280: 160
Helicopter (see Fairey)
Hendon (see Handley Page)
Henson, W. S.: 76
Herndon Jr, H.: 109
Herring, A.: 134
Hervé, Capt: 138
Hewitt-Sperry flying-bomb: 144, 145
Hewlett, Mrs H. B.: 91
Heyford (see Handley Page)
HH-3 (see Sikorsky)
HH-46 Sea Knight (see Boeing
  Vertol)
Hicks, Lt G. R.: 98
Hicks, Sgt L.: 70
Hiller HJ-1 Hornet: 50, 51
Hiller XH-44: 49
Hinadai (see Handley Page)
Hindenburg: 37, 38, 39
Hinkler, Sqn Ldr H. J. L.: 106
Hiryu: 162, 163
Hitchcock, Postmaster-Gen: 91
Hitler, A.: 158
HJ-1 Hornet (see Hiller)
HL-10 (see Northrop/NASA)
HMS *Africa*: 136
HMS *Argus*: 145
HMS *Ark Royal*: 142, 158, 170, 182,
  216
HMS *Ben-My-Chree*: 142, 143

HMS *Egret*: 164
HMS *Engadine*: 144
HMS *Foyle Bank*: 225
HMS *Furious*: 145, 146, 147, 150,
  159
HMS *Hibernia*: 137
HMS *Hermes*: 170, 184, 185
HMS *Implacable*: 168
HMS *Indefatigable*: 168
HMS *Invincible*: 184, 185
HMS *Maplin*: 159
HMS *Ocean*: 170
HMS *Redoubt*: 148
HMS *Victorious*: 192
'Hokum' (see Kamov)
Holcombe, Capt K. E.: 182
Holland, R.: 17
Holloway, Aircraftsman V.: 225
Hooke, Robert: 76
Hopkins, Lt-Col J. R.: 182
Hornet (see de Havilland)
Horsa (see Airspeed)
Hosho: 149, 150, 156
Hotchkiss, 2nd Lt E.: 137
Howell, N.: 130
HP45 (see Handley Page)
HPA Toucan: 219
HRP-1 (see Piasecki)
HTK-1 (see Kaman)
Huber, D.: 70
Hubbard, Wg Cdr: 180
Hubbard Air Service: 96
Hudson (see Lockheed)
Hudson, Lt W.: 173
Huff-Daland/Keystone B-3A: 195,
  196
Hughes, H.: 128, 221
Hughes
  GAR-1 Falcon: 178
  H4: 128, 214, 220, 221
  OH-6A: 62
  XH-17: 58
Hunt, Cdr J. R.: 39
Hunter (see Hawker)
Hurricane (see Hawker)
Hydravion: 88
Hydrogen
  first dem of lifting properties: 11
  first isolated: 11
  first use of name: 16

I

I-1 (see Polikarpov)
I-15 (see Polikarpov)
I-16 (see Polikarpov)
Ibis: 28
Il-22 (see Ilyushin)
Il-86 (see Ilyushin)
Ilya Mouromets (see Sikorsky)
Ilyushin
  DB-3: 163
  Il-22: 171
  Il-86: 124, 125
IM-99 Bomarc (see Boeing)
Immelmann, Leut M.: 142, 224
Imperial Airways: 102, 107, 108,
  113, 114, 115
Indeev, L. A.: 60
Indian National Airways: 112
Indian Trans-Continental Airways:
  113
Inouye, Vice-Adm S.: 162
Instone Air Lines: 103
Integral (see Breguet)
Intrepid: 18
Irvin, Capt W. W.: 180
Irvine, L. I.: 67
Italia: 164
Italia: 35

J

J1 (see Junkers)
J7W Shinden (see Kyushu)
J-29 (see Saab)
Jabara, Capt J.: 225

Jackintell, S.: 70
Jahnow, Oberleut R.: 139
James, J. H.: 102
Janello, G.: 99
Jannus, A.: 67, 95
Janusz, M.: 21
Japanese National Volunteer
  Combat Force: 133
Jatho, K.: 74, 75
Javelin (see Gloster)
Jefferson, T.: 16
Jeffries, Dr J.: 14
Jenkins, Flt Lt N. H.: 107
Jenny (see Curtiss)
Jensen, V.: 130
JetRanger III (see Bell)
JetStar (see Lockheed)
Jetstream 31 (see British Aerospace)
JN-4 (see Curtiss)
Johnson, A.: 7, 108, 109
Johnson, A. M. ('Tex'): 194
Johnson, Gp Capt J. E.: 230
Johnson, President L. B.: 183
Jones, Capt O. P.: 117
Jones Williams, Sqn Ldr A. G.: 107
Jordan, Capt: 150
JRM Mars (see Martin)
Ju 52/3m (see Junkers)
Ju 88 (see Junkers)
June Bug: 82
Junkers, H.: 99
Junkers
  F 13: 99
  G 23: 104
  J1: 143, 146
  Ju 52/3m: 104, 156, 193
  Ju 88: 158, 159, 165

K

K-225 (see Kaman)
Ka-1 (see Kayaba)
Ka-22 Vintokryl (see Kamov)
Ka-32 (see Kamov)
Kaga: 162
Kaman HTK-1: 52
Kaman K-225: 52
Kamov, N.: 44
  'Hokum': 58
  Ka-22 Vintokryl: 8, 61
  Ka-32: 62
Karel, K. E.: 70
Kartveli, A.: 199
Kasler, Maj J.: 182
Kästner, Oberleut: 142, 224
Kauper, H. A.: 94
Kawasaki C-1: 183
Kawasaki T-4: 186
Kayaba K-1: 47
KB-29 (see Boeing)
KC-1 (see Kellett)
KC-135 (see Boeing)
KD-1 (see Kellett)
Keane, Lt O. G.: 102
Keck, Lt-Gen J. M.: 191
Keck, Maj T. J.: 191
Kellett, Sqn Ldr R. G.: 192
Kellett
  KC-1: 47
  KD-1: 45, 46
  KH-15: 53
  XH-8: 49
  YG-1: 45
Kelly, Lt O. G.: 102
Kennedy, President J. F.: 219
Kepner, Capt W. E.: 21
KH-15 (see Kellett)
Ki-20 (see Mitsubishi)
Ki-27 (see Nakajima)
Kidd, Flt Sgt A. K.: 70
King, Capt W. A. C.: 27
King's Cup Air Race: 101
Kites: First
  aerial bombers: 133
  experiments by S. F. Cody: 66
  exponent of box-kite: 66

witness/recorded F on man-
  carrying: 64
Kites: Most
  effective dem of man-lifting: 71
Kittinger, Capt J. W.: 70
Klieforth, H. E.: 71
KLM (Royal Dutch Airlines): 100,
  121, 131
Knabe, Herr: 26
Knapp, B.: 129
Knight, J.: 98
Knight, Maj W. J.: 221, 239
Köhl, H.: 106
Kolibri 1 (see Borgward)
Komarov, Col V. M.: 217, 218
Komet (see Dornier)
Kopets, I.: 62
Korean War: 164, 173, 225
Korolev, S.: 172
Krebs, Lt A.: 26
Kress, W.: 79
Kubasov, V.: 220
Kukkonen, Sgt: 158
Kuparanto, R. J.: 17, 65
Kyushu J7W Shinden: 199
Kyushu Q1W Tokai: 164

L

LA-4 (see Lake)
Lafayette Escadrille: 144, 147
La France: 26
Lahm, Lt F. P.: 20, 134
Lake LA-4: 219
Lamb, D. I.: 138
Lambert, Sgt L.: 171
La Mountain, J.: 18
Lancaster (see Avro)
Lancastrian (see Avro)
Langhoff, Leut: 142
Langley, S. P.: 73, 78, 79
Large American f-b: 146
Latham, H.: 85, 86, 87, 128, 129
Launoy, M.: 41
Lavoisier, M.: 9, 16
Learoyd, Flt Lt R. A. B.: 225
Lebaudy brothers: 27
Le Breton, Lt: 137
le Bris, J. M.: 66
Le Brix, Lt Cdr: 106
Lecointe, S.: 148, 149
Leduc O.10: 213
Leduc O.21: 213
Lee, Capt H. P.: 19
Leete, B. S.: 105
Lefebvre, E.: 86
Legagneux, G.: 84, 86
Legion Cóndor: 156
Le Grand: 93
Le Gustav: 14
le Normand, S.: 65
Leonov, A.: 217, 220
Letchford, Sgt F.: 158
Letov S1: 148
Lightning (see English Electric)
Lilienthal, O.: 71, 72
Lillywhite, R. J.: 95
Lindbergh, Capt C.: 7, 105
Lindstrand, P.: 7, 22
Ling-Temco-Vought F8U Crusader:
  69, 199
Link, E. A.: 151
Link Trainer: 151
Lippisch, Dr A.: 210
Lityvak, Jr Lt L.: 231
Ljebedy: 28
Lockheed
  AC-130: 183
  Altair: 113
  C-5 Galaxy: 183, 185, 186, 189
  C-130 Hercules: 56, 182
  Constellation: 117
  F-94 Starfire: 173
  F-104 Starfighter: 119, 180
  Hudson: 157, 158, 161
  JetStar: 119
  P2V-1 Neptune: 171

P-3B Orion: 182
P-38 Lightning: 165, 198, 230,
  231
P-80 (F-80) Shooting Star: 117,
  164, 172, 174, 231
SR-71: 182, 191
T-33A: 186
TriStar: 186
U-2: 178, 180, 181
Vega: 106, 108, 110, 111, 112
XC-35: 210
XFV-1: 214
Lomonosov, M. V.: 41
London–Manchester Air Race: 88,
  89
Longmore, Sqn Cdr A.: 139
Long Range Monoplane (see Fairey)
Longton, Flt Lt W. H.: 102
López, F. S.: 19
Loraine, R.: 90
Los Angeles: 34, 37
Los Angeles Airways: 50
Lovell, J.: 218
Lowe, Flg Off P.: 70
Lowe, T. S. C.: 18
LS3 (see Rolladen-Schneider)
Lufbery, R.: 229
Luke, 2nd Lt F.: 24, 227
Lunardi, V.: 14, 15
Lunar Module: 218
Luukkanen, Lt E.: 158
LVG CII: 145
Lynch, B.: 171
Lynx (see Westland)

M

M2-F2 (see Northrop/NASA)
M5K (see Fokker)
M8 (see Fokker)
M-52 (see Miles)
M.52bis (see Macchi)
Macchi
  C200 Saetta: 156
  M.52bis: 150
  MC 72: 129
MacCready, Dr P.: 220, 221
MacLaren, Maj A. S.: 95
Macmillan, Capt N.: 102
Macready, Lt J. A.: 102
MacRobertson Race: 112, 113
Madison, J.: 16
Magennis, Mr C. S.: 87
Maia (see Short-Mayo)
Maitland, L. J.: 106
Majendie, Capt A. M.: 119
Maloney, J.: 67
Mammoth: 24
Mangin, M.: 19
Manly, C. M.: 79
Mannock, Maj E. ('Mick'): 228
Mantle, Act Seaman J. F.: 225
Mappleback, Lt G.: 140
Marco Polo: 63, 64
Marix, Flt Lt R. L. G.: 140
Marsden, Capt J. T. A.: 119
Marseille, Haupt H.-J.: 230
Martens, Herr: 69
Martin, Glenn: 67
Martin
  130 Clipper: 114, 115
  B-57: 174
  JRM Mars: 188, 189, 194
  TM-61 Matador: 175
  XB-48: 171
Martin, Maj F.: 103
Martin Marietta SV-5P Pilot: 218
Martlet (see Grumman)
Mason, M.: 17
Masson, D.: 138
Mathers, Corp: 95
Maxim, Sir H.: 126
May, Lt W. R.: 227
Mayfly: 29
MB-3 (see Thomas Morse)
MB-E1 (see Militky)
MC-4 (see McCulloch)

MC72 (see Macchi)
McCallin, L.: 221
McCampbell, Cdr D.: 227
McClean, F. K.: 84, 92, 93
McClellan, Gen: 18
McConnell, Capt J.: 227
McCulloch MC-4: 52
McCullough, P.: 21
McCurdy, J. A. D.: 84, 86, 89
McDivitt, J.: 218
McDonnell
  F2H-1 Banshee: 173
  FD-1 (FH-1) Phantom: 169, 171
  XF-85 Goblin: 212
McDonnell Douglas
  F-4 Phantom II: 123, 181, 182,
    183, 200, 225
  F-15 Eagle: 184, 186
  F/A-18 Hornet: 185
McDonnell Douglas/British
  Aerospace AV-8B Harrier II:
    185, 186
McDowall, Wg Cdr A.: 165
McGwire, R.: 15
McIntosh, Wg Cdr R. H.: 109
McIntyre, Flt Lt D. F.: 111
McMaster, Sir F.: 101
McPherson, Flg Off: 157, 225
MD.450 Ouragan (see Dassault)
MD.452 Mystère (see Dassault)
Me 163 Komet (see Messerschmitt)
Me 209 (see Messerschmitt)
Me 262 (see Messerschmitt)
Me 321 Gigant (see Messerschmitt)
Me 323 (see Messerschmitt)
Meagher, Capt A.: 120
Mellin: 27
Mercury (see Short-Mayo)
Messenger (see Sperry)
Messerschmitt
  Bf 109: 154, 155, 158, 165, 190,
    230
  Me 163 Komet: 164, 210
  Me 209: 190
  Me 262: 161, 163, 165, 167
  Me 321 Gigant: 68, 199
  Me 323: 68
  P.1101: 214
Messiha, Dr K.: 64
Metallballon: 26
Meteor (see Gloster)
Meteor NF11 (see Armstrong
  Whitworth)
Meurisse, M.: 87
Meusnier, Lt J.-B. M.: 25
MH-53E Sea Dragon (see Sikorsky)
Mi-6 (see Mil)
Mi-8 (see Mil)
Mi-12 (see Mil)
Mi-24 'Hind' (see Mil)
Mi-26 (see Mil)
Mi-28 'Havoc' (see Mil)
Michelob Light Eagle (see MIT)
Mier, M.: 101
MiG-9 (see Mikoyan-Gurevich)
MiG-15 (see Mikoyan-Gurevich)
MiG-17 (see Mikoyan-Gurevich)
MiG-21 (see Mikoyan-Gurevich)
MiG-23 (see Mikoyan-Gurevich)
MiG-25 'Foxbat' (see Mikoyan-
  Gurevich)
MiG-29 'Fulcrum' (see Mikoyan-
  Gurevich)
Mikoyan-Gurevich
  MiG-9: 170
  MiG-15: 174, 183, 199, 225, 228,
    231
  MiG-17: 181, 182
  MiG-21: 184
  MiG-23: 184
  MiG-25 'Foxbat': 184
  MiG-29 'Fulcrum': 186
  Ye-266M: 192
Mil
  A-10 (see Mi-24)
  Mi-6: 60
  Mi-8: 62

Mi-12: 58, 59, 60
Mi-24 'Hind': 56, 58, 60
Mi-26: 60
Mi-28 'Havoc': 58
Miles M-52: 210
Militky MB-E1: 219
Miller, B.: 121
Millichap, Capt R. E.: 120
Milling, Lt T. de W.: 137, 138
Mirage III (see Dassault)
Mirage 2000 (see Dassault-Bregue
Mirage G (see Dassault)
'Mistell-Programm': 165
MIT Michelob Light Eagle: 221
Mitchell, Gen W. ('Billy'): 187
Mitchell, R. J.: 99, 100, 196
Mitchell U-2 Superwing: 129
Mitsubishi
  1MF1: 148, 150
  A5M: 157
  A6M Zero-Sen: 154, 159, 166,
    167
  G4M: 198
  Ki-20: 187
  T-2: 183
Mock, J.: 121
Model 47 (see Bell)
Model 200 Monomail (see Boeing
Model 206L LongRanger II (see
  Bell)
Model 209 HueyCobra (see Bell)
Model 247 (see Boeing)
Model 307 Stratoliner (see Boeing
Model 314 (see Boeing)
Model 367-80 (see Boeing)
Model 707 (see Boeing)
Model 727 (see Boeing)
Model 737 (see Boeing)
Model 747 (see Boeing)
Model A (see Wright)
Model B (see Wright)
Model B-8B Gyro-Boat (see
  Bensen)
Model CL-4S (see Boeing)
Model F (see Curtiss)
Model J (see Standard)
Moisant, J. B.: 89
Moll, J. J.: 113
Molland, Flg Off H.: 178
Mollison, J. A.: 110, 111
Moni (see Monnet)
Monnet Moni: 129
Monroe, J.: 16
Montgolfier, E.: 10, 11
Montgolfier, J.: 10, 11, 23
Moore, Lt L. A.: 39
Moore-Brabazon, J. T. C.: 84, 87, 8
Moorhouse, Lt W. B. R.: 92, 224
Morane-Saulnier
  M-S 405: 155
  M-S 406: 155
  Parasol: 31, 228
  Type M: 140
  Type N: 143
Morris, Lt L. B. F.: 226
Morrish, Flt Sub-Lt C. R.: 146
Mortimer, R. W.: 69
Morton, J. G.: 62
Moseley, Capt C. C.: 101
Mosquito (see de Havilland)
Mould, Pil Off P. W.: 158
Moy, J.: 77
Mozhaiski, A. F.: 78
M-S 405 (see Moraine-Saulnier)
M-S 406 (see Moraine-Saulnier)
Multiplane: 78, 81
Murphy, Lt A. W.: 100
Murray, Wrt Off E. J.: 181
Musgrave, Flt Lt J. G.: 191
Mustin, Lt Cdr H.: 143
MX-324 (see Northrop)
MXY-7 Ohka (see Yokosuka)
Myers, Maj J.: 165

N

NACA, foundation: 95

Nakajima
  A4N1: 156
  G5N Shinzan: 158
  Ki-27: 156
NASA Space Shuttle: 209, 218, 219, 220
NASA Space Shuttle Carrier: 220
Navy/Curtiss NC-4: 97
NC-4 (see Navy/Curtiss)
NC 223.4 (see Centre)
Nelson, Lt E.: 103
Nemer, Cdr H.: 127
Nesterov, Lt P. N.: 94, 140
Nettleton, Sqn Ldr J. D.: 161
Newell, W.: 67
Newman, L. M.: 22, 24
Nicholetts, Flt Lt G. E.: 107
Nicholson, Flt Lt J. B.: 229, 230
Nieuport
  17: 229
  28: 148
  Type IV: 94
Nieuport-Delage
  29: 148, 149
  62: 196
Nimrod (see Hawker-Siddeley)
No. 2 biplane (see Short)
Nobile, U.: 35
Nord Gerfaut: 215
Nord Griffon: 216
Nordair: 123
Norge: 35
North American
  B-25 Mitchell: 162
  B-45 Tornado: 172
  F-82 Twin Mustang: 173
  F-86 Sabre: 119, 171, 172, 176, 225, 231
  F-100 Super Sabre: 176, 178
  OV-10 Bronco: 183
  P-51 Mustang: 119, 129, 159, 191
  RB-45: 176
  X-15A: 217
  X-15A-2: 209, 221
  XB-70A Valkyrie: 217
Northrop
  B-35: 212
  F-89 Scorpion: 172, 178, 179
  MX-324: 210
  P-61 Black Widow: 171, 211
  SM-62 Snark: 180
  X-4 Bantam: 212, 213
  XP-79B: 210
  YB-49: 212
Northrop/NASA HL-10: 219
Northrop/NASA M2-F2: 218, 219
Nott, J.: 24
Notts, B.: 70
Nowotny, Maj W.: 163, 167
Nulli Secundus: 27
NY-2 (see Consolidated)
NYP Monoplane (see Ryan)

O

O/10 (see Handley Page)
O.10 (see Leduc)
O.21 (see Leduc)
O/400 (see Handley Page)
Oberth, Prof H.: 209
Obregon, Gen A.: 138
OH-6A (see Hughes)
Old, Maj-Gen A. J.: 180
Oldest route still operated by original airline: 131
Onofrio, C.: 117
Opel-Hatry Rak-1: 209
Operation
  'Barbarossa': 193
  'Black Buck': 185
  'Colossus': 160
  'Downfall': 133
  'Full Flow': 194
  'Junction City': 182
  'Mercury': 188
  'Overlord': 193
  'Rolling Thunder': 181

'Vittles': 172
Omen: 10
Otto, N.: 78
OV-10 Bronco (see North American)
Overstrand (see Boulton Paul)
Ovington, E. L.: 91

P

P1 (see English Electric)
P2V1 Neptune (see Lockheed)
P-3B Orion (see Lockheed)
P.7 (see PZL)
P.11 (see PZL)
P.24 (see PZL)
P-26 (see Boeing)
P-35 (see Seversky)
P-38 Lightning (see Lockheed)
P-51 Mustang (see North American)
P-61 Black Widow (see Northrop)
P-80 (F-80) Shooting Star (see Lockheed)
P.108 Balliol (see Boulton Paul)
P.1101 (see Messerschmitt)
P1127 Kestrel (see Hawker Siddeley)
Page, C.: 20
Page, Cdr L. C.: 181
Pålson Type 1: 95
Pan American Airways: 113, 114, 115, 116, 117, 121, 122
Panavia Tornado: 184, 186, 189
Pangborn, C. E.: 109
Papin, M.: 43
Parachute: First
  dem in Europe of quasi-parachute: 65
  descent by woman from A: 67
  descent from A in USA: 67
  descent from A over UK: 67
  descent from balloon by living creatures: 65
  descent by from balloon in USA: 65
  design seen in published form: 64
  documented jump outside China: 65
  ejection-seat escape from moving A on ground: 69, 178
  escape from disabled A in USA: 69
  known design for: 64
  manned descent by in UK: 65
  man to descend by from damaged A & survive: 65
  public dem of parachute of new design: 65
  recorded free-fall jump from A: 67
  recorded/successful quasi-parachute jumps: 64
  successful descent by man from airborne vehicle: 65
Parachute: Greatest
  altitude from which a man has fallen: 70
  altitude of successful escape from A: 70
  free-fall record by woman: 70
  free-fall record ratified by FAI: 70
  height for delayed drop by UK group: 70
  known landing altitude: 70
  number of parachute jumps in 24 hours: 70
Parachute: Largest
  all-woman free-fall formation: 69
  free-fall formation: 69
  free-fall star formation: 69
Parachute: Longest
  delayed drop achieved by man: 70
  recorded descent: 69
  recorded gap between jumps: 69
Parachute: Most
  amazing rescue by: 71
  northerly jump: 71

Parasol (see Morane-Saulnier)
Parke, Lt W.: 137
Parke, Sub-Lt: 159
Parker, J. L.: 114, 188
Parmalee, P. O.: 90, 135
Parmentier, K. D.: 113
Parnall Pixie: 102
Parschau, Leut: 224
Passarola: 9
Pathfinder Force, RAF: 161, 163
Patteson, C.: 99
Paul, Lt B.: 134
Paulhan, L.: 88, 89, 134
'Pave Tack' weapon delivery: 184, 185
Pavlova, T.: 70
PBY Catalina (see Consolidated)
PC-9 (see Pilatus)
Peck, Capt B. A.: 95
Pegasus Flash: 129
Pégoud, A.: 94
Peltier, Mme T.: 82
Pequet, H.: 91
Percival Gull: 114
Perot Jr, H. R.: 57, 60
Peter, Leut: 145, 193
Peter, Ms R.: 23
Petter, W. E. W.: 177
Pfalz D.IIIa: 148
Phillips, W. H.: 40, 41, 78, 81
Piasecki
  H-21 Workhorse: 52, 55
  HRP-1: 49
  PV-3: 49
Piazza, Capt: 136
Piccard, Prof A.: 20
Pigeon post, first official: 19
Pilatus PC-9: 189
Pilcher, P. S.: 71, 72
Pilot: First
  air Victoria Cross: 224
  American killed 1WW: 144
  American to F after Wrights: 82
  American-trained to shoot down enemy A 1WW: 148
  American woman: 91
  Austrian to F: 84
  British to lose his life while F: 89
  British to survive spin: 90
  certificated woman: 88
  gallantry award to marine aviator: 224
  German to F: 82
  German active duty officer to gain licence: 135
  great UK ace of 1WW: 225
  jet fighter ace, 2WW: 167
  jet fighter ace, Korea: 225
  killed flying a powered A: 86
  military to get Brevet de Aéro Club de France: 135
  naval officers to F: 135
  of Escadrille Américaine to gain air victory: 144
  of fixed-wing A to gain an 'astronaut's wings': 217
  of German Air Service killed on active service 1WW: 139
  of jet A to gain victory over another jet A: 166
  RAF to survive supersonic ejection: 178
  regular serving US to die in action 2WW: 159
  RFC officer killed on military flying duties: 137
  Scottish: 87
  to fly under all of London's Thames bridges: 92
  to gain licence in Germany: 135
  to hold licence for turbine-powered civil transport: 118
  to make solo F across both N & S Atlantic: 111
  to make solo F E–W of South Atlantic: 111
  to make solo F UK–South

America: 111
  to make sustained inverted F: 94
  to perform a loop: 94
  to perform, recover from & dem recovery from a spin: 137
  to survive supersonic ejection: 178
  to take off successfully from towed barge: 148
  true fighter leader 1WW: 224
  UK Army officer to gain Pilot's Certificate: 223
  UK gallantry decoration to in 2WW: 225
  UK woman: 91
  US aces of Vietnam War: 225
  US combat victories in Vietnam: 181
  US in American squadron to gain combat victory: 147
  US Navy student to solo in turbojet: 180
  US to be shot down in war: 20
  US under American colours to become ace 1WW: 147
  US victory Korean War: 173
  USAF aces of Vietnam War: 225
  USAF combat victories in Vietnam: 182
  woman to F solo: 83
  four most successful 1WW
    Austrian-Hungarian: 232
    Belgian: 233
    French: 232
    Imperial Russian: 233
    Italian: 232
    US: 232
Pilot: German who scored 100-plus victories v. Western Allies: 233, 234
Pilot: Greatest
  ace 1WW: 226
  Allied ace 1WW: 226
  'balloon buster' 1WW: 226
  decoration for gallantry to Royal Canadian Navy 2WW: 227
  number of A destroyed in one sortie by US Navy: 227
  number of combat victories Korean War: 227, 228
  US 'balloon buster' 1WW: 227
Pilot: Highest
  scoring Allied in Battle of Britain: 226
  scoring and German leading ace 2WW: 230
  scoring French 1WW: 228
  scoring German in combat with Western Allies: 230
  scoring Luftwaffe with 150-plus victories 2WW & Spanish Civil War: 235
  scoring of RNAS 1WW: 229
  scoring Soviet woman: 231
  scoring UK 1WW: 228
  scoring UK 2WW: 230
  scoring UK/Empire 1WW: 228, 229
  scoring US 1WW: 229
  scoring US 2WW: 230
  scoring USMC Korean War: 231
  six most successful German 1WW: 232
Pioneer: 20
Piper
  Aztec: 124
  Comanche 260: 122
  Cub: 117
Pitcairn, H.: 44
Pixie (see Parnell)
Pixton, H.: 94
Platt-le-Page XR-1: 49
Pocock, G.: 71
Pohl, Haupt: 158
Polikarpov
  I-1: 150
  I-15: 153, 197

I-16: 153, 154, 157
Ponche, M.: 91
Pond, Capt C. F.: 136
Porte Baby: 144
Post, W.: 108, 111, 112
Potez 25: 195
Potez 630: 198
Powers, F. G.: 180
Prather, Lt Cdr V. A.: 23
Pratte-Read PR-GI: 71
Prévost, M.: 93, 128
PR-GI (see Pratte-Reid)
Prier, P.: 91
Primard, M.: 91
Prinz Eugen: 157, 230
Projekt X: 210
Prudhommeau, Corp: 140
PS-1 (see Shin Meiwa)
Ptacek, S.: 220
Pulitzer Trophy Races: 101
Pup (see Sopwith)
PV-3 (see Piasecki)
PV-3 (see Westland)
PZL
   P.7: 151
   P.11: 198
   P.24: 159

Q

Q1W Tokai (see Kyushu)
Qantas Empire Airways: 113, 121
QH-50A (see Gyrodyne)
Queensland & Northern Territory
   Aerial Service (QANTAS):
   101, 106
Quénault, Corp: 140
Quimby, H.: 91

R

R VI (see Zeppelin-Staaken)
R-4 (see Sikorsky)
R4D (see Douglas)
Rader, P.: 138
Radley-England Waterplane: 94
Rak-1 (see Opel-Hatry)
Rankin, Lt-Col W. H.: 69
Rastorgueva, S.: 223
Rawlinson, Mr A.: 88
Raynham, F.: 90
RB-45 (see North American)
RB Racer (see Dayton-Wright)
Read, Lt-Cdr A. C.: 97
Rees, Lt T.: 226
Reid, L. G.: 113
Reitsch, H.: 46
Renard, Capt C.: 26
Republic
   F-84 Thunderjet: 174, 176
   F-105 Thunderchief: 178, 182
   P-47 Thunderbolt: 165, 199
République: 28
Reynolds, G. W. H.: 192
RH-53D (see Sikorsky)
Richey, H.: 113
Richie, Capt R. S.: 225
Richter, Lt J. P.: 150
Rickenbacker, E.: 190, 229
Riddick, Mr: 13
Robert brothers: 13, 25
Roberts, Capt T. C.: 182
Robertson, G.: 71
Robinson, Lt W. L.: 32, 144, 225
Roc (see Blackburn)
Rockwell, Lt K.: 144
Rockwell B-1B: 186
Rodgers, C.: 91
Roe, A. V.: 81, 85, 92
Röeland, M.: 138
Rogers, W.: 112
Rohlfs, E.: 46, 54
Rolladen-Schneider LS3: 70
Rolls, Hon C. S.: 83, 89
Roma: 164
Romain, J.: 15
Ross, Cdr M. D.: 23

Rosseau, Mr: 14
Rotachute: 69
Rota Mk I (see Avro)
Rothermere, Lord: 113
Rotodyne (see Fairey)
Rotorcraft: First:
   1 km distance record: 44
   all H squadron of Royal Navy: 51
   armed autogyro: 47
   ASW H squadron of US Navy: 52
   autogyro for ground/submarine
     attack: 47
   autogyro with rotor spin-up
     mechanism: 45
   composites-built man-powered H:
     58
   cross-country H delivery F: 48
   dem of successful cyclic pitch
     control: 44
   des for convertiplane: 41
   entirely successful coaxial rotor H:
     49
   entirely successful H: 45
   E–W X-Atlantic F by H: 52
   ex night H service: 50
   F model H: 41
   F of Oehmichen No. 2 H: 43
   FAA H ops from frigates: 55
   free H by man-carrying H: 42
   French convertiplane: 52
   H airmail service in UK: 50
   H des and built for military
     service: 48
   H flown during 1WW and
     intended for military use: 43
   H mine countermeasures
     squadron of US Navy: 56
   H model with pressure-jet rotor
     drive: 41
   H night airmail service in UK: 50
   H squadron in RAF: 50
   H station in New York: 50
   H tested from water (probably):
     43
   H tested from ship's gun platform:
     47
   H to cross English Channel: 49
   H to dem basic cyclic control: 43
   H to enter limited production: 46
   H to fly successfully: 45
   H to lift a man from the ground:
     42
   H with 8-blade main rotor: 60
   H with engine in fuselage nose: 50
   H with turboshaft engine: 52
   H with twin turboshaft engines:
     52
   H with USAAF 'R' designations:
     49
   in-action use by H of TOW anti-
     armour missiles: 56
   international H flight into central
     London: 52
   international H service: 53
   jet-driven H: 48
   large VTOL transport H in UK:
     54
   non-stop coast–coast H flight
     across North America: 55
   non-stop X-Atlantic F by H: 55
   non-stop X-Pacific F by H: 56
   non-stop US X-continental F by
     H: 54
   op purpose-des European attack
     H: 57
   op rotating-wing A in RAF
     service: 44
   partially successful full-size UK H
     to fly: 43
   pass carried in an autogyro: 44
   pilotless ASW H of US Navy: 55
   (possibly) purpose-des air-to-air
     combat H: 55
   post 2WW German H: 54
   practical of any type: 44
   RAF rotary-winged A: 44
   real transport H: 46

recognized self-propelled model
   H: 41
rotary-wing A to fly English
   Channel: 44
RTW flight by H: 57
RTW solo flight by H: 57
scheduled H service: 50
scheduled mail service: 46
self-propelled model H (possibly):
   41
Soviet attack H des with tandem
   two-seat layout: 58
Soviet autogyro to F: 44
Soviet purpose-des attack H: 56
specially-des ASW H ordered for
   Royal Navy: 55
specially-des combat H into
   service: 55
successful & practical non-
   German H: 47
successful autogyro for US des: 44
successful gyroplane: 44
successful production tandem
   twin-rotor H: 49
successful UK convertiplane: 54
suggestion of cyclic pitch control
   for: 42
support mission by US H in
   Vietnam: 55
tandem-rotor H for USAAF: 52
tandem-rotor H to gain CAA
   type approval: 52
tests in USA of H with
   intermeshing rotors: 49
tilt-rotor convertiplane to F: 53,
   54
to be literally a 'flying boat': 54
to fly carrying 3 persons: 43
to make intentional roof landing:
   45
twin-rotor twin-engined H des
   and F in UK: 50
two-seat autogyro: 44
Type Approval Certificate for
   commercial H: 50
UK-built H in RAF service: 50
UK-designed/built production H:
   50
UK scheduled H pass service: 51
UK sustained/regular scheduled
   H pass services: 51
US Army rotorcraft: 45
US certificated ramjet-powered
   H: 50, 51
US ex delivery of mail by H: 50
US H unit operating in Vietnam:
   55
US Navy H assault carrier: 54
Rotorcraft: Heaviest
   production H flown: 60
Rotorcraft: Highest
   H landing/take-off: 62
Rotorcraft: Largest
   H built outside USSR: 59
   H ever flown: 59
   rotor fitted to an engine-powered
     H: 58
Rotorcraft: Longest
   first over 1 km H distance record:
     62
Rotorcraft
   military force with most H: 62
   most extensively-built non-
     military autogyro: 62
   only autogyro squadron of RAF:
     45
   purpose-des attack H with coaxial
     contra-rotating rotors: 58
   with slowest turning rotors: 58
World altitude record (current)
   autogyros: 61
   convertiplanes: 61
   helicopters: 62
   H, set by woman: 62
World distance record (current)
   autogyros, in closed circuit: 62
   for autogyros: 62

H flown by woman: 62
H in closed circuit: 62
H in straight line: 62
World speed record (current)
   for autogyros: 60
   for convertiplanes: 61
   for convertiplanes in 100 km
     circuit: 60
   for H: 60
   H flown by woman: 62
   H RTW flight: 60
   H over 100 km circuit: 60
   H over 500 km circuit: 60
   H over 1000 km circuit: 60
Worst accident involving H: 62
Rouilly, M.: 43
Rowe, Lance-Corp R.: 32
Rowley, R. J.: 129
Royal Aero Club: 79, 84, 88, 102,
   103
Royal Aircraft Factory
   BE2c: 31, 32, 144, 224, 225
   BE2e: 100
   BE8: 139
   FE2b: 146, 195, 224, 226
   SE5: 101, 224, 225, 228, 229
Royal Society: 11
Royal Vauxhall Balloon: 17
Rudat, Haupt H.: 165
Rutan, D.: 7, 126, 222
Rutland, Flt Lt F. J.: 144
Ryan NYP Monoplane: 105
Ryan X-13 Vertijet: 216
Rymer, Capt R.: 118

S

S1 (see Letov)
S.6B (see Supermarine)
S-16 (see Sikorsky)
S.26 (see Short)
S.33 (see Short)
S.38 (see Short)
S-51 (see Sikorsky)
S-51 (see Westland/Sikorsky)
S55 (see Savoia-Marchetti)
S-55 (see Sikorsky)
S-58 (see Sikorsky)
S-65 (see Sikorsky)
S.68 (see Short)
S-76A (see Sikorsky)
SA 315B Lama (see Aérospatiale)
Saab J-29: 172, 173
Sabena: 52
Sadler, J.: 14,17
Sadler, W.: 17
Sage, Mrs L. A.: 15
Salmond, Maj Gen W.: 95
Samson, Lt C. R.: 136, 137, 139,
   140, 148
Santos-Dumont, A.: 26, 64, 81, 85,
   208
Saunders-Roe SR45 Princess: 214
Saunders-Roe SR A/1: 211
Savitskaya, S.: 223
Savoia-Marchetti S55: 152
Sayer, Flt Lt P. E. G.: 209
SB-2 (see Tupolev)
SB4 Sherpa (see Short)
SB5 (see Short)
SBC Helldiver (see Curtiss)
SC.1 (see Short)
Scandinavian Airlines System (SAS):
   119
Schall, Haupt F.: 167
Scharnhorst: 157, 230
Schiegg, U.: 13
Schilling, Col D. C.: 174
Schirra, W.: 218
Schleicher AS-W12: 70
Schneider Trophy Contests: 93, 94,
   99, 152, 196
Schutte-Lanz SL XI: 32, 144
Schwaben: 29
Schweibold, J.: 62
Schweizer SGS 2-32: 70
Scimitar (see Supermarine)

Scott, B.: 89
Scott, C. W. A.: 113
Scott, D.: 218
Scott, J.: 134
Scott, S.: 122, 124, 125
Scout (see Bristol)
SE5 (see Royal Aircraft Factory)
SE.210 Caravelle (see Sud-Est
  Aviation)
Sea Dart (see Convair)
Sea Eagle (see Supermarine)
Sea Fury (see Hawker)
Sea Gladiator (see Gloster)
Sea Harrier (see British Aerospace)
Sea Hornet (see de Havilland)
Sea Hurricane (see Hawker)
Sea Lion (see Supermarine)
Sea Mosquito (see de Havilland)
Sea Otter (see Supermarine)
Sea Venom (see de Havilland)
Seki, Lt Y.: 166
Selfridge, Lt T. E.: 132, 134
Sentinel 5000: 11
Seversky P-35: 155
Seys, Sqn Ldr R. G.: 69
SGS 2-32 (see Schweizer)
SH-3A Sea King (see Sikorsky)
Shaw, H. ('Jerry'): 121, 131
Shawnee (see Piasecki H-21)
Shenandoah: 34
Shepard, A. B.: 217
Sherman, Lt T. C.: 138
Shetland (see Short)
Shin Meiwa PS-1: 189
Shin Meiwa US-1: 189
Shoecroft, J.: 22
Shoho: 162
Shokaku: 162
Short, E.: 83
Short
  184: 142, 143
  Belfast: 181
  C-class: 114, 115
  No. 2 biplane: 84, 87
  S.26: 135
  S.33: 92
  S.38: 136
  S.68: 93
  SB4 Sherpa: 214
  SB5: 214, 215
  SC.1: 216
  Shetland: 185
  Stirling: 160
  Sturgeon: 170
Short brothers: 83, 84, 85
Short-Mayo Maia: 116
Short-Mayo Mercury: 8, 116, 130
Siebert, Oberleut L.: 167
Siemens-Schuckert D VI: 190
Sikorsky, I.: 47, 93
Sikorsky
  CH-53E Super Stallion: 59
  HH-3: 55, 56
  Ilya Mourometz: 93, 139, 141, 142,
    187
  MH-53E Sea Dragon: 56
  R-4: 48
  RH-53D: 56
  S-16: 141
  S-51: 50
  S-55: 50, 52, 53
  S-58: 55
  S-65: 56
  S-76A: 60
  SH-3A Sea King: 55
  UH-34: 189
  XR-4: 48
Silver City Airways: 117, 121, 122
Silver Dart: 84
Simon, Corp: 148
Simonet, Mlle: 15
Simons, Maj D. G.: 21
Sippé, Flt Lt S. V.: 141
Sirocco (see Aviasud)
Skrzhinskii, N.: 44
Skua (see Blackburn)
Skyrocket (see Douglas)

SL XI (see Schutte-Lanz)
Slayton, D.: 220
SM-62 Snark (see Northrop)
Smith, Capt C. K.: 106, 107, 113
Smith, Capt L. H.:150
Smith, Capt R. M.: 95, 100
Smith, Cdr H.: 182
Smith, D.: 57
Smith, G. F.: 178
Smith, H.: 148
Smith, Lt K.: 100
Smith, Lt L. H.: 103
Snipe (see Sopwith)
SO 1310 Farfadet (see Sud-Ouest)
SO 9000 Trident (see Sud-Ouest)
SOCATA TB 10 Tobago: 125
Solar Challenger: 220
Solar One: 220
Sommer, R.: 131
Sopwith
  Camel: 34, 147, 148, 195
  Cuckoo: 145
  Gnu: 102
  Pup: 145, 146, 147
  Snipe: 149
  Tabloid: 94, 138, 140
  Triplane: 144, 229
Soryu: 162
Sowrey, 2nd Lt: 32
Soyuz 1: 218
Soyuz 19: 219, 220
Space Shuttle (see NASA)
Space Shuttle Carrier (see NASA)
SPAD XIII: 190
Spanish Civil War, start: 156, 196
Spencer, S.: 27
Spenser-Gray, Sqn Cdr D. A.: 140
Sperry, L. B.: 209
Sperry Messenger: 35
Spitfire (see Supermarine)
SR A/1 (see Saunders-Roe)
SR45 Princess (see Saunders-Roe)
SR-71 (see Lockheed)
Stack, T. N.: 105
Stafford, T.: 218, 220
Stainforth, Flt Lt G. H.: 152
Stamer, F.: 209
Standard Model J: 95
Steill, B.: 17
Stevens , Capt A.: 20
Stirling (see Short)
Stits, D.: 127
Stits Baby Bird: 127
Stoney, Capt T. B.: 120
St Petersburg–Tampa Airboat Line:
  94
Stratocruiser (see Boeing)
Stringfellow, J.: 76
Sturgeon (see Short)
Stuwer, J.: 14
Sud-Est Aviation SE.210 Caravelle:
  120
Sud-Ouest SO 1310 Farfadet: 52
Sud-Ouest SO 9000 Trident: 213
Sukhomlin, I.: 128
Superchicken III: 22
Supermarine
  Attacker: 175
  S.6B: 152
  Scimitar: 180
  Sea Eagle: 103
  Sea Lion: 99
  Sea Otter: 157
  Spitfire: 158, 159, 192, 196, 197
  Swift: 175, 177
Super Sportster (see Gee Bee)
Suring, Prof: 20
SV-5P Pilot (see Martin Marietta)
SVA 5 Primo (see Ansaldo)
Swedish Air Lines: 104
Sweeney, Maj C. W.: 168
Swift (see Supermarine)
Swordfish (see Fairey)
Sycamore (see Bristol)

T

T-1 (see Fuji)
T-2 (see Fokker)
T-2 (see Mitsubishi)
T-4 (see Kawasaki)
T-18 Tiger (see Thorp)
T-33A (see Lockheed)
Tables
  Selected maximum speeds of X-
    15: 238
  World absolute distance records:
    241, 242
  World absolute height records:
    239, 240
  World absolute speed records:
    236, 237, 238
Tabloid (see Sopwith)
Takagi, Vice-Adm T.: 162
Taube (see Etrich)
Taylor, Capt P. G.: 113
Taylor, D.: 124
Taylor, F.: 129, 191
TB-3 (see Tupolev)
TB 10 Tobago (see SOCATA)
TBD Devastator (see Douglas)
TBF Avenger (see Grumman)
Teesdale, Sgt K. J.: 70
Templer, Capt J. L. B.: 19
Tereshkova, Jr Lt V. V.: 217
Terski, V.: 131
Testu-Brissy, P.: 17
Thible, Mme: 14
Thirtle, Sqn Ldr J.: 70
Thomas, G. H.: 95
Thomas Morse MB-3: 148
Thompson, Cdr: 157
Thompson, Lord: 36
Thompson, Lt S. W.: 147
Thorp T-18 Tiger: 124
Tibbets Jr, Col P. W.: 168
Tirpitz: 192
Tissandier, G.: 19, 26
Tissandier, P.: 84
To, F.: 220
TM-61 Matador (see Martin)
Tornado (see Panavia)
Toucan (see HPA)
Tournachon, F.: 18
Towers, Cdr J. H.: 97, 138
Transall C.160: 183
Transcontinental & Western Air
  (TWA): 108, 116
Trans-Mediterranean Airways: 124
Transon, A.: 17
Tremml, G.: 221
Trewin, Asst Paymaster G. S.: 144
Trident (see Hawker Siddeley)
Triplane (see Sopwith)
TriStar (see Lockheed)
Trouvé, G.: 77
Trumpf III: 38
TSR.2 (see BAC)
Tu-12 (see Tupolev)
Tu-104 (see Tupolev)
Tu-114 (see Tupolev)
Tu-144 (see Tupolev)
Tubavion: 91
Tupolev, A. N.: 101, 103
Tupolev
  ANT-1: 101
  ANT-2: 103
  SB-2: 158
  TB-3: 152
  Tu-12: 171
  Tu-104: 120
  Tu-114: 128
  Tu-144: 122
Turbo Centurion (see Cessna)
Twiss, Lt-Cdr L. P.: 215
Type IV (see Nieuport)
Type VI (see Blériot)
Type VII (see Blériot)
Type X (see Voisin)
Type XI (see Blériot)
Type XII (see Blériot)
Type XIII (see Blériot)

Type 1 (see Palson)
Type 142 (see Bristol)
Type 173 (see Bristol)
Type 707 (see Avro)
Type F (see Avro)
Type M (see Morane-Saulnier)
Type N (see Morane-Saulnier)
Typhoon (see Hawker)
Tyson, G.: 188, 214
Tytler, J.: 14

U

U-2 (see Lockheed)
U-2 Superwing (see Mitchell)
U-570: 157
Ugaki, Adm M.: 167
UH-34 (see Sikorsky)
ULD-1: 24
Ulm, C. T. P.: 106
United Air Lines: 108
US-1 (see Shin Meiwa)
USAF formation: 171
USS Akron: 37
USS Antietam: 176, 177
USS Birmingham: 135
USS Constellation: 181, 225
USS Coral Sea: 171, 181
USS Enterprise: 162, 163, 164
USS Franklin D. Roosevelt: 55, 169,
  171, 184
USS Hancock: 181
USS Hornet: 55, 162
USS Jupiter: 148
USS Kalinin Bay: 167
USS Kitkun Bay: 167
USS Langley: 148, 149, 150
USS Lexington: 162
USS Macon: 37
USS Maddox: 181
USS Mannert L. Abele: 168
USS Midway: 181
USS Mississippi: 138
USS Nimitz: 189
USS North Carolina: 143, 145
USS Pennsylvania: 135, 136
USS Princeton: 175
USS Saratoga: 178
USS Sicily: 174
USS St Lo: 167
USS Thetis Bay: 54
USS Ticonderoga: 181
USS Valley Forge: 174
USS Wake Island: 169
USS West Virginia: 168
USS White Plains: 167
USS Yorktown: 162, 163

V

V-1 flying-bomb: 165, 199
V-2 (A-4) rocket: 154, 165, 166,
  172
Valiant (see Vickers)
Valier, M.: 209
Vampire (see de Havilland)
van de Haegen, Oberleut O.: 31
van Deman, Mrs R.: 86
van Orman, W. T.: 21
van Ryneveld, Lt-Col P.: 100
Varney Speed Lines: 104
VC10 (see Vickers)
VE-7SF (see Vought)
Védrines, J.: 94
Vega (see Lockheed)
Ventry, Lord: 38
Veranzio, F.: 64, 65
Vernon (see Vickers)
Vertol H-21C: 54
Verville-Packard 600: 101
Vickers
  Destroyer EFB1: 138
  FB5 Gunbus: 142
  Valiant: 175, 180
  VC10: 131
  Vernon: 149
  Victoria: 151

Viking: 100, 117
Viscount: 117, 118, 119, 125
Vimy: 98, 100, 101, 103
Wellesley: 36, 192
Wellington: 36, 160, 162
Victor (see Handley Page)
Victoria (see Vickers)
Vietnam War, start of: 181
Viking (see Vickers)
Ville d'Orléans: 19
Vimy (see Vickers)
Virgin Atlantic Flyer: 7, 11, 22, 23, 24
Viscount (see Vickers)
VJ-22 Sportsman (see Volmer)
VJ-23 Swingwing (see Volmer)
Vlaicu, A.: 89
Vlaicu I: 89
Voisin, C.: 82
Voisin, G.: 82
Voisin brothers, 64
Voisin Type X: 141
Voisin-Farman I: 81
Volmer VJ-22 Sportsman: 130
Volmer VJ-23 Swingwing: 125
von Braun, W.: 154
von Gronau, Capt W.: 108
von Guericke, O.: 9
von Hiddessen, Lt F.: 140
von Hunefeld, Baron: 106
von Karman, Dr Ing T.: 43
von Ohain, Dr H. J. P.: 209, 210
von Opel, F.: 109
von Parseval, A.: 20
von Petroczy, Oberleut S.: 43
von Richthofen, Rittmeister M.: 226, 227
von Rosenthal, Lt Baron: 140
von Sigsfeld, B.: 20
von Tiedemann, Lt R.: 135
von Zeppelin, Count F.: 26, 28, 39
Voskhod 1: 217
Voskhod 2: 217
Voss, Lt W.: 147
Vostok 1: 216
Vostok 6: 217
Vought
    F4U Corsair: 174, 175, 192, 225, 227
    F-8 Crusader: 178
    VE-7SF: 150
Vought-Sikorsky VS-300: 47

Voyager: 7, 126, 222
VS-300 (see Vought-Sikorsky)
Vulcan (see Avro)
Vulovic, V.: 228

W

W8b (see Handley Page)
WA-116/F/S (see Wallis)
WA-121/Mc (see Wallis)
Waco CG-4: 69
Wakefield, Sir C.: 32
Wal (see Dornier)
Walden, Dr H. W.: 87
Walden III: 87
Walker, J. A.: 221
Wallace (see Westland)
Wallis, B. N.: 36
Wallis, Wg Cdr K. H.: 60, 61, 62
Wallis WA-116/F/S: 60, 62
Wallis WA-121/Mc: 61
Walsh, L.: 90
Walsh, V. C.: 90
Wapiti (see Westland)
Warneford, Flt Sub-Lt R. A. J.: 31
Warsitz, E.: 210
Washington: 18
Washington, G.: 16
Wasp (see Westland)
Waterfall, Lt V.: 140
Waterplane (see Radley-England)
Waterton, Sqn Ldr W. A.: 175, 176
Webb, T. H.: 95
Wee Bee (see Beardmore)
Wehner, Lt: 227
Welch, L.: 69
Wellesley (see Vickers)
Wellington (see Vickers)
Wellman, W.: 29
Welsh, Dr K. H. V.: 106
Wessex (see Westland)
West, Ensign J. C.: 169
West Australian Airways: 101
Westenra, Hon Mrs R.: 109
Westland
    Lynx: 60
    PV-3: 111
    Wallace: 111
    Wapiti: 195
    Wasp: 55
    Wessex: 55
Westland/Sikorsky Dragonfly: 50, 51

Westland/Sikorsky S-51: 50, 51
Wheeler, Dr J.: 71
White, E.: 218
Whitehead, G.: 79
Whitley (see Armstrong Whitworth)
Whittle, F.: 209
Wiederkehr, Ms D.: 24
Wilkins, Capt G. H.: 106
William, D.: 71
Willows, E. T.: 28
Wilson, D. C.: 92
Wilson, Gp Capt H. J.: 170
Windham, Capt W. G.: 91
'Window': 162
Winslow, Lt A.: 148
Wintgens, Lt K.: 142
Wise, J. C.: 18, 19
Wisseman, Lt K.: 228
Wolf, Ms C.: 24
Wölfert, Dr K.: 26
World War
    end of 1WW: 148
    official end of 2WW: 168
Wren (see English Electric)
Wright, O.: 64, 67, 74, 80, 82, 132, 133, 134
Wright, W.: 64, 67, 80, 82, 83, 84, 86, 130, 133
Wright
    Flyer: 64, 67, 74, 75, 80, 89, 133
    Flyer II: 80
    Flyer III: 75
    Model A: 84, 86, 134
    Model B: 90, 137
    No. 1 glider: 64, 67, 133
    No. 2 glider: 64, 67, 133
    No. 3 glider: 64, 67, 75, 133
Wright brothers: 67, 73, 74, 75, 79, 133, 134, 208
Wrigley, Capt H. N.: 100
Wronieki, Sgt Maj: 148

X

X-1 (see Bell)
X-2 (see Bell)
X-3 (see Douglas)
X-4 Bantam (see Northrop)
X-5 (see Bell)
X-13 Vertijet (see Ryan)
X-15A (see North American)
X-15A-2 (see North American)

XB-48 (see Martin)
XB-70A Valkyrie (see North American)
XC-8A Buffalo (see de Havilland Canada)
XC-35 (see Lockheed)
XF-85 Goblin (see Consolidated)
XFY-1 (see Convair)
XFV-1 (see Lockheed)
XH-8 (see Kellett)
XH-17 (see Hughes)
XH-C-1A (see AIDC)
XNBL-1 (see Barling)
XP-47J Thunderbolt (see Republic)
XP-79B (see Northrop)
XR-1 (see Platt-le-Page)
XR-4 (see Sikorsky)
XV-3 (see Bell)

Y

Y1B-9A (see Boeing)
Yak-9 (see Yakovlev)
Yak-15 (see Yakovlev)
Yak-18 (see Yakovlev)
Yakovlev, A. S.: 170
Yakovlev
    Yak-9: 173
    Yak-15: 170, 176
    Yak-18: 231
Yamshikova, O.: 170
Yarry, M.: 22
YB-49 (see Northrop)
Ye-266M (see Mikoyan-Gurevich)
Yeager, Capt C. ('Chuck'): 209, 211
Yeager, J.: 7, 126, 222
Yegorov, B.: 217
YG-1 (see Kellett)
Yokosuka E14Y1 Glen: 162
Yokosuka MXY-7 Ohka: 168
Yokoyama, Lt T.: 159
Young, J.: 218, 220

Z

Zambecarri, Count F.: 13
Zeppelin-Staaken R VI: 147, 187
Zimmer, E.: 108
Zurovec, W.: 43
Zuyeva, T.: 62
Zvonariev, Capt: 157